LANGUAGE AND COGNITION
IN SCHIZOPHRENIA

LANGUAGE AND COGNITION IN SCHIZOPHRENIA

Edited by
STEVEN SCHWARTZ
University of Texas Medical Branch

LAWRENCE ERLBAUM ASSOCIATES, PUBLISHERS
1978   Hillsdale, New Jersey

DISTRIBUTED BY THE HALSTED PRESS DIVISION OF
JOHN WILEY & SONS
New York   Toronto   London   Sydney

Lawrence Erlbaum Associates, Inc., Publishers
62 Maria Drive
Hillsdale, New Jersey 07642

Distributed solely by Halsted Press Division
John Wiley & Sons, Inc., New York

Library of Congress Cataloging in Publication Data

Main entry under title:

Language and cognition in schizophrenia.

    Includes bibliographical references and indexes.
    1. Schizophrenics—Language.   I. Schwartz, Steven.
RC514.L32   616.8'982'07   77-15648
ISBN 0-470-99343-X

Printed in the United States of America

Contents

Contributors ix

Preface xi

1. **Referent Communication Disturbances in Schizophrenia**
Bertram D. Cohen **1**

    Experimental Paradigm   4
    Theory of Referent-Communication Processes   6
    Experiments with Schizophrenic Patients   8
    Clinical Implications   21
    Appendix   26
    References   33

2. **Communicability Deficit in Schizophrenics Resulting from a
More General Deficit**
*Kurt Salzinger, Stephanie Portnoy, and
Richard S. Feldman* **35**

    Problems of Specification of Schizophrenia   36
    The General Deficit in Schizophrenia   37
    The Study of Verbal Behavior   40
    Some Experiments in Verbal Behavior   43
    Conclusion   51
    References   51

3.   Remembering of Verbal Materials by Schizophrenic
     Young Adults
     Soon D. Koh **55**

         Research Strategy and Subjects   56
         Experimental Findings   64
         Discussion and Interim Conclusions   88
         References   95

4.   Schizophrenic Thought Disorder: Why the Lack of Answers?
     Paul H. Blaney **101**

         Discriminating Power   102
         Isolating Cognitive Processes   106
         Degree of Disorganization   109
         Relationships Among Theories of Cognitive
            Deficit   110
         Conclusion   115
         References   115

5.   Distractibility in Relation to Other Aspects of Schizophrenic
     Disorder
     Thomas F. Oltmanns and John M. Neale **117**

         Introduction   117
         Definitions   119
         Diagnostic Issues   120
         Subjective Accounts of Perceptual Experience   135
         The Course of the Disorder   126
         Genetic Predisposition: Schizotypic Signs   129
         The Effects of Antipsychotic Medication   131
         Information Processing: Some Possible
            Mechanisms   135
         Conclusions   138
         References   139

6.   Personal Constructs among Schizophrenic Patients
     Lawrence G. Space and Rue L. Cromwell **147**

         The Kelly Rep-Grid Paradigm   147
         Analysis of Rep-Grid Protocol   150
         Personal Constructs and Related Research with
            Schizophrenics   156
         Rep Grids of Schizophrenics   165
         A Viewpoint about Schizophrenia   187

The Role of Conceptual Breakdown   188
References   189

7. **Hemispheric Asymmetry and Schizophrenic Thought Disorder**
    Algimantas Shimkunas **193**

    The Plurality of Thought Disorder   193
    Construct Validity of Schizophrenic Thought   193
    An Analogy for Schizophrenic Thought   195
    Patterns of Asymmetry in Cortical Functions   196
    Left-Hemisphere Functions   198
    Right-Hemisphere Functions   202
    Interhemispheric Interaction   207
    Lateral Asymmetry in Schizophrenia   209
    Bilateral Transfer and Conceptual Disorganization
        in Schizophrenia   213
    Hemispheric Asymmetry and Cognitive Deficit in
        Schizophrenia   215
    Attention-Perceptual Operations   215
    Cognitive Operations   216
    Conclusion   227
    References   228

8. **Language and Cognition in Schizophrenia: A Review
    and Synthesis**
    Steven Schwartz **237**

    Introduction   237
    Associationistic Approaches to the Study of
        Schizophrenic Language   238
    Nonassociative Approaches to Schizophrenic
        Language   259
    A Schema for the Study of Schizophrenic Language   271
    References   272

Author Index   277

Subject Index   285

Contributors

Paul H. Blaney,* Department of Psychology, The University of Texas, Austin, Texas 78712

Bertram D. Cohen, Institute of Mental Health Sciences, Rutgers Medical School, Piscataway, New Jersey 08854

Rue L. Cromwell, Department of Psychiatry, University of Rochester, Rochester, New York 14642

Richard S. Feldman, Biometrics Research Unit, New York State Psychiatric Institute, 722 West 168 Street, New York, New York 10032

Soon D. Koh, Psychosomatic and Psychiatric Institute, Michael Reese Hospital and Medical Center, 2959 South Ellis Avenue, Chicago, Illinois 60616

John N. Neale, Department of Psychology, State University of New York, Stony Brook, Stony Brook, New York 11790

Thomas F. Oltmanns, Department of Psychology, Indiana University, Bloomington, Indiana 47401

Stephanie Portnoy, Biometrics Research Unit, New York State Psychiatric Institute, 722 West 168 Street, New York, New York 10032

Kurt Salzinger, Biometrics Research Unit, New York State Psychiatric Institute, 722 West 168 Street, New York, New York 10032 also at Polytechnic Institute of New York

Steven Schwartz, Department of Psychiatry, University of Texas Medical Branch, Galveston, Texas 77550

Algimantas Shimkunas, Department of Psychology, University of Missouri, Columbia, Missouri 65201

Lawrence G. Space, Department of Psychiatry, University of Rochester, Rochester, New York 14642

*Now at Department of Psychology, University of Miami, Coral Gables, Florida 33124

Preface

About three decades ago, a book entitled *Language and Thought in Schizophrenia* was published to wide critical acclaim. Its editor, J. S. Kasanin, writing in the volume's Preface, stated:

> Language is probably one of the most momentous and most baffling products of the human mind—a phenomenon that is handed down by social inheritance from generation to generation. . . . It is yet far from clear just how facts accumulated (about language) can be coordinated and explained.

Thirty years later, it is unfortunately still not possible to explain all of the facts accumulated about language in general or about the communication problem of schizophrenics specifically. This is not to say that no progress has been made in all of these years. Indeed, despite the similarity of their titles, there is virtually no overlap between contents of the earlier volume and the present one. Whereas the writers in Kasanin's book were involved in an inductive enterprise developing theoretical explanations from an examination of the speech of schizophrenic patients, the authors of the present chapters largely take the opposite approach, deducing the behavior of schizophrenics from more general psychological theories of language, learning, and cognition. This shift from induction to deduction reflects more than just a change in style. It also shows today's greater reliance on laboratory experimentation as opposed to the clinical case–study method so popular in the earlier volume. The emphasis on carefully controlled laboratory research has had its payoff in a remarkable increase in our knowledge of the characteristics of schizophrenic communication. The contributions to this volume reflect this new knowledge, and the contributors include the leading figures in the field of schizophrenic research. Taken as a whole, their chapters cover the breadth and variety of current approaches to the study of schizophrenic cognition and language.

The eight chapters may be divided into three parts. The first, consisting of four chapters, is concerned with recent developments in the laboratory study of schizophrenic language. Chapter 1 by Cohen and Chapter 2 by Salzinger, Portnoy, and Feldman are reviews of very different research programs, both aimed at clarifying the nature of the schizophrenic communication deficit. Koh's chapter on schizophrenic verbal memory integrates this complex area into the mainstream of current experimental information–processing research. Chapter 4 by Blaney is concerned with general theoretical issues in the study of schizophrenic language and thought. It serves to organize the preceding chapters and sets the stage for the next chapters.

Part two consists of three chapters, each concerned with various aspects of schizophrenic cognition. The chapter by Oltmanns and Neale is concerned with the study of attentional processes. The hypothesis that distractibility is an important aspect of schizophrenic behavior is explored in depth in their chapter. Reviewing experiments conducted using different research and diverse theoretical strategies, they conclude that, indeed, distractibility is a crucial variable in the explanation of schizophrenic cognition. Space and Cromwell's chapter on personal constructs deals with schizophrenia from the viewpoint of Kelly's theory of personality. The last chapter in this section by Shimkunas reviews a great deal of literature in the area of physiological psychology, brain functions and attention, in trying to relate the biological fact of hemispheric asymmetry to the schizophrenic thought disorder. The final section consists of a single chapter by the editor, which attempts to review and integrate the work in schizophrenic language and cognition. The chapter contrasts the various experimental methodologies used to validate theories of schizophrenic language and cognition and serves to place the first seven in perspective. It points out areas of agreement and disagreement, indicates problems and unanswered questions and also possible directions for future research and theorizing.

I am indebted to many people for their assistance in helping me to prepare this volume. I would like to acknowledge the advice, hints, support, and guidance of Larry Erlbaum in all phases of the book's preparation. I am also grateful for the invaluable help of my wife, Carolyn. Finally, many thanks are due to the colleagues and friends whose advice is reflected in the best aspects of this book.

STEVEN SCHWARTZ

LANGUAGE AND COGNITION
IN SCHIZOPHRENIA

1

Referent Communication Disturbances in Schizophrenia

Bertram D. Cohen

Rutgers Medical School

Disturbances in the use of language are among the most convincing indications of a schizophrenic psychosis. Yet, as cryptic or disorganized as schizophrenic speech may sound, it rarely (if ever) includes hard instances of agrammatism or word-finding deficits. It is a disturbance of communication rather than of language per se; its most dependable feature is that listeners find the patient's referents too elusive to grasp. Thus, measures of "communicability" are among the most effective discriminators of schizophrenic speech samples and are clearly superior to measures of style, structure, or thematic content (Salzinger, 1973). Accordingly, the emphasis in this paper is on disturbances of the referential process itself.

Putting the issue this way requires some understanding of the *normal* referent-communication process, one that can permit investigators to pinpoint components of the process as possible "loci" of schizophrenic disturbances. Therefore, basic to the work presented here is an empirically derived conception of how normal speakers select utterances to make it possible for their listeners to know what they are talking about and, also, how normal listeners use speakers' utterances to identify their referents. Previous investigators in this field have rarely paid much attention to the need for an explicit conception of normal referent communication, perhaps because of the assumption that normal processes are so obvious that they can be taken for granted. To provide background for our own conception of normal and pathological referent communication, I first review briefly the major approaches to schizophrenic language and thought and the normal referent communication processes that they imply.

A productive place to start is Bleuler's (1911) 65-year old analysis of schizophrenia as a cognitive disorder. Bleuler's theory deals with "ideas" and "associations," which were, of course, the popular concepts of eighteenth and nineteenth century psychology. Ideas were psychological representations of objects and events, and associations were the relational "threads" that connected ideas. For Bleuler, associations came in two main categories: *logical* and *autistic.* Bleuler believed that logical associations are the dominant forms of association in the normal adult. They occur more frequently than autistic associations and are, in effect, models of reality. Thus, if one's associations are predominantly logical, one is not likely to combine ideas in a bizarre, delusional, or incoherent manner. Autistic associations, in contrast, give rise to combinations of ideas that are likely to be analytically or empirically false. For Bleuler's normal adult, autistic associations, in effect, are held in check by logical associations and intrude into thought—and through thought into speech—only during moments of high emotional stress. With the onset of schizophrenia, the single crucial change was, for Bleuler, the "loosening" of the associations, a psychopathological process that he assumed to attack principally the logical associations, with the result that the autistic associations are permitted freer access to expression.

Bleuler's theory can be viewed either as a *hierarchic model* or as a *control model.* As the hierarchic model, the emphasis is on changes in the schizophrenic speaker's hierarchically ordered *repertoire* of associations in which the relative strengths of autistic associations have been increased. From the control viewpoint, the emphasis is instead on the schizophrenic speakers' loss of organizational control of their thought processes; that is, the loosening of the logical associations diminishes the speaker's power to control associative *selection.* Under these conditions, one's thoughts become autistic in the sense that they are determined by fortuitous contiguities in experience or by partial or inessential similarities among ideas. It is important to note that the control model permits the same associations to be logical in one context but autistic in another. The control model emphasizes failure in a mechanism that selects contextually appropriate associations; the hierarchic model emphasizes pathological changes in the repertoire itself.

Contemporary "interference theories" (Buss, 1966) of schizophrenic deficit appear to be of the hierarchic type. These twentieth century conceptions speak of "responses" in place of ideas, and associations are seen as relations among responses (or between responses and stimuli). Broen and Storms (1966), for example, proposed a theory in which responses that are, for the normal adult, low in frequency of occurrence and contextually inappropriate accrue larger relative strengths in the associative repertoires of schizophrenic patients. Therefore, they are more likely to intrude into thought and language.

A difficulty with such hierarchic theories is that they equate the appropriateness of a given association with its relative dominance in the associative repertoire from which it is selected. Such a theory would require the normal adult to possess as many repertoires as there are contexts if he were to speak or think "appropriately." Aside from questions of parsimony, this type of conception also fails to consider the large diversity of situations in which an unusual association to a referent is not only recognized (by nonschizophrenics) as appropriate but even as astute, witty or creative.

In contrast to the Broen–Storms theory is the Chapmans' (1973) dominant-response hypothesis. Whereas the Broen–Storms theory views schizophrenic performance in terms of the increased strengths of normally weak responses, the Chapmans view the schizophrenic patient as someone whose verbal behavior is unduly influenced by what are normally the *strongest* responses in his associative repertoire. This type of interference-by-dominant-associations conception is reminiscent of the theory proposed 35 years earlier by Kurt Goldstein (1944), in which schizophrenic "concreteness" was seen as an inability to shift one's attention from some single, salient feature of a referent object regardless of that feature's pertinence to the context in which it was perceived or communicated.

The Chapman and Goldstein theories are variations on a control model in the sense that they posit deficits in the patient's ability to resist interference from strong but inappropriate associations, meanings or descriptions of a referent object. Presumably, normal adults are able to neutralize the power of such salient or dominant responses to scan their repertoires for responses that are more pertinent to the momentary context. How do normals manage this? These theories may specify a normal outcome but are silent about the process through which this outcome is achieved.

Sullivan (1944) is relatively unique among theorists in this field because, although lacking precision and detail, he did explicitly propose a conception of the normal speaker's referential process and then attempted to explain schizophrenic communication in terms of certain disturbances in the normal process. He postulated a self-editing process whereby normal speakers pretest their utterances against an implicit "fantastic auditor" before saying them aloud to listeners. Insofar as this inner listener is an accurate representation of the speaker's real listener, the pretest helps the speaker edit out utterances that may prove too cryptic, misleading, or unacceptable to an actual listener. Schizophrenic speech, according to Sullivan, occurs either when the speaker fails to pretest utterances altogether or pretests them against an invalid fantastic auditor, that is, one that fails to represent the actual listener realistically.

Though brief, I hope my reference to Bleuler and more recent investigators highlights the two principal ways in which disorders of referent communication are explained: disorders in the speaker's *repertoire* of associations, meanings, or descriptions of a referent, and disorders in the *selection* mechanism through which the speaker edits out contextually inappropriate (cryptic, ambiguous, or misleading) responses before they intrude into overt speech.

In the following sections I (1) describe and illustrate an experimental paradigm for studying referent communication; (2) outline a theoretical model that accounts for behavior in these experimental situations and incorporates both repertoire *and* selection (self-editing) components; (3) examine a number of studies designed to analyze schizophrenic speaker disturbances in terms of the model; and (4) consider implications of the data and theory for the psychopathology and treatment of these disturbances.

EXPERIMENTAL PARADIGM

The basic experimental situation has involved the presentation of an explicit set of stimulus objects to a speaker with one of the objects designated as his referent. The speaker's task is to provide a verbal response so that his listener can pick out the referent from the set of objects. The listener's task is to identify the referent from the stimulus set on the basis of the speaker's response.

In early studies (Rosenberg & Cohen, 1964) words were used as the referent and nonreferent objects. A speaker was shown pairs of words and was instructed to provide a third word, one that neither looked nor sounded like either of the words in the stimulus pair, as a "clue" (referent response) for a listener. Although artificial, this use of single-word responses and single-word referent stimuli permitted investigators to take advantage of word-association norms to estimate certain quantitative properties of the associative repertoires from which speakers selected responses in this situation. It should be clear, however, that the use of the paradigm was limited neither to verbal stimuli nor to single-word speaker responses. Later studies involved nonverbal referent objects and speakers' responses that consisted of continuous discourse.

The data shown in Table 1.1 were obtained in an early exploratory application of the paradigm with 18 speaker–listener pairs. This table includes the speaker-response distributions from three word pairs. For any given word pair, the speaker provided a clue word for a listener who was seated facing away from him in the same room. In each instance, the speaker was shown the word pair with the referent word underlined, and the listener was shown the same word pair with neither word underlined. The listener's task was to indicate to the experimenter, by pointing, a choice of the referent after hearing the speaker's response.

Synonym pairs were found to be especially instructive because many of the responses associated with the referent in such word pairs were likely to overlap with responses to the nonreferent thus accentuating a contextual factor that the speaker had to confront if he or she was to communicate effectively, that is, if the subject was to avoid "overincluding" the nonreferent. The distributions of speakers' responses shown in this table are representative of results obtained for pairs of synonyms.

The content of many of the responses to these high-overlap word pairs reflects the speaker's specific relationship to the listener. That is, speakers and listeners were self-selected pairs (in this pilot study— from the same college subculture, geographical region, and era, which may have made possible the effective use of such responses as *academic* and *riders* to FREEDOM: or *queer* to the referent

TABLE 1.1

Speaker-Response Frequencies and Listener Errors in Sample Protocols from Eighteen
Speaker–Listener Pairs (Word-Communication Task)

Freedom[a]–Liberty			Command–Order			Gay–Cheerful		
academic	2		general	3	(1)	queer	5	
rider(s)	2		hair	2		Ben	1	
bondage	1		allied	1		exhilarated	1	
bus	1		army	1		fairy	1	
circus	1	(1)[b]	chain	1		happy	1	
democracy	1		cigarette	1		homo	1	
four	1		direct	1	(1)	homosexual	1	
Fromm	1		exclamation	1		joyful	1	
jail	1	(1)	force	1		light	1	
land	1		Fritz	1		liquor	1	
nondetermined	1		hunger	1		lively	1	(1)
sexual	1		military	1		Paris	1	
slave	1		official	1		party	1	
slavery	1		short	1		wild	1	
speech	1	(1)	tell	1				
unchained	1							

[a]The first word in each pair was the referent.
[b]The number of responses that led to listener errors are shown in parentheses.
(From Cohen, 1976. Reprinted with permission of the New York Academy of Sciences.)

GAY, a pejoratively toned association that would surely be less evident among similar college students today. Other more individualized examples are the response *Fromm* to FREEDOM by a speaker who was, at that time, enrolled in the same Psychology of Personality course as her listener and the response *Fritz* to COMMAND by a speaker who belonged to the same fraternity as his listener, a fraternity which included a member nicknamed "Fritz the Commander." Such responses were much less frequent when the listener was a stranger to the speaker.

Although, as indicated, a number of the speaker responses reflect special features of the interpersonal relationships between speakers and listeners, it is also clear that the speakers' repertoires of associations to any given referent were similar enough to those of other "normal adults" in the same general linguistic community to communicate adequately most (if not all) of the 149 referents used in this exploratory study. In fact, Rosenberg and Cohen (1966) later confirmed the hypothesis that all but a very small proportion of the speakers' responses to the referents in these word pairs can also be found in word-association distributions obtained using the referent words alone in standard free word-association tests. There is, however, an important difference between the speaker-response distributions and those obtained from free word association. The proportions of responses of any given "type" are often drastically changed because the speaker's selection of a response from his repertoire of associations to the referent takes into account the associative strengths of the response word to both the referent and the nonreferent. Thus, a response that is a strong associate of the referent is not likely to appear as a popular speaker response if it is also a high-frequency associate of the nonreferent. In contrast, a weak or unusual associate of the referent may be used if the speaker happens to think of it and if its relation to the nonreferent is even more tenuous. On the listeners' side, the results suggest that the listeners' choices also were functions of the relative associative strengths linking the speakers' responses to the referent and the nonreferent. Listeners' errors were more likely to occur when these differences were small or actually favored the nonreferent, which sometimes happened.

On the basis of these observations, we constructed and then tested formal models of speaker and listener processes in which quantitative parameters were estimated from large group word-association and speaker-response norms. Mathematical versions of these models have been published (Rosenberg & Cohen, 1964, 1966). Further tests and extensions of this theory have been made using a variety of nonverbal referent stimulus displays, including facial expression photographs (Rosenberg & Gordon, 1968), snowflake designs (Rosenberg & Markham, 1971), and fictitious animal drawings (Rosenberg, 1972) in studies of young children and Munsell colors (Farnsworth, 1957) in later studies of schizophrenia (Cohen, Nachmani, & Rosenberg, 1974; Kantorowitz & Cohen, 1977).

THEORY OF REFERENT-COMMUNICATION PROCESSES

The speaker process, as shown in Figure 1.1 is assumed to consist of a two-stage process in which the stages are termed *sampling* and *comparison*. When confronted with a display containing referent and nonreferent objects, the model

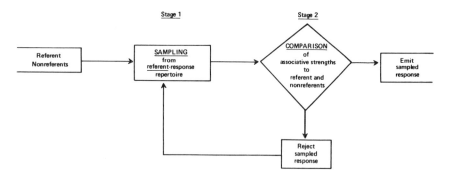

FIG. 1.1   Diagram of the 2-stage normal speaker's referential process.

assumes that the speaker will begin by sampling a response from his repertoire of linguistic units associated with the referent. (The "units" can be names, descriptions, meanings, word associations, and so forth, depending upon the demands of the particular setting.) The speaker's repertoire usually contains many possible responses to any given referent, and the probability that any given response will be sampled is proportional to the strength of its association with the referent. For example, when single-word referent and nonreferent stimulus displays were used, it was shown that the probability with which a speaker response is sampled can be estimated by its relative frequency as a free word associate of the referent (Rosenberg & Cohen, 1966). However, having sampled a response, the speaker does not necessarily emit it. The probability of emission depends instead upon the second or comparison stage which follows the sampling stage.

In the second stage, the speaker implicitly compares the associative strengths of his sampled response to referent and nonreferent objects. The conditional probability that the speaker will emit (or reject) the sampled response is determined by its relative associative strength to referent and nonreferent stimuli. The stronger the association with the referent, relative to the nonreferent, the higher the probability that the speaker will emit the sampled response in order to communicate the referent. If instead its associative strength to a nonreferent is similar to or larger than its association with the referent, the sampled response will more probably be rejected, and the entire two-stage cycle will be repeated. That is, the speaker again samples, compares, and either emits or recycles and repeats the two-stage process. Ultimately, a response is sampled, passes the comparison-stage test, and is expressed, thus terminating the speaker's referential process.

The process for the listener is considered to be essentially similar to the speaker's comparison stage because given the speaker's emitted response, the probability that the listener will correctly choose the referent is also determined by the relative associative strengths of the speaker's response to referent and nonreferent objects. This correspondence between speaker and listener comparison is instructive because it highlights the speaker's comparison stage as a self-editing function in which the speaker implicitly takes the role of listener to pretest the communicability of his utterances prior to their emission (or rejection) in interpersonal communication. It is important, therefore, that speaker and listener share substantial portions of their referent-response repertoires if accurate and fluent referent communication is to be maintained.

Our conception of the speaker's comparison stage as a self-editing function in which the speaker implicitly projects himself into the listener's role has antecedents not only in Sullivan's (1944) "fantastic auditor" construct but also in Piaget's (1926) conception of socialized (nonegocentric) speech, Mead's (1934) "generalized other," and Vygotsky's (1962) theory of the process through which inner speech is transformed into external speech.

EXPERIMENTS WITH SCHIZOPHRENIC PATIENTS

In an initial study (Cohen & Camhi, 1967), 72 hospitalized schizophrenic patients and the same number of normal hospital employees were assigned randomly to speaker or listener roles in the word communication task.[1] Each of the speakers was shown a list of word pairs and asked to provide clue words that would later be delivered to an individual listener. The design had four types of speaker–listener pairs assembled: (a) a schizophrenic speaker with a schizophrenic listener; (b) a schizophrenic speaker with a normal listener; (c) a normal speaker with a schizophrenic listener; and (d) a normal speaker with a normal listener.

The results given in Table 1.2 are for communication accuracy and include the average proportion of correct referent choices by the 18 listeners in each of the four speaker–listener combination groups.

These results indicate: (1) the schizophrenics were inferior to normals in the speaker role; (2) there was no significant difference between the schizophrenics and normals in the listener role; and (3) there were no special interactions between speaker and listener diagnosis. For example, schizophrenic speakers achieved no better accuracy in communication with schizophrenic than with normal listeners.

How can one account for the specific schizophrenic deficit in the speaker role? In terms of the theory, one can attribute a speaker deficit to the sampling stage of the two-stage speaker process with the assumption that the associative repertoires from which schizophrenic patients sample are deviant, an hypothesis that is consistent with the findings of many studies of free word association in schizophrenia (Buss, 1966). However, if deviant associative repertoires are crucial to the schizophrenic speaker deficit, one can also expect a schizophrenic listener deficit because a listener's choices are determined by the same associative strengths that determine a speaker's sampling probabilities. Therefore, the failure of the findings to indicate a schizophrenic listener deficit tends to contradict the hypothesis that schizophrenic speaker deficits are due to deviant sampling repertoires.

An alternative interpretation implicates the speaker's comparison stage as the locus of the schizophrenic deficit. If a schizophrenic is unable to make the requisite comparison of associative strengths, the self-editing decisions will be faulty and will lead to the emission of poor speaker responses. Here, too, however, the relative adequacy of the schizophrenic listener's performance suggests that the speaker's ability to make these comparative judgments is also

---

[1] In each experiment to be reviewed, the schizophrenic and control groups were comparable in age, education, and gender and, unless otherwise stated, patients were under maintenance dosages of tranquilizing medication.

TABLE 1.2
Communication Accuracy: Average Proportion Correct
Referent Choices in Each Speaker—Listener Group

	Listeners	
Speakers	Schizophrenic	Normal
Schizophrenic	.66	.67
Normal	.72	.74

(From Cohen & Camhi, 1967. Copyright 1967 by the American Psychological Association. Reprinted by permission.)

intact because the listener's comparison process is formally identical to the speaker's comparison stage.

Another way to implicate the speaker's comparison (or self-editing) stage derives from the conception of the speaker role as a two-stage process in which comparison is combined with sampling. In contrast, the listener role is a one-stage process involving only comparison, the sampling having been accomplished for the listener by his speaker. Thus, faulty integration of the comparison stage with the sampling stage rather than faulty comparison per se might be responsible for the schizophrenic speaker deficit. This hypothesis was tested in two follow-up studies.

In one of these experiments, Nachmani and Cohen (1969) used recall and recognition tasks as analogues of the speaker and listener roles in referent communication. This analogy was based on the Rosenberg—Cohen (1966) theory that recall involves a two-stage process similar to the speaker model, and recognition involves a one-stage process similar to the listener model. The results of the experiment are indeed parallel to the Cohen—Camhi speaker and listener results. Schizophrenic patients were inferior to controls (nonpsychotic psychiatric patients) on the recall but not on the recognition tests. These findings were interpreted to support the hypothesis that faulty self-editing is responsible for schizophrenic deficits in recall or in speaker-communication tasks.

Further evidence of the culpability of the speaker's self-editing stage was provided by the results of an experiment by Lisman and Cohen (1972), in which a word-association task was used as an analogue of the speaker role. Lisman and Cohen reasoned that the occurrence of deviant word associations by schizophrenic subjects, when compared to normals, could be explained by either a one-stage or a two-stage model of the process through which individuals find and emit responses in (free response) word-association tests. The one-stage model involves only a sampling stage, and deviant performance by schizophrenics is attributed to deviant associative (sampling) repertoires. According to the two-stage model, the process starts with a sampling stage in which the subject samples a potential response from his repertoire of word associates of the stimulus word; then, in a self-editing stage, the sampled response is compared with criteria of appropriateness supplied by the subject as in free word association or by an experimenter as in controlled word association (Rothberg, 1967). The outcome is a decision to emit or reject the sampled response (and then re-sample, and so on) depending upon how appropriate it is to the relevant criterion. Thus, deviant word associations can occur despite the presence of a nondeviant repertoire. The deviancy is attributable instead to faulty self-editing during the two-stage process.

In the Lisman–Cohen experiment, schizophrenic and normal subjects were administered word-association tests under standard (free) and controlled (idiosyncratic) conditions. In the idiosyncratic condition, the subjects were instructed to respond with a word they believed other people would *not* be likely to think of as an associate of the stimulus word. The point of these instructions was to pit the self-editing stage against the tendency of the sampling stage to favor common but then inappropriate associations.

The results show that the normals were much better able than the schizophrenics to edit out common responses following the idiosyncratic instructions. In fact, the patients' word associations under this condition were *more common* than the normals', although they were more deviant under the standard word-association condition. These results confirm predictions from the two-stage model and clearly favor a faulty self-editing hypothesis in contrast to one that posits a deviant sampling repertoire as the basis for schizophrenic responses in word-association tasks.

Another feature of the Lisman–Cohen experiment is their comparison of the effects of "steep-slope" and "flat-slope" stimulus words. Steep-slope stimuli are words with strong dominant (popular) associates; flat-slope stimuli, in contrast, are words with relatively weak (low frequency) popular associates.

Indicated by the results depicted in Figure 1.2 is the schizophrenics' inability to edit out common associations when given idiosyncratic instructions. This inability is much more pronounced with steep- rather than with flat-slope stimulus words presumably because of the increased strength of the common responses to these stimuli. Under this condition, predictions from the two-stage model are similar to predictions from the Chapman and Chapman (1973) dominant-response-bias model. Both models predict the comparatively high commonality of the schizophrenics' (versus the normals') responses under idiosyncratic instructions and the exaggeration of this effect on the steep-slope list.

The two-stage model, however, is also compatible with the comparatively low commonality indicated in Figure 1.2 for the schizophrenics' responses under standard (free) word-association instructions. According to the probabilistic two-stage model, schizophrenics are no more likely than normals are to sample deviant word associations but fail more often to edit them out prior to expres-

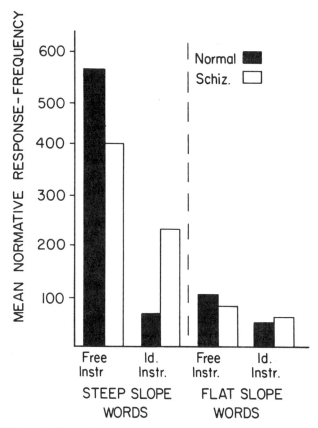

FIG. 1.2 Effects of diagnosis, instructions, and stimulus word type on mean normative response frequency in the experiment by Lisman and Cohen (1972).

sion. The two-stage model thus offers a possible resolution of the apparently contradictory implications of the Chapman and Chapman (1973) and Broen (1968) interference theories. Whereas the Chapmans consider schizophrenics to be especially vulnerable to interference from normally strong (high-frequency) responses, according to Broen the interference comes instead from normally weak (low-frequency) responses. The two-stage model permits either type of interference depending upon which response has been sampled and what contextual criterion the self-editing stage has failed to satisfy.

The evidence reviewed so far tends strongly to implicate the self-editing stage as the locus of the schizophrenic speaker deficit. Aside from the original Cohen–Camhi experiment, however, the follow-up studies described above are only indirectly related to referent communication. Accordingly, an experiment involving the direct use of a referent-communication task was designed (Cohen et al., 1974) with the demands placed on the speaker's self-editing function systematically manipulated. Also, the experiment involved communication via continuous discourse. This permitted a more detailed analysis of the speaker disturbance than was possible in any of the prior studies where the subjects had been limited to single-word utterances.

The stimulus materials were sets of Munsell color discs which were presented to individual speakers with one of the discs in a display designated as the speaker's referent. The sets of colors varied in hue similarity (and number) to manipulate the self-editing requirements of the display. Because colors similar in hue tend to evoke overlapping descriptions, the more similar (and numerous) the colors in the displays, the more rigorous the self-editing requirements placed on the speaker.

The speakers were 24 acute, nonparanoid schizophrenics not receiving medication at the time of the experiment and 24 normal hospital employees. To measure communication accuracy, a panel of 24 normal listeners who had not served in the speaker role were given the speakers' color descriptions via audio tape recordings with the appropriate stimulus displays. The communication accuracy results are shown in Figure 1.3.

It is apparent that both groups of speakers achieved progressively poorer communication accuracy with increases in the self-editing requirements of the displays and that this decrease clearly was much sharper for the schizophrenics, who showed little or no deficit when display similarity was minimal. These

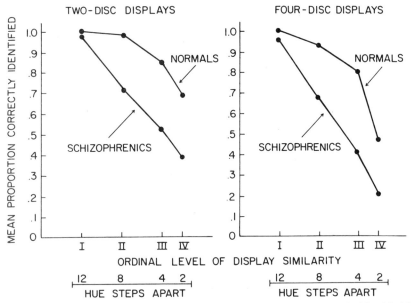

FIG. 1.3 Communication accuracy: Mean proportion of referents correctly identified by the listener panel. (From Cohen, Nachmani, & Rosenberg, 1974. Copyright 1974 by the American Psychological Association. Reprinted by permission.)

results confirmed the hypothesis that schizophrenic speakers suffer from a self-editing deficit. Further analyses of the speakers' responses then were made with the aim of specifying the nature of this malfunction. Three different models of the self-editing malfunction were considered. I outline and then evaluate each of them in turn by reference to certain quantitative properties of the speakers' responses.

The first hypothesis, termed the *Tower of Babel Model,* reconsiders the notion that schizophrenic speakers base their comparison-stage decisions on idiosyncratic associative strengths, at least in situations in which culturally dominant responses (the common color names in this experiment) are inadequate. This model is similar to Sullivan's conception that schizophrenic speech lacks "consensual validity" insofar as the patients pretest their utterances against an idiosyncratic rather than a socially representative fantastic auditor. The fantastic auditor functions for normals as an internal representation of cultural referent-response norms. If schizophrenic speakers pretest their responses instead against idiosyncratic referent-response norms, they may go through the same 2-stage response-selection process as normal speakers but may nevertheless fail to communicate accurately to other persons. However, their messages should be meaningful to themselves. That is, if they served as listeners to their own speaker responses, they should have no more difficulty in identifying their referents than normal speakers who were asked to identify their own referents on the basis of their (the normals') speaker-role descriptions. A strong case could be made for the Tower of Babel Model if, instead of the impaired communication accuracy scores found when the listener panel was used, the patients showed levels of accuracy equal to the normals when speakers served as their own listeners.

This hypothesis was tested by placing speakers in the listener role and feeding back to them their own speaker-role descriptions a week after they had served in the speaker role.

The self-accuracy findings shown in Figure 1.4 disconfirm the Tower of Babel Model. The results are similar to those obtained with the independent listener panel. That is, the schizophrenic speaker deficit was found even when the speakers served as their own listeners.

The second hypothesis is called the *Impulsive Speaker Model.* It asserts that schizophrenic speakers fail to self-edit altogether. In Sullivan's terms, patients function without a fantastic auditor to modulate their utterances prior to their overt expression. In our terms, patients sample from a nondeviant repertoire and emit responses without going through a self-editing stage. Such a truncated, one-stage (sampling only) model implies that speakers' descriptions of a referent will be independent of the contextual constraints provided by the nonreferents from which it is to be distinguished. Thus, if speakers sample the common color name — the most probable referent description in this experiment — they will emit it regardless of its "overinclusion" of the nonreferent. This will produce a steep decrease in communication accuracy (to themselves or others) with in-

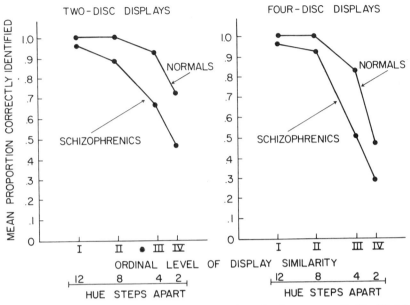

FIG. 1.4 Communication accuracy: Mean proportion of referents correctly identified by the speaker himself. (From Cohen et al., 1974. Copyright 1974 by the American Psychological Association. Reprinted by permission.)

creases in display similarity, a prediction that is consistent with the results shown in Figures 1.3 and 1.4.

The Impulsive Model also has implications for two other properties of speakers' responses: utterance length and response time. Normal speakers usually increase the lengths of their color descriptions as display similarity increases (Krauss & Weinheimer, 1967) because the typically short common color name will not distinguish the referent color under high or even moderate levels of display similarity and will probably be replaced by longer and more elaborate forms of description if speakers intend to communicate accurately to listeners. In addition to utterance length, normal speakers will also increase their response times (the time between the presentation of a display and the initiation of a description) as display similarity increases because the more similar the colors, the more likely speakers will need to recycle a number of times before sampling a description that passes the self-editing stage and is emitted.

In contrast to these expectations for normal (two-stage process) speakers, the Impulsive Model speakers should show no such progressive similarity-induced increases either in utterance length or response time because their referent descriptions are not influenced by a self-editing stage; that is, the responses are context-free.

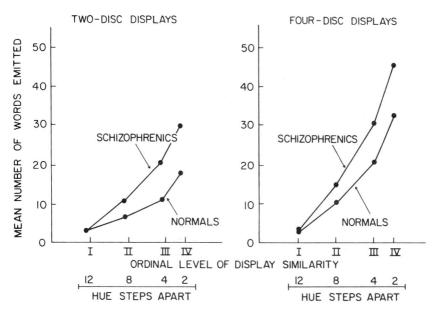

FIG. 1.5   Mean length of a description. (From Cohen et al., 1974. Copyright 1974 by the American Psychological Association. Reprinted by permission.)

The results for utterance length and response time are shown in Figures 1.5 and 1.6. Clearly, the data disconfirm the Impulsive Speaker Model to be an explanation of these patients' self-editing impairments. Not only do the findings show no evidence of insensitivity to the display similarity variable, but instead, the patients' progressive increases in both measures *exceeded* those of the normal speakers. Possibly, the patients were trying harder to communicate, although they were succeeding less.

The third hypothesis is termed the *Perseverative Speaker Model*. According to this model, speakers sample from a nondeviant repertoire and engage in normal editing-stage activity but continually resample the same inadequate response after each rejection of it. Ultimately, because of the probabilistic nature of the comparison stage, the response is emitted. When looked at in terms of this model, the schizophrenic speakers' fantastic auditor can be depicted as accurate but impotent. Their vetos are astute, but they cannot make them stick.

This implicit perseveration hypothesis is related to the "disattention deficit" conception proposed by Cromwell and Dokecki (1968) who viewed schizophrenic patients as deficient in the ability to "disattend from" a stimulus after having attended to it. In the present context, this is analogous to speakers' inability to ignore a sampled and rejected response.

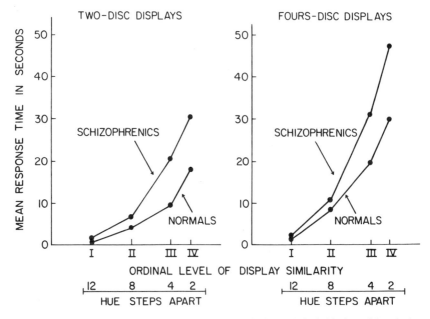

FIG. 1.6   Mean time between the presentation of a display and the initiation of description. (From Cohen et al., 1974. Copyright 1974 by the American Psychological Association. Reprinted by permission.)

The data needed to evaluate the Perseverative Speaker Model are those already presented in Figures 1.3, 1.4, 1.5, and 1.6. The Perseverative Model entails the same predictions as the Impulsive Model with respect to communication accuracy (Figures 1.3 and 1.4) and utterance length (Figure 1.5) but is different with respect to response time (Figure 1.6).

For communication accuracy, the Perseverative Model calls for the same progressively steeper-than-normal decrements with increasing display similarity as did the Impulsive Model because according to both models the common color description is the one most likely to be sampled and (ultimately) emitted regardless of the nonreferents in the display. The predictions from both models are consistent with the sharp drops in schizophrenic communication accuracy shown in Figures 1.3 and 1.4.

A second prediction from this common feature of the Impulsive and Perseverative Models—the emission of the initially sampled response regardless of the nonreferents in the display — is that utterance lengths will not change with increases in display similarity. The findings (Figure 1.5) clearly disconfirmed this prediction from the Perseverative Model for the same reasons given above for the Impulsive Model. The schizophrenic speakers gave progressively even longer descriptions than the normals with increases in display similarity.

Because of its inclusion of an active but ineffectual self-editing stage, the Perseverative Model, in contrast to the Impulsive Model, predicts progressive increments in response time with increases in display similarity, a prediction that is quite consistent with the results shown in Figure 1.6. In respect to response time, therefore, the Perseverative Model is superior to the Impulsive Model as an account of these schizophrenic speakers' self-editing problems and, if not for the exaggerated increments in utterance length, the Perseverative Model would account adequately for all findings.

What is the source of the schizophrenic speakers' abnormally protracted descriptions? At this juncture it can prove to be helpful to examine some examples from the speaker-response protocols of both groups with attention given to the composition of the longer schizophrenic descriptions. Samples are provided in the appendix to this chapter.

The following descriptions, extracted from the Appendix, are typical of those produced under conditions of minimal challenge to the speakers' self-editing stage — a two-disc, low-similarity display in which the referent, a purple blue, was 12 Farnsworth–Munsell hue steps from a red nonreferent.

Normal Speaker 2: "Purple."
Normal Speaker 3: "Purple."
Normal Speaker 7: "This is purple blue."
Schizophrenic Speaker 2: "The bluer."
Schizophrenic Speaker 4: "Blue."
Schizophrenic Speaker 10: "Purple."

The appropriateness of the schizophrenic responses and their comparability to the normal responses is consistent with both the Impulsive and the Perseverative Models. Both predict that the common color names will be the most likely to be given by the schizophrenics. At the same time, these responses are highly acceptable to normal speakers in this low-similarity situation.

In contrast, the following examples produced by the same normal and schizo-phrenic speakers are typical of those given under conditions in which the speakers' self-editing stage was subjected to a much more rigorous challenge. These are descriptions of a red referent in a display containing a highly similar (slightly yellower) nonreferent two hue steps distant.

Normal Speaker 2: "Both are salmon colored. This one, however, has more pink."
Normal Speaker 3: "My God this is hard. They are both about the same except that this one might be a little redder."
Normal Speaker 7: "They both are either the color of canned salmon or clay. This one here is the pinker one."
Schizophrenic Speaker 2: "Make-up. Pancake make-up. You put it on your face and they think guys run after you. Wait a second! I don't put it on my face and guys don't run after me. Girls put it on them."
Schizophrenic Speaker 4: "A fish swims. You call it a salmon. You cook it. You put it in a can. You open the can. You look at it in this color. Salmon fish."

Schizophrenic Speaker 10: "This is the stupid color of a shit ass bowl of salmon. Mix it with mayonnaise. Then it gets tasty. Leave it alone and puke all over the fuckin' place. Puke fish."

The examples confirm the impression that the normal and schizophrenic protocols became increasingly different both in length and in content as display similarity was increased. As the self-editing demands increased, both groups complained about the difficulty of the required discriminations. The normals' comments, however, were more pertinent to the task, and their utterances retained the character of coherent color descriptions even for the most challenging displays. One frequent normal-speaker tendency was to describe a nonreferent to exclude it. Another tendency was to express first a common color name (for example, "salmon") and then, after noting its overinclusive character, to shift to other units of description that particularized the referent disc (for example, "more pink" or "a little redder").

Although initial units of the schizophrenics' descriptions often consisted of the same overinclusive common response to the referent as the normals', later units appeared instead to be drawn from associations to prior components of the strings, resulting in chains of loosely connected elements rather than in coherent descriptions. Perhaps the single most distinctive feature of the schizophrenics' lengthy utterances was this tendency for responses to lose their connection with the referent. References to the objective stimuli (the discs) were replaced by a bewildering variety of intraverbal associations. As can be seen among the examples in the Appendix, these included instances of clang association, condensation, neologism, alliteration, and a number of private individual stereotypies (for example, Hilda and her anatomy) among other forms of sheer free-associative word play. At times, schizophrenic speakers attempted to impose narrative or expository forms on their responses which, however, did not improve their referent communicability. For example, Schizophrenic 8 in the Appendix slipped from "green things" to "a dashboard light at night" and "fifty miles an hour tonight." Schizophrenics 3 and 4, having sampled "salmon," continued with instructions about cans, cooking, vinegar, or eating. Schizophrenic 5 attempted, in one of his descriptions, to confer a semblance of order on what was otherwise a loose chain of associations by turning it into a lecture on agriculture and nutrition.

At times, the content of the patients' utterances also reflected feelings of frustration in the face of difficult challenges to their self-editing capabilities. The normals' difficulty comments were more specific and were usually followed by a separate, attempted description. The patients were more prone to react with implicit anger, which then colored (or off-colored) their descriptions. For example, one patient, after commenting on the sameness of the colors in a high-similarity display, warned the listener "not to be fooled" and then alluded to the referent as "full of tricks" and to the nonreferents as "liars" and "punks" who were "scared shit" and "yellow bastards."

Whether they were associations to prior words or to feelings, these *responses* rather than the referents served as the major source of the schizophrenics' verbal excess. An adequate model of the schizophrenic speaker deficit would need to include this switch in the source from which the speaker samples new responses.

The Perseverative-Chaining Model

This model is identical to the Perseverative Model but has the addition of a two-stage "chaining" process. The chaining process begins immediately after the initially sampled and implicitly perseverated response has been either emitted or terminated without express verbalization. In either case, in the chaining process, the speakers (1) sample each new response from a repertoire of verbalizations associated with a just prior response rather than with the referent; (2) express the sampled-but-rejected responses overtly; and (3) continue to sample and reject in this overt fashion until a reponse passes the probabilistic self-editing stage, and the patients stop talking.

The implicit perseverative process accounts for the schizophrenics' increments in response latency, and the overt chaining process accounts for the abnormal increments in utterance length. Both occur under conditions requiring increasingly rigorous self-editing. The key assumption with regard to the perseverative process is the schizophrenics' inability to reject a sampled response or, at least, to make the rejection stick. As mentioned earlier, this is analogous to the "disattention deficit" posited by Cromwell and Dokecki (1968). It is also tempting to relate it to a possible habituation deficit in schizophrenia at a level that may implicate neurophysiological processes (Venables, 1973). The key assumption of the chaining process – that each successive component of a schizophrenic utterance is more likely to be sampled from the patients' associations to a just prior response in the string rather than from the referent – is consistent with Salzinger's (1973) "immediacy hypothesis." Also, the role of the dominant response – the response most likely to be sampled but rejected in high-similarity displays – is consistent with the influence accorded dominant responses by the Chapmans (1973). Finally, the hypothesized tendency to escape from the perseverative response via tangential inter-response associations is (perhaps too loosely) reminiscent of Mednick's (1958) theory of bizarre-thought generation in schizophrenia. As an interesting related touch, I am tempted to refer here to Auster's (1975) review of a schizophrenic patient's extraordinary biographical account, in French, of his radical attempt to escape from aversive perseverative responses by disconnecting entirely from the English language, his mother tongue.

Referent Communication in Chronic Schizophrenia

The findings leading to the construction of the Perseverative-Chaining Model were obtained from acute, first admission, nonparanoid schizophrenics. It is possible that changes occur in the referential functions with increasing chronicity of schizophrenia. Cohen et al., (1974) pointed out that the perseverative and chaining tendencies indicated by their patient group might be specific to the psychopathology of the early stages of schizophrenia when the patient still persists in the struggle to communicate effectively. In later stages of the disorder, referent communication might be better described by the Impulsive Speaker Model insofar as long-term patients might be more prone to express, with no (or minimal) attempts to self-edit, sampled but inappropriate responses once they have learned to anticipate the futility of their attempts to reject them.

In a recent study, Kantorowitz and Cohen (1977) administered a variation of the color-description task to 30 long-term patients selected from the wards of a custodial Veterans Administration hospital. Fifteen were classified as reactive schizophrenics and 15 as process schizophrenics on the basis of Phillips Scale ratings. The length of hospitalization varied from about 6 to 9 years for the reactive, and 7 to 10 years for the process patients. Kantorowitz and Cohen also tested 15 normal hospital employees.

As anticipated, both groups of patients showed poorer communication accuracy than the normals when measured by the referent choices of a (normal) listener panel. However, in contrast to the acute patients seen in the previous color-description study, both groups of long-term patients showed little change in response to increases in display similarity either in their response latencies or in their utterance lengths. Compared to the process group, the reactives did show somewhat sharper similarity-related increments in response latency and utterance length, but the differences were nonsignificant. One interesting finding was that the combined patient groups showed significantly faster speaker-response times (overall) than the normals.

Qualitatively, the patients' descriptions rarely went beyond common color names or phrases, even for the high similarity displays. This fact, together with the relative speed of response shown by the patients, suggests that their referent communication process conforms to the Impulsive Speaker Model.

One further finding of interest emerged when the patients were divided into two equal N groups on the basis of clinical judgments of the prevalence of paranoid versus nonparanoid features in their current clinical status. At either of the two levels of similarity used in this study, the paranoids' utterance lengths were significantly shorter than the nonparanoids. No other differences between these two groups were found.

This paranoid—nonparanoid difference may represent a difference in style that is manifest in situations where the patient is likely to sample responses that are contextually or interpersonally inappropriate but difficult to reject and replace with responses that are more appropriate. The paranoids' terseness is consistent with a generalized pattern of suspicious, self-guarded behavior; the nonparanoids' verbosity instead seems to represent a superficially more open style, one in which the patient maintains a semblance of verbal contact with listeners.

It is, of course, not possible to make very strong inferences from a comparison of the acute (Cohen et al., 1974) and chronic (Kantorowitz & Cohen, 1977) color-description studies because they differed in many ways other than the patients' lengths of hospitalization. However, I am inclined to regard chronic schizophrenia as a condition that develops as patients gradually (or suddenly) yield more and more to the "pull" of referent stimuli rather than continue the struggle to edit out sampled but inappropriate responses. As this process develops, contextual cues become less effective as determinants of thought and speech; and perhaps, as a means of dealing with this handicap, chronic schizophrenic patients learn to avoid situations that are likely to involve novel or ambiguous interpersonal circumstances.

CLINICAL IMPLICATIONS

In this section, I extend the ideas presented earlier in this chapter to some clinical issues concerning the psychopathology and treatment of communication disturbances in schizophrenia. These extensions are frankly speculative and involve assuming the validity of the two-stage model of the normal speaker process and the hypothesis that the schizophrenic speaker deficit involves a basic impairment of the ability to reject sampled responses (the perseverative deficit). In addition, I make some further assumptions concerning the nature of anxiety in schizophrenia and its link to the basic speaker deficit.

Psychopathology

There is a consensus among clinical investigators that anxiety is an important determinant of psychological dysfunction in schizophrenia. For present purposes, I use the term "anxiety" to refer to an aversive state elicited by the *anticipation of social punishment contingent upon the emission of a sampled response.* By "social punishment," I mean such listener reactions as censure, rebuff, ridicule, contempt, and so on. There is extensive clinical and experimental documentation of the influence of these interpersonal sources of anxiety on psychological deficit in schizophrenia (Rodnick & Garmezy, 1957).

In common with other investigators (for example, Mednick, 1958; Broen & Storms, 1966), I also attribute energizing (Spence & Spence, 1966) properties to this anticipatory state because, as applied in the present theory, it magnifies the perseverative deficit. Thus, to the extent that schizophrenic speakers anticipate social punishment for the emission of a sampled response, there is an *increase* in the probability that the punishable response is perseveratively resampled. The speakers are denied access to acceptable alternative responses to the referent, even though their underlying sampling repertoires may be adequate. Instead, they are caught in a vicious circle. The more they fear the consequences of emitting sampled responses, the more the responses resist rejection.

How can speakers cope with the fact that their sampling is perseverative? There may be as many variations in these forms of adaptation as there are variations in stages of illness and other sources of heterogeneity in schizophrenia. It may be possible, however, to describe a relatively small number of main clinical categories of speakers' defensive adaptations within the framework of the present theory. These defensive adaptations, include (1) referent shifts; (2) nonresponse; and (3) social withdrawal.

Referent shifts. If speakers cannot effectively reject punishable responses to referents, they can break the perseverative cycle by shifting to different referents. One way to do this is via chaining. The speakers sample fresh responses from the sets associated with the perseverative responses rather than from the referents. If the new responses are also punishable, they can repeat the chaining process. Ultimately, this should produce a response they preceive to be innocuous but which may be remote from the original referent and, from the listeners' standpoint, seriously tangential to the conversational context. Presumably, if the speakers were sensitive to the possibility that their listeners may react aversively to a tangential response, they will continue the chaining process. In the end, however, their decision to emit may involve misjudgment of the contextual relevance of their responses.

Referent shifts based on the chaining process are likely to be most prominen in early schizophrenia when the speaker is still struggling to communicate. In the studies reviewed earlier in this chapter, we have seen chaining occur most readily in early, acute patients (Cohen et al., 1974) and least, if at all, in long-term patients (Kantorowitz & Cohen, 1977). This is not to say that long-term schizophrenics may not also resort to chaining under conditions of interpersonal pressure to communicate, conditions in which other, typically more passive, forms of avoidance (for example, nonresponse or social withdrawal) fail to prevent or remove the threat of punishment.

Another form of referent shift is one in which speakers sample new responses from the sets associated with perceptually convenient objects in the immediate external environment, responses which they may then emit no matter how tenuous their relation to the initial referents or to the conversational flow. Examples of this form of schizophrenic communication disturbance are described by Woods (1938, pp. 297–298).

A third type of referent shift comes via the paranoid mechanism of substituting a delusional topic for the initial referent. Paranoid speakers have recourse to learned sets of self-protective responses associated with delusional themes. The responses that are then sampled from the sets associated with the delusional referents relieve the speakers of the need to sample alternative responses to the initial referent and thus remove the immediate threat of social punishment. Such speakers may not impress their listeners as being quite as disorganized as those described in the first two forms of referent shift but may impress listeners instead with their "stickiness" or rigidity and the tiresome monotony with which they return to their characteristic themes.

Paranoid patients are considered to have better prognoses than nonparanoids.

In any case, they are less likely to be found among the long-term patients in state hospital populations (Strauss, 1973). The tendency to shift to delusional referents seems, therefore, to be more likely in patients with relatively short durations of illness who have not yet given up the attempt to engage in interpersonal communication. The content of delusional responses, however, often produces aversive reactions in the listener. In time, therefore, speakers can learn either to modify the content so that it is less aversive (less bizarre) or resort instead to more passive forms of defense, such as nonresponse. The relatively sparse utterances of the Kantorowitz and Cohen (1977) paranoid, compared to their nonparanoid, speakers are consistent with the latter possibility. Though paranoid, they were chronic schizophrenics averaging 8 years of hospitalization.

Nonresponse. If speakers sample responses they perceive to be punishable and are unable to edit them out, they can choose not to respond altogether. The speakers thus remove the perceived risk of social punishment contingent upon the expression of the responses. Bleuler (1911) described schizophrenic "blocking" as an abrupt stop in a speaker's discourse that, when resumed, deals with content unrelated to the preblock discourse. This symptom can be explained by a punishment–avoidance function of the abrupt stop supplemented by some form of referent shift during the silent interval.

If speakers adopt nonresponding as a generalized strategy for dealing with the ubiquitous threat that they may at any time sample punishable responses, they may discontinue speech altogether. Some instances of functional muteness in schizophrenia may have such a basis.

Less extreme forms of generalized nonresponse are more likely to be encountered in long-term patients for whom this adaptation is complementary to the social withdrawal adaptation to be described next. Interestingly, the Kantorowitz and Cohen (1977) findings suggest that long-term process schizophrenics use shorter utterance lengths than either (equally long-term) reactive schizophrenics or normal control speakers.

Social withdrawal. The several forms of referent shift and nonresponse described above may each succeed, from the speakers' viewpoint, in removing the immediate threat of social punishment. However, each also involves a failure of communication from the listeners' standpoint. Tangential responses, responses with delusional or boringly repetitive content, or silence are each likely to result in aversive listener reactions which the speakers may in time perceive as confirmation of their anticipations of rebuff, contempt, ridicule, and so forth. In the long run, therefore, it is not surprising that attempts to self-edit, which are exaggerated in early schizophrenia (Cohen et al., 1974), are given up by long-term patients because they are futile – given up to the extent that their referent communication processes can be described by the one-stage sampling process (Impulsive Speaker Model).

Communication via the one-stage (sampling only) model may be a feasible adjustment if the speakers are able to avoid contact with any or all interpersonal situations in the presence of which they may possibly sample inappropriate and socially punishable responses. Thus, long-term schizophrenics may seek or drift into settings in which ambiguous interpersonal referents are rarely encountered, that is, settings in which the dominant response is appropriate because little or no self-editing is required. Such simplified environments may appear to be especially well suited to the communication skills of chronic, long-term patients of the type Cromwell (1972) termed "high-redundancy" schizophrenics. These milieux are often found in highly routinized custodial institutions. In such settings, also, listeners (staff or other persons) may in effect collude in the speakers' defensive adjustment by ignoring inappropriate responses if they happen to occur or by treating them as signs of illness rather than as attempts to communicate.

Treatment

In the present context, I consider the perseverative tendency – the impaired ability to reject sampled responses – to be the primary deficit. In contrast, the various defensive adjustments outlined above are secondary symptoms. The present theory does not deal with the etiology of the primary deficit. If its etiology was known and an effective cure for the primary deficit resulted from this knowledge, then the schizophrenic speaker disturbances would presumably be eradicated as a consequence. However, because the etiology of the primary deficit is unknown, rehabilitation seems to be a more realistic objective. Following is an outline of such an approach, one that attempts to modify or prevent the secondary communication disturbances rather than to eliminate the primary deficit. One further qualification is that the approach may be feasible mainly with younger patients during periods of relative remission. In any event, my own experience with this approach is limited to younger post psychotic patients who are still motivated to do something positive about their interpersonal relationships.

Common to the various secondary defensive reactions is the speakers' attempt to escape from or avoid their perseverative response pattern which they assume implicitly or explicitly will lead to punitive listener reactions and, hence, results in an increase in anxiety. This anxiety-producing assumption is often but not always groundless. Groundless or not, however, the anxiety makes sampled responses even more difficult to reject. The first step in the therapeutic program, therefore, is to reduce the speakers' anticipation of social punishment. Although the basic perseverative deficit is not thereby completely removed, its strength can be sufficiently diminished so that whatever residual ability the patients may have to sample alternative responses (rather than to shift referents, block or withdraw) will be maximized.

The first step in the program can be achieved in a setting in which the speakers feel secure about the interpersonal consequences of their responses. That is, therapeutic personnel must consist of "real listeners" who can, by their own example and reactions, encourage the speakers to acknowledge and express their own sampled responses (feelings, perceptions, thoughts, and communications) fully and accurately regardless of how inappropriate they may seem. Listeners (1) provide the speakers with their own reactions to the speakers' overt responses, whether these reactions are affectively positive or negative; (2) when necessary, assist the speakers to label their referents; and (3) expect the speakers to do likewise for them. The schizophrenic speakers can thus learn that many of their assumptions about their listeners' reactions are groundless and, even when they are not groundless, the real consequences are not catastrophic.

I have recently begun exploring the efficacy of outpatient groups in which both patients and staff (including students) participate as co-equal members, with each member's purpose being to develop and refine essential interpersonal communication skills for himself. This experience suggests that professional personnel are able to provide much more effective interpersonal feedback to schizophrenic patients under these conditions than under more traditional therapy conditions in which their roles as listeners (or speakers) are qualified by their perceived status as formal psychotherapists.

Group meetings are conducted similarly to T-Group (Back, 1972) sessions in which the norms of participant behavior are intrinsic to the therapeutic process. Development of norms is initiated in part by an example of the leader's own behavior, instruction as needed, and the use of specially designed events within which norm-relevant behavior can occur naturally and in especially salient forms. These norms encourage spontaneous self-disclosure in relation to the ongoing situation and intermember feedback that (1) is informational rather than judgmental; (2) refers to specific acts rather than generalized traits; (3) is immediate rather than delayed; and (4) distinguishes clearly between the feedback-giver's personal feelings versus his opinions about the recipient's behavior or state of mind.[2]

Such a therapeutic regimen is designed to provide schizophrenic speakers with skills not only for the effective labelling of their own referents, but also for the accurate assessment of their listeners' reactions. *A fundamental goal of the program is the development of the speakers' ability to discriminate between their assumptions and the actual reactions of their listeners.* Probably most people, schizophrenic or normal, can profit from experiences that sharpen these kinds of interpersonal communication skills. Schizophrenics (or preschizophrenics), however, have an especially profound need for such training.

[2] Patients participating in these groups were encouraged to continue whatever medication (antipsychotic or anti-anxiety) their clinical condition warranted. It may also be important to point out that the skills required to conduct this type of program are considerable. Extensive formal preparation and experience is recommended, both in the processes and leadership of small training groups *and* in clinical psychopathology.

CONCLUSIONS

The research summarized in this chapter attests to the usefulness of an explicit conception of normal referential processes as a basis for the study of referent communication pathology. The two-stage model of the normal speaker process provides a theoretical basis for distinguishing empirically between hierarchical and control models of disordered referent communication in schizophrenia. The results, taken as a whole, clearly favor some form of control model and indicate that a fundamental deficit in schizophrenia is the inability to reject a sampled response, a problem that patients may adapt to differently depending upon the stage of illness and other sources of heterogeneity in schizophrenia. As tentative as the Perseverative-Chaining and Impulsive Speaker Models are as representations of early- and later-term patients' attempts to deal with (or surrender to) the fundamental deficit, these models seem to accord with clinical experience and, from the standpoint of research or practice, to have useful implications for a theoretically consistent functional classification of communication disturbances in schizophrenia, their clinical course and their treatment.

APPENDIX

A sample of speaker protocols from the color description
experiment by Cohen, Nachmani, and Rosenberg (1974).

Included in this appendix are referent-color descriptions at each of the four levels of display similarity for the two- and four-disc displays. The referent and nonreferent stimulus colors are identified by their Farnsworth–Munsell Disc numbers (Farnsworth, 1957). The descriptions were provided by the same 12 normal and 12 schizophrenic speakers throughout. The patients were initially diagnosed by an intake psychiatrist or psychologist whose diagnosis was later concurred with by three other diagnosticians (two psychiatrists and one psychologist) at a treatment planning conference. They were acute, first-admission males seen in a short-term residential psychiatric setting in the greater New York City area. In each case there was agreement by all four diagnosticians that the patient (1) was schizophrenic, (2) showed symptoms of language and thought disorder and (3) showed a predominantly nonparanoid presenting picture. The patients were not administered psychotropic medication during the study period.

TWO-DISC DISPLAY, LOW SIMILARITY
(TWELVE HUE STEPS APART)

Referent color: Disc #62   Nonreferent color: Disc #74
Norm 1: Bluest.
Norm 2: Purple?
Norm 3: Purple.

Norm 4: The purple one.
Norm 5: It's purple.
Norm 6: Blue!
Norm 7: This is purple blue.
Norm 8: Purple.
Norm 9: Purple.
Norm 10: The purple blue.
Norm 11: Purple. (Pronounced Purpool!)
Norm 12: Bluer.

Schiz 1: The blue one.
Schia 2: The bluer?
Schiz 3: A blue one.
Schiz 4: Blue.
Schiz 5: Blue.
Schiz 6: It's blue. Makes me sick.
Schiz 7: Another blue! (Disgusted tone of voice).
Schiz 8: A purple blue.
Schiz 9: Peerpul.
Schiz 10: Purples.
Schiz 11: Purple.
Schiz 12: Purple.

TWO-DISC DISPLAY, HIGH SIMILARITY
(TWO HUE STEPS APART)

Referent color: Disc #50   Nonreferent color: Disc #58

Norm 1: It's the greener blue.
Norm 2: This is the greener blue.
Norm 3: The greener blue.
Norm 4: This one is the blue.
Norm 5: Oh this is blue. The other has purple.
Norm 6: Yellowish!
Norm 7: This one here is aquamarine.
Norm 8: The bluer one.
Norm 9: This is the blue one.
Norm 10: Blue. The other is purple.
Norm 11: A beautiful Carribean like blue.
Norm 12: This is the very light bluish color.

Schiz 1: This one is a lighter blue, and has more green.
Schiz 2: The color of lighter blue water.
Schiz 3: A ha. A nice blue. Bar Mitzvah blue!
Schiz 4: This is the color of a lady's eye shadow. Blue.
Schiz 5: This is a lighter blue than the other one.
Schiz 6: A pretty shitty ditty shade of blue if I ever saw one.
Schiz 7: A blue color of dirty sea water.
Schiz 8: Sea blue? I mean see the sea blue!
Schiz 9: A blue only matched by Hilda's eye. Rip it out! Fast!
Schiz 10: A tender blue. It caresses me well.
Schiz 11: A blue meanie. John Lennon made it.
Schiz 12: This is just the blue for bathrooms.

TWO-DISC DISPLAY, MODERATE-HIGH SIMILARITY
(FOUR HUE STEPS APART)

Referent color: Disc #35   Nonreferent color: Disc #39

Norm 1: This is the lighter of the two greens.
Norm 2: Both are light green. This one is lighter.
Norm 3: These are both greenish blue, but this one has some more green.
Norm 4: Both are grassy green. This one has more pure green.
Norm 5: This seems like a richer purer green. The other has more bluish tint.
Norm 6: The greener.
Norm 7: This one is really a much lighter color green.
Norm 8: This is the lighter green.
Norm 9: This is clearly a purer green. Lighter too.
Norm 10: This is by far the greenest.
Norm 11: Here is the greener of the two of them.
Norm 12: This is a Kentucky blue grass green. Not blue, but a lighter grassy green.

Schiz 1: What's with green? Huh? Again green, this one is like paint. The other one is
          more like grass, and the one like paint. The one like paint.
Schiz 2: How blue I am. (singing) If I were blue, I'd like to be this green instead, I really
          like it. You could put it in a salad and eat.
Schiz 3: "Vell" a green here, a green there. Of course it's lighter. But that's a description?
          You need a special green and all it is is lighter. Lighter.
Schiz 4: Green like the eyes of a virgin. After she fucks her eyes become darker like the
          other one. Virgin eye green.
Schiz 5: Green (SHOUTS)! Hold on, the other is too! In the garden such a green is
          unlikely. Too synthetic! The other is more gardenreal (*one word*), piecemeal,
          oatmeal green, greenreal, filmreal, greenreal.
Schiz 6: This fuckin green here pisses me off. It will get you angry too! The angry green.
Schiz 7: This isn't such a bad green. Reminds me of a picnic on the green. Yes! Picnic
          green.
Schiz 8: Green things. Whappa Whappa doo. The green thing is like a dashboard light at
          night. Fifty miles an hour tonight.
Schiz 9: This is green pea soup pea soup green. Eat this one and no lentils in it.
Schiz 10: The eentsy beentsy spider went up his mother's *spot*. Out came the rain the color
          of green snot.
Schiz 11: This says GO (shouts). It's a traffic light. The other isn't a light so it means stop.
Schiz 12: Such a natural color. Real nature. If you had a tree, some grass, maybe some
          flowers in your room you'd paint it this color like so.

TWO-DISC DISPLAY, HIGH SIMILARITY
(TWO HUE STEPS APART)

Referent color: Disc #2   Nonreferent color: Disc #4

Norm 1: In order to describe this color best, you have to look at the lightness. It's lighter.
Norm 2: Both are salmon colored. This one, however, has more pink.
Norm 3: My God this is hard. They are both about the same, except that this one might be
          a little redder.
Norm 4: Didn't you show me this one before with the other color to describe? Well, this
          one is the lightest.

Norm 5: These are clay colors. They seem identical. But the one to talk about has more white in it.

Norm 6: These are the same things. There just is no difference!

Norm 7: They both are either the color of canned salmon or clay. This one here is the pinker one.

Norm 8: This one looks like clay from a ceramics class.

Norm 9: The two are the same. Almost the same. This one has more red there.

Norm 10: This looks like salmon. The other looks like clay.

Norm 11: Your colors are the same as mine and these are both the same. Perhaps its a bit redder.

Norm 12: This reminds me of clay color. The other does too, but this one, the one I'm talking about is a more likely clay than the other.

Schiz 1: Now I'll tell you the one I'm talking about. The one I'm talking about is so much like the other that they both are alike, except that it's more mushy looking.

Schiz 2: Make-up. Pancake make-up. You put it on your face and they think guys run after you. Wait a second! I don't put it on my face and guys don't run after me! Girls put it on them.

Schiz 3: Oy vehs mir! This is what a color is? This is what I have to talk about? This here? Such a color? Like a can of salmon. Maybe some vinegar. Eat.

Schiz 4: A fish swims. *You* call it a salmon. You cook it. You put it in a can. You open the can. You look at it in this color! Salmon Fish.

Schiz 5: If you and I could go for a walk and look at flowers, look at flowers you would never see one like this. Never! Don't think about flowers. It *is* fish eye.

Schiz 6: They're both the same and don't be fooled. Life is full of tricks and so is this color. Other colors are liars. These aren't liars. They're not yellow like are punks. Punks are scared shit and they're yellow-bastards-orangy.

Schiz 7: Looks like clay. Sounds like gray. Take you for a roll in the hay. Hay day. May day. Help! I just can't. Need help. May day.

Schiz 8: This thing here is the thing there too and this other thing is this thing. So the things are same things. Same color things but its different too.

Schiz 9: What do you mean? What do you think I mean? That's what the other guy is saying to me when he hears me saying that this is the lighter one.

Schiz 10: This is the stupid color of a shit ass bowl of salmon. Mix it with mayonnaise. Then it gets tasty. Leave it alone and puke all over the fuckin place. Puke fish.

Schiz 11: This is what happens to blood if you leave it in the sun and it bleaches. The skin gets tan like the niggers, but the blood gets whiter.

Schiz 12: Now listen to me again! Suppose I had to paint your house you'd say paint this color and I'd say no. All painters are crazy you'd say. Maybe so, but what do you know from paint. Light paint dries slow – schmuck.

FOUR-DISC DISPLAY, LOW SIMILARITY (TWELVE HUE STEPS APART)

Referent color: Disc #49   Nonreferent colors: Discs #61, #73, #85

Norm 1: Blue.

Norm 2: The blue.

Norm 3: This blue one.

Norm 4: Blue.

Norm 5: Blue.

Norm 6: Blue.

Norm 7: Blue.
Norm 8: It's blue.
Norm 9: This is blue.
Norm 10: Blue.
Norm 11: Blue.
Norm 12: A pretty little blue.

Schiz 1: Light blue with green.
Schiz 2: Greenest.
Schiz 3: Light blue?
Schiz 4: The lightest blue.
Schiz 5: Carribean.
Schiz 6: The fuckin light blue.
Schiz 7: This blue relaxes me.
Schiz 8: It's the only blue thing.
Schiz 9: Hilda's eye. Please come home. (starts crying)
Schiz 10: Very touching blue.
Schiz 11: Blue blue.
Schiz 12: We see here a blue.

FOUR-DISC DISPLAY, MODERATE-LOW SIMILARITY (EIGHT HUE STEPS APART)

Referent color: Disc # 18   Nonreferent colors: Discs #26, #34, #42
Norm 1: This one is the mustard green.
Norm 2: The green with the yellow.
Norm 3: This one is the yellowest green.
Norm 4: These go in big green jumps, and this is the least green. Yellowish.
Norm 5: The yellowest of the four greens.
Norm 6: This is the yellower one.
Norm 7: Compared to the other three, this one is yellower.
Norm 8: This is a mustard yellow green like color.
Norm 9: This looks like the yellowest one.
Norm 10: A mustardy yellow with the brown.
Norm 11: A mustard yellowish slightly green.
Norm 12: This does have some green in its yellow. Mostly yellow.

Schiz 1: Mustard green and shit.
Schiz 2: This one really has a lot of yellow.
Schiz 3: From colors you don't know. The man downstairs has a tie just this color. Go look!
Schiz 4: This color stinks! No sex appeal. The other colors have sex. The darkest has syrup dripping from the cunt. (Sorry Doc! *aside*)
Schiz 5: Mustard plants aren't the color of mustard, but this is. Why is turd in mustard?
Schiz 6: This is the only one that looks like shit. All the others don't. The shitty one.
Schiz 7: The others have green and go away to blue. Yellow?
Schiz 8: This is the only yellow thing in the green things. The green things are the nicer green things.
Schiz 9: The yellowest greenie on the table. Why don't you – hey you! – look for the yellow one.
Schiz 10: Muck! Like swamps with snakes and *crocodillos* that swim in scum like this.

Schiz 11: This is my puss. It blops (sounds like BLOP – gn) in the balls until I squirt it in the toilet.
Schiz 12: This is the Dutchboy color called mustard yellow antique.

FOUR-DISC DISPLAY, MODERATE-HIGH SIMILARITY (FOUR HUE STEPS APART)

Referent color: Disc #38   Nonreferent colors: Discs #42, #46, #50

Norm 1: This is the lightest green. The one without any blue.
Norm 2: If you mix green and blue, this has no blue.
Norm 3: They are all along a blue green scale. I'm catching one. This one seems to have the purest green.
Norm 4: Again we have the greenies. This one is sort of the greenest. The others seem to have a lot more blue.
Norm 5: This is the greenest one. The others have a bit more blue in them. The greenest.
Norm 6: This is the lightest and most real green.
Norm 7: This is really the lightest green and I think we saw this one before. Light green.
Norm 8: The lightest of the greens. The others become blue like the ocean or sea.
Norm 9: This is a very good green. The others have much more blue.
Norm 10: This is the greenest one. The others have some blue.
Norm 11: This is a green! Boy! The others seem to be going toward sea water blue. Greenest.
Norm 12: This is a grass colored green, while the others surely appear to have elements of bluish shading in them all.

Schiz 1: Clean green. The one without the cream. Don't see this color on planes, it looks like moss, boss!
Schiz 2: The last time I saw green I felt blue. A few minutes ago, no? You want me to sing and not talk, and this sings.
Schiz 3: Why so much green? In the Torah, they say green fields and maybe this one is from the Torah. Yes! This is the one "He" spoke about, *if you know what I mean (whispering)*. This is a green field where life grows much.
Schiz 4: Again fucking! This is the green that hasn't been fucked yet. All the others are dirty fuckers and you can tell they get laid a lot. This would be the worst lay!
Schiz 5: Leaves is a poem by a poet who looked at this color when he saw the poem in his brainside. Barnside. Brainstorms make poets. God makes these leaves.
Schiz 6: Too many fuckin words all comin to mind. Why don't they stop when all you gotta do is say the lightest green. That's not enough. No!
Schiz 7: I feel so shitty when the colors are the same. Are they? I used to talk colors o.k. Now I can't. A green which is grassy assy green.
Schiz 8: Green things. These things are easy things cause the thing is the green green thing and not the not so green green thing. The greenest thing is the it.
Schiz 9: This is green like vegetables in a salad with dressing that covers the green so its covered over green salad. Mazola green.
Schiz 10: This is the national color. All across the nation there are phone booths of this color. Telephone green.
Schiz 11: This is a hospital? No! You're a driving teacher and this is a test to see if I know green lights. In China red lights mean go, green stop.
Schiz 12: President Kennedy with all his money couldn't grow the lawn. Jackie pissed up the place. So they painted the lawn green. This is the color of a lawn that's painted green.

FOUR-DISC DISPLAY, HIGH SIMILARITY
(TWO HUE STEPS APART)

Referent color: Disc #9   Nonreferent colors: Discs #11, #13, #15

Norm   1: All of these are very close together. Their color is all mustard brown. You have to
          pick out the one that has I guess the most brown.
Norm   2: They could all really be the same color with more or less brown. This one has the
          most of brown.
Norm   3: Dammit! These are all alike! So little difference! The one that's important seems
          to be the brownest. That's right. The brownest. It's got no yellow.
Norm   4: We've seen this group of colors before, too! This one is a murky brown. The
          others are brown too and you can sort of line them up by the amount of brown.
Norm   5: These really look shitty. Lousy brown colors. The one that I'm describing has the
          most brown in it compared to the other ones.
Norm   6: These again all look alike. This one is more brown.
Norm   7: This is like a spectrum from brown to mustard. Each one is really close together,
          but if you look at the extremes then this one is the brownest of them all.
Norm   8: This is the brownest of the four colors. The others have more or less yellow in
          them by a comparison.
Norm   9: The three *other* colors have increasing amounts of yellow. This one has the least
          yellow and the most brown. The brownest one.
Norm 10: At first I thought the more colors there are the harder it is. Not so. The brownest.
Norm 11: The others have yellow tint in them. This one has a peculiar brown color to it.
          Sort of a golden brown that has become tarnished or weather worn, faded,
          rusted.
Norm 12: These, of course, are part of the brown yellow spectrum. If you look carefully for
          the one that has the least yellow, the most brown, and this will be the one.

Schiz 1: Four pieces of shit. 1, 2, 3, and 4, and you want to know which piece of shit.
          Well here goes. The one that's the one is the brownest with the most shit in it.
Schiz 2: When you read old bibles, old books, the pages turn colors. They already turned
          colors. This turned color because it is old. The others – I saw 'em before
          no? – are not so old. From them you could read a better story. Newer story.
          More sex. A hotter sexier story.
Schiz 3: This too! This you call a color? Brown, Hitler wore brown and you give me
          Hitler! But I'll tell you 6 million, 4 and a half million, what's the difference. My
          parents got out alive Baruch Hashem. We went to Israel and the desert was brown
          and they say Hitler was dead. But they caught Eichman, brown!
Schiz 4: A truck I saw had a brown like this and it was moving so fast that I remembered
          the color. Brown trucks move fast like hell. Faster than green trucks. Faster then
          blue trucks, and this would be the fastest moving truck around.
Schiz 5: Oranges grow in citrus groves. Tomatoes grow in patches. Potatoes grow in fields.
          Grapes . . . where do they grow? Vines? . . . This has life to it. It is more alive
          than any color. It has Vitamin C. Vitamin C is life and comes from citrus like
          lemons, limes, grapefruit, oranges. This has Vitamin C in it.
Schiz 6: This looks like shit! The same shit as before, only this shit is after you eat corn. I
          had shit like this after my operation. It came poppin out all over the place, the
          nurse came and wiped it up. I wish she had just came. Nurses are good shit
          cleaners.
Schiz 7: Tell ya what I'm gonna do. Not talk about blue. Gonna talk about a brown and
          go to town. Brown and yellow make us mellow. The brown to town. They call
          me mellow yellow (*singing!*). Can't get rid yellow. (*tone of despair*)

Schiz 8: The things are more things. Brown things. Yellowish brown things. Yellowish things. The thing is the brown thing, not the yellow things which get in the way of all things.

Schiz 9: I never saw anything like this before. The only thing like it is the crap in Hilda's cunt, and you don't know what that looks like unless you screwed Hilda's crappy cunt. Not her — just her crappy cunt. Do you?

Schiz 10: A few means two. Now there are four — close the door on the brownish yellows. Lock them out. Lock them out. Only let the brownies through the keyhole. Fill the room with girl scouts in brown. Brownshirts.

Schiz 11: Four niggers all trying to make it in the white world: My world. They're all commie pinkos. One of them has some doubts and doesn't bleach his skin so he's really Uncle Tom. Look out for him. Try and find an honest nigger.

Schiz 12: Hello my name is Jacob. I paint houses and this is a brown for the outside. Its good for shingles, garage doors. Latex paint dries quick but what you really need is an oil base because it is glossy sheen.

ACKNOWLEDGMENTS

This chapter is adapted from an address (Cohen, 1975) to the New York Academy of Sciences, Psychology Section, April 21, 1975. Beyond additional material in the section, *Experiments with Schizophrenic Patients,* this chapter includes an entirely new section, *Clinical Implications,* and an appendix containing a much larger set of illustrative speaker protocols than presented in any previous publication based on this research. The research has been supported in part by NSF Grant GS-40265 and is, in large measure, the outcome of a long and satisfying collaborative relationship with Professor Seymour Rosenberg of Rutgers University.

REFERENCES

Auster, P. One-man language. (Review of *Le schizo et les langues* by L. Wolfson). *New York review of books,* February 6, 1975, 30–31.

Back, K. W. *Beyond words: The story of sensitivity training and the encounter movement.* New York: Russel Sage Foundation, 1972.

Bleuler, E. *Dementia-praecox and the group of schizophrenias.* New York: International Universities Press, 1950. (Originally published, 1911).

Broen, W. E. *Schizophrenia: Research and theory.* New York: Academic Press, 1968.

Broen, W. E., & Storms, L. H. Lawful disorganization: The process underlying a schizophrenic syndrome. *Psychological Review,* 1966, *74,* 265–279.

Buss, A. H. *Psychopathology.* New York: John Wiley & Sons, 1966.

Chapman, L., & Chapman, J. *Disordered thought in schizophrenia.* New York: Appleton-Century-Crofts, 1973.

Cohen, B. D. Referent communication in schizophrenia: The perseverative-chaining model. *Annals of the New York Academy of Sciences,* 1976, *270,* 124–141.

Cohen, B. D., & Camhi, J. Schizophrenic performance in a word-communication task. *Journal of Abnormal Psychology,* 1967, *72,* 240–246.

Cohen, B. D., Nachmani, G., & Rosenberg, S. Referent communication disturbances in acute schizophrenia. *Journal of Abnormal Psychology,* 1974, *83,* 1–13.

Cromwell, R. Strategies for studying schizophrenic behavior. *Psychopharmacologia*, 1972, *24*, 121–146.

Cromwell, R. L., & Dokecki, P. R. Schizophrenic language: A disattention interpretation. In S. Rosenberg & J. H. Koplin (Eds.), *Developments in applied psycholinguistics research*. New York: Macmillan, 1968.

Farnsworth, D. *The Farnsworth–Munsell 100 hue test for the examination of color discrimination manual*. Baltimore: Munsell Color Co., 1957.

Goldstein, K. Methodological approach to the study of schizophrenic thought disorder. In J. S. Kasanin (Ed.), *Language and thought in schizophrenia*. Berkeley: University of California Press, 1944.

Kantorowitz, D., & Cohen, B. D. Referent communication in chronic schizophrenia. *Journal of Abnormal Psychology*, 1977, *86*, 1–9.

Krauss, R. M., & Weinheimer, S. Effect of referent similarity and communication mode on verbal encoding. *Journal of Verbal Learning and Verbal Behavior*, 1967, *6*, 359–363.

Lisman, S. A., & Cohen, B. D. Self-editing deficits in schizophrenia. *Journal of Abnormal Psychology*, 1972, *79*, 181–188.

Mead, G. H. *Mind, self, and society*. Chicago: University of Chicago Press, 1934.

Mednick, S. A. A learning theory approach to research in schizophrenia. *Psychological Bulletin*, 1958, *55*, 316–327.

Nachmani, G., & Cohen, B. D. Recall and recognition free learning in schizophrenics. *Journal of Abnormal Psychology*, 1969, *74*, 511–516.

Piaget, J. *The language and thought of the child*. New York: Harcourt, 1926.

Rodnick, E. H., & Garmezy, N. An experimental approach to the study of schizophrenia. In M. R. Jones (Ed.), *Nebraska Symposium on Motivation*. Lincoln, Nebraska: University of Nebraska Press, 1957.

Rosenberg, S. The development of referential skills in children. In R. L. Schiefelbusch (Ed.), *Language of the mentally retarded*. Baltimore: University Park Press, 1972.

Rosenberg, S., & Cohen, B. D. Speakers' and listeners' processes in a word-communication task. *Science*, 1964, *145*, 1201–1203.

Rosenberg, S., & Cohen, B. D. Referential processes of speakers and listeners. *Psychological Review*, 1966, *73*, 208–231.

Rosenberg, S., & Gordon, A. Identification of facial expressions from affective descriptions: A probabilistic choice analysis of referential ambiguity. *Journal of Personality and Social Psychology*, 1968, *10*, 157–166.

Rosenberg, S., & Markham, B. Choice behavior in a referentially ambiguous task. *Journal of Personality and Social Psychology*, 1971, *17*, 99–106.

Rothberg, M. The effect of "social" instructions on word-association behavior. *Journal of Verbal Learning and Verbal Behavior*, 1967, *6*, 298–300.

Salzinger, K. *Schizophrenia: behavioral aspects*. New York: John Wiley & Sons, 1973.

Spence, J. T., & Spence, K. W. The motivational components of manifest anxiety: Drive and drive stimuli. In C. D. Spielberger (Ed.), *Anxiety and behavior*. New York: Academic Press, 1966.

Strauss, M. E. Behavioral differences between acute and chronic schizophrenics: Course of psychosis, effects of institutionalization or sampling biases? *Psychological Bulletin*, 1973, *79*, 271–279.

Sullivan, H. S. The language of schizophrenia. In J. S. Kasanin (Ed.), *Language and thought in schizophrenia*. Berkeley: University of California Press, 1944.

Venables, P. Input regulation and psychopathology. In M. Hammer, K. Salzinger & S. Sutton (Eds.), *Psychopathology: Contributions from the social, behavioral, and biological sciences*. New York: John Wiley & Sons, 1973.

Vygotsky, L. S. *Thought and speech*. Cambridge, Massachusetts: MIT Press, 1962.

Woods, W. L. Language study in schizophrenia. *Journal of Nervous and Mental Disease*, 1938, *87*, 290–316.

2
Communicability Deficit in Schizophrenics Resulting from a More General Deficit

Kurt Salzinger

New York State Psychiatric Institute,
and Polytechnic Institute of New York

Stephanie Portnoy
Richard S. Feldman

New York State Psychiatric Institute

A basic premise of this chapter is that the oft-reported peculiar schizophrenic language, though constituting a good entree to gaining an understanding of the abnormality of schizophrenia, is not itself the underlying problem that the schizophrenic individual has to contend with. Because we are talkers rather than doers, and because language has two important functions in the human being, one to control one's own behavior and the other to communicate with other individuals or to influence them, any major difficulty influences speech. Finally, whatever one's theoretical position with respect to language behavior, all agree that language behavior is very complex and for that reason also is an ideal index of any general behavioral difficulty.

Knowing all of this, one may ask why language in schizophrenia is not the major focus of the difficulty. The answer lies in the multiplicity of differences between schizophrenics and normals, differences that are as plentiful as grains of sand on a beach. All of the differences in the functioning of schizophrenics and normals cannot be explained in terms of language behavior, and trying to do so is to bend the facts until they break. Needed is a concept that supercedes but also explains all of the particular differences. Finally, we believe that any explanation of the behavior of the schizophrenic must view that behavior in a dynamic fashion; schizophrenic behavior, like normal behavior, is controlled by the genetic foundations laid down in the germ plasm of the individual, but it expresses itself through the force which we have come to call behavior theory variables in psychology.

PROBLEMS OF SPECIFICATION OF SCHIZOPHRENIA

No discussion of any behavior related to schizophrenia can be engaged in without pointing out the critical problem of identifying those individuals who supposedly suffer from this malady. Despite the fact that we have studied "schizophrenics" for some 21 years now, we have steadfastly held to the opinion that this diagnostic category is not reliable. When one of us wrote a book on schizophrenia (Salzinger, 1973b), he felt compelled to explain his own peculiar behavior of describing a phenomenon whose reliability he doubted. How is it, if it is so difficult to decide who is schizophrenic, that he not only does research on such people but also managed to write a whole book about them? That issue is dealt with in the introduction to the book; the conclusion reached is that schizophrenia is a unicorn. There is no sense burdening readers with the entire argument for that point here, because, if interested, they can find it spelled out in the book. Here, let us simply state that schizophrenia, like the unicorn, has a voluminous literature, much of it interesting but often written without aware-ness of the writings of others, and that the lack of awareness has in both cases produced much conflict with respect to what the phenomenon actually is. Thus, we are told in the Old Testament that the unicorn is a two-horned animal, and in the psychiatric literature that at least one category of schizophrenia, pseudo-neurotic schizophrenia, is essentially a neurosis gone on too long. Yet, despite (or maybe partly because of) the terrible state of description and location of the unicorn we call schizophrenia, people so labelled do exist; many of them inhabit our hospitals and remain for long periods of time; others live in the community limited by their peculiarity of behavior − a form of peculiarity which not only makes them annoying to others but which also makes them susceptible to being used and abused by others in the community who offer them half-way houses and welfare hotels. The lack of reliability is not an argument for the nonexis-tence of these people; it is an argument for further study.

The problem is essentially one of finding a common core for at least some of the people labelled schizophrenic. The common core we find may well describe other patients equally behaviorally incapacitated. Our boundaries for the cate-gory of schizophrenia, at least with respect to hospital populations in the United States, stem from the fact that these are people who have been placed in state hospitals and that they are in the age range of 18 to 45. In our studies, most of the patients admitted to the hospital in that age range are labelled schizophrenic.

There are, of course, a great many complications. Patients so labelled have been influenced not only by the primary effects of schizophrenia but also by the interaction of whatever the basic incapacity may be with the environment as mediated by the laws of behavior theory. This requires careful measurement free of the artifacts that accompany most experiments with schizophrenic patients, and yet it requires that we study behavior significant in the life of the schizophrenic. It requires that we study behavior that must have been influenced, if not produced, by the learning process, and yet that we disentangle the basic deficit from its interaction with the environment. Furthermore, this procedure requires that we slowly change the category of schizophrenia itself as we collect more data and empirically arrive at new groupings of patients. Sutton (1973) has suggested the "iterative method" as a way of using empirical data to increase the homogeneity of a diagnostic category: An exact test is used to distinguish one diagnostic category from another; then, the part of the interview data on which is based the diagnosis that best relates to the objective test data is employed to confirm the objective test data of a new group of patients.

It seems to us that one must use theoretical considerations as another way of making the diagnostic categories more homogeneous. If a theory states that a particular form of behavior or stimulus control is characteristic of schizophrenic patients, then, having decided on the measurement of that characteristic and assuming that it does distinguish schizophrenics from others, one can make that group more homogeneous by selecting the patients who have extreme values of that characteristic. Whether the homogenization of the diagnostic category is entirely empirical, as suggested by Sutton, or whether it is theoretically stimulated, there can be no question that it is sorely needed. We suggest here that the Immediacy Hypothesis presents an opportunity for homogenization of the diagnostic category.

THE GENERAL DEFICIT IN SCHIZOPHRENIA

The Immediacy Hypothesis states that schizophrenic behavior is primarily controlled by stimuli that are immediate in the environment. This means that when there are several stimuli acting simultaneously upon a schizophrenic, the one that controls behavior is the one that comes closest to the occasion for the response. For example, if a schizophrenic subject is instructed to try to counteract the effect of an anchor stimulus in an absolute judgment situation, and only after a while the anchor is presented and immediately thereafter the stimulus to be judged, then the schizophrenic's behavior will be controlled by the anchor stimulus much more than will the corresponding behavior of a normal individual (Salzinger, 1957). On the other hand, if that same anchor stimulus is presented at an earlier time, the effect becomes reduced (Wurster, 1965). When the schizophrenic patient is provided with a card sorting task but also systematically presented with distracting stimuli, it will be found that the schizophrenic will be much more affected by the irrelevant stimuli than will the normal individual

(Chapman, 1956). Constancy experiments show that the retinal image is more important than object constancy in governing the perceptions of schizophrenics compared to normals (Weckowicz, 1964). In our conditioning work, we have found that schizophrenics' responses extinguish faster than normals' (Salzinger & Pisoni, 1960), showing once again the effect of the immediacy of stimuli, this time by the diminution of response in the absence of the supporting stimuli (the reinforcers). We have reviewed a large number of experiments with respect to the Immediacy Hypothesis (Salzinger, 1971a, 1971b, 1973b), and the results seem to fit rather nicely.

A question that may be asked is how this theory relates to the spate of other theories now becoming so plentiful. Without presenting extensive detail, we can say that the Immediacy Hypothesis is simpler. That is, it requires only one process in explaining the aberrant behavior, namely, that stimuli closer to the occasion for a response have more control over responses than stimuli more remote. This is in contrast with other theories that suggest that schizophrenics have difficulty disattending (which, it would seem, not only requires concern about how stimuli get control over responses but also an additional process to explain how stimuli release responses). By positing that the schizophrenic may have a deficit in both processes, one is certainly complicating the picture, and Cromwell and Dokecki (1968), who generated this theory, may well have introduced the complication earlier than needed. Certainly, at this point, there is no indication of the need for a two-process theory. We also maintain that our theory is more general than others because it pertains not only to verbal behavior but to other kinds of behavior, including the processing of stimuli, motor responses, conditioning, and so forth. (See Salzinger, 1973b, for a fuller comparison of the Immediacy Hypothesis to other theories.)

A word needs to be said about the relationship of the Immediacy Hypothesis to some internal process. Because we are contending that the schizophrenic is an individual who begins life with a tendency to respond to stimuli that are more immediate, we ought to be able at least to point in the general direction of where the deficit may be found. This is not the place to go into details of any biochemical basis for schizophrenia. Nevertheless, it is interesting to look at the recent findings (Snyder, 1974) on the effectiveness of those tranquilizers thought to be specifically antischizophrenic and at amphetamine, which elicits schizophrenic-like behavior. The tranquilizers apparently block the dopamine receptors, thus keeping those specialized neurons from releasing the neurotransmitters that allow one neuron to activate another. It is also interesting that amphetamines can release norepinephrine or dopamine directly into the synaptic cleft, that is, the connection between neurons. The link from this biochemical set of findings to the Immediacy Hypothesis is that responding to the most immediate stimulus may be produced by the potentiating effect of amphetamine or some such substance (presumably found in schizophrenic patients) when even slight external stimulation occurs. It should be pointed out that the amphetamine model of psychosis is far from established. Nevertheless, the potential relationship between the amphetamine-psychosis model and the Immediacy Hypothesis suggests the following test: Determine the effectiveness of immediate stimuli as compared to those that are more remote in animals administered amphetamine. Although no direct tests of this kind have been made, the animal data on DRL (Differential Reinforcement of Low rates) schedules of reinforcement seem to show a greater degree of responding to the more immediate than to the more remote stimuli (Sidman, 1955).

It remains for us to speak of the interaction of the Immediacy Hypothesis and the laws of acquisition and maintenance of behavior. No theory which fails to take the laws of behavior into account can explain a phenomenon such as schizophrenia, which is obviously a long-range affliction, whether episodic, as Zubin (1975) has recently suggested, or whether a slow insidious deteriorating process, as the more classical conception of schizophrenia suggests. The behavior-theory model, with its concept of reinforcement contingency, is most helpful in explaining the interaction of the postulated deficit and the ultimate effect on behavior. The concept of reinforcement contingency states that behavior (classes of responses) is emitted on certain occasions (discriminative stimuli) that precede or accompany the behavior, and that the behavior has certain consequences (reinforcing events) that follow the behavior. In following the Immediacy Hypothesis, it must be assumed that a great many of the discriminative and reinforcing stimuli that act upon the schizophrenic individual are of an immediate nature. Obviously, a great many *but not all* of the controlling stimuli for normals are also immediate in nature. What happens when the vast preponderance of the controlling stimuli are immediate? Individuals so controlled are expected to respond to stimuli that normal individuals often ignore. Sorting-test behavior is obviously an example of such inappropriate behavior, but in life there are a great many other examples, such as the paranoid responding to unimportant stimuli. The normal individual must ignore a large number of impinging stimuli and yet respond to others. A conversation held by two individuals unrelated to, but within earshot of, ` someone else must not be assumed to relate to that person. A response to immediate stimuli, however, may produce the "misunderstanding" so typical of patients called paranoid because they respond to such extraneous stimuli in the same way as they do to remarks addressed directly to them.

To take but one other example of the Immediacy Hypothesis and its interaction with the laws of behavior theory, we now examine the consequence of immediacy on the production of conditioned reinforcement. A great many stimuli accompany the occurrence of primary or conditioned reinforcers; those accompanying stimuli become candidates for turning into conditioned reinforcers. The stimuli that are closer always become the conditioned reinforcers for the schizophrenic individual; hence, stimuli thought to be incidental by normal individuals come to control the behavior of schizophrenics. There are obviously many other ways in which the principle of immediacy interacts with the laws of behavior theory. Many of these ways have already been sketched out in the publications cited. The kinds of effects we have described are the ones that are expected to become somewhat permanent in the behavioral repertory of the schizophrenic individual.

The variables of behavior theory ought to be expected to influence the testing of various theories in other ways as well, however. Thus, the environment of the ward and the hospital in general that is now being much more frequently discussed in reference to patients can be conceptualized in terms of behavior-theory variables. Salzinger and Salzinger (1973) described data relevant to this issue, so we need only to point out here that the particular reinforcement contingency effective on the ward from which the patient is drawn for confirmation or disconfirmation of the theory being tested should have some importance in controlling the results obtained. One possibility is that the patients are kept under deprivation conditions in which no response results in any consequence with the exception of some violent behavior, and then the consequence is very aversive. Such a patient can be expected to be much more susceptible to social reinforcement than a patient who is already being reinforced socially in his or her ward environment. Approval in solving a word problem or in a reaction time or sorting task can be expected, under such circumstances, to go much further with a deprived patient than with a patient already receiving considerable social reinforcement. To test a theory, information about the ward climate should be gathered; one effective way of doing that is by observing the behavior of the staff and the patients to determine the reinforcement contingencies effective there. By using the same mode of analysis for both the test situation and the ward-life situation, predictions can be made about the kinds of effects to be expected — effects not related to the theory being tested or even to the patients, but rather to the temporary environment in which the individual resides just before being tested. Because there has yet been little effort to study this problem in a systematic way, investigators will have to begin work on it.

So far, we have discussed the theory that we want to apply to schizophrenic behavior. The argument has been made that the theory must apply to verbal behavior, even that verbal behavior may be the best testing ground for schizophrenic behavior theories, but we have also argued that the theory must be general enough to explain all the anomalies of schizophrenia, many of which are clearly outside the province of verbal behavior. We must now explain how the Immediacy Hypothesis can be translated into its effects in verbal behavior.

THE STUDY OF VERBAL BEHAVIOR

The importance of language behavior derives from two sources: its regulatory function, in which the verbal behavior directs control of one's own behavior, as in problem solving or self-control, and its communicative function, in which one person essentially seeks to influence another through verbal behavior. Sometimes that influence seems almost trivial because the only accomplishment of the communication may be to keep the other interlocutor with the speaker; at other times, the effect of the influence is the procurement of more tangible reinforcers, but influence is clearly always a part of communication.

Earlier research (Kasanin, 1944) into language of schizophrenics on an objective basis took the route of studying their problem-solving behavior as in sorting tests, proverb interpretation and the like. The speech of schizophrenics and its communicative value were always clinically examined and otherwise wondered at. Comparisons to poetry have run rampant, and so have the clinical interpretations of what the schizophrenic patient actually means when he or she emits this manifestly uncommunicative speech. Outstanding exceptions to this soft-minded approach have been the work of Whitehorn and Zipf (1943) and the Johnson (1944) book compiling a number of dissertations, which examined the rate of repetition of words in speech and writing. More recent work has been reviewed in Chapman and Chapman (1973), Vetter (1968, 1975), and in our own research papers (Hammer & Salzinger, 1964; Salzinger, 1973b; Salzinger, Portnoy, & Feldman, 1964b, 1966; Salzinger, Portnoy, Pisoni, & Feldman, 1970).

Before reviewing the work on the objective measurement of language behavior, a comment is needed on the rule-governed approach to language that is still being used to gain an understanding of language, although its most virulent form, the generative grammatical approach, is definitely on the wane. We have already commented critically elsewhere on the nature of the generative model (Salzinger, 1967, 1968, 1970, 1973a, 1975; Salzinger & Eckerman, 1967; Salzinger & Feldman, 1973). Because a number of students of psychopathology seem to be getting interested in the notion of rule-governed behavior, it is useful to make some comments on that kind of approach. The first point to be remembered is that rules are concepts, not facts. Secondly, rules are not stimuli or even processes that actually control the behavior of the speaker or, for that matter, of the hearer. At their best, rules are concepts that are not inconsistent with the behavior that is being examined. Unfortunately, too frequently the rules are made by investigators who are untroubled by exceptions to those rules because they have the theory-saving concepts of "competence" and "performance." Performance is thought to reflect underlying competence only some of the time, so when a response pattern does not follow the rule established, the investigators simply resort to the explanation that performance (*mere* performance) is unfortunately affected by variables unrelated to the person's competence and, therefore, can be disregarded when the exception arises. In the field of abnormal psychology, too many such concepts already exist. Therefore, we need not borrow untestable theories from linguistics in order to have vague thinking.

What are the advantages of the study of language behavior as an index to pathology? There are both methodological and substantive ones. First, we examine the methodological ones. Most patients are capable of speech; that is, they are capable of at least a few minutes of speech. Our research (Salzinger, Portnoy, & Feldman, 1964a) has shown that although only about 40% of the patients selected by no other criterion than being between the ages of 18 and 45, with a diagnosis of schizophrenia in both the distribution hospital and the hospital in which we were testing the patients, seem capable of speaking for a period of 30 minutes without being asked questions, virtually 100% can speak for the short period of time necessary to accumulate the kind of speech sample long enough for the cloze procedure (a communicability measure). Therefore, the first point to be made on methodology is that speech is relatively easy to obtain from the kinds of patients we are interested in studying. We should add to this that speech is a relatively stable form of behavior in our society because it is well practiced from early childhood and central in any kind of social intercourse.

Thirdly, because people talk much of the time, they are used to being asked to talk or are used to being engaged in conversation. This is very important in circumventing the problem of cooperativeness which plagues any psychological techniques requiring patients to do something specific, such as lifting a finger as soon as a stimulus appears, recalling a word, defining a word, tapping as fast as possible, or saying what they see on some peculiar-looking but symmetrical picture. Because of the nature of the procedures employed to analyze the resultant speech samples, the patients do not even have a clue about what the experimenter is looking for. What better way exists to circumvent the problem of cooperativeness than to present a task when the subject does not know a task is being presented or how the material will be analyzed? In addition, recording equipment enables investigators to record, under relatively noisy conditions, the kinds of speech samples necessary for analysis. This equipment allows the transformation of the material rapidly and efficiently into a form that is amenable to analysis either by working on the written form directly, as in the type-token ratio analysis already mentioned; in grammatical or in content analysis (for example, Gottschalk, 1967); or in some transmuted form to be tested on a new group of people, as in the cloze procedure. The same kind of material also lends itself to other kinds of analysis, such as vocal analysis (Starkweather, 1967; Waskow, 1967). Finally, the nature of speech yields a rather large sample of responses related to one another, thus allowing the examination not only of a large sample of behavior but also of the way in which the responses of that sample interrelate.

The substantive advantage of using speech for analysis is that it is the essence of social intercourse. Without speech or communication of some sort, no person can long exist in our society. Furthermore, speech demonstrates the extent to which an individual can influence others. In addition, the extent to which an individual's verbal behavior can be modified through reinforcement may be taken as an index of that individual's more general susceptibility to social influence. Because of the naturalness of the speaking procedure, we found it possible to condition (and measure the rate of such conditioning) both schizo-phrenic and nonpsychiatric, physically ill patients in the course of what un-doubtedly seemed to be nothing more than another clinical interview (Salzinger & Pisoni, 1958, 1960, 1961). The response class being conditioned was verbal (self-referred affect), and the reinforcement was verbal, consisting of such well-used expressions as "Yeah," "Yes," "I see," and "I can understand that." Our findings, in short, were that the schizophrenics were as easily conditionable as the normal controls, the only difference arising when we examined the rate of extinction. The schizophrenics' responses extinguished more rapidly than did the normals'. When the immediate stimulus (in this case the reinforcer) was re-moved, the response rate decreased more rapidly, indicating that only when the stimulus was right there, as it was during the entire conditioning period, were the schizophrenics changing their response rate. We must emphasize here again that the subjects, whether normal or schizophrenic, did not realize that they were subjects or that an experiment was taking place. Finally, because verbal behavior is used to control oneself, examination of the intactness of the verbal response interrelationships provides us with some indirect information on the ability of the subjects to make use of their verbal behavior for problem solving. In brief, the examination of verbal behavior provides us with information on the extent to which a person can influence others or, for that matter, can be influenced by others and the extent to which self-influence (that is, self-control) is possible in such a person.

SOME EXPERIMENTS IN VERBAL BEHAVIOR

No psychologist studying behavior can avoid making the assumption that behav-ior is lawful, predictable, and controllable. With respect to language behavior, this assumption is, if possible, even more obvious. Language is nothing if it is not predictable. Because of predictability, understanding between people takes place. The basis for one of the procedures we have been using to study what we have first called comprehensibility and then communicability is exactly this kind of predictability. The method was named "cloze" procedure by Taylor (1953). A good way to explain how it works is to think of a conversation taking place over a bad telephone connection. If the interlocutors are clear in what they say, then missing words once in a while ought not to influence the communicability of the messages very much; to the extent that they are unclear, however, the mutilation involved in the noisy telephone line is probably just enough to prevent understanding.

An important variable in determining the amount of understanding, when part of a message is distorted, must depend on how well individuals know one another, and indeed, we have done research (Hammer, Polgar, & Salzinger, 1969; Salzinger, Hammer, Portnoy & Polgar, 1970) that shows the power of such variables. Here our concern was to construct methods of quantitative measurement of the degree of communicability. Whatever else could be said about schizophrenic speech, much of it manifested a quality of only vague understandability. Having shown successfully that the communicability of speech varied with the statistical approximation to English as measured by the cloze procedure (Salzinger, Portnoy, & Feldman, 1962), we felt ready to examine the speech of schizophrenic patients. We took the first 200 words of the monologues we had been collecting both from schizophrenic patients and from matched normal controls who were patients with physical ailments and who had resided in the general medical hospital for approximately as long as had the schizophrenic patients with whom we were comparing them. Having learned earlier that speech depends to a large extent on the speech community from which the individual speaker comes, we matched the normals and schizophrenics not only on sex, age, and education, but also on speech community. We defined the latter in terms of such criteria as ethnic group membership and birthplace of the parents. The success of this kind of grouping was borne out by a study we did on type-token ratio (Hammer & Salzinger, 1964), which showed significant differences among such groupings. Before presenting the cloze procedure results, it is pertinent to comment on the type-token ratio results of our experiment. Like many other investigators, we found that the schizophrenics had a tendency to repeat words more than did the normals. Assuming that everybody avoids repeating exact words, in terms of the Immediacy Hypothesis, this means that schizophrenics "consider" repetition over shorter spans than do normals.

Let us now look at the cloze procedure results. Our cloze procedure consists of preparing a typescript of the first 200 words of each monologue and substituting a blank of standard length for every fifth word. A group of normal subjects is then given these mutilated typescripts and is told that these are actual speech samples with every fifth word deleted. They are asked to guess the missing words. The results for the first 100 words are that 11 out of 13 pairs show better communicability (guessability) in the normal than in the schizophrenic samples. For the second 100 words, only one out of the 13 pairs shows better communicability for the schizophrenic than for the normal, with 12 going in the predicted direction. Figure 2.1 shows a summary of the findings. Although the normal samples get the larger correct guessing scores and the first 100 words do not differ from the second, the schizophrenic samples clearly (and significantly) obtain lower scores on the second 100 words than on the first, with both being significantly lower than the normal scores.

The Immediacy Hypothesis predicts that the speech of schizophrenics should be more difficult to understand than the speech of normals because the response-produced stimulus control in the former extends over shorter spans than in the latter. Shorter spans of response-produced stimulus control suggest less coherence of the material, with more tangential material coming up because individual words, or even phrases, evoke later words and phrases depending on

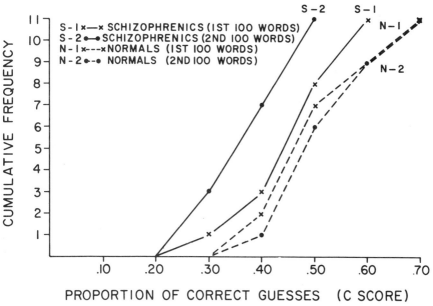

FIG. 2.1 Cumulative frequency of schizophrenic and normal subjects as a function of proportion of correct guesses to total guesses (C score). S-1 and S-2, and N-1 and N-2, refer respectively to the first and second 100 words of the schizophrenic and normal passages. (From Salzinger, Portnoy, & Feldman, 1964b. Reprinted by permission of The New York Academy of Sciences.)

the context in which they are emitted. If that context tends to fade sooner for one population than for another, more tangential remarks can be expected, that is, remarks that are connected to the preceding words but not to all the preceding words.

The second result — that the second 100 words were even less communicable than the first — suggests, because the 200 words were spoken continuously without any questions or other remarks by the experimenter during their course of utterance, another bit of evidence in favor of the Immediacy Hypothesis. The effect of external stimuli (the instructions with their suggested topics, and so forth) that got the speaker going can be expected to become progressively weaker and might largely have worn off by the time the speaker emitted the second 100 words. Therefore, one would expect the schizophrenic to show more of the tangential effect than even before, being now entirely dependent on response-produced stimuli. A question persisted on this result, however. Is the reduction in communicability from the first 100 to the second 100 words a function of the reception (does the "hearer" get more and more confused in reading the material?) or does the speaker tend, as already suggested, to relate successive emissions of verbal behavior to relatively short preceding segments of utterance, thus confusing the hearer? The manner in which we originally tested the changing communicability with time did not allow us to disentangle the two factors from one another. Therefore, we readministered the passages to new groups of clozers. Each clozer received the first half (first 100 words) first for "clozing" followed by the second half, in some passages, and the reverse (that is, the second half first followed by the first half second) in others. The results were no different from the original ones; the order of clozing had no effect. Apparently, the changing communicability was entirely a function of the speaker rather than of the hearer.

In a further effort to evaluate the significance of the cloze procedure, we related the cloze scores (the number of words correctly guessed for each passage) to the number of days that the patients spent in the hospital out of 180 days of follow-up. Those patients whose speech samples received the higher cloze-procedure scores remained in the hospital for a shorter period of time than those whose speech received lower cloze scores. The correlation was −.47, significant at better than the .05 level. When we correlated the cloze procedure scores to number of days in the hospital, separately for the first 100 and the second 100 words, the first 100-word scores correlated −.29 with number of days in the hospital, and the second correlated −.48. Only the second 100-word correlation was statistically significant. For the schizophrenic—normal difference, the immediacy effect based on the response-produced stimuli left a greater mark on the second 100 words than on the first.

These rather tantalizing results led us to the next experiment. If it is true that the schizophrenic patients left dependent on their own response-produced stimuli tend to respond preponderantly to those words closest to them at the time of utterance, then we should be able to test for this effect directly. Selecting blanks on the basis of high and low cloze-procedure scores and part of speech (function or lexical words) from the passages of 20 schizophrenics and normals matched with respect to age, sex, education, and speech community, we presented each blank in the following different contexts: the two words surrounding it, 4, 8, 16, and 28 words surrounding the blank, one-half on each side. Looking at the overall results (Figure 2.2), it is clear that an increase in context causes an increase in the correct guessing of the missing words. Note that at low context the schizophrenic speech appears to evoke a larger number of correct guesses than the normal speech, and then, as the normal curve grows faster than the schizophrenic curve, eventually the normal material is clearly superior to the schizophrenic material.

The next figure (Figure 2.3) gives a much more detailed picture of what happens to the various classes of words. In general, the graph shows that the schizophrenic speech samples increase less in predictability than do the normal samples. This difference is most marked in the class of function words, such as "and," "but," "of," "for," and "to." One may expect exactly this result, given

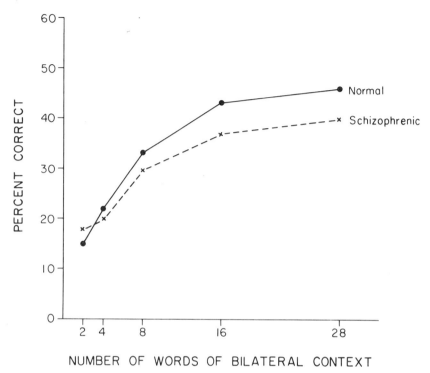

FIG. 2.2 Percent of correct words guessed to schizophrenic and normal speech segments as a function of the number of words of bilateral context.

that function words derive their meaning almost exclusively from the words among which they are embedded. If we look at the normals' high function and the schizophrenics' high function words, remembering that the word "high" refers to highly predictable words in the original administration of the cloze procedure, we find that at low context values the schizophrenic speech is more highly predictable, whereas at high context the situation reverses itself, with normal speech being more predictable. This provides direct evidence for schizophrenic speech having interrelationships among words over short spans, although normal speech has such relationships over relatively long spans. Schizophrenic speech being more predictable than normal speech at low contexts suggests that those closer words are more closely related to one another than are the more remote words. In the normal case, there continues to be an increase in the number of correct guesses, with an increase in context, thus showing that as one goes further and further away from a particular word, there continue to be bits of information related to that word.

Since that experiment, we have become interested in the problem of unilateral context. The data are now being analyzed, but at least one interesting result has

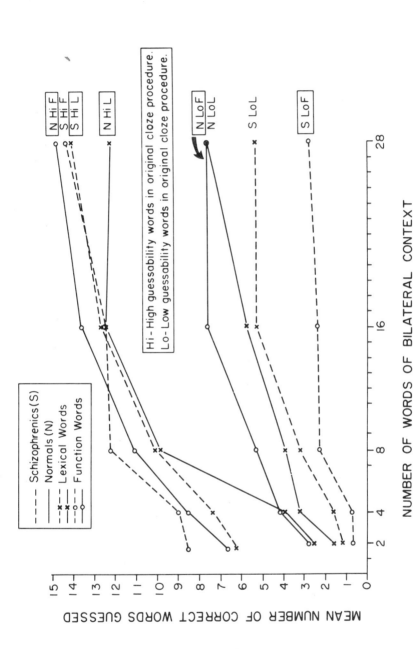

NUMBER OF WORDS OF BILATERAL CONTEXT

FIG. 2.3 Mean number of correct words guessed to schizophrenic and normal speech segments as a function of number of words of bilateral context, with type of word as a parameter. (The boxed word types designate statistically significant trends (p < .05) over increasing degrees of bilateral context.) (From Salzinger, Portnoy, Pisoni, & Feldman, 1970. Copyright 1970 by the American Psychological Association. Reprinted by permission.)

already emerged. We used the same speech segments employed for the study just described, presenting the same blanks in the bilateral context form, and also in a unilateral form in which we presented only left context (that is, material that preceded the particular blank) and also right context only (that is, material that followed the blank). The results for the response class of high function words, which we found of particular interest in the last study, again show data of interest (see Figure 2.4). The bilateral results (and here note that we are looking at contexts up to *14* words to make it comparable to the unilateral context) are very much like those obtained originally; at low contexts the schizophrenic speech segments call forth a greater number of correct guesses, and by the time the context increases to 14 words, there is no difference between the normal and the schizophrenic speech, again showing a different distribution of relatedness of words to one another. With schizophrenic speech, most of the related words are very close, and with normal speech the related words stretch out over longer spans.

Now, let us look at the unilateral results. The left context does not seem to differentiate the schizophrenic from the normal passages at all. On the other hand, the right context (which is, of course, most logically relevant to function words) shows the schizophrenic speech segments to be approximately as predictable as the normal for low context, but the normal speech segments are clearly superior for high context.

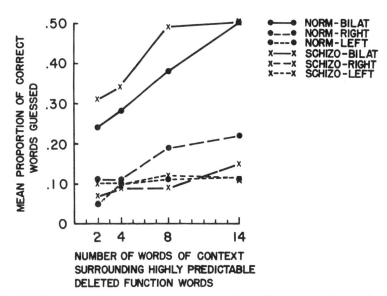

FIG. 2.4 Mean proportion of correct words guessed to schizophrenic and normal speech segments as a function of number of words of context (both bilateral and unilateral) surrounding highly predictable deleted function words.

There is one other interesting result that has come from this study so far. When we compared the effect of a given amount of context in the bilateral condition to the same amount of context in the unilateral condition, we found that bilateral context evoked a significantly larger number of correct guesses than unilateral context for schizophrenic speech segments for all values of context (2, 4, 8, and 14 words), whereas for normal speech, bilateral context was superior to unilateral context only at high levels of context (8 and 14 words). Thus again, we find that the degree of remoteness of words from one another clearly differentiates the schizophrenic from the normal speech segments. For schizophrenic speech, it makes a clear difference whether the context words are more removed from the word to be guessed by even one word because even at the 2-word context, bilateral context was superior to unilateral context.

One other study remains to be described. We set out to compare the Immediacy Hypothesis with McGhie and Chapman's (1961) "lapse-of-attention hypothesis." The lapse-of-attention hypothesis says essentially that schizophrenic patients suffer from fluctuations of attention, as opposed to the attraction or control by immediate stimuli which is what the Immediacy Hypothesis postulates. In one of our studies (Salzinger, Portnoy, & Feldman, 1966), we devised a measure for that kind of phenomenon in speech. The measure consisted simply of asking a group of normal subjects to convert the unpunctuated transcripts into sentences by marking them off by means of parentheses by crossing out any words that did not seem to fit into the sentences at all. These words that did not seem to fit at all (we have called them "intrusions") constitute the measure of attention lapse, in the sense that such words presumably must have come from some other stimulation – from stimulation unrelated to what the person was saying before. We then constructed new cloze-procedure passages from the original speech samples by first removing the intrusions and then, from these shortened speech samples, deleting every fifth word and substituting blanks. The proportion of correct guesses obtained for these passages was then compared to the proportion of correct guesses for the corresponding complete passages (including intrusions) from which the same words to be guessed had been deleted. The two kinds of passages showed no difference in guessability, and the differences between schizophrenics and normals were the same in both cases. We concluded that in schizophrenics the intrusions constituted only an extreme consequence of the communicability deficit, whereas in normals (where there was no significant correlation between communicability and the number of intrusions) the small number of intrusions is unrelated to the general ability to communicate. Also of interest in this study was our *post hoc* analysis of the blanks that were preceded or followed by intrusions and those that were not adjacent to such intrusions. Although the normal passages were reduced in communicability by having an intrusion adjacent to the blank, the schizophrenic passages were reduced in communicability by twice as much. Again, we find that the word immediately adjacent is the critical one for understanding schizophrenic speech but only partially significant for normal speech. In other words, schizophrenic speech, to be understood, must have the short-range related words present; if one of these short-range words is not at all related, then a great loss in communicability is inevitable.

CONCLUSION

What can we say on the basis of all these studies? It seems quite clear to us. Schizophrenic patients suffer from a general deficit that produces inefficient functioning in most of their behavior. This is true for their ability to solve problems, to control self, to react fast enough, to have an objective view of the world (as opposed to paranoid ideas), and to speak and write in a way that is understandable to their audience. As important as speech production and speech reception are, the present evidence and the Immediacy Hypothesis suggest that communication difficulties are the secondary product of a tendency to respond to immediate stimuli rather than the source of the schizophrenic problem.

REFERENCES

Chapman, L. J. Distractability in the conceptual performance of schizophrenics. *Journal of Abnormal and Social Psychology,* 1956, *53,* 286–291.

Chapman, L. J., & Chapman, J. P. *Disordered thought in schizophrenia.* New York: Appleton–Century–Crofts, 1973.

Cromwell, R. L., & Dokecki, P. R. Schizophrenic language: A disattention interpretation. In S. Rosenberg & J. H. Koplin (Eds.), *Developments in applied psycholinguistic research.* New York: Macmillan, 1968.

Gottschalk, L. A. Theory and application of a verbal method of measuring transient psychologic states. In K. Salzinger & S. Salzinger (Eds.), *Research in verbal behavior and some neurophysiological implications.* New York: Academic Press, 1967.

Hammer, M., Polgar, S. K., & Salzinger, K. Speech predictability and social contact patterns in an informal group. *Human Organization,* 1969, *28,* 235–242.

Hammer, M., & Salzinger, K. Some formal characteristics of schizophrenic speech as a measure of social deviance. *Annals of the New York Academy of Sciences,* 1964, *105,* 861–889.

Johnson, W. Studies in language behavior: I. A program of research. *Psychological Monographs,* 1944, *56.* (2, Whole No. 255)

Kasanin, J. S. (Ed.). *Language and thought in schizophrenia.* Berkeley: University of California Press, 1944.

McGhie, A., & Chapman, J. Disorders of attention and perception in early schizophrenia. *British Journal of Medical Psychology,* 1961, *34,* 103–116.

Salzinger, K. Shift in judgment of weights as a function of anchoring stimuli and instructions in early schizophrenics and normals. *Journal of Abnormal and Social Psychology,* 1957, *55,* 43–49.

Salzinger, K. The problem of response class in verbal behavior. In K. Salzinger & S. Salzinger (Eds.), *Research in verbal behavior and some neurophysiological implications.* New York: Academic Press, 1967.

Salzinger, K. On the operant conditioning of complex behavior. In J. M. Shlien & H. Hunt (Eds.), *Research in psychotherapy* (Vol. 3). Washington, D.C.: American Psychological Association, 1968.

Salzinger, K. Pleasing linguists: A parable. *Journal of Verbal Learning and Verbal Behavior,* 1970, *9,* 725–727.

Salzinger, K. An hypothesis about schizophrenic behavior. *American Journal of Psychotherapy,* 1971, *25,* 601–614. (a)

Salzinger, K. The immediacy hypothesis of schizophrenia. In H. Yaker, H. Osmond, & F. Cheek (Eds.), *The future of time.* Garden City, New York: Doubleday, 1971. (b)

Salzinger, K. Inside the black box, with apologies to Pandora. A review of Ulric Neisser's Cognitive Psychology. *Journal of the Experimental Analysis of Behavior,* 1973, *19,* 369–378. (a)

Salzinger, K. *Schizophrenia: Behavioral aspects.* New York: John Wiley & Sons, 1973. (b)

Salzinger, K. Are theories of competence necessary? In D. Aaronson & R. W. Rieber (Eds.), *Developmental psycholinguistics and communication disorders. Annals of the New York Academy of Sciences,* 1975, *262,* 178–196.

Salzinger, K., & Eckerman, C. Grammar and the recall of chains of verbal responses. *Journal of Verbal Learning and Verbal Behavior,* 1967, *6,* 232–239.

Salzinger, K., & Feldman, R. S. (Eds.) *Studies in verbal behavior: An empirical approach.* New York: Pergamon Press, 1973.

Salzinger, K., Hammer, M., Portnoy, S., & Polgar, S. K. Verbal behaviour and social distance. *Language and Speech,* 1970, *13,* 25–37.

Salzinger, K., & Pisoni, S. Reinforcement of affect responses of schizophrenics during the clinical interview. *Journal of Abnormal and Social Psychology,* 1958, *57,* 84–90.

Salzinger, K., & Pisoni, S. Reinforcement of verbal affect responses of normal subjects during the interview. *Journal of Abnormal and Social Psychology,* 1960, *60,* 127–130.

Salzinger, K., & Pisoni, S. Some parameters of the conditioning of verbal affect responses in schizophrenic subjects. *Journal of Abnormal and Social Psychology,* 1961, *63,* 511–516.

Salzinger, K., Portnoy, S., & Feldman, R. S. The effect of order of approximation to the statistical structure of English on the emission of verbal responses. *Journal of Experimental Psychology,* 1962, *64,* 52–57.

Salzinger, K., Portnoy, S., & Feldman, R. S. Experimental manipulation of continuous speech in schizophrenic patients. *Journal of Abnormal and Social Psychology,* 1964, *68,* 508–516. (a)

Salzinger, K., Portnoy, S., & Feldman, R. S. Verbal behavior of schizophrenic and normal subjects. *Annals of the New York Academy of Sciences,* 1964, *105,* 845–860. (b)

Salzinger, K., Portnoy, S., & Feldman, R. S. Verbal behavior in schizophrenics and some comments toward a theory of schizophrenia. In P. Hoch & J. Zubin (Eds.), *Psychopathology of schizophrenia.* New York: Grune & Stratton, 1966.

Salzinger, K., Portnoy, S., Pisoni, D. B., & Feldman, R. S. The immediacy hypothesis and response-produced stimuli in schizophrenic speech. *Journal of Abnormal Psychology,* 1970, *76,* 258–264.

Salzinger, K., & Salzinger, S. Behavior theory for the study of psychopathology. In M. Hammer, K. Salzinger, & S. Sutton (Eds.), *Psychopathology: Contributions from the social, behavioral, and biological sciences.* New York: John Wiley & Sons, 1973.

Sidman, M. Technique for assessing the effects of drugs on timing behavior. *Science,* 1955 *122,* 925.

Snyder, S. H. *Madness and the brain.* New York: McGraw–Hill, 1974.

Starkweather, J. A. Vocal behavior as an information channel of speaker status. In K. Salzinger & S. Salzinger (Eds.), *Research in verbal behavior and some neurophysiological implications.* New York: Academic Press, 1967.

Sutton, S. Fact and artifact in the psychology of schizophrenia. In M. Hammer, K. Salzinger, & S. Sutton (Eds.), *Psychopathology: Contributions from the social, behavioral, and biological sciences*. New York: John Wiley & Sons, 1973.

Taylor, W. L. Cloze procedure: A new tool for measuring readability. *Journalism Quarterly,* 1953, *30,* 415–433.

Vetter, H. (Ed.). *Language behavior in schizophrenia*. Springfield, Illinois: Charles C. Thomas, 1968.

Vetter, H. Psychopathology and atypical language development. In D. Aaronson & R. W. Rieber (Eds.), *Developmental psycholinguistics and communication disorders. Annals of the New York Academy of Sciences,* 1975, *263,* 140–155.

Waskow, I. E. Vocal measures and drug effects. In K. Salzinger & S. Salzinger (Eds.), *Research in verbal behavior and some neurophysiological implications*. New York: Academic Press, 1967.

Weckowicz, T. E. Shape constancy in schizophrenic patients. *Journal of Abnormal and Social Psychology,* 1964, *68,* 177–183.

Whitehorn, J. C., & Zipf, G. K. Schizophrenic language. *Archives of Neurology and Psychiatry,* 1943, *49,* 831–851.

Wurster, S. A. Effects of anchoring on weight judgments of normals and schizophrenics. *Journal of Personality and Social Psychology,* 1965, *1,* 274–278.

Zubin, J. Vulnerability – A new view of schizophrenia. Distinguished Scientist Award Lecture of Section III, Division 12 Presented at the meeting of the American Psychological Association, Chicago, Illinois, August, 1975.

3
Remembering of Verbal Materials by Schizophrenic Young Adults

Soon D. Koh

Michael Reese Hospital and Medical Center

During the last several years, research at our laboratory has been focused on understanding how schizophrenics encode and store verbal materials in memory and eventually retrieve them for adaptive use in a variety of tasks. It has been assumed that, if memory is an essential component of higher mental operations, the commonly observed schizophrenic dysfunctions in language and thought may be a reflection of more basic deficits in the memory system.

Human memory has hardly been a respectable topic of research under the general climate of behaviorism because it is an invisible middle ground between the stimulus events in the world and the behaviors that follow. This climate, however, seems to be diminishing in recent years as it becomes apparent that no theory positing one-to-one connections between stimuli and responses can satisfactorily account for human languages and behaviors (Bransford, Barclay, & Franks, 1972; Chomsky, 1959; Neisser, 1967). People respond not to the stimulus events per se but to the encoding or interpretation of these events, adopting strategies and selecting response alternatives based on their personal knowledge of the world. The memory system is found to be an important determinant of these adaptive behaviors. Contemporary researchers have been able to identify and demonstrate the significant role memory plays in perception (Broadbent, 1958; Haber, 1968, 1969), concept formation (Hunt, 1962; Solso, 1974, 1975), learning (Estes, 1975a, 1975b, 1976), language performance (Chomsky, 1965; Miller & McNeill, 1969), and thinking (Newell & Simon, 1972). For example, memory may have little to do with linguistic competence, which deals primarily with the abstract syntactic and semantic structures of language, but it imposes rather serious constraints on linguistic performance

(Chomsky, 1965; Miller & McNeill, 1969). Verbal messages always occur in temporal sequence from past to future, therefore, forcing people to produce or interpret a message as it occurs through time. In listening to speech, for instance, the acoustic features of the message must be transformed into phonemic, semantic, syntactic, and thematic units simultaneously or, in close succession as the message proceeds, they must be constantly referred to the subjective lexicon and factual knowledge stored in the permanent memory. Furthermore, the information coded at each stage is tentative and subject to constant revision pending the contents of the message that follows. In addition, people must often go beyond the information provided, making inferences on the basis of prior knowledge. Indeed, these are complicated operations to be performed within a short time span, especially because the capacity of immediate memory is limited (Broadbent, 1958, 1971; Miller, 1956). Accordingly, strategies to reduce the vast amount of information into far fewer memory units must be invented or derived, so that immediate memory can handle the message until it is appropriately comprehended. Linguistic performances presume efficient mnemonic strategies in addition to learning, problem-solving and thinking because information overload and temporal processing are involved in all of these activities.

In this chapter, I present the findings from experiments I have participated in and interpretations they suggest regarding the capabilities and limitations of schizophrenic young adults in remembering verbal information. These studies are still in progress and have merely touched the surface of the problem, but when the results from various experiments are combined, some provisional generalizations can be made. The young schizophrenics that have been investigated find it difficult to remember verbal materials. This recall deficit is apparently not attributable to some permanent structural impairment in their memory system. Instead, it probably results from their insufficient attentional efforts and inefficient mnemonic strategies, problems that may well be remediable. It should be noted, however, that these generalizations are based on the particular schizophrenic sample that has been investigated and the research techniques that have been employed.

RESEARCH STRATEGY AND SUBJECTS

As stated above, the information-processing approach suggests ways to pry open the invisible human memory, making its contents and the processes which underlie it more visible and manipulative. The strict conceptual formulation and the research approach and tools generated by this approach are a great asset for the inquiry into the schizophrenic memory system. The information-processing approach views human memory to be an open system, consisting of a series of structural components and the executive control processes that regulate the flow of information through the components (Atkinson & Shiffrin, 1968; Murdock,

1974; Norman, 1970). These exectutive control processes, which are synony-
mous with mnemonic strategies, are invented, derived, modified, and used at the
option of the subject. Investigators generally postulate three structural components: the short-term sensory memory (STSM), the short-term memory (STM),
and the long-term memory (LTM). In the case of verbal memory, these structural divisions seem justified because of differences in the storage capacity, the
coding format, and the characteristics of information loss and information retrieval (Craik & Lockhart, 1972). In brief, the STSM has a large capacity, but its
modality-specific contents are lost quickly, usually within two seconds. The
STM can store only five to seven items, encoded largely in phonemic form; these
items can be retained for up to 30 seconds. The LTM can store an unlimited
quantity of items for an unlimited length of time. The contents of the LTM are
largely transformed into semantic codes.

Recently, however, investigators have become increasingly concerned with the
permanent memory structure, tending to view it to be separate from the LTM.
Instead of attributing an unlimited capacity to the LTM, Greeno and Bjork
(1973), for example, conceived of the LTM as a system which can store only
dozens of items for a duration of a few minutes to several hours. The permanent
memory refers to the person's virtually permanent store of knowledge about
concepts and past events. In his influential paper, Tulving (1972) has distinguished the semantic memory and the episodic memory. Episodic memory is a
person's store of experiences that are temporally dated, spatially located, personally experienced and context-bound. Semantic memory, in contrast, is "a
mental thesarus, organized knowledge a person possesses about words and other
verbal symbols, their meaning and referents, about relations among them, and
about rules, formulas, and algorithms for the manipulations of these symbols,
concepts and relations" (Tulving, 1972, p. 386). Miller's (1972) lexical memory
and Atkinson, Herrmann, and Wescourt's (1974) lexical and event-knowledge
store seem to convey similar notions. Traditionally, students of human memory
have been mostly concerned with episodic memory and "pure memory processes" that are not influenced by the personal knowledge that the subject brings
to the experiment. I believe that separation of semantic memory has heuristic
and conceptual advantages for my purposes because I am trying to understand
how schizophrenics utilize their knowledge to meet the episodic task demands
set by the experimenter. The adequacy of a person's semantic memory and his
efficiency in utilizing the relevant information already in his repertoire are,
therefore, both critical determinants of his mnemonic strategies.

The information-processing model described above, however, should be recognized as an analogue, not as a theory to be proven or disproven. On the whole,
the model can adequately account for the findings on verbal memory, but Craik
and Lockhart (1972) have recently warned investigators against strict adherence
to such a multiple-storage model. First, no sharp lines can be drawn among its
components, and no one-to-one correspondence exists between the structural

components and the executive control processes. Furthermore, Craik and his associates (Craik & Jacoby, 1975; Craik & Tulving, 1975; Lockhart, Craik, & Jacoby, 1975) have demonstrated that the depth or elaboration of processing (that is, the control process) alone is equally suitable for explaining human memory. For my purposes, however, both the structural and control-process aspects are helpful in the formulation of experimentally testable questions. I find the model to be valuable because it allows me to segment the overall problem of schizophrenic memory, and it thereby enhances conceptual precision and objectivity and suggests ways to attack each segment separately.

Needless to say, there is an inherent flaw in such a "separatist" approach because human memory is essentially an inseparable whole. Any artificial separation of its component processes is bound to produce findings of limited generality and interpretation. Thus, the overall research strategy I have adopted to minimize this inherent flaw and maximize the virtues of the information-processing model is that of converging operations (Garner, Hake, & Eriksen, 1956) or constructive replication (Lykken, 1968). In converging operations, no single experiment is conceived of as being decisive. When two or more independent experiments, specifically designed to clarify a given theoretical construct, converge on a mutually reinforcing result, the construct gains validity. The problem that investigators have to solve in designing the converging operations is which variables to control and which variables to activate in each experiment. The information-processing model is especially helpful here. That is, the explicit assumptions that human memory consists of an array of components, each accomplishing certain operations upon the information flow, and that these components are organized and sequenced to allow an overall mnemonic performance help us to interpret the findings from one experiment, to design a follow-up experiment, and to integrate the various piecemeal findings into a coherent perspective. The schizophrenic features that remain invariant over these converging operations are, in my opinion, more genuine and credible than the features depicted by a single experiment.

Schizophrenic Subjects

The protean manifestations of schizophrenia, the difficulty in defining and identifying a schizophrenic patient, and the ethical and clinical considerations to be taken into consideration in using the patient for experimental studies all impose severe limitations on investigators. These limitations help to explain the current status of confusion in the theorizing and the perplexing inconsistency in experimental findings on schizophrenic psychopathology. Perhaps the best that any investigator can do is to describe in detail the clinical qualities of the schizophrenic subjects, the selection procedures adopted, and the compromises made in conducting such research. If this information was provided, interpretations of and generalizations from experimental findings could be made more appropriately.

The schizophrenic subjects who participated in our studies were inpatients at the Psychosomatic and Psychiatric Institute of the Michael Reese Hospital in Chicago. These schizophrenics as well as nonschizophrenic psychiatric inpatient controls were diagnosed and selected by an independent clinical research team from the Institute's comprehensive research program on schizophrenia of which the project that I am associated with is a part. The demographic characteristics of the schizophrenic and nonschizophrenic patients who served as subjects in several studies are summarized in Table 3.1. (Only those who participated in the

TABLE 3.1

Actuarial Characteristics of the Schizophrenic Patients and Nonschizophrenic Psychiatric Patients Participating in Earlier Studies

Characteristic	Schizophrenic N = 59 (M = 33; F = 26)	Nonschizophrenic N = 31 (M = 9; F = 22)
Age		
Mean	21.6	22.4
(SD)	(2.2)	(3.7)
Years in school		
Mean	13.7	13.1
(SD)	(1.6)	(1.9)
Vocabulary score[a]		
Mean	13.2	12.7
(SD)	(2.3)	(2.3)
Months in hospital[b]		
Median	2.8	2.0
(Range)	(0–16)	(.3–20)
Medication[c]		
N	38	9
Median	480 mg	143 mg
(Range)	(135–1275)	(31–1350)
Marital status		
Single, N	55	20
Married, once married, N	4	12
Socioeconomic index[d]		
Mean	2.43	2.50
(SD)	(1.22)	(1.42)

[a]The Wechsler Adult Intelligence Scale vocabulary scaled scores.

[b]The previous and current hospitalization combined.

[c]The daily doses of phenothiazine medication in terms of chlorpromazine, converting the dose level of other drugs by the Cole and Davis (1969) table.

[d]The Hollingshead and Redlich (1958) 6-point index, ranges from 1 (highest position) to 6 (lowest position).

earlier experiments and who completed the Minnesota Multiphasic Personality Inventory are included.) They were all born in the United States, had a mean age of 21 to 22 and were whites from middle or upper socioeconomic backgrounds, in terms of the Hollingshead and Redlich (1958) index. Most of them were single, although the incidence of marriage was noticeably higher in the non-schizophrenic females. Their Wechsler Adult Intelligence Scale (WAIS) vocabulary levels were above average. Approximately 63% of the schizophrenics and 29% of the nonschizophrenics were receiving phenothiazine medication. The median length of hospitalization, including all previous admissions was approximately 2 to 3 months for both groups.

Grinker (1975) and Grinker and Holzman (1973) have detailed the diagnostic procedures used by the clinical team and the characteristic features of the schizophrenics whom the team has selected for the project. In brief, each young adult admitted to the Institute was interviewed by the Institute's Director (Roy R. Grinker, Sr.) after becoming sufficiently remitted from sustained psychotic disturbances. This tape-recorded semistructured interview was then rated by the team members (two psychiatrists, one clinical psychologist and one social worker), using the Schizophrenia State Inventory. In addition, pertinent information was collected on the patient's current and past clinical psychodynamic status. The diagnostic criteria centered around the patient's previous and current perceptual distortion, interpersonal aversiveness, anxiety, lapses in reality testing, associative dyscontrol, ambivalence, and affective disturbance. The following clinical qualities that distinguished these schizophrenics from nonschizophrenic young patients have been summarized by Grinker (1975, p. 191): (a) the presence of disordered thinking, even though its manifestations may be subtle; (b) a strikingly diminished capacity to experience pleasure, particularly in interpersonal relationships; (c) a strong characterological dependency upon people; (d) a noteworthy impairment in competence; and (e) an exquisitely vulnerable sense of self-regard. The subcategories of the 59 schizophrenics classified by the clinical team were 29 chronic, 10 paranoid, 7 acute chronic, and 6 schizoaffective (see Grinker, 1975, for definitions).

The Minnesota Multiphasic Personality Inventory (MMPI) was individually administered one to five days after the patient satisfactorily completed the experimental task. Although the MMPI has been used as a screening device for the normal controls, the information was obtained from the patients simply to provide an independent description of them. In each experiment, there were a few patients who refused to complete the MMPI or who were discharged before it could be administered. The mean MMPI profiles of the two groups are illustrated in Figure 3.1.

The schizophrenic configuration matches the elevated Depression–Psychasthenia–Schizophrenia (2–7–8) code type. According to Gilberstadt and Duker's (1965) MMPI Handbook, this profile is typical of pseudoneurotic schizophrenia, chronic undifferentiated schizophrenia, anxiety reaction in schiz-

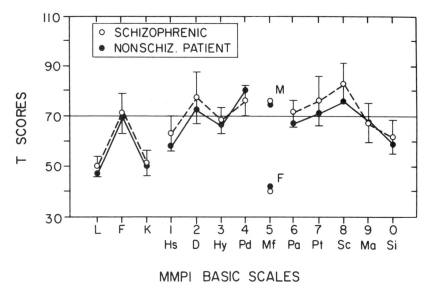

MMPI BASIC SCALES

FIG. 3.1 Mean MMPI profiles for schizophrenics and nonschizophrenic psychiatric patients. (The MMPI basic scales: L, F and K are the three validity scales; other scales, from
left are, Hypochondriasis, Depression, Hysteria, Psychopathic Deviate, Masculinity–Femi-
ninity, Paranoia, Psychasthenia, Schizophrenia, Hypomania, and Social Introversion. M and
F refer to male and female. The vertical line indicate ± .5 SD range of the schizophrenics).

oid personality, and depressive reaction in schizoid personality. The particular
schizophrenic groups participating in each of our studies have rather consistently
shown the 2–7–8 code type. The nonschizophrenics, on the other hand, have
shown a combination of a mildly elevated 2–7–8 type and a moderately
elevated Psychopathic Deviate (Scale 4) code type, a typical profile of character
disorders. According to the diagnosis of the clinical team, this group includes
monopolar and bipolar depression and character disorders. Statistical analyses
showed, however, that the MMPI was not quite successful in differentiating the
schizophrenic group from the nonschizophrenic group classified by the clinical
team.

First, none of the MMPI subscale differences between the two groups was
significant. One clinical psychologist and I then independently classified each
subject's MMPI configurations.[1] The consensual classification that we finally
reached, by relaxing the classification rules somewhat and adjusting our mutual
discrepancies, is summarized in Table 3.2. The six configurations grouped
together in the upper portion of Table 3.2 had the primary and/or secondary
labels of schizophrenia; the remaining seven configurations did not (Gilberstadt
& Duker, 1965). That is, the MMPI configurational matching correctly identified

[1] I would like to thank Dr. Mary Rootes for her participation in this MMPI matching.

TABLE 3.2

MMPI Clinical Code Type and Psychiatric Diagnosis for Schizophrenic and Nonschizophrenic
Psychiatric Patients

	Psychiatric diagnosis		
Gilberstadt–Duker code type (primary diagnosis)	Schizophrenic N (%)	Nonschizophrenic N (%)	Total N (%)
Schizophrenic configuration			
2–7–8 (Pseudoneurotic or chronic undifferentiated schizophrenia	19 (32)	8 (26)	27 (30)
8–9 (Schizophrenic reaction, catatonic)	6 (10)	2 (6)	8 (9)
8–2–4 (Personality pattern disturbance, paranoid)	3 (5)	3 (10)	6 (7)
8–6 (Schizophrenic reaction, paranoid)	6 (10)	0	6 (7)
7–8 (Psychoneurosis, obsessive-compulsive)	3 (5)	1 (3)	4 (4)
8–1–2–3 (Schizophrenic reaction, simple)	2 (3)	1 (3)	3 (3)
Nonschizophrenic configuration			
4 (Personality trait disturbance, Passive-aggressive personality, aggressive)	3 (5)	4 (13)	7 (8)
4–3 (Personality trait disturbance, emotionally unstable personality)	3 (5)	3 (10)	6 (7)
2–7–4 (Anxiety reaction with alcoholism, passive-aggressive personality)	3 (5)	2 (6)	5 (6)
9 (manic depressive reaction, manic)	4 (7)	1 (3)	5 (6)
4–9 (Sociopathic personality disturbance, anti-social reaction)	0	2 (6)	2 (2)
2–7 (Psychoneurosis, anxiety reaction)	1 (2)	0	1 (1)
1–2–3–4(Personality trait disturbance with anxiety, depression, psychological reaction)	1 (2)	0	1 (1)
Normal configuration	3 (5)	4 (13)	7 (8)
No matching, but disturbed configuration	2 (3)	0	2 (2)
Total	59 (99)	31 (99)	90 (101)

39 (65%) of 59 psychiatrically diagnosed schizophrenics but incorrectly identified 15 (48%) of 31 nonschizophrenics to be schizophrenics. The chi-square test applied to this table was not statistically significant.

The relative significance of the MMPI subscales in discriminating the two psychiatrically separated groups and their maximized discriminability were examined by means of the stepwise procedure of discriminant analysis (Nie, Hull, Jenkins, Steinbrenner, & Bent, 1975). This procedure first selects the best subscale for differentiating the two groups. A second subscale is then selected that would best be able to improve the discrimination when combined with the first subscale. The subsequent subscales are selected in the same way until the remaining subscales add no further improvement. The present application revealed seven subscales to be important. They were in the order of their contributions (in terms of the standardized coefficient): Pd (.476), Sc (−.299), Mf (−.264), Pa (−.249), L (−.220), K (−.196), and D (−.163). The absence of Pt in the above list resulted from its high correlations with Sc (r = .81) and D (r = .76) that were already selected. Overall, these seven subscales separated the two groups with only a moderate degree of success as indicated by a canonical correlation of .558 and Wilks' lambda of .703 for the discriminant function. That is, the proportion of variance in the two groups explained by the discriminant function was only .31. Although these findings are somewhat disappointing, they may have resulted because the nonschizophrenic group was a mixture of heterogeneous subgroups and the sample size was small.

Finally, I would like to emphasize that these patients were not psychotic. During the entire period of each study, which included the clinical team's diagnostic evaluation, the administration of the MMPI and the WAIS vocabulary scale, and the successful completion of the experimental sessions, they were free from sustained psychotic disturbances. Most of them were at the postpsychotic phase or at the middle or terminal phase of recuperation (see Kayton, 1973). The term schizophrenia, as the clinical team has conceived it, does not necessarily imply psychosis, a behavioral term applicable to many different types of severe illness. The interest in studying these nonpsychotic forms of schizophrenia (for example, schizophrenia in remission, ambulatory and latent schizophrenia, schizoid character, and schizotype) stems from the team's belief that they may represent the "prototype" of schizophrenia and may reflect the most genuine schizophrenic syndrome. It is assumed that long-standing sociocultural deprivation and the accompanying schizophrenic adaptation, long-term hospitalization and long-term medication, severity of illness, and other factors that may obscure the unique features of schizophrenia are believed to be much less prevalent in the nonpsychotic schizophrenic young adults that participated than in acutely or chronically psychotic schizophrenics.

The diagnostic procedure adopted by our clinical research team, the demographic characteristics of the patient subjects (Table 3.1), the supplementary diagnosis based on MMPI configurations suggest that the schizophrenic patients who have been studied are comparatively free from the "nonschizophrenic" factors listed above. The stringent requirements set for the selection of patient subjects, the informed consent required, and various clinical considerations have necessarily kept the sample size of schizophrenics in each study small. However, because the schizophrenic subjects in these studies have been drawn from a single subject pool and selected and diagnosed by a single clinical team, using a consistent procedure, and because the converging experiments have been designed to verify and elaborate the previous findings, and schizophrenic features revealed by this project should be genuine and reliable.

EXPERIMENTAL FINDINGS

Because most of project's studies have been published in full form elsewhere, presented only in this section are the principal findings and experimental design. By doing so, I hope to provide an adequate empirical base for discussing and drawing interim conclusions about the mnemonic processing of verbal materials by schizophrenics. There are four groups of experiments to be reported: (a) studies on schizophrenics' free-recall performance and their accompanying organizational strategies; (b) converging studies that are relevant in clarifying the locus and nature of schizophrenics' deficits in recall and mnemonic organization; (c) studies on schizophrenics' short-term memory processes; and (d) one study that examines those strategies used by schizophrenics that are primarily nonorganizational and nonverbal in nature.

Free Recall and Mnemonic Organization

The idea that immediate memory has a limited capacity led Miller (1956) to postulate unitization or chunking mechanisms and Broadbent (1958) to postulate filtering mechanisms to be the means by which the memory system can deal with information economically. Although these two mechanisms appear to be closely interwoven in the memorizing of input materials, there is an important conceptual distinction. Although the filtering process is primarily a one-to-one mapping between stimulus features and internal representations, the unitization process is primarily a many-to-one mapping between the two variables. The unitization process, therefore, involves grouping, classification, and organization; it implies a higher level of information processing than does the filtering process because unitization depends on the appropriate filtering of stimulus features. In the recent revision of his theory, Broadbent (1971) has included the categorizing process to be distinct from the filtering process.

Several investigators of schizophrenia have adopted the notion of a filtering mechanism and have presented some evidence that schizophrenics are defective in this filtering – that is, in the ability to reject all stimulus features not demanded by the current processing task. This interpretation of schizophrenia appears to be in harmony with the well-known phenomena of schizophrenic overinclusiveness and vulnerability to distraction (see Chapman & Chapman, 1973; McGhie, 1970). On the other hand, less is known about the unitization mechanism involved in schizophrenic remembering; only in recent years have investigators started to tackle this important concept (Koh, Kayton, & Berry, 1973; Larsen & Fromholt, 1976; Traupmann, 1975). In the following three studies, therefore, the unitization processes involved in the memorizing and remembering of verbal materials by schizophrenics have been examined, using a free-recall paradigm.

In free recall, the subject is shown a list of words and is asked to recall as many items as possible. What is "free" about free recall is that the subject is allowed to recall the items in any order he or she wishes; thus, the procedure offers an opportunity to make inferences about the mnemonic strategy that the subject adopts. If the free-recall trials are repeated, using a single list but varying the presentation order each time (multitrial free recall), then the number of words recalled, needless to say, increases, and the recall order tends to become fixed as the trials progress. This stereotyped recall order, in spite of the varied input order, suggests that mnemonic organization is taking shape. Two organizational indices can be extracted from the recall data: categorical clustering and subjective organization. Categorical clustering reflects the degree to which the subject discovers and uses in his or her organization the categorical features provided by the experimenter. Subjective organization, on the other hand, is independent of the experimenter's taxonomy and reflects the degree to which the subject imposes his or her own idiosyncratic organization on the stimulus list.

Recall of word lists. In a study done by Koh et al. (1973), schizophrenics, nonschizophrenic patients and normals recalled a list of "unrelated" words in one session; in another session they recalled a list of words consisting of five examplars from each of four conceptual categories. The words were presented at a 2-second rate, and the subject's free recall was tape-recorded. There were nine study–and–recall trials.

For the categorizable list, the recall performance was lowest for the schizophrenics highest for the normals and intermediate for the nonschizophrenics. An analysis of variance applied to these recall data indicated that the group difference, the trial effect, and the group-by-trial interaction were significant.[2] The significant interaction resulted from a slow rate of recall learning in the schizophrenics. The same trend was found in the recall of the unrelated list. The group and trial effects were significant, but their interaction was not.

Categorical clustering was indexed by Bousfield and Bousfield's (1966) stimulus category repetition (SCR) measure. Because this measure reflects the degree to which the subject uses the conceptual categories provided by the experimenter, it was applicable only to the recall of the categorizable list. The mean SCR scores over trials were 1.61 for the schizophrenics, 6.61 for the normals, and 3.87 for the nonschizophrenics. An analysis of variance indicated that the group difference, the trial effect, and the group-by-trial interaction were significant. These results correspond to the two groups' recall performance. The schizophrenics' categorical clustering increased with the trials, but their learning rate was significantly slower than the normals'.

Subjective organization was indexed by Mandler and Dean's (1969) bidirectional intertrial repetition (ITR) measure. Because this measure is defined as the extent to which the subject recalls a pair of words in contiguity on two successive recall trials and because it reflects the degree of organization the

---

[2] The rejection region for the statistical tests in this paper encompassed p values of less than .05.

subject imposes on the to-be-remembered items, it is applicable to the recall of both the categorizable and the unrelated lists. For the categorizable list, the mean ITR scores over trials were .12 for the schizophrenics, .29 for the normals, and .25 for the nonschizophrenics. Again, the group effect, the trial effect and the group-by-trial interaction were all significant. The mean ITR measures for the unrelated list were .16 for the schizophrenics, .20 for the normals, and .15 for the nonschizophrenics. The group effect and the group-by-trial interaction were not significant here.

To assess the functional relationship between recall and organizational strategies, product–moment correlations were computed. Both the ITR and SCR measures were corrected for chance clustering and recall performance (see Bousfield & Bousfield, 1966; Mandler & Dean, 1969). The correlation coefficients between the recall and the ITR scores for the unrelated list were .39 for the schizophrenics, .69 for the normals, and .68 for the nonschizophrenics; the coefficients for the categorizable list were, respectively, .35, .63 and .66. The correlations between the recall and the SCR scores for the categorizable list were .79 for the schizophrenics, .67 for the normals, and .28 for the nonschizophrenics. On the whole, however, the strategic significance of mnemonic organization was more conspicuous in the normals than in the schizophrenics.

Recall of anomalous and normal sentences. In another study done by Koh, Kayton, and Schwarz (1972), it was assumed that the schizophrenic deficits in recall and organization might be more clearly demonstrated if the to-be-recalled materials were strings of words in which syntactic and semantic rules were systematically varied. Using Marks and Miller's (1964) procedure, three types of word strings were constructed: the random word list, the anomalous sentence, and the normal sentence. Each type consisted of five strings of five words each. The syntactic structure of each normal and anomalous sentence was adjective–noun–verb–adjective–noun. The anomalous sentence violated semantic rules (*"Hot wildcats deter dried needles"*), and the word list violated both semantic and syntactic rules (*"Children bouquets distressed colorful create"*). Words of each type were presented at a 2-second rate; a blank slide was shown for 2 seconds between the strings. There were four trials for each type of word string; each trial was followed by a written free recall. The order of the strings varied over trials and over subjects, but the order of the words within each string remained the same. The word list was presented first, the anomalous sentence next and the normal sentence last. Schizophrenics and normals participated in the experiment.

The recall performance was scored both in terms of the number of words correctly recalled (regardless of recall order) and in terms of the number of complete strings correctly recalled. Figure 3.2 shows the results. For the word recall, the normals performed significantly better than the schizophrenics in all three types of word strings. For both groups, the word recall improved as

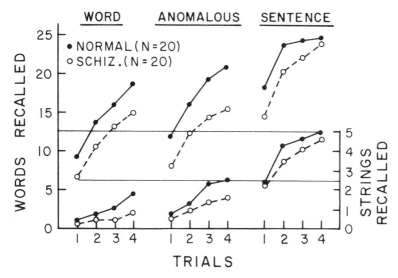

FIG. 3.2 Mean number of words recalled and mean number of complete word-strings recalled as a function of trials.

subjects advanced from the word list to the anomalous sentence to the normal sentence, and there were no significant group-by-string-type or group-by-trial interactions. The normal sentence task was too easy for the normal subjects, as the pronounced ceiling effect shows in Figure 3.2. For the complete string recall, the normals again performed significantly better than the schizophrenics in all three types of strings. This time, however, the group-by-trial interaction was significant for the word list and for the anomalous sentence, indicating a slow rate of learning of the complete strings by the schizophrenics.

It was assumed that in this task the input order would offer an organizational strategy because the input order of the five words in each string (including the word list) was fixed, although the string order varied on each trial, and because the fixed position of the words corresponded to syntactic rules in the anomalous and normal sentences. Therefore, the degree to which the subject retained the input order of the string in his recall (the input–output concordance) was assessed by means of Bousfield and Bousfield's (1966) unidirectional intertrial repetition (ITR) measure. That is, the ITR was defined here as the number of pairs of words in the subject's recall that repeated the input contiguity. The mean ITR scores over trials (corrected for chance and for recall performance) for the word list, and anomalous sentence, and the normal sentence were, respectively, .31, .45 and .82 for the schizophrenics and .41, .62 and .92 for the normals. The normals' ITR scores were significantly higher than those of the schizophrenics in all three types of strings. Again, the group-by-trial interactions were significant for the word list and for the anomalous sentence, indicating the schizophrenics' slower learning.

Recall of affective word-lists. In still another study conducted by Kayton and Koh (1975) it was hypothesized that schizophrenics are suffering from affective disturbances, most especially from a pleasure deficit (Meehl, 1962; Rado, 1956). Therefore, they are probably inefficient in detecting and utilizing the affective features of to-be-remembered words, so that their free recall of an affect-laden word list and their mnemonic organization based on affective features should prove to be defective. On the other hand, Osgood (1964; Boucher & Osgood, 1969) has noticed a strong and pervasive tendency in normal people to use evaluatively positive (good, pleasant) words more frequently, diversely, and easily than evaluatively negative (bad, unpleasant) words. This so-called "Polly-anna tendency" led the project team to expect that the normals' free recall and mnemonic organization would be better for pleasant words than for unpleasant words. Schizophrenics, nonschizophrenics, and normals recalled affective words, which were presented sequentially at a 2-second rate. In addition, each subject provided a pleasantness rating for each word. The data analysis was based on the subject's own pleasantness ratings. The mean pleasantness ratings among the three groups were quite comparable (r's, .93 to .96). The words rated by one of the four graded-pleasant categories were defined as the pleasant words, those rated by one of the four unpleasant categories as the unpleasant words, and those rated by the indifferent category as the neutral words for each subject.

The percentage of recalls of the three groups are displayed in Figure 3.3 on the left panel. The schizophrenics' overall recall was significantly inferior to that of the other two groups. There was no significant group-by-trial interaction. The recall performance was analyzed separately for the pleasant, unpleasant, and neutral words. The between-group analysis revealed that the schizophrenics' performance was significantly inferior to that of the other groups in the recall of pleasant words but not in the recall of unpleasant and neutral words. The learning rate over trials was parallel among the groups in all of these comparisons. Because the number of neutral words was small, the results from the neutral-word recall may be less reliable. The within-group comparison indicated that, although the normals' pleasant-word recall was significantly better than their unpleasant-word recall, such a differential recall was completely absent in the schizophrenics' recall and nonsignificant in the nonschizophrenics' recall. These findings are consonant with the hypothesized pleasure-deficit in schizo-phrenics and the Pollyanna tendency in normals. By contrast, the nonschizo-phrenics seem to have recalled the pleasant and unpleasant words equally well.

Subjects in this experiment could have organized the to-be-remembered words into higher memory units in at least three ways: (a) affective clustering based on pleasantness features; (b) input—output concordance based on the list order; and

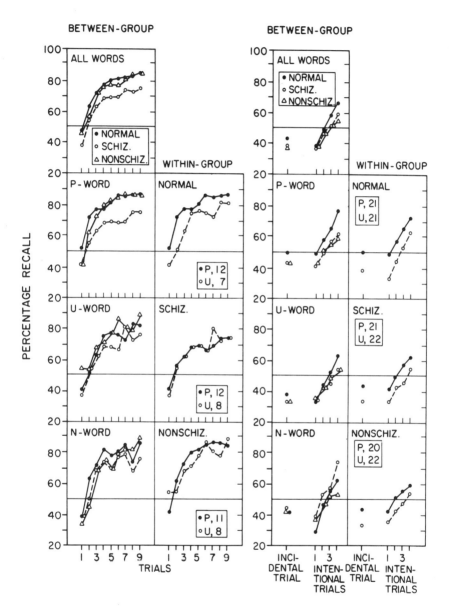

FIG. 3.3 Left panel, mean percentage recall as a function of trials (from Kayton & Koh, 1975. Copyright 1975, The Williams & Wilkins Co., Baltimore); right panel, mean percentage recall in incidental and intentional learning sessions (from Koh, Kayton, & Peterson, 1976. Copyright 1976 by the American Psychological Association. Reprinted by permission.) (There were four trials for the intentional learning session. P, U and N refer to pleasant, unpleasant and neutral, respectively, and the numbers following P and U indicate the mean numbers of pleasant and unpleasant words rated by each group, respectively. The within-group comparisons for the neutral words are not shown).

(c) subjective organization based on each subject's own idiosyncratic scheme. Affective clustering was defined here as the contiguous recall of pleasant, unpleasant, or neutral words, respectively, assuming that the affectively related words would cluster in recall despite the variable input order. The adjusted ratio of clustering (Roenker, Thompson, & Brown, 1971) was computed to be a measure of affective clustering.[3] For the pleasant words, the median scores over subjects and trials were −.01 for the schizophrenics, .11 for the nonschizophrenics, and .13 for the normals; for the unpleasant words the scores were, respectively, .01, −.01 and .09. The difference between the pleasant-word and unpleasant-word clusterings was significant only in the normals. Both input—output concordance and subjective organization were assessed by Mandler and Dean's (1969) bidirectional ITR measure. The ITR measure for subjective organization reflects the concordance between the two successive outputs (recalls), but for input—output concordance it reflects the concordance between the input (list order) and the corresponding output (recall). The subjective organization of all three groups increased rapidly as the trials progressed and showed no group difference. The overall means for the schizophrenics, nonschizophrenics, and normals were, respectively, .21, .19 and .21. The input—output concordance, on the other hand, rapidly decreased over the trials. Nevertheless, the normals' scores (.11) over trials was significantly higher than the schizophrenics' (.05) and the nonschizophrenics' (.07). The recall showed small and nonsignificant correlations with the affective clustering measure (r's, .21 to .43).

In summary, these three partially overlapping experiments present convincing evidence that schizophrenic young adults have difficulty in remembering verbal materials ranging from an "unrelated" word list to affective word lists to sentences. These experiments, furthermore, present evidence that the recall deficit of schizophrenics is attributable in part to their inefficiency in mnemonic organization. The schizophrenics were inferior to the normals in categorical clustering, in subjective organization, in input—output concordance, in improving organizational strategies over trials, in learning complete word-strings, and in clustering pleasant words more readily than unpleasant words. The schizophrenics' recall performance was partially a function of these inefficiencies in mnemonic organization. However, organizational measures based on output consistency provide an incomplete index of mnemonic organization. The free-recall paradigm encourages the subject to form multiple associations because the recall order is free to vary, and the input order is varied by the experimenter over trials. Consequently, the use of this paradigm militates against finding a single output consistency over trials. There are also organizational strategies that

---

[3] There is no simple best measure of mnemonic organization. The measure by Roenker et al. (1971) was used here because it is presumably less contaminated by the number of categories recalled and the distribution of the total items recalled across categories.

operate at cross purposes, such as input—output concordance versus output consistency and affective clustering between opposite categories (for example, joy—weep). The occurrence of these and other complex strategies will reduce the magnitude of the organizational indices that have been adopted. Furthermore, the meager number of affective clusterings found by Kayton and Koh (1975) may have resulted in part from the pleasantness categories corresponding to a loosely ordered affective continuum. Using different experimental paradigms, converging experiments were conducted to clarify further the nature of mnemonic organization in schizophrenia.

Converging Experiments on Mnemonic Organization

Three major questions are addressed in this section: (a) whether the schizophrenics' recognition memory is intact, as one would expect from the currently prevailing theory that mnemonic organization is essential for recall but not for recognition; (b) whether schizophrenics' recall deficiency disappears if mnemonic organization is experimentally induced at the acquisition stage; and (c) whether the schizophrenics' deficits in the recall and mnemonic organization of verbal materials result essentially from inadequacies in the semantic structure of the permanent memory.

Recognition memory. In the study by Koh, Kayton, and Berry (1973), a follow-up experiment was conducted to examine the schizophrenics' recognition memory. We adopted the theoretical formulation that mnemonic organization is important for recall but not for recognition (see Anderson & Bower, 1972; Kintsch, 1970b, 1974). According to this generation—recognition model, in recall the to-be-remembered item has to be implicitly searched for and retrieved before a recognition check is made. Retrieval is seen as a process that operates on a structure or semantic network in the permanent memory. In recognition, this initial process is bypassed; only required is a recognition check. In this study, it was assumed that, if organizational inefficiency is indeed an important determinant of the schizophrenics' recall deficit, then these patients should demonstrate intact recognition memory.

Schizophrenics and normals engaged in repeated recognition tasks that employed 40 words and 40 consonant—vowel—consonant (CVC) nonsense syllables. The words for study consisted of 20 high-frequency and 20 low-frequency words; the nonsense syllables for study consisted of 20 high-association and 20 low-association syllables. Each of the study items was presented on a screen at a 2-second rate, and the subject was asked to read each item aloud as it was shown. For the recognition test, the subject was asked to mark all the items he or she could recognize as old items on an answer form that contained 40 study items and 40 corresponding distractors in mixed order. The word list was tested twice; the syllable list was tested three times. A new set of distractor items was used on each repeated test.

The d' value of signal-detection theory was adopted to be a measure of each subject's recognition memory. An analysis of variance applied to the word recognition yielded no group difference, although there were significant frequency and trial effects. The interactions were not significant. The recognition memory for the low-frequency words was better than that for the high-frequency words, as other investigators (for example, Shephard, 1967) have found. An analysis of variance applied to the d' values for the nonsense-syllable recognition, however, indicated significant group, association, and trial effects, with no significant interactions. Further analyses revealed that the schizophrenics' recognition on the first trial was comparable to the normals', but their recognition on the following two trials for the low-association CVCs tended to be poorer than the normals'. It was assumed that for the low-association CVCs the subject may first have to integrate or chunk the independent elements of each CVC unit before it could be coded appropriately for storage (response integration). That is, the schizophrenics were probably slow and inefficient in the initial organization of low-association CVCs, an interpretation that would appear to be consonant with Koh et al.'s assumption of a schizophrenic dysfunction in mnemonic organization. It was concluded, therefore, that schizophrenics' recognition memory is adequate as long as organizational processes are not critical elements of the task.

Semantic encoding and recall.   Koh, Kayton, and Peterson (1976) studied the effect of experimenter-induced encoding and organization of the to-be-remembered words on the subsequent recall of schizophrenics. In the free-recall paradigm used in the previous studies, the mnemonic strategy was left to be the subject's option. Accordingly, it is not clear whether the schizophrenic recall deficit is caused by some permanent, built-in incapacity unique to schizophrenia or simply caused by a lack of conscious effort to elaborate and organize the to-be-remembered words into higher memory units. There is ample evidence that the encoding process that takes place during the input stage is crucial for remembering (Craik & Lockhart, 1972; Melton & Martin, 1972; Tulving & Thompson, 1973). In this study, therefore, the subject's selective attention and affective-semantic encoding during the acquisition stage were placed under the control of the experimenter by means of the incidental-learning paradigm.

In the typical incidental-learning paradigm, the subject is not instructed to learn but is required to engage in an orienting task to insure that he or she pays attention to and encodes the input materials in the manner determined by the experimenter; an unexpected recall test follows. This procedure permits the experimenter to manipulate the subject's control processes at the input stage through a systematic variation of the orienting task. It has been well documented that an incidental-learning procedure requiring semantic encoding produces a level of recall equivalent to that resulting from an intentional learning procedure, in which the subject is forewarned about the recall test (Craik & Tulving, 1975; Hyde & Jenkins, 1973; Jenkins, 1974; Rosenberg & Schiller,

1971). That is, the semantic encoding, rather than the intention to memorize per se is critical for remembering. Apparently, people ordinarily pay attention to and encode input items according to semantic attributes when they are instructed to learn the materials for a subsequent recall test. One of the orienting tasks often used is rating the input words according to their pleasantness or unpleasantness.

Subjects in the present experiment participated in two sessions, incidental learning and intentional learning. In the first session the orienting task consisted of writing down each of 50 words that appeared on a screen one at a time and then rating each word along a 7-point pleasantness scale. Thus, the subject's attention and affective-semantic encoding of the words were assured. Following, was an unexpected free-recall test. In the second session, which was conducted approximately one week later, the subject was instructed to write down and rate another 50-word list, as in the first session. But the subject was told at the outset that there would be a subsequent recall test. A multitrial free recall followed, repeating the trial four times. That is, both the encoding and the intention to learn were induced in the second session. Schizophrenics, nonschizophrenics and normals completed the two sessions.

In order to examine the three groups' affective encoding or discriminability for the two lists, the product–moment correlations among the groups' pleasantness ratings were computed; they ranged from .96 to .99. That is, the encoding systems among the groups were comparable. Accordingly, any group differences in recall, if found, could not have resulted from encoding differences. The recall performances are summarized in Figure 3.3 on the right panel. The three groups showed no significant differences in the number of words recalled in both the incidental and the intentional sessions. The group-by-trial interaction in the second session was not significant. The recall performance was also separately examined for the pleasant (three subcategories combined), unpleasant (three subcategories combined), and neutral (mid-category) words. The between-group comparison again showed no significant differences, even for the pleasant-word recall. The within-group comparison revealed that all three groups recalled the pleasant words more often than the unpleasant words in both sessions (the Pollyanna tendency). In the incidental recall, the differential recall between the pleasant and unpleasant words was significant for the normals and for the nonschizophrenics but not for the schizophrenics; in the intentional recall, it was significant for the normals and for the schizophrenics but not for the nonschizophrenics. Kayton and Koh's (1975) results from the intentional-recall task in which the encoding operation was not induced at the acquisition stage are shown in Figure 3.3 on the left panel for comparison.

The clustering of output according to pleasantness features was also examined, using Bousfield's (1953) ratio of repetition. Again, a repetition was defined as the contiguous recall of two items for the same pleasantness category, based on the appropriate group mean ratings. The measure was then a simple ratio of the number of obtained repetitions to the number of possible repetitions. For the incidental recall, both the pleasant-word clustering (.53 to .60) and the unpleasant-word clustering (.50 to .58) were substantial, but there were no group differences. For the intentional recall, the mean ratio across the four trials for the pleasant words was significantly higher in the normals (.53) than in either patient group (.44 for both), but the unpleasant-word clustering (.49 to .54) showed no group differences.

This study suggests that schizophrenics are capable of encoding and organizing verbal material according to affective-semantic features and that, once such encoding is appropriately carried out at the acquisition stage, the schizophrenics recall and pleasure deficits are both considerably ameliorated. In other words, the schizophrenic deficits are probably not caused by some irreversible, permanent, structural impairment but by a production deficiency – a failure to use a strategy that is already in their repertoire (Brown, 1975a; Flavel, 1970).

Semantic memory. Thus far, these studies have demonstrated the poor performance of schizophrenics in remembering verbal materials and have identified some of the underlying impairments in their mnemonic control processes. However, a question can be raised about whether this deficit in mnemonic processing and the consequent recall deficit of schizophrenics simply reflects the inappropriate storage structure of their permanent memory. If the schizophrenics' semantic memory is either loosely or constrictively organized, then their mnemonic strategies should suffer. Recent investigators have appeared to be increasingly aware of the significant role played by the semantic memory in episodic memory tasks (Kintsch, 1974; Melton & Martin, 1972; Tulving & Donaldson, 1972). Koh, Kayton, and Schwarz (1974), therefore, investigated the structural component of schizophrenic memory, using the method of sorting. For a subject to sort two or more words into a category, some common feature or features shared by the words have to be extracted by imposing a cognitive structure on the entire set of words. The subject must contact, activate and utilize the subjective lexicon existing in the permanent memory. That is, assuming a functional isomorphism between the storage structure of words and the sorting, the structural features extracted from the sorting were used to infer the network of the internal lexical representation.

Two experiments were conducted. In Experiment 1, schizophrenics, nonschizophrenic patients and normals sorted "unrelated" words and conceptually categorizable words under an undemanding condition. That is, the subject was allowed ample time and as many piles of words and revisions as wished. In Experiment 2, schizophrenics and normals sorted affective words under a time limitation. Koh et al. assumed that the time pressure would generate information overload and would necessitate the use of strategies analogous to those involved in recall tasks.

The hierarchical clustering schemes underlying the sorting were extracted using Johnson's (1967) computer program. This program extracts clusters that range progressively from the cluster of words sorted together by the most subjects to the cluster sorted together by the fewest subjects. The entire clustering scheme depicts a hierarchical network of words based on the interitem similarity perceived by the group. The scheme extracted for each group in Experiment 1 is presented in Figure 3.4. Each node or cluster represents item similarity because it depicts the proportion of subjects who placed the words in the same pile.

These schemes suggested that the mediational features most salient among the three groups' hierarchical clustering schemes were semantic and associative and

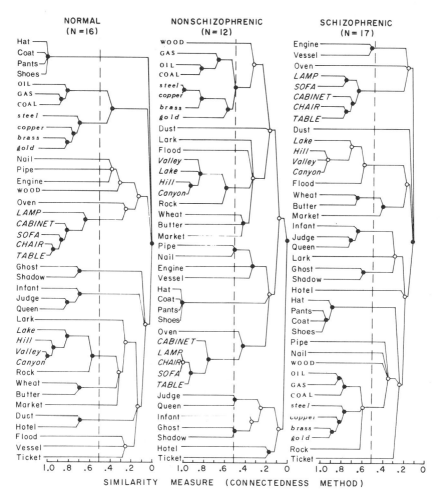

FIG. 3.4 Forty words used for free-sorting and the hierarchical clustering schemes extracted from the sorting. The similarity measure refers to the number of subjects (proportion) who share the clusters. (From Koh, Kayton, & Schwarz, 1974. Copyright 1974 by the American Psychological Association. Reprinted by permission.)

that the schizophrenics' scheme was essentially the same as those of the other two groups. When the nodes in Figure 3.4 were plotted agaisnt the order of cluster extraction (from the strongest to the weakest nodes) to compare the three groups' degree of group consensus or intersubject similarity in the sorting, the distributions of these nodes overlapped, showing no group differences (Koh et al., 1974, Figure 3). Under the demanding condition of Experiment 2, where strategic efficiency was presumably involved, the difference between the schizophrenics and the normals emerged in the topographical similarity of the hierarchical clustering schemes and in the measures of group consensus (Koh et al., 1974, Figures 3 & 4). However, the overall clustering patterns of the two groups, based on the semantic, associative and affective features, were similar. The schizophrenics revealed no clusters that could be considered anomalous. It was noted, however, that the schizophrenics used fewer piles than the normals (and, consequently, more words in each pile) in Experiment 1, but this trend was reversed in Experiment 2. It appears that even under an apparently undemanding condition, the schizophrenics tended to simplify the task by reducing their response alternatives and the variations of word meaning — a control process. Nevertheless, this constrictive strategy was disrupted under the time pressure. Because the schizophrenics' hierarchical clustering schemes were adequate in spite of these strategic variations, it was therefore concluded that the schizophrenics' subjective lexicon is probably not impaired and thus their subjective lexicon may not be responsible for their poor recall and inefficient mnemonic organization.

In summary, these three converging experiments suggest that mnemonic organization is an important process in recall and that the schizophrenics are probably endowed with an adequate subjective lexicon and adequate mnemonic strategies, but that they do not spontaneously and fully utilize these resources in recall tasks. In a recent series of papers, Brown (1975a,b) has elucidated several important topics that the students of human memory should be aware of. On memory deficit, she has suggested three problems to clarify: (a) whether it is caused by the subject's passive, inactive, strategic effort; (b) whether it is caused by the limitation in structural features or control processes; or (c) whether it is caused by a mediational or production deficiency. The production deficiency is remediable by adequate training of the required strategy, but the mediational deficiency is not. Koh et al.'s results seem to characterize the schizophrenic recall deficit to result from passive strategic effort, inefficient mnemonic strategy and production deficiency.

Short-Term Recognition Memory

Recently, there has been a considerable change in the notion of the STM. The format of information stored in the STM was formerly regarded to be primarily acoustic or phonemic in nature (Atkinson & Shiffrin, 1968), but it is now regarded to adopt any format from acoustic to semantic, depending upon the demands of the particular experimental task (Craik & Tulving, 1975). The rehearsal in the STM is no longer viewed as a unitary process. It consists of two different levels of processes: rote maintanence, which contributes little to the LTM storage, and constructive coding, which elaborates the STM items for the LTM storage (Bjork, 1975; Craik & Jacoby, 1975). Investigators, accordingly, are becoming more aware of the active role played by executive control in STM processing and are tending to interpret the limited capacity of the STM to be a consequence of limited control processes rather than of limited storage. As previously stated, however, we prefer to keep the storage concept because the structural features, in contrast with control processes, are also helpful in our conceptualization of the schizophrenic memory system. An important point to note is that the STM processing is essentially automatic, requiring little conscious effort on the part of the subject (for example, Bjork, 1975; Craik & Tulving, 1975; Wickens, 1972). By contrast, the mnemonic organization that the team has been concerned with in the studies described above involve a strategic process that facilitates the storage and retrieval of LTM items, which is relatively unnatural and requires the subject's conscious effort and attention. That is, the constructive coding occurring in the STM can be seen to consist of two levels: low-level coding, which makes the memory items available for recognition check, and high-level coding, which makes them accessible for recall by providing organizational schemes for search and retrieval. Our findings that schizophrenics' long-term recognition memory for verbal materials is intact, although their recall memory is impaired, and that conscious, experimentally induced encoding eliminates their recall deficit lend support to these speculations.

It can be argued, however, that the findings of an intact long-term recognition memory in schizophrenics may have resulted from the use of verbal materials as the stimuli. The overlearned verbal materials would have facilitated both the rote and the constructive rehearsals of the STM items and, in consequence, may have masked a possible impairment. Using stimuli, which were not readily codable in verbal terms, and adopting a delayed comparison method, two studies that examined schizophrenics' STM processing were conducted respectively for numerousness and for picture preference. In a third study, the STM scanning and retrieval of words were investigated by means of the Sternberg (1969, 1971) choice reaction time paradigm.

Short-term perceptual memory. In a study conducted by Koh, Kayton, and Streicker (1976), the subject was presented with a random dot pattern on a screen and was asked to decide whether this pattern had "more" or "less" dots than another dot pattern presented 2 or 8 seconds later. This delayed comparison paradigm (Guilford, 1954; Kinchla, 1973) allows an assessment of the subject's capacity to encode the first (to-be-remembered) stimulus and retain the coded information in his STM store until the second (probe) stimulus becomes available for the comparison. Verbal encoding and linguistic organization presumably have minimal influence on this task.

Two experiments were conducted. In Experiment 1, schizophrenics and normals compared one of eight variable dot patterns to a fixed standard dot pattern that appeared earlier (the standard-comparison condition). Each subject was required to participate in eight consecutive experimental sessions, with the hope of obtaining his or her asymptotic performance. In Experiment 2, schizophrenics and normals completed two sessions in which the comparison task for numerousness was more demanding. That is, on each trial, one of the eight variable stimuli was randomly presented first as the to-be-remembered stimulus, and the fixed standard stimulus followed as a probe (the comparison-standard condition) on half of the blocks in each session, thus, making it difficult to form a durable memory trace for the first stimulus. On the remaining half of the blocks, the standard-comparison condition was employed as in Experiment 1. In addition, the interstimulus or delaying interval (2 or 8 seconds) was always filled with an "unjudged" dot pattern as an extraneous interference. Furthermore, in both experiments, the subject was postexperimentally asked to assign a given scale value based on his or her perception of the numerousness to each of the 18 dot patterns shown on the screen. The scaling procedures used were a 9-point rating scale, the magnitude estimation scale (Stevens, 1975), and the estimation of the actual number of dots. These scale values are believed to reflect the subject's resolving power for numerousness, which is presumably influenced little by the subject's mnemonic control processes.

In the data analyses, the STM strength was estimated by the d' value of signal-detection theory (Banks, 1970; Green & Swets, 1966), thereby eliminating the response bias (β) from the estimation. In the present application of this procedure, the hit rate was defined to be the proportion of the trials on which the subject judged the second stimulus to have more dots than the first, given that it had more dots in fact (p = "more"/more); the false-alarm rate was defined to be the proportion on which he or she judged the second stimulus to have more dots than the first, given that it had less dots in fact (p = "more"/less). This definition permitted an analysis of the data by means of the two-alternative forced-choice procedure. From these conditional probabilities, a 2 by 2 stimulus—response matrix was made for each subject, and the hit and false-alarm rates were estimated by using Hochhaus's (1972) formula.

The results from individual subjects in the two experiments are shown in Figure 3.5, which plots the hit rates against the false-alarm rates. The major diagonal represents zero memory strength (d' = 0). As the point lies further away from the major diagonal toward the upper left corner, the STM, as indexed by the d' value, increases. In both experiments the scatter of these points for individual subjects overlapped, suggesting no group differences. An analysis of variance applied to the d' values from Experiment 1 showed only a significant learning (session) effect. In Experiment 2, the STM of both groups was severely

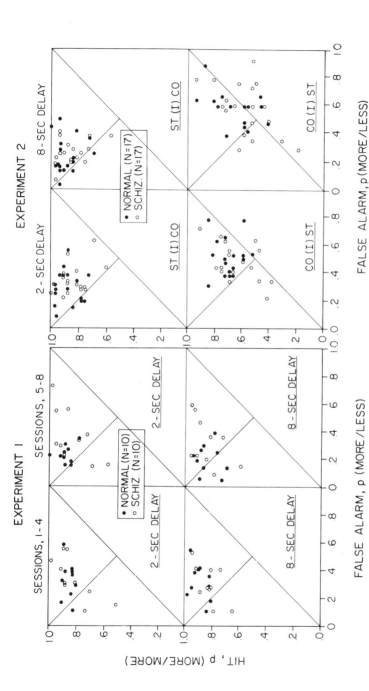

FIG. 3.5 Proportion of hits plotted against proportion of false alarms for each subject. ST ( ) CO, ST(I) CO and CO(I) ST refer to: the fixed stimulus first and the variable comparison stimulus second, with no extraneous stimulus-interpolation between the paired stimuli; the standard first and the comparison second with interpolation, and the comparison first and the standard second with interpolation, respectively. (From Koh, Kayton, & Streicker, 1976. Copyright 1976 by The Williams & Wilkins Co., Baltimore.)

impaired under the comparison—standard condition because of the encoding difficulty and the extraneous interference. Moreover, the STM loss became significant over the 8-second delayed interval. However, the schizophrenics' STM was still comparable to the normals', and it decayed over time at the same rate as the normals'. An analysis of variance showed significant presentation order effect and significant interval-by-presentation interaction. The STM (d') of both groups improved over the 8-second interval in the standard—comparison condition, but it deteriorated over the interval in the comparison—standard condition.

The response bias, as indexed by the β value, indicated a strong tendency to judge the second stimulus to have more dots than the first, but no group difference was found. The product—moment correlations were computed between the individual subject's rating, magnitude estimation and number-of-dots estimation values, respectively, and the actual number of dots; the median r's for the two groups ranged from .82 to .87. The resolving or discrimination power for numerousness in the schizophrenics was as good as that of the normals'. The internal consistency of each subject was further estimated by means of the correlations among the three scales. The median r's for both groups ranged .74 to .82, and the schizophrenics' resolving power for numerousness was as reliable as the normals'.

Short-term memory for pleasantness. In a study by Koh, Peterson, and Streicker (unpublished), the STM process of schizophrenics in a picture preference task was examined, using inkblot pictures as the stimuli and adopting the delayed comparison method. The subject was asked to make a comparison between the pleasantness of an inkblot picture (the probe stimulus) and the pleasantness of another inkblot picture (the to-be-remembered stimulus) shown either 2 or 8 seconds earlier. Again, there are at least two limiting factors in the present study: the subject's capacity to differentiate among "meaningless" inkblot pictures on the basis of the pleasantness—unpleasantness dimension and the subject's capacity to retain the pleasantness impression of the first stimulus until the second inkblot picture has appeared. Koh et al. assumed that, because schizophrenics are suffering from affective disturbances, both their pleasantness discrimination of inkblot pictures and their retention of affective information in the STM may be defective. Consequently, these subjects ought to perform poorly in the present task.

The experimental design for this study, however, was not straightforward because the pleasantness of inkblot pictures lacks appropriate metric counterparts. The two paired pictures, A and B, were presented in the temporal order AB once and in the reversed order BA once, without informing the subject about the repeated presentation of the same two pictures in a pair. Each picture in a pair, therefore, served once as a first (to-be-remembered) stimulus and once as the second (probe) stimulus. If the subject had no STM loss during the delayed interval, he or she would prefer A or B regardless of the presentation order. On the other hand, if the subject's memory for the pleasantness or unpleasantness of the first stimulus were weakened during the interstimulus interval, then the presentation order would influence the affective comparison. That is, if the two pictures in a pair were both equally pleasant, then the second picture would be judged to be more pleasant because the pleasantness memory of the first picture was weakened during the interval. On the other hand, if both the two pictures were equally unpleasant, the second would be judged to be more unpleasant. That is, the decay of affective memory over the delayed interval, therefore, could be estimated by comparing the subject's preference of a picture in the AB presentation and that of the same picture in the BA presentation.

Schizophrenics and normals individually participated in three experimental sessions. The inkblot pictures used were Kodaslides, which included 47 Holtzman inkblot pictures and the 10 Rorschach pictures. A normative pleasantness value for each of the 57 pictures was obtained from 92 undergraduates (50 men and 42 women) prior to the experiment, using a 9-point rating scale. The two pictures in a pair had approximately equal pleasantness on the basis of the normative scale values; that is, pleasant pictures were paired with pleasant and unpleasant pictures with unpleasant. In the first session, 26 pairs were compared twice, and in the second session 22 pairs were compared twice, once in AB order and once in BA order. However, the interstimulus interval (2 or 8 seconds) in the second session was filled with an "unjudged" inkblot picture that was more pleasant or less pleasant than or approximately equal to the paired pictures. The data from the two sessions allowed an evaluation of the subject's preference shift because of the STM delay in terms of the normative pleasantness values of the pairs. The second session, in addition, provided data on the effect of extraneous distraction on the preference shift. In the third session to assess the affective discriminability, the subject was asked to rate the 57 inkblot pictures on a 9-point pleasantness—unpleasantness scale.

Figure 3.6 displays the results. The zero shift means a random shift, but the positive or negative shifts mean a constant shift, analogous to the constant error in psychophysics (see the time-order error, Guilford, 1954). That is, the positive shift means that a picture in a pair was less often preferred when it was presented second than when it was presented first; the negative shift means that it was more often preferred when it was presented second than when it was presented first. The results from both sessions indicated that if the pictures in a pair were both unpleasant (on the normative scale), the second presentation was less often preferred. If they were both pleasant, the second presentation was more often preferred. That is, the unpleasant or pleasant impression of a picture stored in the STM became less unpleasant or less pleasant with the passage of time, suggesting a decay of pleasantness memory trace. The scatters of the points shown in Figure 3.6 indicate that (a) both the schizophrenics and the normals revealed a trend toward a negative preference shift as the pleasantness of the pairs increased in both sessions; (b) the slopes of this trend remained essentially

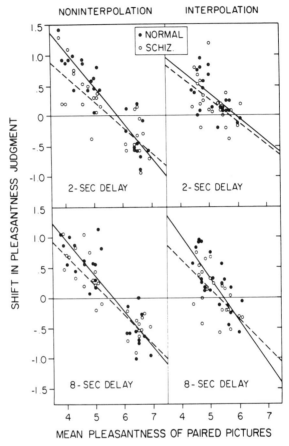

FIG. 3.6 Shift in pleasantness judgment as a function of mean pleasantness rating of paired pictures. (The rating categories shown are: 4, mildly unpleasant; 5, neutral; 6, mildly pleasant; and 7, moderately pleasant. The best-fit lines were computed by the least-squares method.)

the same regardless of the variation of the interstimulus interval and of the extraneous stimulus interference; and (c) the schizophrenics' shift was generally comparable to the normals'.

It would probably be inaccurate, however, to attribute these findings entirely to a possible decay of the STM of pleasantness. First, the measure of memory in this study was contaminated by the subject's response bias (the nonmetric nature of the stimuli did not allow a use of the procedure of signal-detection theory). Second, if STM decay was responsible for the preference shift, the regression lines shown in Figure 3.6 should have been much steeper for the 8-second delay than for the 2-second delay.

The question often raised in psychophysics on the phenomenon of constant error (the time-order error) is whether the subject makes the delayed comparison on the basis of the "sensory-trace" mode or on the basis of the "context-coding" mode (Durlach & Braida, 1969; Guilford, 1954; Helson, 1964). The question for the present study is whether the subject has made the "more pleasant" or "less pleasant" judgment by comparing the second picture to the trace of internal representation of the first picture or to the total context of pictures in the experiment. If the sensory-trace mode is assumed to operate, then memory must simply decay as a function of time and must be highly vulnerable to extraneous stimulation. On the other hand, if the context mode is assumed to operate, then memory must be generally independent of time and extraneous interference. In the context-coding mode it is assumed that the first stimulus is assimilated with or incorporated into the middle magnitude of the series (an adaptation level), and the second stimulus is compared with the overall adaptation level rather than with the representation of the first stimulus. The sensory-trace assumption would explain the preference shift observed in this study to be a result of weakening trace over time, whereas the context-coding assumption would explain the shift to be a result of the subject's "pulling down" the pleasantness or unpleasantness of the first stimulus on the level of the overall adaptation level. Because the present results revealed no noticeable degree of the interval and interference effects, they seem to be more consistent with the context-coding assumption.

The pleasantness—unpleasantness ratings of the schizophrenics and the normals correlated highly with those of the normative ratings obtained in the preliminary experiment (r = .90 for both). The correlation between the ratings of the two experimental groups was also .90. That is, the schizophrenics' affective discriminability was generally adequate. The form of the schizophrenic groups' rating scale, however, was noticeably constrictive. When the patient's scale values were plotted against those of the normative sample and of the normal group, the slope estimated by the least-squares procedure was less than unity. The results of the present experiment led to a conclusion that the STM for pleasantness and the affective differentiation of inkblot pictures are adequate in the schizophrenics.

Short-term memory scanning. In another study by Koh, Peterson, and Szoc (in press), the schizophrenics' STM scanning and retrieval of common English words were examined by means of Sternberg's (1969, 1971) choice reaction-time procedure. In this procedure, the subject first memorizes a few stimuli (memory set), and then a probe stimulus is shown. The subject's task is to choose one of the two response: "yes" if the probe stimulus matches one of the memory-set items or "no" if it fails to match any of them. Sternberg rather consistently found that mean reaction time (RT) is a linear function of the memory-set size (M) and that both "yes" and "no" RTs increase at about the same rate (the slopes, bs, are equal). On the basis of these findings, Sternberg hypothesized that STM scanning in normal subjects is serial and exhaustive. The comparisons for match occur one at a time, and the probe is always tested against every item in the memory set. The choice reaction time (RT) paradigm is seen to involve the following sequential substages: (a) preprocessing or stimulus encoding; (b) comparison of the encoded probe with mnemonic representations of the memory set; (c) decision making or response selection, given the results of the comparison stage; and (d) response executive (Smith, 1968). The intercept in the above linear function is interpreted to represent the time required for Stages a, c and d, while the slope constant (b) represents the scanning or comparison time (Stage b). Interest in this experiment is focused on Stage b. Is the STM scanning time or b of schizophrenics comparable to that of normals, and can their mode of STM scanning be characterized to be serial and exhaustive? If primary-process thought, dreamlike thought, cognitive slippage, and associative dysfunction can be seen to be a consequence of "multiple processing," and if these thought processes characterize schizophrenic thought (Neisser, 1967), then the schizophrenics' scanning may deviate from the serial-and-exhaustive mode.

Two experimental sessions were completed by schizophrenics, nonschizophrenic patients and normals. On each trial, 1, 2 or 4 to-be-memorized words were shown on a screen, one by one; then, a single word was shown as a probe. The subject was instructed to indicate as quickly as possible whether the probe word was one of the memory-set items by pressing the key for "yes" or for "no". The positive and negative probes occurred with equal frequency. Each subject had 72 trials for each of the three memory-set sizes, including 36 trials for "yes" and 36 trials for "no."

Figure 3.7 displays mean RT as a function of M. The mean RTs for the positive probes showed that: (a) the two patient groups' intercepts were significantly higher than the normal group's, indicating their slow overall RT; (b) RT increased with M, but the relationship was nonlinear; and (c) the group-by-M interaction was not significant, suggesting approximately equal scanning time and similar scanning strategies between the normals and the patients. The mean RTs for the negative probes revealed the same trends as above but with the exception that the relationship between the mean RT and M was linear. (The analysis of variance was performed on the logarithmic transformation of the RT.) The RT function for the positive probes could be described by a logarithmic function: for the schizophrenics, mean RT = 635.8 + 81.6 log$_2$ M and for the normals, mean RT = 534.8 + 59.3 log$_2$ M.[4] The RT function for the negative probes was linear: the schizophrenics mean RT = 669.9 + 24.5 M; the nonschizophrenics, mean RT = 611.7 + 44.5 M; and the normals, mean RT = 533.4 + 28.2 M. That is, the schizophrenics' scanning time for the positive probes was 22.3 msec/bit slower and that for negative proves was 3.7 msec/word

----

[4] The logarithm to the base 2 of the number of memory-set items is the amount of information or uncertainty expressed in bits.

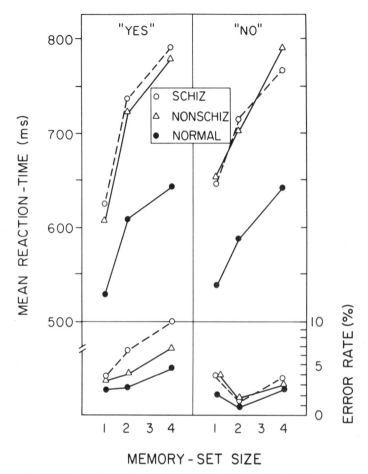

FIG. 3.7   Mean reaction time and mean error rate for positive and negative probes, respectively, as a function of the size of memory set.

faster than the normals', but these differences were not statistically significant (the group-by-M interaction was not significant). The nonschizophrenics' scanning times were similar to those of the other two groups.

Obviously, there is no straightforward fit between the present results from both the normals and schizophrenics and the serial—and—exhaustive assumption. The fast RT for the 4-word memory set for the positive probes implies that a self-terminating, rather than an exhaustive, strategy may have occurred. That is, the subject may have terminated his or her scanning as soon as a correct match had occurred. On the other hand, the comparatively high error rate shown for the 4-word memory set, especially for the schizophrenics, suggests the subject's acceleration of RT at the expense of accuracy (Figure 3.7). It can be speculated further that the process involved in the 1-word memory set is somehow qualitatively different from that in the 2- and 4-word memory sets, resulting in disproportionately fast RTs. For the negative probes, the self-terminating strategy is impossible because the subject had to check all four words to make a "no" response. Briggs and Johnson (1973) have offered another interpretation. If a particular stimulus serves as positive on one trial and as negative on another trial in a session (the variable-set procedure), as in the present procedure, the role played by individual stimuli becomes ambiguous. In such a case, Shannon's (1948) uncertainty measure of the memory set ($\log_2$ M) describes the RT function better, as we found for the positive probes. The logarithmic RT function for negative probes, however, often shows an upward concavity because of extra time expended for rechecking. This also appeared to be the case with our data. In other words, when no match occurs in the scanning or comparison stage, the subject tends to recheck the memory-set items before making the negative response; this rechecking consumes extra time, especially for the long memory-set size. As Figure 3.7 shows, the error rates for the negative probes were considerably lower than those for the positive probes, especially for the 4-word memory set, suggesting that rechecking may have served to reduce the error rate. Briggs (1974) further surveyed the literature on the RT function and found that for the processing of words, but not letters and digits, the RT function is mostly logarithmic. Whatever interpretation can be advanced for the present data, the conclusion would remain the same. The schizophrenics' short-term memory scanning behaves the same as that of the normals. Finally, the markedly high intercept values shown by the two patient groups are probably caused by their slow RT in one or more of the remaining three substage processes. These, however, are topics for seperate investigations.

In summary, these three experiments suggest that the STM processes of schizophrenics may not be impaired if high-level organization and elaboration are not critical parts of the tasks. The various interpretations that have been raised, however, have to be settled in future studies.

Nonorganizational and Nonlinguistic Strategies in Free Recall

The studies summarized thus far are directly or indirectly related to the mnemonic organization that underlies the schizophrenics' recall performance. The general notion emerging from these studies is that the recall performance of schizophrenics is poor whenever organizational strategy based on linguistic features is an important element of memory tasks. It would be an oversimplification, however, to assume that organizational dysfunction is the sole determinant of the schizophrenics' recall deficit. Mnemonic processes or strategies that are not organizational or that are organizational but not linguistic in nature may also be employed at the option of the subject in the free-recall paradigm.

Koh and Kayton (1974), therefore, conducted an experiment to examine the extent to which nonorganizational and nonlinguistic strategies influence the schizophrenics' recall performance. To minimize the output consistency or the organization which occurs over successive recalls, the procedure of single-trial free recall was adopted, using multiple word lists studied and recalled in succession instead of the procedure of multi-trial free recall using a single word list repeatedly over trials. The organizational cues present in the to-be-remembered materials were further minimized by using words that were moderately low in frequency of usage, imagery, concreteness, meaningfulness, and affectivity. In addition, both the immediate-recall and the delayed-recall paradigms were incorporated in he experiment to assess both STM and LTM processes. Schizophrenics and normals completed both a five-trial immediate recall task and a five-trial delayed recall task, learning a different 12-word list on each trial. The subject heard the words binaurally through earphones, and the oral recall was tape-recorded. In the delayed recall, as soon as the subject heard a signal at the end of the list, he or she was required to count numbers aloud until another signal, 10 seconds later, was heard; then the free recall followed. In the no-delay recall, the subject was required to start the free recall immediately after hearing the terminal signal for the list. The mean percentage of recall over trials for the no-delay and delayed conditions, respectively, were 30.8% and 22.8% for the schizophrenics and 39.0% and 32.0% for the normals. The schizophrenics' recall was again significantly poorer than the normals', although organizational variables were kept at a minimum. Both groups revealed a clear proactive inhibition in both recall conditions, recalling progressively less as the trials progressed, but the group-by-trial interaction was not significant. That is, because the build-up of proactive interference is a direct function of item similarity, the semantic encoding that occurs automatically and naturally (Wickens, 1970, 1972) is comparable between the schizophrenics and normals.

Some of the mnemonic strategies that are not primarily linguistic or organizational but that may covary with the schizophrenic recall deficit are the serial position effect, the capacity of the STM and LTM stores, the input–output concordance, instrusion of inappropriate words, and psychomotor retardation. First, the serial position curves, that relate the percentage of words recalled (five trials combined) to their serial position at input, were U-shaped in both groups, showing an elevation that spans the first few serial positions (the primacy effect), another elevation that spans the last few positions (the recency effect), and low recall percentages that span the intermediate positions (see Koh et al., 1974, Figure 2). Investigators generally interpret the recency effect to reflect both STM and LTM components, while the primacy effect and the middle segment are interpreted to reflect solely the LTM component (see Kintsch, 1970b). Moreover, the primacy effect is seen to be evidence for a rehearsal strategy, including some semantic elaboration. When the serial positions were divided into the above three segments for statistical analyses, the schizophrenics' recall tended to be inferior to the normals' in all three segments. That is, although the strategies of rehearsal and direct read-out from the STM store underlie the recall of both schizophrenics and normals, the schizophrenics are comparatively inefficient. The schizophrenic STM deficit found in this experiment, therefore, is at variance with the notion of an intact STM in schizophrenics, which has been advancing thus far. Tulving and Colotla's (1970) procedure, which separates the STM components from the LTM components for the no-delay data, was applied also. The number of words read out from the STM store was 1.9 for the schizophrenics and 2.4 for the normals; this group difference was small but significant. However, it should be noted that the serial position curves resulting from the free-recall paradigm cannot adequately assess the STM store because selective attention, rehearsal, read-out, and other mnemonic processes are all under the subject's control. Accordingly, the subject could have rehearsed and paid more attention to the earlier items in the string at the expense of the middle and later items, or vice versa.

The input–output concordance, as defined above, measures the extent to which the subject retains the input order of the string in his or her recall. This form of organization is based on stimulus contiguity rather than on semantic association. The input–output concordance, indexed by Mandler and Dean's (1969) ITR scores, was significantly higher in the normals than in the schizophrenics. This measure was significantly correlated with the recall performance in the normals, suggesting its strategic significance; but the correlation was not significant in the schizophrenics. The schizophrenics also committed more intrusion errors. The percentage of intrusions based on the total number of words recalled for the no-delay and delay conditions were, respectively, 32% and 27% for the schizophrenics and, respectively, 12% and 12% for the normals. Furthermore, the schizophrenics were significantly slower in emitting the words that they could recall. In the no-delay condition, the emission rate during the first 10 seconds was 2.3 words/log second for the schizophrenics and 3.1 words/log second for the normals; in the delayed condition the rate was 1.8 words/log second for the schizophrenics and 2.7 words/log second for the normals. The schizophrenics' poor recall, therefore, was partially caused by psychomotor retardation.

This study, therefore, demonstrates that in free recall other mnemonic strategies than organizational and linguistic are also operating and that schizophrenics are again inferior to normals in these mnemonic strategies.

DISCUSSION AND INTERIM CONCLUSIONS

What generalizations that bear on the schizophrenics' capabilities and limitations in the mnemonic processing of verbal materials can be drawn from this series of experiments? I have tried to show how and where our various experiments fit into the schizophrenic memory system, using an information-processing model, supplemented by the notion of levels of information processing. Although each of these experiments touches merely a small portion of the vastly complex problems, when their results are examined within the general framework of the model, some modest but meaningful generalizations seem to emerge.

Recall Memory

It is clear that the schizophrenics' recall for verbal materials is poor, regardless of the type of to-be-remembered string employed. Their performance was consistently inferior to that of the normals in the recall of random lists (Koh & Kayton, 1974; Koh et al., 1972; Koh et al., 1973), conceptually and affectively categorizable lists (Kayton & Koh, 1975; Koh et al., 1973), and anomalous and normal sentences (Koh et al., 1972). This conclusion, however, varies partly with the conclusions drawn by Lawson, McGhie, and Chapman (1964), Levy and Maxwell (1968), and Truscott (1970). They found the schizophrenic recall deficit in contextual word strings but not in random word strings. Chapman and Chapman (1973) have rather convincingly argued that this finding may be an artifact resulting from the difference in discriminating power between the random-list tasks (very difficult) and the contextual-list tasks (optimally difficult) used by these investigators. Furthermore, in the studies by Lawson et al. and by Levy and Maxwell, the random-word string was always given on the first trial, and the contextual cues in the strings increased with trials. The significant group-by-organization interaction they found, accordingly, was a joint function of the organization factor and the trial, a difference in learning rate. A better design could include a random presentation or a counterbalanced presentation order of the different strings and an independent estimation of the organizational factor. In the studies cited above, schizophrenics were repeatedly found to be poor also in the recall of random lists.

Throughout these studies, effort has been focused on isolating and independently assessing the mnemonic processes or strategies that are believed to be responsible for the schizophrenic recall deficit. The other investigators just cited viewed the schizophrenic deficit in remembering to be largely caused by their relative inability to detect and utilize the contextual cues that the experimenter has provided in the to-be-remembered word strings. This view is essentially in harmony with the author's interpretation that the schizophrenics' recall deficit is caused by their inefficiency in mnemonic organization. This interpretation, however, is distinct from their more behaviorally oriented interpretation, insofar as an attempt has been made to identify the underlying organizational processes by means of various indices and to treat this measurable construct as a factor that contributes to the recall deficit. Because the mnemonic strategies available to the subject in the free-recall paradigm are many and varied, it is unlikely that the variables manipulated at the input stage can fully account for the subject's recall performance. The problem, then, is whether the organizational indices that have been extracted are valid. In general, the various clustering measures, the measures of subjective organization and the measures of input—output concordance extracted from the free-recall data covaried with the recall performance; in addition, the schizophrenic recall deficit generally covaried with their comparatively meager scores in mnemonic organization. In a recent study, Traupmann (1975) has also demonstrated such a correlation between the schizophrenics' recall deficit and their inefficient subjective organization.

A series of converging experiments conducted to clarify the schizophrenic organizational processes reinforces the above observation. That is, (a) the schizophrenic recall deficit disappears when the encoding and organization of the to-be-remembered words is appropriately induced at the input stage (Koh et al., 1976); (b) the memory of schizophrenics is adequate when the tasks require minimal use of retrieval processes based on the LTM organizational network (recognition memory, Koh et al., 1973; perceptual memory, Koh et al., 1976; affective memory, Koh, Peterson, & Streicker, unpublished; memory scanning. Koh, Peterson, & Szoc, in press); (c) the schizophrenics' deficit in mnemonic organization is not attributable to their permanent memory structure, which suggests their inefficiency in mnemonic control processes or in utilizing their internal resources (Koh et al., 1974); and (d) the schizophrenics' inefficiency in mnemonic strategy is limited to organizational strategies as well as nonorganizational strategies (Koh & Kayton, 1974). Such a finding is not unexpected. After all, the two types of strategies, organizational and nonorganizational, are both aspects of the subject's executive control system.

Recognition Memory

The recognition memory of schizophrenics was found to be intact by previous investigators (Bauman & Murray, 1968; Nachmani & Cohen, 1969). The study by Koh et al. (1973) has confirmed their finding. Traupmann (1975), however, found that recognition memory is impaired in process schizophrenics, although it is not impaired in reactive schizophrenics.

Recently, the notion that recall is sensitive to organizational variables but that recognition is not (generation—recognition theories) has been questioned by Tulving and Thompson (1971, 1973). They found impaired recognition memory in normal subjects when the contexts in which a target item occurred for study and for test were different. In a series of experiments, Mandler (1972) induced different levels of organizational encoding by means of sorting tasks and found a positive relation between the organizational level and the subsequent recognition performance. He hypothesized that subjects make a retrieval check on those items that have weak initial tags by using organizational schemes (postrecognition retrieval check). These findings lead to the belief that if these paradigms developed by Tulving and Thompson and by Mandler are used, a schizophrenic inefficiency in recognition memory may emerge. On the other hand, when contextual variables are not maximized, as was the case in the previously described experiment, recognition memory is apparently little impaired. The important point, however, is not the distinction between recall and recognition but the nature of the psychological processes underlying these tasks. If the contextual variables are maximized in a recognition task, then the task would require mnemonic organization as does the free-recall task.

Short-term Memory

Our studies have rather strongly suggested that schizophrenics are adequate in the encoding of words, of random dot patterns for numerousness and of inkblot pictures for pleasantness; in the short-term retention of coded information; and in the STM search, comparison and retrieval for both nonverbal and verbal information (Koh & Kayton, 1974; Koh et al., 1976; Koh, Peterson, & Streicker, unpublished; Koh, Peterson, & Szoc, in press). In spite of the varying conditions of task difficulty introduced for both the stimulus encoding and the information storage, the schizophrenics were comparable to the normals. These findings are actually contrary to the investigators' expectation because schizophrenic dysfunctions in short-term memory processes were widely hypothesized by previous investigators, for example, an input dysfunction (Venables, 1964), an impaired filtering mechanism (McGhie, 1970) and early stage retardation of information processing (Yates, 1966, 1973).

This discrepancy in experimental findings may have partly resulted from differences in the constructs, the sensory modalities, the research designs, the subject variables, and other features involved in the various experiments. For example, the schizophrenics' deficit in the recall of contextual word strings is seen by McGhie (1970) to be a consequence of a filtering dysfunction, but it could also be interpreted to be a result of an organizational dysfunction. Some of the studies reviewed by McGhie (1970), however, used the free-recall paradigm. This paradigm is not suitable for assessing the locus and nature of a schizophrenic filtering dysfunction, although it is helpful for depicting organizational strategies. The delayed comparison and choice reaction-time procedures that my colleagues and I have used are more direct in clarifying the STM processes of schizophrenics.

If we examine only those studies which have used experimental paradigms similar to ours, there are still some noticeable discrepancies. Using the delayed comparison method, Claridge (1960) found that schizophrenics, when compared to normals, underestimated the loudness of the first of two successively presented tones; he concluded that there is a greater STM trace decay in schizophrenics. Using a simplified version of the method of limits, Ritzler and Rosenbaum (1974) found no STM trace decay for the first-weight memory in schizophrenics, but they found a deficit in proprioceptive encoding. Replications of these two experiments seem to be in order, however, because these investigators did not consider the possible contamination of the memory strength by the subject's response bias. Koh and Peterson (1974) partially replicated Koh et al.'s (1976) delayed comparisons of numerousness using two groups of college students, MMPI 2–7–8 ("pseudoneurotic schizophrenia") students and MMPI normal-type students. The 2–7–8-type students revealed encoding difficulty and greater STM decay under the condition in which the first to-be-remembered dot pattern was varied over trials (comparison–standard condition). This finding is, therefore, at variance with that of Koh et al.'s. There were, however, major procedural differences between the experiments by Koh and Peterson and by Koh et al. In the former, the round area of the dot patterns projected on a wall had a 68-cm diameter, and the subject was tested, most of the time, in a small group; in the latter, however, the area projected on a 40-by-40-cm rear projection screen had a 19-cm diameter, and the subject was tested individually.

These differences must have created more variations within the Koh and Peterson study. For example, there was opportunity for variation in the individual subject's viewing angles, in the area that the foveal vision could cover at any point in time and in the number and direction of eye movements required for the abstraction of a stable internal representation of the first dot pattern. In addition, the assumption that 2–7–8-type students are comparable to hospitalized and clinically diagnosed schizophrenics may be questionable. In regard to the STM scanning and search reflected in the Sternberg choice reaction-time paradigm, Checkosky (see Sternberg, 1975) found that schizophrenics and alcoholics hospitalized in a Veterans Administration hospital and normal college students revealed a linear relationship between the mean RT and the memory-set size. Furthermore, the slope for the RT function was the same among all three groups. Koh, Peterson, and Szoc's (in press) result of nonlinearity in the RT function, therefore, differs from Checkosky's result, although the finding of equal slopes between schizophrenics and normals confirms his conclusion that the short-term scanning of schizophrenics is comparable to that of normals. Checkosky used digits and letters as the stimuli and the fixed-set procedure (in which the same memory set was used for a long series of trials); in contrast, Koh, Peterson, and Szoc used common English words as the stimuli and the varied-set procedure (in which the subject memorized a different memory set on each trial). Some of these and other procedural differences reviewed above are currently being examined at our laboratory through separate investigations. Our current notion that the active but automatic aspects of the schizophrenic STM is intact may require some modifications as these studies progress.

Semantic Memory

As long as the structural component of permanent memory is assessed by means of the subject's performance, there is always the risk that his or her control processes will affect the data. Koh et al.'s (1974) study on the subjective lexicon of schizophrenics by means of the sorting method is no exception because sorting, like recall, requires the subject's active and conscious participation. Mindful of this possible influence, the hierarchical clustering scheme extracted from the schizophrenics' sorting was taken to be evidence for an intact semantic memory because it was found to be comparable to the normals'. There are also some supplementary data in our studies to support the notion of an intact structral memory in schizophrenics. In the studies by Koh et al. (1976) by Koh et al. (1976) and by Koh, Peterson and Streicker (unpublished) described above, the schizophrenics' psychophysical scalings for affective words, for the numerousness of random dot patterns and for the pleasantness of inkblot pictures were obtained; they were generally comparable to those of the normals in terms of the mean scale values. In these tasks, the subjects must not only sort the stimuli into classes but must also order them in asymmetric relations when the imposed constraints are the rules of rating and magnitude-estimation. If the subject's scalings are assumed to reflect his or her internal categorical and relational scheme, these results certainly strengthen the observation resulting from the sorting task. One exception to be noted, however, is that the schizophrenics tended to be constrictive and stereotyped in these seemingly nonstressful tasks, showing the tendency to use a small number of categories in the sorting and rating and using a smaller number of numerals in the magnitude estimation.

Interim Conclusions

Conceptualizing human memory as consisting of the central executive control process and a series of interdependent structural components, each of our experiments has separately examined a small, manageable portion of the schizophrenic memory system. When the findings from these various converging experiments are related to the information processing model of human memory, a few provisional conclusions are possible. First, as far as our young nonpsychotic schizophrenics are concerned, there appears to be no impairment in the structural components of their memory. This conclusion is suggested by their adequate STM and LTM recognition performances as well as by their adequate internal structure of words and their adequate internal schematics for numerousness. Second, the basic difficulty of schizophrenics in the remembering of verbal materials is largely attributable to their inefficiency in the executive control that regulates the flow of information through the structural components. This inefficiency, however, is not obvious (and may even be absent) in the STM processing that requires little high-level organization and elaboration and is more or less automatic and natural. Our findings that schizophrenics performed well in the short-term delayed comparison and scanning for verbal as well as nonverbal stimuli suggest the existence of intact or comparatively unimpaired STM processes in schizophrenia. The notion of active but automatic processing in the STM is also advanced by investigators in psycholinguistics. In human communication, the process of recoding phonetic representations into semantic representations and semantic representations into phonetic representations occurs easily and naturally in the STM, although these processes are complex and require the speaker's and listener's active and conscious participation (Liberman, Mattingly, & Turvey, 1972). The working hypothesis at this stage of our investigation is that STM processes are probably not impaired in schizophrenics. A schizophrenic deficit in executive control, however, emerges when the processes involved in memory tasks are unnatural, requiring high-order stimulus elaboration and mnemonic strategies. Schizophrenics are capable of improving their recall performance; however, these mnemonic processes simply are not as efficient as those in normals. A few works currently in progress at our laboratory were designed to reveal some of the boundary conditions beyond which the schizophrenics' control processes break down. Third, because the schizophrenic deficit in control processes is presumably not attributable to some permanent structural impairment, it must be remediable by inducing appropriate mnemonic strategies in the patients. Recently, Larsen and Fromholt (1976) have presented supporting evidence for the observation that schizophrenics are appropriately equipped with the necessary structures and mnemonic strategies, but they simply fail to utilize these internal resources efficiently and to initiate these strategies spontaneously.

I often feel that the information-processing approach can be viewed to be similar to the dynamic approach of ego psychology. Ego psychology conceives a person to be a hierarchically structured system who searches, analyzes and acts on the environment by manipulating and utilizing his or her knowledge and the objects and events as perceived (Rapaport, 1959, 1960). That is, both approaches posit structural and control components. At the initial input stage, the information is modality-specific and intensity-bound. Following, is a sequence of substages, in which the information is transformed and modified into qualitatively different forms. The executive control or ego regulates the information flow through these substages and compensates for the structural limitations. Furthermore, although our laboratory studies conclude that the schizophrenics' disorders in language and thought are largely caused by their inefficient executive control, our clinical research team attributes these disorders to impaired ego-functioning (Grinker, 1975). Of course, these two approaches differ radically in the data and concepts with which they deal. The significance of the information-processing approach lies in the fact that the theoretical constructs and research techniques that it generates have the virtues of precision and objectivity in clarifying the loci and nature of the internal determinants of behavioral disorders. I am tempted to state that analytic inquiry into schizophrenic ego-functioning is possible by means of laboratory studies and that these studies can help to detail the stage-by-stage processes involved. Perhaps these studies can eventually suggest ways to ameliorate schizophrenic thought and language disorders.

ACKNOWLEDGMENTS

The preparation of this paper and the author's research reported herein were supported by U.S. Public Health Service grants MH-18991, MH-5519, and State of Illinois grant 432-12-RD. I am indebted to my coinvestigators, especially to Lawrence Kayton and Rolf A. Peterson, for their invaluable contributions to the work, and to Roy R. Grinker, Sr., Director of the Psychosomatic and Psychiatric Institute, who has been not only sympathetic to our laboratory studies on schizophrenia but has also spent a great deal of his time and energy in selecting and diagnosing our patient subjects and as serving as the head of the clinical research team described in the text. Special thanks go to James D. Dooling and Endel Tulving for their valuable comments on this manuscript.

REFERENCES

Anderson, J. R., & Bower, G. H. Recognition and retrieval processes in free recall. *Psychological Review,* 1972, *79,* 97–123.

Atkinson, R. C., Herrmann, D. J., & Wescourt, K. T. Search processes in recognition memory. In R. L. Solso (Ed.), *The theories in cognitive psychology.* New York: John Wiley & Sons, 1974.

Atkinson, R. C., & Shiffrin, R. M. Human memory: A proposed system and its control processes. In K. W. Spence & J. T. Spence (Eds.), *The psychology of learning and motivation* (Vol. 2). New York: Academic Press, 1968.

Banks, W. P. Signal detection theory and human memory. *Psychological Bulletin,* 1970, *74,* 81–99.

Bauman, E., & Murray, D. J. Recognition versus recall in schizophrenia. *Canadian Journal of Psychology,* 1968, *22,* 18–25.

Bjork, R. A. Short-term storage: The ordered output of a central processor. In F. Restle, R. M. Shiffrin, N. J. Castellan, H. R. Lindman, & D. B. Pisoni (Eds.), *Cognitive theory* (Vol. 1). New Jersey: Lawrence Erlbaum Associates, 1975.

Boucher, J., & Osgood, C. E. The Pollyanna tendency. *Journal of Verbal Learning and Verbal Behavior,* 1969, *8,* 1–8.

Bousfield, A. K., & Bousfield, W. A. Measurement of clustering and sequential constancies in repeated free recall. *Psychological Reports,* 1966, *19,* 935–942.

Bousfield, W. A. The occurrence of clustering in the recall of randomly arranged associates. *Journal of General Psychology,* 1953, *49,* 229–240.

Bransford, J. D., Barclay, J. R., & Franks, J. J. Sentence memory: A constructive versus interpretive approach. *Cognitive Psychology,* 1972, *3,* 193–209.

Briggs, G. E. On the predictor variable for choice reaction time. Paper presented at the meeting of the Midwestern Psychological Association, Chicago, May 1974.

Briggs, G. E., & Johnson, A. M. On the nature of central processing in choice reactions. *Memory and Cognition,* 1973, *1,* 91–100.

Broadbent, D. E. *Perception and communication.* Oxford: Pergamon Press, 1958.

Broadbent, D. E. *Decision and stress.* New York: Academic Press, 1971.

Brown, A. L. The role of strategic behavior in retardate memory. In N. R. Ellis (Ed.), *International review of research in mental retardation* (Vol. 7). New York: Academic Press, 1975. (a)

Brown, A. L. The development of memory: Knowing, knowing about knowing, and knowing how to know. In H. W. Reese (Ed.), *Advances in child development and behavior* (Vol. 10). New York: Academic Press, 1975. (b)

Chapman, L. J., & Chapman, J. P. *Disordered thought in schizophrenia.* Englewood Cliffs, New Jersey: Prentice–Hall, 1973, (a)

Chapman, L. J., & Chapman, J. P. Problems in the measurement of cognitive deficit. *Psychological Bulletin,* 1973, *79,* 380–385. (b)

Chomsky, N. A review of B. F. Skinner's *Verbal behavior. Language,* 1959, *35,* 26–58.

Chomsky, N. *Aspects of the theory of syntax.* Cambridge, Massachusetts: MIT Press, 1965.

Claridge, G. The excitation–inhibition balance in neurotics. In H. J. Eysenck (Ed.), *Experiments in personality* (Vol. 2). London: Routledge & Kagan Paul, 1960.

Craik, F. I. M., & Jacoby, L. L. A process view of short-term retention. In F. Restle, R. M. Shiffrin, N. J. Castellan, H. R. Lindman, & D. B. Pisoni (Eds.), *Cognitive theory* (Vol. 1). Hillsdale, New Jersey: Lawrence Erlbaum Associates, 1975.

Craik, F. I. M., & Lockhart, R. S. Levels of processing: A framework for memory research. *Journal of Verbal Learning and Verbal Behavior,* 1972, *11,* 671–684.

Craik, F. I. M., & Tulving, E. Depth of processing and the retention of words in episodic memory. *Journal of Experimental Psychology: General,* 1975, *1,* 268–294.

Durlach, N. I., & Braida, L. D. Intensity perception: I. Preliminary theory of intensity resolution. *Journal of the Acoustic Society of America,* 1969, *46,* 372–383.

Estes, W. K. (Ed.). *Handbook of learning and cognitive processes* (Vol. 1). Hillsdale, New Jersey: Lawrence Erlbaum Associates, 1975. (a)

Estes, W. K. (Ed.). *Handbook of learning and cognitive processes* (Vol. 2). Hillsdale, New Jersey: Lawrence Erlbaum Associates, 1975. (b)

Estes, W. K. (Ed.). *Handbook of learning and cognitive processes* (Vol. 3). Hillsdale, New Jersey: Lawrence Erlbaum Associates, 1976.

Flavell, J. H. Developmental studies of mediated memory. H. W. Reese & L. P. Lipsitt (Eds.), *Advances in child development and behavior* (Vol. 5). New York: Academic Press, 1970.

Garner, W. R., Hake, H. W., & Eriksen, C. W. Operationism and the concept of perception. *Psychological Review,* 1956, *63,* 317–329.

Gilberstadt, H., & Duker, J. *A handbook of actuarial MMPI interpretation.* Philadelphia: Sander, 1965.

Green, D. M., & Swets, J. A. *Signal detection theory and psychophysics.* New York: John Wiley & Sons, 1966.

Greeno, J. G., & Bjork, R. A. Mathematical learning theory and the new "mental forestry." *Annual Review of Psychology,* 1973, *24,* 81–116.

Grinker, R. R. *Psychiatry in broad perspective.* New York: Behavioral Publications, 1975.

Grinker, R. R., & Holzman, P. S. Schizophrenic pathology in young adults. *Archives of General Psychiatry,* 1973, *28,* 168–175.

Guilford, J. P. *Psychometric methods* (2nd ed.). New York: Harper & Row, 1954.

Haber, R. N. (Ed.). *Contemporary theory and research in visual perception.* New York: Holt, Rinehart & Winston, 1968.

Haber, R. N. *Information-processing approaches to visual perception.* New York: Holt, Rinehart & Winston, 1969.

Helson, H. *Adaptation-level theory: An experimental and systematic approach to behavior.* New York: Harper & Row, 1964.

Hochhaus, L. A table for the calculation of d' and β. *Psychological Bulletin,* 1972, *77,* 375–376.

Hollingshead, A. B., & Redlich, F. C. *Social class and mental illness.* New York: John Wiley & Sons, 1958.

Hunt, E. B. *Concept learning: An information processing problem.* New York: John Wiley & Sons, 1962.

Hyde, T. S., & Jenkins, J. J. Recall for words as a function of semantic, graphic, and syntactic orienting tasks. *Journal of Verbal Learning and Verbal Behavior,* 1973, *12,* 471–480.

Jenkins, J. J. Can we have a theory of meaningful memory? In R. L. Solso (Ed.), *Theories in cognitive psychology.* Hillsdale, New Jersey: Lawrence Erlbaum Associates, 1947.

Johnson, S. C. Hierarchical clustering schemes. *Psychometrika,* 1967, *32,* 241–254.

Kayton, L. Good outcome in young adult schizophrenia. *Archives of General Psychiatry,* 1973, *29,* 103–110.

Kayton, L., & Koh, S. D. Hypohedonia in schizophrenia. *Journal of Nervous and Mental Disease,* 1975, *161,* 412–420.

Kinchla, R. A. Selective processes in sensory memory: A probe-comparison procedure. In S. Kornblum (Ed.), *Attention and performance IV.* New York: Academic Press, 1973.

Kintsch, W. Models for free recall and recognition. In D. A. Norman (Ed.), *Models of human memory.* New York: Academic Press, 1970.

Kintsch, W. *The representation of meaning and memory.* Hillsdale, New Jersey: Lawrence Erlbaum Associates, 1974.

Koh, S. D., & Kayton, L. Memorization of "unrelated" word strings by young nonpsychotic schizophrenics. *Journal of Abnormal Psychology,* 1974, *83,* 14–22.

Koh, S. D., Kayton, L., & Berry, R. Mnemonic organization in young nonpsychotic schizophrenics. *Journal of Abnormal Psychology,* 1973, *81,* 299–310.

Koh, S. D., Kayton, L., & Peterson, R. A. Affective encoding and consequent remembering in schizophrenic young adults. *Journal of Abnormal Psychology,* 1976, *85,* 156–166.

Koh, S. D., Kayton, L., & Schwarz, C. Remembering of connected discourse by young nonpsychotic schizophrenics. *Abstract Guide, Twentieth International Congress of Psychology,* 1972, 407. (Abstract)

Koh, S. D., Kayton, L., & Schwarz, C. The structure of word-storage in the permanent memory of nonpsychotic schizophrenics. *Journal of Consulting and Clinical Psychology,* 1974, *42,* 879–887.

Koh, S. D., Kayton, L., & Streicker, S. Short-term memory for numerousness in schizophrenic young adults. *Journal of Nervous and Mental Disease,* 1976, *163,* 88–101.

Koh, S. D., & Peterson, R. Perceptual memory for numerousness in "nonpsychotic schizophrenics." *Journal of Abnormal Psychology,* 1974, *83,* 215–226.

Koh, S. D., Peterson, R. A., & Streicker, S. *Short-term memory for picture preferences in schizophrenic young adults.* Unpublished manuscript.

Koh, S. D., Peterson, R. A., & Szoc, R. Short-term memory scanning for words in schizophrenic young adults. *Journal of Abnormal Psychology,* in press.

Larsen, S. F., & Fromholt, P. Mnemonic organization and free recall in schizophrenia. *Journal of Abnormal Psychology,* 1976, *85,* 61–65.

Lawson, J. S., McGhie, A., & Chapman, J. Perception of speech in schizophrenia. *British Journal of Psychology,* 1964, *110,* 375–380.

Levy, R., & Maxwell, A. E. The effect of verbal context on the recall of schizophrenics and other psychiatric patients. *British Journal of Psychology,* 1968, *114,* 311–316.

Liberman, A. M., Mattingly, I. G., & Turvey, M. T. Language codes and memory codes. In A. W. Melton & E. Martin (Eds.), *Coding processes in human memory.* Washington, D.C.: Holt, Rinehart & Winton, 1972.

Lockhart, R. S., Craik, F. I. M., & Jacoby, L. L. Depth of processing in recognition and recall: Some aspect of a general memory system. In J. Brown (Ed.), *Recognition and recall.* London: John Wiley & Sons, 1975.

Lykken, D. T. Statistical significance in psychological research. *Psychological Bulletin,* 1968, *70,* 151–159.

Mandler, G. Organization and recognition. In E. Tulving & W. Donaldson (Eds.), *Organization of memory.* New York: Academic Press, 1972.

Mandler, G., & Dean, P. J. Seriation: The development of serial order in free recall. *Journal of Experimental Psychology*, 1969, *81*, 207–215.

Marks, L. E., & Miller, G. A. The role of semantic and syntactic constraints in the memorization of English sentences. *Journal of Verbal Learning and Verbal Behavior*, 1964, *3*, 1–5.

McGhie, A. Attention and perception in schizophrenia. In B. A. Maher (Ed.), *Progress in experimental personality research* (Vol. 5). New York: Academic Press, 1970.

Meehl, P. E. Schizotaxa, schizotypy, schizophrenia. *American Psychology*, 1962, *17*, 827–828.

Melton, A. W., & Martin, E. (Eds.). *Coding processes in human memory*. Washington, D.C.: Holt, Rinehart & Winston, 1972.

Miller, G. A. The magical number seven, plus and minus two: Some limit on our capacity for processing information. *Psychological Review*, 1956, *63*, 81–96.

Miller, G. A. Lexical memory. *Proceedings of the American Philosophical Society*, 1972, *116*, 140–144.

Miller, G. A., & McNeill, D. Psycholinguistics. In G. Lindzey & E. Aronson, (Eds.), *The handbook of social psychology* (2nd ed.). Reading, Massachusetts: Addison–Wesley, 1969.

Murdock, B. B. *Human memory: Theory and data*. Hillsdale, New Jersey: Lawrence Erlbaum Associates, 1974.

Nachmani, G., & Cohen, B. D. Recall and recognition free learning in schizophrenia. *Journal of Abnormal Psychology*, 1969, *74*, 511–516.

Neisser, U. *Cognitive psychology*. New York: Appleton–Century–Crofts, 1967.

Newell, A., & Simon, H. A. *Human problem solving*. Englewood Cliffs, New Jersey: Prentice–Hall, 1972.

Nie, N. H., Hull, C. H., Jenkins, J. G., Steinbrenner, K., & Bent, D. H. *SPSS: Statistical package for the social sciences*. New York: McGraw–Hill, 1975.

Norman, D. A. *Models of human memory*. New York: Academic Press, 1970.

Osgood, C. E. Semantic differential technique in the comparative study of cultures. *American Anthropology*, 1964, *66*, 171–200.

Rado, S. *Psychoanalysis of behavior: Collected papers*. New York: Grune & Stratton, 1956.

Rapaport, D. The structure of psychoanalytic theory: A systematic attempt. In S. Koch (Ed.), *Psychology: A study of science* (Vol. 3). New York: McGraw–Hill, 1959.

Rapaport, D. On the psychoanalytic theory of motivation. *Nebraska Symposium on Motivation* (Vol. 17). Lincoln: University of Nebraska Press, 1960.

Ritzler, B., & Rosenbaum, G. Proprioception in schizophrenics and normals: Effects of stimulus intensity and interstimulus interval. *Journal of Abnormal Psychology*, 1974, *83*, 106–111.

Roenker, D. L., Thompson, C. P., & Brown, S. C. Comparison of measures for the estimation of clustering in free recall. *Psychological Bulletin*, 1971, *76*, 45–48.

Rosenberg, S., & Schiller, W. J. Semantic coding and incidental sentences recall. *Journal of Experimental Psychology*, 1971, *90*, 345–346.

Shannon, C. E. A mathematical theory of communication. *Bell System Technical Journal*, 1948, *27*, 379–423; 623–656.

Shephard, R. N. Recognition memory for words, sentences, and pictures. *Journal of Verbal Learning and Verbal Behavior*, 1967, *6*, 156–163.

Smith, E. E. Choice reaction time: An analysis of the major theoretical positions. *Psychological Bulletin*, 1968, *69*, 77–110.

Solso, R. A. (Ed.) *Theories in cognitive psychology: The Loyola symposium*. Hillsdale, New Jersey: Lawrence Erlbaum Associates, 1974.

Solso, R. L. (Ed.) *Information processing and cognition: The Loyola symposium.* Hillsdale, New Jersey: Lawrence Erlbaum Associates, 1975.

Sternberg, S. Memory scanning: Mental processes revealed by reaction-time experiments. *American Scientist,* 1969, *57,* 421–457.

Sternberg, S. Decomposing mental processes with reaction-time data. Paper presented at the meeting of the Midwestern Psychological Association, Detroit, May 1971.

Sternberg, S. Memory scanning: New findings and current controversies. *Quarterly Journal of Experimental Psychology,* 1975, *27,* 1–32.

Stevens, S. S. *Psychophysics: Introduction to its perceptual, neural and social prospects.* New York: John Wiley & Sons, 1975.

Traupmann, K. L. Effects of categorization and imagery on recognition and recall by process and reactive schizophrenics. *Journal of Abnormal Psychology,* 1975, *84,* 307–314.

Truscott, I. P. Contextual constraint and schizophrenic language. *Journal of Consulting and Clinical Psychology,* 1970, *35,* 189–194.

Tulving, E. Episodic and semantic memory. In E. Tulving & W. Donaldson (Eds.), *Organization of memory.* New York: Academic Press, 1972.

Tulving, E., & Colotla, V. A. Free recall of trilingual lists. *Cognitive Psychology,* 1970, *1,* 86–98.

Tulving, E., & Donaldson, W. (Eds.). *Organization of memory.* New York: Academic Press, 1972.

Tulving, E., & Thompson, D. M. Retrieval processes in recognition memory: Effects of associative context. *Journal of Experimental Psychology,* 1971, *87,* 116–124.

Tulving, E., & Thompson, D. M. Encoding specificity and retrieval processes in episodic memory. *Psychological Review,* 1973, *80,* 352–373.

Venables, P. H. Input dysfunction in schizophrenia. In B. A. Maher (Ed.), *Progress in experimental personality research.* New York: Academic Press, 1964.

Wickens, D. D. Encoding categories of words: An empirical approach to meaning. *Psychological Review,* 1970, *77,* 1–15.

Wickens, D. D. Characteristics of word encoding. In A. W. Melton & E. Martin (Eds.), *Coding process in human memory.* Washington, D.C.: Holt, Rinehart & Winston, 1972.

Yates, A. J. Psychological deficits. *Annual Review of Psychology,* 1966, *17,* 111–114.

Yates, A. J. Abnormalities of psychomotor functions. In H. J. Eysenck (Ed.), *Handbook of abnormal psychology.* San Diego, California: Robert R. Knapp, 1973.

4

Schizophrenic Thought Disorder: Why the Lack of Answers?

Paul H. Blaney

The University of Texas at Austin

When I embarked about eight years ago on the study of language disorder in schizophrenia, it seemed reasonable that the way to obtain the whole picture on this topic was to read as much of the research and theoretical literature in this and related areas as possible. I expected to learn the answers to some questions and to learn what the unanswered questions were. Given the sheer bulk of the research in this field of study, my expectation was not unreasonable. If the schizophrenic psychological deficit lies in the impairment of a particular function or finite group of functions, should not its nature be virtually self-evident to a person examining the incredibly wide variety of tasks on which schizophrenics have been tested in well-controlled studies? The fact is, of course, that it does not. My quest was doomed; a complete picture was not obtainable.

Instead, a huge but relatively fruitless literature exists. One possible inference is that the whole enterprise of trying to characterize schizophrenic psychological deficit is futile. That is, perhaps the visible psychological symptoms are too far removed from the underlying malfunction which is their source. Research in this area may possibly never be able to answer any important questions. As an alternative, it seems profitable to try to understand why progress has been so slow.

There are a number of technical and methodological pitfalls in the study of schizophrenia that may provide answers. These research pitfalls have been described well by Chapman and Chapman in their recent book (1973a, Section II), by Salzinger in his book on schizophrenia (1973, pp. 27–31), and by Cromwell in his article in *Psychopharmocologia* (1972). I will not attempt to mention all of these pitfalls. Instead, a discussion of those pitfalls which are of special import follows.

DISCRIMINATING POWER

The first pitfall is the one noted by Chapman and Chapman in their book (1973a) and in a 1973(b) *Psychological Bulletin* article. (Also see Chapman & Chapman, 1975.) Sophisticated researchers have known for a long time that comparing schizophrenics with controls on only one task is not very revealing because the finding of a schizophrenic deficit is so ubiquitous. A finding needs to be more than just a possible instance of nonspecific deficit to be of worth. A solution appeared to be to compare schizophrenics and controls on more than one task; a task showing substantially more deficit than another could be said to be tapping some specific aspect of the schizophrenic deficit. Indeed the strategy of using group X test interactions in the search for a differential deficit is an excellent one. Chapman and Chapman noted, however, that the desired interaction can emerge for purely psychometric reasons – the test showing the most apparent schizophrenic deficit may do so merely because it is the most discriminating. Chapman and Chapman have described two aspects to discriminating power: reliability and difficulty level. Because these issues are not easily grasped, they are discussed here in a simpler manner than they were in early writings. Described here also is an additional source of ambiguity which, I believe, may be present when the differential deficit design is used.

Reliability.

Concerning reliability, consider for the purpose of the argument a simple model in which a test's variability has two components, a systematic component and a random component. A reliable test, of course, has much systematic and little random variance. The important point is that *randomness is a great equalizer.* That is, the random component of a test's variability will not differentiate groups. To the extent that the random component is large, it will tend to counter any true systematic group difference and drive the means toward each other. Thus, how far apart two group means on a test are depends upon how far apart they really are (in terms of systematic component) and how much of these tests' variability is random. Likewise, if two tests differ in the extent to which they differentiate two groups (that is, there is a group X test interaction), this may mean that the two groups differ more on what one test measures than on what the other one does or that one test has a larger random component than the other. Accordingly, unless the magnitude of the random component is controlled (that is unless the tests are equated for reliability) a group X test interaction cannot yield an unequivocal interpretation.

One way of getting an intuitive grasp of the phenomenon underlying the spurious impact of differences in reliability is in terms of a couple of better known psychometric effects. There are, in fact, two such effects that are manifestations of similar processes. The first is regression to the mean. Consider that offspring of tall parents tend to be shorter than they are; it is the randomness involved in genetic transmission that results in this shift toward the mean. Likewise, it is the randomness associated with unreliability which drives a set of scores toward the mean and leads to a diminution of obtained differences between groups. The second well-known psychometric effect to which the Chapmans' argument can be related is summarized in the statement: "The reliability of a test puts an upper limit on its correlation with other variables." An obvious correlary of this statement is that two variables which (if equally reliable) would correlate equally with a given criterion, will show unequal correlations with that criterion if one is more reliable than another. If one assumes the schizophrenia–nonschizophrenia dichotomy to be the "criterion," the last sentence constitutes a restatement of the Chapmans' argument in correlational rather than analysis-of-variance terms. That is, just as a difference between the magnitude of two correlations with a single criterion may be due to the fact that one predictor variable had lower reliability than the other (putting greater constraints on its ability to correlate with anything), then, likewise, a less reliable measure can be expected, with all other things being equal, to foster less separation of means on a criterion variable than a more reliable measure would.

My impression is that when people get confused about the confounding role of realiability in the group X test design it is because they think that the reliability of a test has no impact upon the *mean* of scores obtained on it. The common error is to think that a less reliable test will merely yield a distribution having greater variance than a more reliable test. This is not so. A less reliable test will, with all other things being equal, yield a distribution whose mean is closer to *whatever the mean score would be if scores were generated randomly* than a more reliable test will. Only when the mean of randomly generated scores happens to be identical to the mean of true scores will the reliability of the test have no impact on the mean.

Difficulty Level.

The impact of item difficulty upon discriminating power is most easily understood in terms of the most extreme case, commonly known as a "ceiling effect." If a group X test interaction resulted from one of the tests having, for instance, too few difficult items for the true magnitude of the between groups difference on it to be manifest, the interaction would readily be mistrusted. It would be said that the interaction was caused by a ceiling effect on one variable. The import of Chapman and Chapman's argument is that such effects can occur and can result in artifactual group X test interactions even when they are not blatant enough to force investigators to label them as ceiling effects.

Chapman and Chapman's (1973a, 1973b, 1975) use of the term "difficulty" should not be interpreted to imply that the artifact involved is specific to ability tests. To apply their argument to nonability situations, the expression "the percentage of persons responding to an item in a particular direction" (with that direction uniform across items insofar as interpetation is concerned) needs only to be substituted for the expression "difficulty level." The more general term is, of course, p+ value. The artifact applies in any circumstance (a) where there is a mode toward which scores gravitate, to the extent that they are unreliable and (b) where scores can be influenced by a failure to include sufficient numbers of items having a particular p+ value. The relevance of this point to the study of schizophrenic deficit is that the artifact must be feared even in situations where the designation of one response as "correct" and another as "incorrect" is not clear.

It Matters.

The relevance of this methodological pitfall for hypotheses regarding schizophrenia should be emphasized. Most studies using the differential deficit strategy involve the following logic: the two tasks used are similar, but one has an added feature which will hopefully directly indicate a special weakness of schizophrenics. The threat lies in the added feature which almost always makes the experimental task more difficult than the control task, and this, as noted above, may cause the tests to differ in discriminating power. Indeed, it would probably be hard to avoid a group X test interaction when two tests differ substantially in difficulty level. When, as appears most commonly, the control task is quite easy and thus not very discriminating, although the task having the feature to which schizophrenics are allegedly vulnerable is somewhat more difficult, the psychometric effect strongly biases in favor of support of the hypothesis. If the control task is moderately difficult, and the experimental task is extremely difficult, the artifactual bias favors an interaction effect opposite to prediction. This situation rarely occurs, though.

Because the psychometric artifact then usually biases experiments' results according to prediction, whether or not the hypothesis is true, the differential deficit design (in which two or more tasks are compared) leaves investigators in the same quandary that studies comparing schizophrenics with controls on just one task do. Positive results supporting almost any hypothesis are so easy to obtain that such results have little consequence. In short, the designs traditionally used even by psychologists functioning at a reasonable degree of methodological sophistication have rendered it inordinately easy to obtain results in favor of their hypothesis regarding schizophrenic deficit, regardless of what that hypothesis was or how closely it matched objective reality.

Validity and Discriminating Power.

In the draft of this paper presented at the 1975 American Psychological Association convention, I stated that these problems vanish when the differential deficit design is executed according to the canons recommended by Chapman and Chapman (1973a, 1973b, 1975), that is, with tests equated for discriminating power. I am now convinced that this matter is more complex still and is not so easily dealt with.

Recall that it is because reliability and difficulty level can influence the difference between obtained means that they are such a menace. Yet another potential source of such influence is validity. The model described above assumes that all systematic (reliable) variance is construct-relevant (valid). This is not a very realistic assumption. Tests are often more reliable than they are valid. The presence of a construct-irrelevant but systematic source of variance can influence the degree of difference between means.

A few hypothetical examples may help. For each example, imagine that the design calls for the comparison of schizophrenics and controls on two tests, with the focus of interest upon a potential group X test interaction (differential deficit). For simplicity, imagine that both tests are perfectly reliable and that they both have ample items through a wide range of difficulty, so that differential discriminating power as Chapman and Chapman have discussed it is not a problem. Test A is alleged to measure cognitive process X; Test B supposedly measures process Y. If schizophrenics show a greater deficit, relative to controls, on Test A than on Test B, the conclusion that schizophrenics have some special difficulty with X may seem safe. There are several circumstances in which the conclusion may be incorrect and in which, instead, schizophrenics have no more trouble with X than with Y, the obtained pattern of results notwithstanding. Each circumstance involves the presence of (an) additional source(s) of reliable variance in the test(s).

For the first example only 50% of the variance in Test A is attributable to X, while 80% of the variance in Test B is attributable to Y, and in both tests all the remaining variance is attributable to the reliable measurement of process Z. If schizophrenics have a greater specific deficit on process Z than on X and Y, the obtained interaction can emerge even if there is no real differential deficit involving X and Y. (Indeed, this interaction pattern is obtained even if both X and Y have *no* ability to distinguish schizophrenics from controls.)

For the next example, imagine that 80% of the variance in Test A is attributable to X, while 50% of the variance in Test B is Y variance. In both tests all the remaining variance is attributable to Z' a process that is reliably measured but that does not covary with the schizophrenia—control dichotomy at all. Here again, the obtained interaction can emerge in the absence of any true differential deficit. In this case Z', through reliable variance, has the same effect as unreliable variance; it drives group means together. The extent of this impact is related to its percentage of variance in a particular test (greater on Test B than on Test A).

In yet another instance, Test A involves 50% X and 50% Z, while Test B involves 50% Y and 50% Z'. As above Z differentiates schizophrenics from controls; Z' does not. This too leads to a greater deficit on Test A than on Test B, even if X and Y are equivalent in their ability to distinguish schizophrenias from controls. This can, incidentally, happen even if Z is considerably less effective at distinguishing these two groups than are X and Y.

These contrived examples undoubtedly underplay the complexity of real situations. More commonly, a given test may have several sources of reliable but nonvalid variance, some of which distinguish groups, and some of which do not. Studies often involve comparisons between tests that probably have markedly different mixes of valid and nonvalid variance, although this is minimized when tests being compared are quite similar.

To summarize, the role of validity in the assessment of differential deficit appears to involve two major aspects: the percentage of reliable variance which is construct-irrelevant and the extent to which the construct-irrelevant variance is related to the schizophrenia—control dichotomy. Insofar as two tests differ on either aspect, even though the tests have equal discriminating power, there is a risk that a group X test interaction (or lack thereof) may be misleading.[1] Such an interaction effect, if the tests have been equated for discriminating power, will not be spurious with regard to the tests themselves; the locus of potential error is the relationship between what is true of the tests and what is true of the processes they are alleged to assess.

Regrettably, I have no general prescription for ensuring that tests are equated for validity. What is needed, of course, is some way of ascertaining what the sources of systematic variance in a set of scores are and how much variance each accounts for. Factor analysis is the usual way of doing this, but it works only if the units into which the scores are broken for the analysis (that is, items) differ substantially from one another in their loading on the various sources of systematic variance. As long as items are similar to one another, factor analysis will declare the test to be homogeneous; if each of these similar items depends upon several sources of variance, the true picture regarding the sources of variance in the total score will go unrevealed. The problems involved in equating tests for validity are related to the subtlety of the matter of construct validity generally.

ISOLATING COGNITIVE PROCESSES

The second reason I offer for the missing progress is closely related to this. It concerns what I perceive to be a failure to exert enough care in operationalizing constructs. The problem is that the test tasks used, although ostensibly tapping

---

[1] I believe that there is a special instance in which, even though the two equally reliable tests differ in their ratios of construct-relevant to irrelevant variance, there is no risk of misinterpretation of an interaction term in the differential deficit design. It is when (a) the construct-irrelevant processes tapped in the two tests are equally differentiating of schizophrenics from controls *and* (b) this irrelevant variance is no less differentiating than is the less differentiating of the two target constructs, nor more differentiating than is the more differentiating of the two constructs.

one cognitive function, are usually open to alternative interpretations and, moreover, almost inevitably reflect multiple sources of variance. For example, at one point I was interested in the concept of behavioral *rigidity* as it applied to schizophrenic functioning. By collecting as many articles as possible that claimed to address the topic, I found that a remarkable diversity of tasks had been used to stand for rigidity and that they tended to bear no obvious relationship to one another. This is a case of a construct being operationalized in a somewhat scattered fashion, but cases of the reverse are not hard to find, that is, operations that have been used by several different researchers to represent quite dissimilar constructs. Related to this, an interesting didactic device is to describe commonly used test tasks to classes and ask students to speculate on what the task may be used to measure. The diversity of reasonable responses is usually overwhelming, even with some of our more carefully designed measures.

It would behoove investigators to be more aware of the issue of construct validation. Although the distinction between face validity and construct validity is commonly understood, it is forgotten when tasks to test hypotheses regarding a cognitive deficit are developed. However, the solution does not lie merely in worrying about having a task which measures a construct validly. Most complex cognitive functions cannot be embodied in tasks which do not embody other cognitive functions as well. It is hard to have a task which does not, for instance, require attention, information processing, memory *and* response selection. It is usually futile to argue about whether a task, for example, really measures short-term memory or really measures attention, because a person grossly defective in either would do poorly on virtually all of the tasks schizophrenics are likely to be tested on.

There are several solutions that have been used, but my impression is that they have all been underexploited. One that is especially suitable is the tactic of designing two minimally different tasks and comparing performance on them. Although, for instance, it is difficult to imagine a single task that taps only memory, it is easier to imagine two tasks which differ only in the extent to which they tap memory. This tactic involves the differential deficit design. It was noted above that the differential deficit design can be a good way to cope with the problem of a nonspecific deficit and, in particular, that the use of minimally different tests reduces the likelihood that tests will have different construct-irrelevant systematic variance. Here it is suggested that this is a good strategy for isolating specific psychological functions. Again, it is totally successful only when the tests differ in just one aspect and when the tests are matched for discriminating power.

Following is an example from my own research taken from a study which is currently in progress. I will not describe the entire study, but instead just mention the relevant aspects. The hypothesis, drawn mainly from the work of Bertram Cohen and his associates, is that schizophrenics do not screen their communications for adequacy by considering the needs of a listener. As has usually been the case for testing such hypotheses, subjects are cast in the role of a clue-giver in a modified version of the game Password shown on television. As modified for this study, their task is actually a multiple-choice paper and pencil task, and the guesser is hypothetical. The subject is given two words, one of which is underlined (that is, the referent). The hypothetical guesser knows what the two words are but not which one is the referent. The subject's task is to help the guesser choose the referent, and the subject is given two clues of which the better must be chosen. The objectively better, correct clue is the one which does a better job of distinguishing the two initial words. The inferior, incorrect clue, however, is more closely related to the referent than the correct one is, but it fails to differentiate the referent from the nonreferent. That is, a subject needs to overcome an associative response bias and consider the perspective of the guesser to make the correct response.

With such a task, very careful control procedures are obviously needed to eliminate the possibility that an inferior performance on the part of schizophrenics is caused by a nonspecific deficit. A vocabulary test was chosen to be the control task. Persuant to the strategy of having the tasks minimally different, this test consisted of multiple choice questions, and the incorrect option was more closely associated to the stimulus than was the correct option. Moreover, items were selected so that the mean associative difference between the correct and incorrect options was the same for the vocabulary test as for the communication task. That is, the tests were equated quantitatively for the extent to which the incorrect option was associatively closer to the cue word than to the correct option. The tests, of course, were equated for discriminating power. The control task thus controls not merely for level of general intellectual functioning but also for specific aspects of the communication task, and, in particular, for the tendency to succumb to associative distractors.

To summarize the argument, although it would be difficult to conceive of a task that measures only the extent to which a person edits communications in deference to the needs of a listener, it is reasonable to claim that this quality has been isolated as the only one in which the two tests differ. Although it is not quite to the point that this example is intended to make, a qualifying comment is in order. These two tasks are minimally different, but they do differ in at least one respect other than the desired one; the communication task is a more complex one. If schizophrenics do more poorly on this task, it will be possible to attribute the difference to the complextiy aspect of it and not to the communication aspect of it. Thus, the results will not be entirely free of ambiguity.

Moreover, although this ambiguity merely illustrates that the goal of the perfect control task is elusive, there is another source of ambiguity that is of greater methodological import. It stems from the inevitability that, although we are interested mainly in what the experimental task has that the control task does not, the control task has some challenge to the subject that the experimental task does not. This is because a specific source of difficulty is generally introduced to this task to make it as difficult as the experimental task. In the example, the essentially simpler vocabulary control task had to be matched for difficulty level with the communication task, and this was achieved by using words whose correct definition was especially obscure. That is, the tasks differ in two ways. The communication task has a communication component, but the vocabulary task has difficult words. This state of affairs is inescapable, at least as long as investigators lack a standard operationalization of the nonspecific deficit shown by schizophrenics. Often, though, this ambiguity is not too troublesome. In the example, for instance, if a group X task interaction emerges with schizophrenics showing a greater deficit on the communication task than on the vocabulary task, the effect may have been caused by a special schizophrenic superiority at defining obscure words (coupled with a nonspecific schizophrenic deficit, manifest equally in the two tasks). Because the chances of such a superiority appear minute, the ambiguity is purely academic, and the conclusion that the results reflect a special difficulty with the communication task seems quite safe.

To return to the original point of the example, a strong strategy for the pinpointing of particular functions is to compare schizophrenics' performance, relative to normals', on two tasks which differ as minimally as possible.

DEGREE OF DISORGANIZATION

Most writers who critique research on language in schizophrenia give ample attention to the need to consider subgroups of schizophrenics rather than to treat schizophrenics as a single homogeneous group. This accounts for the lack of attention given to this point in the present paper. There is one dimension, however, which is often ignored in lists of within-sample dimensions which is deserving of consideration: degree of disorganization, that is, degree of psychotic decompensation. Indeed, Chapman and Chapman (1973a) in their book (which must usually be viewed as definitive) asserted:

> Studies using cognitively intact [schizophrenic] patients can scarcely be expected to yield useful evidence concerning the nature of the cognitive disturbance in schizophrenia. (p. 186)

Their claim may seem unassailable. If there exist schizophrenics lacking any cognitive anomaly, studying them will not be informative about the nature of thought disorder in thought-disordered schizophrenics. However, it seems reasonable, with Meehl (1962), to assume that *all* individuals belonging to the schizophrenic genotype have some sort of cognitive defect. In this case, the study of intact patients may be an ideal way to understand the essence of the schizophrenic cognitive defect. Such individuals can be expected to manifest a minimal nonspecific deficit, rendering more discernable any specific deficit present.

The question of cognitive deficit in schizophrenia should be seen as embodying two components. What cognitive defect, if any, is associated with vulnerability to psychotic decompensation? Also, what are the cognitive concomitants of the actual decompensation? Answers to the first question are most likely to come from studies of remitted schizophrenics (or, better still, from studies of pre-schizophrenics, as when the high risk strategy is used). Moreover, it may be that an understanding of the processes of decompensation must await an understanding of the cognitive vulnerabilities of the intact schizophrenic.

In short, I am suggesting that the common failure to sort schizophrenic subjects into disorganized and remitted subgroups may be one reason for the missing progress.

RELATIONSHIPS AMONG THEORIES OF COGNITIVE DEFICIT

Turning now from methodological concerns to a theoretical issue in accounting for the missing progress in this field, it can be stated most generally that one reason for the slow progress lies in the failure of theoretical positions to articulate one with another. In most cases, if any two models of the schizophrenic deficit are compared, it is difficult to state their similarities and their differences. They are not so likely to conflict as to nudge against each other while passing by on different planes. The essence of one theory is likely to appear indifferent to, rather than in conflict with, the essence of another theory. Related to this, studies are remarkably rare whose purpose is one of pitting one theory against another and seeing which one wins empirically.

One reason for this state of affairs appears to be the penchant theorists of cognitive deficit have for theories that go beyond being descriptive and have an explanatory component. That is, it is common for cognitive-deficit hypotheses to be generated from proposed anomalies in noncognitive (neurological, motivational) systems. Care must be taken not to overstate objections to such theories. After all, cognitive processes do not exist in a vacuum. Research hypotheses have to come from somewhere; hypotheses lacking any theoretical context at all and generated by whim cannot usually be expected to be of much value. But explanatory theories are all too easy to come by in this area. Various psychological and neurological processes are so interdependent and schizophrenic cognitive deficit is so diffuse that one can probably start with almost any psychological or neurological anomaly and make a plausible case for how that anomaly was the source of much schizophrenic symptomatology. Indeed, a number of elaborate causal theories have emerged whose major virtue appears to be their intuitive appeal.

At any rate, explanatory theories, when there is a lack of a widely accepted, precise *description,* can be justified only in terms of their potential for suggesting descriptive hypotheses. The pitfall, when a theory has both a descriptive and an explanatory component, is to view those components to be inseparable. Given the present stage of knowledge, it is wise to try to give the most attention to the descriptive implications of theories and treat whatever else is part of them as an intellectually intriguing component. Doing so should be of assistance in comparing those aspects of theories with one another that are germane to the question which most needs to be answered. "What is it about the thinking of schizophrenics which is different from the thinking of nonschizophrenics?"

In any case, I am attempting now to clarify the relationships of the theories with one another. The sample of theories discussed includes: Salzinger's (1971) immediacy hypothesis; Cromwell and Dokecki's (1968) disattention theory; Cohen's (Cohen & Camhi, 1967) editing deficit theory; Storms and Broen's (1969) response disorganization theory; and Chapman and Chapman's (1973a) normal error bias theory.[2] I believe that no univariable taxonomy can begin to capture the differences among the theories. Three areas of difference that are especially interesting are focused on with no pretense that these three exhaust the subtle differences among the theories.

Assumptions About Normality.

The first is of special interest because it accounts in large part for the reason why theories do not articulate easily with one another. Any theory of a deficit inevitably makes some assumptions about normality. A theory of what is wrong in schizophrenia implies a norm from which schizophrenia is a deviation. A theory about inappropriate responses must be more or less linked with a notion about how appropriate responses are generated. Psychology in general, and the study of normal cognitive functioning in particular, are beset with pluralism. This pluralism is reflected somewhat in the assumptions which the various theories of a schizophrenic deficit make regarding normal functioning. These theories differ not only in what the assumptions are but also in how explicit a role they play in the theory.

Storms and Broen's theory, and Mednick's (1958) before it, are, in an explicit and detailed fashion, related to the Hull–Spence notion of how normal, appropriate responses are generated. Appropriate responses are those with the highest response potential, given a relevant learning history. In effect, correct responses are ones having the greatest associative relationship to whatever stimuli are

---

[2] In fairness to the authors involved, I should mention that I am *not* dealing with Cromwell's (1968) redundancy theory, nor with Cohen, Nachmani, and Rosenberg's (1974) "perseverative-chaining" elaboration of their model, nor with Broen's (1973) theoretical emphasis on narrowed cue utilization, nor with any theoretical statements offered in other chapters of the present book. In addition, I am disregarding certain aspects of immediacy as Salzinger has discussed it, because I believe that he has used the term immediacy to cover diverse phenomena, endangering the construct's coherence and unity. That is, the discussion of his theory is limited to what appears to be the primary thrust of the immediacy position.

present. Cohen and his collaborators are just as explicit in stating that responses generated by normal associative processes are appropriate only part of the time, and that normal cognitive functioning entails a screening of responses against criteria of adequacy. For instance, in a communication context, responses are screened for whether or not the response communicates. Chapman and Chapman evidently subscribe to a similar view. This issue of whether associative processes alone govern the responses of normals is not germane to Salzinger's hypothesis or to Cromwell and Dokecki's. These two share as their crucial assumption the view that the normal organism functions in such a way as to weight the various stimuli or information which reach it at various points in time and space, that is, to proportion in an adaptive fashion the extent to which the various stimuli are utilized in governing behavior. No other theory has anything in it which runs contrary to this assumption.

To summarize, all of the theories appear to start with responses being generated by an associative process or something akin to it. One theory specifies a second, screening stage for the selection of responses, and another theory seems to imply this. Two other theories note that cues must be dealt with in a space and time continuum and suggest that there is an adaptive integration of present with distant cues. Recall that I have still spoken only of what these theories presume about normal persons, giving normal responses.

Locus of Deficit.

The theories vary with regard to where the schizophrenic deficit is localized: at the point of input, during internal processing, or at the point of output. Or at least they appear to. Cromwell and Dokecki offer a disattention theory, suggesting an input locus. Salzinger does likewise by focusing primarily on stimulus immediacy. Cohen's theory is explicit in placing the defect at an intermediate, processing stage. Storms and Broen's is an output theory inasmuch as it claims that schizophrenics suffer from response disorganization. Chapman and Chapman are explicitly neutral, refusing to be wedded either to a stimulus or a response hypothesis.

This dimension is offered as one in which the theories vary mainly to repudiate it. The distinction has no operational import with respect to most of the experiments cited to support the various theories. These experiments use tasks which require a subject to attend, process, and respond. For instance, it is difficult — and perhaps, in principle, impossible — to distinguish operationally *response interference* from *stimulus distractibility*. This dimension never appears pivotal in the predictions generated by these theories. For example, Cromwell and Dokecki's theory, with its claim that schizophrenics fail to disattend from stimuli present in the environment, predicts just what would be predicted by a theory which says that schizophrenics fail to inhibit responses to stimuli present in the environment.

Therefore, this dimension does not provide a basis on which experiments should be designed which compare the existing theories. This is not to say that the question of the locus of the dysfunction is uninteresting. It is, in fact, an important one, one that will require the application of rather new and sophisticated designs, such as Briggs and Swanson (1970) have developed. Such research will eventually have to cope with what will probably be an extremely difficult methodolgial task, the task of equating the indexes reflecting the various input—processing—output loci with one another for discriminating power.

Constraint Utilization.

The third area of difference among the theories is that of which constraints schizophrenics are most likely to utilize. This issue transcends the stimulus—response dimension and is perhaps the most useful in contrasting the theories. I choose to talk about "constraints" being "utilized" as a way of maintaining theoretical neutrality; by these terms I only imply that there are contingent probabilistic relationships between characteristics of stimuli and the responses of the organism. By calling a constraint supersalient, I am saying that errors result from its overutilization. An undersalient constraint is one whose underutilization accounts for errors. The issue, then, concerns the way the theories define the cues and constraints that are more salient in influencing the experience and behavior of schizophrenics (and which are less so) than is the case with non-schizophrenics. Phrased in terms of responses, what responses interfere? Phrased in terms of input, what stimuli distract?

Salzinger's hypothesis, or at least the primary thrust of it, is quite explicit in this area. The constraints that are overutilized are those that are associated with stimuli that are proximal in time or space; those which are underutilized are those which are distant. Cromwell and Dokecki's hypothesis, although very similar to Salzinger's, speaks more of constraint utilization being overextended in time; a stimulus following an attended-to stimulus is underutilized.

Cohen's theory appears to have two forms; one defines the class quite specifically, and one does not. In the strong, specific form, the constraints which are undersalient for schizophrenics are those that involve the perspective and needs of other individuals. This is the form that the theory takes when tested by means of diadic interaction paradigms (Cohen & Camhi, 1967; Cohen, Nachmani, & Rosenberg, 1974). The class of constraints becomes less easily specified when the theory is tested using nondiadic paradigms (Lisman & Cohen, 1972; Nachmani & Cohen, 1969); it appears to consist of any criteria of response appropriateness that may be applicable in a given situation. In either form of the theory, however, the class of supersalient constraints evidently consists of simple stimulus—response associative bonds.

Storms and Broen's theory is, in essence, a theory of the equalization of constraints; those that should be salient are less so, those that should be less salient are more so. All constraints which are low salient for normals are higher in salience for schizophrenics; all constraints that are high salient for normals are less so for schizophrenics.

Chapman and Chapman define the undersalient class in terms of those constraints which are most likely to be undersalient for normals. Supersalient constraints, similarly, are those most likely to be supersalient for normals. That is, given that normals do make errors, whatever processes are involved in these errors also account for the errors schizophrenics make. There are as many reasons for schizophrenics' errors as for normals' errors; in each case the error tendency is quantitatively exaggerated in schizophrenia.

In comparing the theories, note first that Chapman and Chapman's theory potentially encompasses each of the others except Storms and Broen's. In listing "recency of stimuli" as a response bias to which schizophrenics yield excessively, Chapman and Chapman (1973a, p. 121) made it clear that both Salzinger's and Cromwell and Dokecki's hypotheses can be taken as instances of their more generalized theory. If it is assumed that some inappropriate responses in normals result from the individual's failure to take the role of the other, then the strong form of Cohen's theory also comes under the purview of the Chapman theory. Indeed, as long as a theory focuses on a kind of error which corresponds to a normal response bias, the theory is automatically subsumed as a tenet of the Chapmans' theory. Accordingly, it is useless to think of pitting the Chapmans' theory against Salzinger's or Cromwell and Dokecki's or Cohen's in the sense of generating opposing hypotheses.[3] In fact, none of these theories are mutually exclusive of any of the others.

This is not to say, however, that they are equally satisfactory characterizations of the class of constraints. The Chapmans' theory defines the class most broadly, and it remains to be seen if this breadth is necessary. Davis and Blaney (1976) have recently obtained evidence indicating that the Chapmans' hypothesis may not apply to schizophrenics who are not manifesting psychotic disorganization when tested and that the specific, role-taking version of Cohen's hypothesis may be more appropriate with respect to relatively intact schizophrenics. More data are needed.

Chapman and Chapman have chosen not to commit themselves to any elaborate model of what cognitive malfunction may underlie the schizophrenic excessive yielding to normal biases. Their hypothesis, however, does appear to entail the assumption that there is a function that keeps normals from always succumbing to their response biases and that this function is suppressed (or lazy)

---

[3] This claim may seem at variance with a recent study (Chapman, Chapman, & Daut, 1976) that appears to have pitted the Chapman theory against Cromwell and Dokecki's. In fact, however, this study pitted Cromwell and Dokecki's (1968) explanation for a prior finding (Chapman, Chapman, & Miller, 1964) against an explanation based on the Chapman theory. That is, it was not a matter of comparing the two theories, but rather a matter of comparing two explanations for a finding.

in schizophrenia. The screening or comparison stage that Cohen and his associates describe appears to be no more nor less than an embodiment of this assumption, at least in the weak version of their theory. Cohen's theory is, of course, more descriptive than explanatory in this regard because it merely verbalizes the notion that responses are inadequately screened for appropriateness. Assuming that this general conceptual strategy proves fruitful, I foresee that an eventual theoretical task will be to add some psychological substance to both Cohen's and the Chapmans' theories, something which ties these notions to a broader theory of internal self-supervision of cognitive functioning in normals.

CONCLUSION

There is reason to hope that progress toward an understanding of schizophrenic thought disorder may be accelerated if research strategies include the following elements:

a. A focus upon the question: What are the defining characteristics of circumstances in which schizophrenics give an excess of inappropriate responses? The testing of hypotheses regarding the reasons that they make such responses should be a lesser priority.

b. The use of the differential deficit design in such a way that the performance of schizophrenics is compared with that of controls on tests which differ, if possible, in only one respect. In particular, tests should be equated for discriminating power.

c. As an alternative means for the isolating cognitive functions, the use of procedures borrowed from research on normal cognitive functioning. Such procedures may, at least within the suppositions of a given model, yield relatively pure measures of a specific function, but their use does not obviate the need for some control over the problem of a nonspecific deficit. The differential deficit design, with measures equated for discriminating power, still appears to be necessary.

d. Insofar as possible, attention to the question posed in (a) above not with respect only to the differences between schizophrenics and nonschizophrenics, but also with respect to differences as a function of dimensions of psychotic symptomatology. Of particular interest is the question: What are the defining characteristics of circumstances in which relatively asymptomatic schizophrenics give an excess of inappropriate responses?

REFERENCES

Briggs, G. E., & Swanson, J. M. Encoding, decoding, and central functions in human information processing. *Journal of Experimental Psychology,* 1970, *86,* 296–308.
Broen, W. E., Jr. Limiting the flood of stimulation: A protective deficit in chronic

schizophrenia. In R. Solso (Ed.), *Contemporary issues in cognitive psychology: The Loyola Symposium.* Washington, D.C.: Winston, 1973.

Chapman, L. J., & Chapman, J. P. *Disordered thought in schizophrenia.* New York: Appleton–Century–Crofts, 1973. (a)

Chapman, L. J., & Chapman, J. P. Problems in the measurement of cognitive deficit. *Psychological Bulletin,* 1973, *79,* 380–385. (b)

Chapman, L. J., & Chapman, J. P. Alternatives to the design of manipulating a variable to compare retarded and nonretarded subjects. *American Journal of Mental Deficiency,* 1975, *79,* 404–411.

Chapman, L. J., Chapman, J. P., & Daut, R. L. Schizophrenic inability to disattend from strong aspects of meaning. *Journal of Abnormal Psychology,* 1976, *85,* 35–40.

Chapman, L. J., Chapman, J. P., & Miller, G. A. A theory of verbal behavior in schizophrenia. In B. A. Maher (Ed.), *Progress in experimental personality research* (Vol. 1). New York: Academic Press, 1964.

Cohen, B. D., & Camhi, J. Schizophrenic performance in a word-communication task. *Journal of Abnormal Psychology,* 1967, *72,* 240–246.

Cohen, B. D., Nachmani, G., & Rosenberg, S. Referent communication disturbances in acute schizophrenia. *Journal of Abnormal Psychology,* 1974, *83,* 1–13.

Cromwell, R. L. Stimulus redundancy and schizophrenia. *Journal of Nervous and Mental Disease,* 1968, *146,* 360–375.

Cromwell, R. L. Strategies for studying schizophrenic behavior. *Psychopharmacologia,* 1972, *24,* 121–146.

Cromwell, R. L., & Dokecki, P. R. Schizophrenic language: A disattention interpretation. In S. Rosenberg & J. H. Koplin (Eds.), *Developments in applied psycholinguistics.* New York: Macmillan, 1968.

Davis, K. M., & Blaney, P. H. Overinclusion and self-editing in schizophrenia. *Journal of Abnormal Psychology,* 1976, *85,* 51–60.

Lisman, S. A., & Cohen, B. D. Self-editing deficits in schizophrenia: A word-association analogue. *Journal of Abnormal Psychology,* 1972, *79,* 181–188.

Mednick, S. A. A learning theory approach to research in schizophrenia. *Psychological Bulletin,* 1958, *55,* 316–327.

Meehl, P. E. Schizotaxia, schizotypy, schizophrenia. *American Psychologist,* 1962, *17,* 827–838.

Nachmani, G., & Cohen, B. D. Recall and recognition free learning in schizophrenics. *Journal of Abnormal Psychology,* 1969, *74,* 511–516.

Salzinger, K. An hypothesis about schizophrenic behavior. *American Journal of Psychotherapy,* 1971, *25,* 601–614.

Salzinger, K. *Schizophrenia: Behavioral aspects.* New York: John Wiley & Sons, 1973.

Storms, L. H., & Broen, W. E., Jr. A theory of schizophrenic behavioral disorganization. *Archives of General Psychiatry,* 1969, *20,* 129–144.

5

Distractibility in Relation to Other Aspects of Schizophrenic Disorder

Thomas F. Oltmanns[1]
John M. Neale

State University of New York at Stony Brook

INTRODUCTION

Virtually all descriptions of schizophrenia place heavy emphasis on thought disorder as a primary feature of the disorder. Relying on observations of schizophrenics' verbal behavior, Bleuler (1950), for example, postulated that a "loosening of associative threads" was the most important feature of the disorder. Bleuler's view has heavily influenced the definition of schizophrenia as it now appears in the American Psychiatric Association's Diagnostic and Statistical Manual (DSM-II) and the forthcoming DSM-III. Kurt Schneider (1959), whose writings have had a greater impact on European definitions of schizophrenia, has also described instances of thought disorder (primarily delusions of control) among his pathognomonic signs for the diagnosis of schizophrenia. Hence, there is widespread agreement that an understanding of thought disorder would greatly increase our understanding of schizophrenia itself.

Research attacking the problem of thought disorder has tried to account for it using further concepts. In recent years, one popular notion has been that schizophrenics are impaired in a number of abilities which fall loosely under the rubric of "attention." This construct is then typically invoked to explain the phenomena of disordered speech. For example, Maher (1972) has reviewed the data concerning formal properties of schizophrenic language and has concluded that one primary characteristic is an atypical propensity for previously uttered

---

[1] Now at the Department of Psychology, Indiana University, Bloomington, Indiana 47401.

words and syllables to intrude in the individual's speech. Maher speculates that this disturbance may be related to problems of attention.

> The attentional disturbances believed to affect the processing of sensory input . . . also underlie the failure to inhibit associations from intruding into language utterance. Intrusions of associations into language may be regarded as similar in character to the "intrusions" of background auditory and visual stimuli into the perceptual processes of the schizophrenic patient. Attentional focusing of the patient is assumed to fluctuate so that vulnerability to distraction varies from moment to moment. Intrusions occur when attentional focusing is broad and are absent when it is narrow. (p. 12)

Thus, defective attentional mechanisms may mediate the production of schizophrenics' unusual patterns of verbal communication.

In attempting to gather empirical support for such proposals, investigators have compared the performance of schizophrenics and controls on measures designed to tap "attention-related" processes. For example, Lawson, McGhie, and Chapman (1967) required schizophrenics, other psychiatric patients, and normal subjects to recall lists of digits in both the presence and absence of distracting stimuli. Finding that the performance of the schizophrenic patients deteriorated significantly more than any other group in the presence of auditory distraction, these investigators concluded that a particular form of attentional problem, heightened susceptibility to auditory distractors, is indeed an important element of schizophrenia. Other investigators have employed the same paradigm with a variety of tasks. Schizophrenics have been found to be impaired in a number of attention-related abilities: perceptual span (Neale, 1971); extra-dimensional shifts (Nolan, 1974); dichotic listening (Hawks & Robinson, 1971; Payne, Hochberg, & Hawks, 1970; Wishner & Wahl, 1974); auditory signal detection in the presence of background noise (Broen & Nakamura, 1972) and continuous performance (Orzack, Kornetsky, & Freeman, 1967). On the other hand, a substantial number of investigations have failed to find attention-specific deficits in schizophrenics' performance in size estimation (Kopfstein & Neale, 1971; Spohn, Cancro, & Thetford, 1976), digit-span performance in the presence of distraction (Taylor & Hirt, 1975) and delayed auditory feedback (Levine, Pomeranz, & Toscano, 1974; Watson, 1974). Generally, a consistent pattern of results has not emerged.

A substantial portion of this confusion stems from the inadequacy of "attention" as a hypothetical construct and inconsistencies in the operations which have been used to index it. The problems associated with multiple, and often unrelated, measures of attention in schizophrenia research have been amply documented (Neale & Cromwell, 1970; Zubin, 1975). In brief, attention has come to mean too many things to too many people, reducing its explanatory utility to a low level. Thus, it seems best *not* to continue invoking attention as a global mechanism whose dysfunction may account for aberrant behavior but rather to move on to consider more discrete abilities such as maintenance of a readiness to respond or the ability to deal effectively with distracting input.

Such a shift may produce a more easily interpretable set of data regarding schizophrenics' cognitive abilities. However, further difficulties arise from the use of the usual cross-sectional research design comparing the performance of schizophrenics and controls on some cognitive measure.* The nonexperimental nature of the variable of primary interest (diagnosis) makes the interpretation of differences between schizophrenics and controls difficult (Chapman & Chapman, 1973; Oltmanns & Neale, in press). "Schizophrenic deficits" may often be spurious, reflecting the operation of third variables. Even if the deficit appears valid, there remains the directionality or cause–effect problem. Thus, we believe that further progress in understanding schizophrenia will come from moving beyond the traditional cross-sectional design.

This goal may be accomplished in several ways, and we try in this chapter to illustrate several potentially fruitful avenues for investigation. Our focus is on the notion that distractibility is an important element in schizophrenia. In general, we follow Maher's (1972) suggestion that the best explanatory hypotheses about schizophrenic language are those that relate these abnormalities to other perceptual or cognitive abilities. We also want to extend this logic and argue that the most promising research designs are those which allow the integration of data on information processing with etiological variables, specific clinical symptoms, and treatment factors. As Reiss (1975) has pointed out, results from a cross-sectional design can be buttressed by considering their relationship to other variables known to be associated with schizophrenia. When looking at distractibility, for example, the demonstration that schizophrenics are more distractible than controls is only minimally enlightening, *vide supra*.

If this specific phenomenon can be integrated with a network of related data and propositions – or a nomological net (Cronbach & Meehl, 1955) – then the significance of distractibility to the development and treatment of schizophrenic symptoms may become apparent. After we have considered definitions of both distractibility and schizophrenia, we then discuss several issues pertinent to current models of the disorder, beginning with a consideration of patients' own descriptions of their perceptual experiences. An outline of the potential relationship between genetic predisposing factors and distractibility follows before we turn to the role of distractibility in the course of schizophrenia. Our final discussion deals with the effects of antipsychotic medication, specifically the amelioration of perceptual disturbance. Having established such a network of relationships, we conclude with a consideration of cognitive mechanisms involved in distraction and their potential relevance to disordered speech.

DEFINITIONS

Distractibility

For our purposes, distractibility may be operationalized as that deterioration in performance on a perceptual or cognitive task which accompanies the introduction of greater amounts of irrelevant stimulation. For example, in our studies, distraction has been indexed by the contrast between subjects' performance on a digit-span task in the presence and absence of extraneous numbers. This definition should be distinguished from Chapman's principle of associative intrusion (Chapman, 1956, 1958; Rattan & Chapman, 1973) which refers to multiple aspects of a *single* stimulus. Distractibility is an element of the broader "interference theory" which has been proposed as generally descriptive of schizophrenics' cognitive deficit (Lang & Buss, 1965) but has not been shown to be empirically related to problems of response competition (Broen, 1968) or difficulties in shifting the focus of attention (Zubin, 1975), which are also subsumed under that heading. With this definition in mind, we turn first to the relationship between distractibility and diagnosis.

DIAGNOSTIC ISSUES

Clearly, for our discussion to proceed, distractibility must be related to the diagnosis of schizophrenia. Indeed, this is the usual point of most cross-sectional deficit research. However, most deficit research stops there and thus remains uninteresting. Typically, such studies do not report diagnostic reliability, who did the diagnoses, or which criteria were used. All of these are crucial points for elaborating a relationship between a cognitive variable and schizophrenia.

Most discussions of the diagnosis of schizophrenia begin with the well-worn issue of the heterogenity of schizophrenic behavior, noting that Bleuler initially posited the existence of more than a single disorder. Indeed, more careful specification of patient-selection criteria and analyses of the relationship between certain symptomatic and demographic variables and task performance have, in some cases, clarified otherwise puzzling results (for example, Harris, 1957). Most investigators during the past decade have dichotomized their schizophrenic samples along the dimensions of chronicity, premorbid adjustment, and paranoid symptomatology. Generally, nonparanoid schizophrenics with a poor premorbid social adjustment have been found to be a more homogeneous group of patients who perform less adequately on experimental tasks than either paranoid or good-premorbid patients.

Although this use of individual-difference constructs in subclassifying schizophrenics has been an improvement over earlier procedures, it has also raised further problems and has failed to deal with larger diagnostic issues. The simultaneous utilization of numerous systems of dichotomization has sometimes resulted in statistically significant, but conceptually unlikely, triple- and quadruple-order interactions that are in many ways as ambiguous as simple comparisons between gross schizophrenic groups and normal subjects. More importantly, without specifying more exactly the fundamental criteria for schizophrenia by which the original sample is selected, major cross-study sampling differences have gone unresolved. Therefore, before discussing more particular aspects of the disorder, we first consider some current data relating to the definition of schizophrenia and the relation of these data to distractibility.

Criteria for Schizophrenia

At the New York Psychiatric Institute between 1931 and 1953, the percentage of patients diagnosed as schizophrenic at admission rose from roughly 20% to nearly 80% (Professional Staff of the Cross-National Project, 1974). The same percentage at London's Maudsley Hospital remained relatively constant between 15 and 20%. This very dramatic difference in epidemiological patterns, and related observations, led to the development of two large-scale international studies of diagnostic practices in psychiatry, the United States–United Kingdom Cross-National Study (Zubin, 1969) and the International Pilot Study of Schizophrenia (World Health Organization, 1973). Some of the issues raised by these teams of investigators and the initial data they have produced have significant relevance to researchers interested in cognitive variables.

The major finding of the cross-national study has been that the diagnosis of schizophrenia is used much more broadly in the United States than in Great Britain (for example, Cooper, Kendell, Gurland, Sharpe, Copeland, & Simon, 1972; Gurland, Sharpe, Simon, Kuriansky, & Stiller, 1972). European diagnosticians have continued to follow a more conservative system in the Kraepelinian tradition. They rely heavily on the presence of first-rank symptoms described by Schneider (1959) as pathognomonic for the disorder. One primary distinction between diagnostic practices in the two countries centers on seriously disordered patients who exhibit significant signs of depressed mood, retardation or anxiety in the presence of an otherwise schizophrenic picture. In the United States, most of these patients are labeled schizophrenic. In England, they are not. Perhaps it is even more alarming that such systematic variations in diagnostic criteria may even exist between different wards of the same hospital (Gurland, Sharpe, Stiller, & Barrett, 1973).

This situation poses an obvious problem for deficit researchers. How may results obtained from different samples of schizophrenics be compared? Clearly, the establishment of adequate reliability of classification does not solve the dilemma. The eventual acceptance of a single set of diagnostic criteria for schizophrenia will depend on their demonstrated empirical utility. Because no current system has yet met this test, the best procedure for investigators to follow is to collect and report descriptive data that may then be used in multiple classifications. The innovative work of Gottesman and Shields (1972) on the genetics of schizophrenia has established an admirable precedent in this regard. They asked 12 diagnosticians, using varying criteria, to classify all of their probands and co-twins as being either schizophrenic or not schizophrenic. The system that was most useful in distinguishing between monozygotic and dizygotic concordance rates lay midway between the broadest American criteria and the most conservative European standards.

We have recently adopted a similar approach in our investigations of distractibility in schizophrenia (Oltmanns, Ohayon, & Neale, in press). Our dependent measures consisted of two sets of neutral and distractor digit-span tests. The first set was composed of shorter-length strings: 5-digit distractor and 6-digit neutral sequences. The second, longer sets of items were composed of 6-digit distractor and 7- and 8-digit neutral strings. Each of these pairs of neutral and distractor tests had been previously matched for psychometric variables affecting discriminating power (Oltmanns & Neale, 1975). This precaution was employed to avoid the potential artifactual production of group X task interactions by the use of unmatched control and experimental tasks (Chapman & Chapman, 1973).

After testing 47 psychiatric patients on an admissions ward and 24 normal subjects, we classified the patients as either schizophrenic or nonschizophrenic according to two different sets of criteria, the DSM-II diagnoses assigned by the hospital staff and our own diagnoses made by applying the Research Diagnostic Criteria (RDC) for functional psychiatric disorders (Spitzer, Endicott, & Robins, 1975) to material contained in the patients' clinical histories. These latter criteria reflect a more conservative standard and systematically exclude patients with primary affective symptoms from the schizophrenic category. Two independent raters agreed on schizophrenic–nonschizophrenic classification in 84% of the cases diagnosed using the RDC.

The data for these comparisons are presented in Table 5.1. When the patients were grouped according to hospital diagnoses (31 schizophrenics and 16 nonschizophrenics), none of the groups were found to be distractible; their scores on the distractor tests were not significantly lower than on the respective neutral tests. However, when the patients were grouped according to the RDC (21 schizophrenics and 20 nonschizophrenics[2]), the schizophrenic group was found to be significantly distractible, although the nonschizophrenic and normal groups were not.

These data may, in part, account for previous contradictions in studies of schizophrenic distractibility. For example, the investigations of McGhie and his colleagues (McGhie, 1970) repeatedly found a deficit in schizophrenics' cognitive performance in the presence of distraction. Taylor and Hirt (1975) found that although the introduction of response delays in a digit-span task differentially impaired the performance of process schizophrenics in comparison to reactive schizophrenics and normals, the addition of varying degrees of distracting stimuli during these delays affected all three groups equally. Whereas

[2] Four of the patients diagnosed by the hospital as schizophrenic were considered manic by the RDC. These patients were included in this second nonschizophrenic group. However, in the interest of maintaining clear distinctions between the groups, we excluded from this analysis the other 6 patients in the "other schizophrenic" group, whom we considered to be primarily schizo-affective disorders.

TABLE 5.1

Means and Standard Deviations of Percentage Correct on Each Test by Psychiatric Patients
Classified as Either Schizophrenic or Nonschizophrenic on the Basis of Hospital Diagnosis
and the Research Diagnosic Criteria

Test	Schizophrenics		Nonschizophrenic Patients		Normals	
	$\overline{X}$	SD	$\overline{X}$	SD	$\overline{X}$	SD
Hospital diagnosis	N = 31		N = 16		N = 24	
Pair 1						
5-digit distractor	.57	.23	.73	.18	.83	.17
6-digit neutral	.64	.22	.81	.17	.87	.13
Pair 2						
6-digit distractor	.40	.22	.60	.21	.72	.20
7- and 8-digit neutral	.46	.19	.61	.19	.71	.22
RDC diagnosis	N = 21		N = 20		N = 24	
Pair 1						
5-digit distractor	.52	.22	.71	.21	.83	.17
6-digit neutral	.65	.18	.74	.23	.87	.13
Pair 2						
6-digit distractor	.37	.22	.57	.21	.72	.20
7- and 8-digit neutral	.43	.18	.57	.20	.71	.22

McGhie's patients were sampled from European hospital populations, Taylor and
Hirt's patients were diagnosed by staff in American hospitals. In general, our
current data indicate that distractibility characterizes only a specific group of
schizophrenics who meet a conservative set of criteria for the disorder.

Individual Symptoms and Specificity to the Disorder

One important by-product of the renewed interest in diagnosis has been a
focusing of attention on symptoms of schizophrenic disorder. As Strauss, Carpenter, and Bartko (1974) have indicated, most investigators concerned with
theories of the nature of "fundamental" disturbances in schizophrenia have
shown little interest in describing symptomatology, and vice versa. Since Bleuler
first suggested the possibility of an underlying cognitive defect central to the
disorder (that is, loosening of "associative threads"), the investigation of cognitive disturbance has been pursued with a fervent zeal that has often blinded
researchers to more elementary, logical issues.

Most investigators have sought to relate a particular psychological deficit to
schizophrenia as a whole, although it appears that their primary interest is

thought disorder in schizophrenic patients. Such a strategy ignores the possibility that thought disorder may not be present in all schizophrenic patients and that it may also be found in some patients who are not schizophrenic (for example, Korsakoff's syndrome). Indeed, recent data suggest that thought disorder may also be a prominent symptom in manic illness and that the form of language disturbance in the two disorders has not been sufficiently clarified to allow for their distinction (Andreasen, Tsuang, & Canter, 1974). Gurland, Fleiss, Cooper, Kendell, and Simon (1969) found in the Cross-National Study that the mutual manifestation of paranoid delusions and incoherent speech often blurred distinctions between schizophrenic and manic-depressive patients. Although incoherent speech has been found in the IPSS to be one of 12 differential symptoms which best discriminate between schizophrenics and nonschizophrenic, psychotic patients (Carpenter, Strauss, & Bartko, 1974), this symptom has been shown to also be present in other disorders.

Laboratory investigations have tentatively verified these clinical reports. Breakey and Goodell (1972) found that Bannister's Grid Test for schizophrenic thought disorder did not distinguish between schizophrenic and manic patients. Andreasen and Powers (1974) administered Payne's battery of tests for overinclusion to groups of schizophrenics and manics. They found that manic patients were *more* overinclusive than schizophrenics and normals.

Because the logic of deficit research begins with an interest in disordered thought, and because this symptom is not universally typical of schizophrenic disorder or solely limited to it, the implicit identification of the symptom and the disorder in studies that simply compare schizophrenic and control subjects is misleading. As Bannister (1968) suggested, it may be more pragmatic to correlate task performance with ratings of areas of pathological behavior rather than broad diagnostic categories. Given that schizophrenia often reflects interpersonal and affective, as well as cognitive, disturbance, a specified deficit could be related to any or all of these problems. But because distractibility is presumed to be related to disordered thought and language, we should be able to show this more specific relationship. At issue, of course, is whether we can expect to find a unitary underlying process to account for such diverse manifestations of disorder. Regardless of our individual biases on this issue, the most efficient approach to deficit research is probably to correlate task performance with diagnostic categories *and* ratings of individual symptoms.

We have demonstrated this realtionship with the sample of patients already discussed. For each of our 21 schizophrenic patients who fit the RDC, a distractibility index was computed by subtracting performance on the distractor items from the score on the corresponding neutral test. The written record of each patient's most recent hospitalization was also rated for the presence and severity of 52 particular symptoms (for example, depressed mood, loss of appetite, lack of insight, slowed speech, auditory hallucinations) on a 4-point scale using a modified version of the Casé Record Rating Scale (Strauss, 1974). These symptoms were grouped into 12 rational clusters (for example, delusions, depression, anxiety—restlessness), and correlations were computed between these scores and the distraction indices. The only symptom cluster which correlated significantly with distractibility was the presence of formal thought disorder (r = .55, p < .05) as defined by Spitzer, Endicott, and Robins and including incoherence, loosening of associations, illogical thinking, and poverty of content of speech. Thus, it appears that when distractibility is present in schizophrenia, it is associated with unusual speech patterns. The more specific functional analysis of this relationship may lead to a better understanding of at least *one* important element of schizophrenia.

In sum, it appears that research on schizophrenics' cognitive abilities may benefit from more specific definitions of both attentional abilities and the disorder itself. Given improvement in these areas, what other aspects of schizophrenic disorder may provide useful clues to the *significance* of perceptual and cognitive anomalies?

SUBJECTIVE ACCOUNTS OF PERCEPTUAL EXPERIENCE

The clinician's and researcher's starting point in organizing hypotheses concerning schizophrenia must be clinical observation (for example, noting the presence and typical characteristics of incoherent speech). Important clues to the possible source of such disordered behavior come from the patients' own reports of their perceptual and cognitive experiences during acute psychotic episodes. In experimental psychology, objective task-performance patterns have, in many instances, provided reliable measures of underlying cognitive processes (for example, Levine, 1966), but introspection has also been a valuable supplementary source of information (for example, DeSoto, London, & Handel, 1965). As the study of human cognitive processes has returned to prominence in experimental psychology and subjective data have regained a measure of respectability, clinical investigators have shown a renewed interest in phenomenological information. Ideally, experimental hypotheses concerning disordered thought should be related to these first-hand descriptions of schizophrenia. For our present purposes, we hope to find that distractibility is indeed a prominent phenomenological feature of the disorder, not merely a laboratory fiction.

The first published accounts of schizophrenia were case histories written by patients who had subsequently recovered from the experience. Freedman (1974) has reviewed over 50 such reports. She found that the most frequently mentioned perceptual and cognitive disturbances were problems in focusing attention and concentration. Perhaps the best known of these accounts, probably by virtue of its detail, eloquence and close relation to currently popular notions of attention (Broadbent, 1958, 1971), was written by MacDonald (1964).

So the mind must have a filter which functions without our conscious thought, sorting stimuli and allowing only those which are relevant to the situation in hand to disturb consciousness. And this filter must be working at maximum efficiency at all times, particularly when we require a high degree of concentration. What happened to me in Toronto was a breakdown in the filter, and a hodgepodge of unrelated stimuli were distracting me from things which should have had my undivided attention. (pp. 175−176)

An additional account has recently been given by Vonnegut (1975) who writes:

> The problem is that schizophrenia makes you so goddammed fragile. I was reacting appropriately, but to so many different things, so strongly, and in such a personal way that it didn't look that way to anyone else. More important, my being that fragile and reactive meant I couldn't do many things I wanted to do. I was so distractible that even very simple tasks were impossible to complete. (p. 209)

These data provide a stimulating insight into the "inner world" of schizophrenic experience. Nevertheless, they are obtained from patients, who, by virtue of their motivation and creative abilities are certainly atypical of the disorder. McGhie and Chapman (1961) interviewed a sample of 26 newly admitted schizophrenics, more typical of the general hospital populations − at least in Scotland − and asked them to describe their recent experiences. These patients reported a pronounced change in their attentional and perceptual abilities, particularly the ability to selectively organize and control incoming information.

This report was later substantiated by Freedman and Chapman (1973) who interviewed groups of schizophrenic *and* nonschizophrenic patients at intake using a standardized questionnaire. They found that, among other experiences, the schizophrenic group more frequently reported inability to focus attention and impaired perception of speech. They also more frequently noted impaired concentration, which was attributed to factors other than preoccupation with personal problems.

Most importantly, although schizophrenics did indeed report "attentional" problems significantly more often than nonschizophrenics, these difficulties were reported by only half of the schizophrenics interviewed. Because Freedman and Chapman's criteria for schizophrenia were presumably American in orientation, their subgroup of schizophrenics with attention-related difficulties *may* have been primarily those who would also have fit more rigorous standards − at least, this pattern would be suggested by our data (Oltmanns et al., in press) using objective measures of distractibility. Future investigations may benefit by employing subjective, as well as behavioral, measures of distractibility with the same patients to determine the potential relationship between these areas of disturbance.

THE COURSE OF THE DISORDER

Until recently, most studies of schizophrenic thought have focused on patients who were hospitalized during the period of investigation. More often than not, these subjects had been institutionalized for many years. The development of this research strategy was based on two primary factors. First, as Kraepelin had originally conceptualized the disorder, schizophrenia was supposed to follow a chronic deteriorating course. Thus, studying chronic patients should reveal the same features present at an earlier period, but with the potential advantage of seeing them in an exacerbated and more easily detectable form. Second, knowledge of both etiological and treatment factors was limited. Therefore, the study of cognitive variables was largely confined to that aspect of the disorder which was best understood and most easily observable (that is, the chronic, hospitalized patient).

During the past two decades, knowledge of both the etiology and course of schizophrenic disorder has increased substantially. The advent of major tranquilizers has drastically reduced the average length of hospitalization, and fewer patients are now following the deteriorating course described by Kraepelin. The certain implications of genetic factors in the transmission of schizophrenia has led to speculation concerning the nature of premorbid dispositions (for example, Meehl, 1962). Although many investigators have hypothesized that cognitive and perceptual factors may be involved in the earliest stages of the disorder, there are very few data to substantiate this belief. The investigation of psychological deficit has, in this sense, lagged far behind advances in other areas.

With regard to distraction, a few investigations have sought to determine its relationship to the course of the disorder. The earliest data were provided in the form of comparisons between relatively newly admitted and chronic patients. For example, Rappaport (1967, 1968) tested a group of 90 acute schizophrenics within two days of their admission to the hospital, 71 "nonacute" schizophrenics who had been hospitalized at least several weeks, 12 chronic schizophrenics and 37 normals. They were required to shadow messages consisting of sequences of 30 random numbers which were presented simultaneously to both ears. In addition to this neutral condition, the subjects were also asked to perform the task in the presence of increasing numbers of distracting messages which were spoken simultaneously with the relevant message, but which were only presented to one ear. For example, in the 7-voice condition, the subject would hear the relevant voice in both ears (spatially localized in the center of his head), three irrelevant voices to the left ear only, and three irrelevant voices in the right ear only.

The presence of these distracting stimuli did not substantially affect the performance of normal subjects or nonacute patients. The scores of chronic schizophrenics were not greatly disrupted, although they were more distracted than normals. In contrast, most of the very recently admitted schizophrenics, who were symptomatically acutely disturbed, were very substantially impaired in the presence of increasing amounts of irrelevant distraction, although their scores on the neutral task did not differ significantly from the other groups. Thus, there appears to be a covariation of gross aspects of psychotic behavior and more subtle problems in processing auditory information in the presence of distraction.

Our data (Oltmanns et al., in press) also indicate that a subset of relatively newly admitted schizophrenics are more distractible than chronic patients. However, McGhie and his colleagues did not find this pattern (McGhie, 1970). They found chronic patients to be as distractible as acutes, with an overall tendency for hebephrenic patients in either category to be most distractible. This inconsistency is most easily attributed to the fallacious assumption that cross-sectional data may be used in making longitudinal inferences. Strauss (1973) has clearly indicated that in cross-sectional analyses of schizophrenic patients, the acute—chronic dimension is confounded with other variables (for example, paranoid status and premorbid adjustment). Thus, the most useful study would be one which followed patients over a period of time and tested them at different intervals of their adjustment.

Blum, Livingston, and Shader (1969) have performed such a study, following 10 schizophrenic patients over the course of several weeks. All patients were given both neutral and distractor digit-span tests (after McGhie, Chapman, & Lawson, 1965), the standard digit-span items of the WAIS, an equivalence measure developed by Olver and Hornsby (1966), and a sentence completion task. Clinical status was assessed daily. Patients were tested initially during the first two weeks of hospitalization. Four were assigned to a placebo condition, three were given haloperidol and the remaining three received thioridazine. All patients were retested between 60 and 75 days after their first session. The only cognitive measure that was associated with changes in clinical status was distractibility. This relationship endured regardless of medication status. The seven patients who showed clinical signs of improvement also showed less disruption by distraction on retesting. The three who deteriorated on the Behavioral Disturbance Index (a psychopathology rating scale completed independently by two observers) also were more impaired by distraction at retesting. These data suggest an interesting relationship but should not be overemphasized because the three patients whose distraction scores deteriorated were also the least impaired at initial testing, and, therefore, regression factors may have played an important role in their fluctuation. Nevertheless, they are among the only longitudinal data available on distractibility.

One other interesting study has been reported by Wohlberg and Kornetsky (1973). They tested 16 schizophrenic patients "in remission" who had been out of the hospital for at least a year since their most recent admission. Fourteen were no longer receiving medication. The test required the patients to observe a screen on which letters were briefly displayed in a sequential fashion. The subject was asked to press a lever if he saw an "X" preceded by an "A." Errors were scored if the subject either failed to respond to a critical stimulus (omission) or if he responded inappropriately (commission). In a distraction condition, flashing lights appeared at the periphery of the subject's visual field or regular and irregular metronome beats were played to the subject through stereo headphones. In the presence of distracting stimuli, the schizophrenics in remission made more omission errors than a group of normal subjects.

Thus, the tentative indications are that although distractibility is an important element of schizophrenic disorder, the extent of the disruptive influence of irrelevant stimuli fluctuates over the course of the illness. The most distractible patients are those who are experiencing an acute schizophrenic episode. As clinical manifestations, including signs of thought disorder and confused speech, subside, so do more subtle laboratory measures of distractibility. Nevertheless, even those patients who have improved sufficiently to stay out of the hospital for over a year and be removed from medication are still more susceptible to distraction than normal individuals. This pattern supports the notion that distractibility *may* be both causally implicated in disorders of language (Maher, 1972) and associated with the genetic predisposition to schizophrenia – a "schizotypic" characteristic (Meehl, 1962).

GENETIC PREDISPOSITION: SCHIZOTYPIC SIGNS

Data from a variety of sources (Fischer, 1973; Kety, Rosenthal, Wender, Schulsinger, & Jacobsen, 1975; Rosenthal, 1975) have recently confirmed the indications of previous investigators (for example, Kallmann, 1938, 1946; Slater, 1953) that there is an important genetic factor operative in the etiology of schizophrenia. At the same time, these studies have emphasized that the factors that are transmitted are genotypic rather than phenotypic in character. Both Meehl (1962) and Rosenthal (1970) have proposed diathesis–stress models for the disorder which postulate the existence of hereditary predisposing characteristics that *may* interact with environmental (biological or psychological) stress to precipitate the clinical signs of schizophrenia. Unfortunately, neither of these etiological factors has yet been specified in any greater detail. Based on the data reviewed thus far, it seems possible that an exaggerated susceptibility to distraction may be an important element of the schizotypic diathesis.

There are some inferential data that support this notion. The same type of patients who demonstrate strong genetic loadings for the disorder may also be the most distractible. Gottesman and Shields (1972) found that diagnostic criteria somewhat more conservative than American standards (but less stringent than the most conservative European criteria) provided the best discrimination between monozygotic and dizygotic concordance rates. This pattern may indicate that the patients who fit these criteria represent a more homogeneous group who share a particularly salient hereditary predisposition. We used relatively similar criteria to identify a subset of acute schizophrenics who were more susceptible to distraction than either normals or nonschizophrenic psychiatric patients (Oltmanns et al., in press). The implication of these parallel findings is also supported by a study reported by Orzack and Kornetsky (1971). They divided a group of chronic schizophrenics into "poor attenders" and "good attenders" on the basis of performance on the Continuous Performance Task. Poor attenders were those patients who more often failed to respond to a critical stimulus which was presented intermittently between extraneous, distracting cues. Orzack and Kornetsky then compared the two schizophrenic groups for family history of mental illness, a rather broad category including schizophrenia, alcoholism, depression, paranoia, manic depression, and suicide. A significantly higher proportion of poor attenders had a history of familial psychiatric disorder than was found in the good attending group. The same pattern was found after limiting the extent of affected relatives to siblings. The significance of these data are somewhat diminished by the broad categories of disturbance included under "mental illness." However, it may be safe to assume that a substantial portion of the disorders recorded were schizophrenic because the hereditary components in both schizophrenia and severe depressive disorders appear to be fairly specific (Winokur, Morrison, Clancy, & Crowe, 1972). This may also be true of alcoholism.

Thus, generally the same type of schizophrenic patients seem to show both distractibility *and* the operation of salient genetic etiological features. To more directly implicate distractibility as a schizotypic factor, more elaborate data concerning individuals who are genetically predisposed but not clinically disordered is necessary. This evidence is not yet available. However, two primary research strategies have been outlined which may shed light on this question. One potentially fruitful avenue of investigation involves the study of schizophrenics' offspring. These individuals are genetically "at risk" for the future development of the disorder. Approximately 15% will eventually become schizophrenic themselves (Heston, 1966), but they have not yet manifested clinical signs of disturbance. Because they share 50% of their genes with their schizophrenic parent, it should be possible to detect behavioral differences between high-risk children and offspring of normals and other psychiatric groups *if* there are behavioral correlates of the genetic predisposition (Meehl's schizotypic signs).

Some preliminary, cross-sectional comparisons between the children of psychotic and normal mothers indicate that the offspring of schizophrenics *may* be differentially impaired in attention-related abilities. Grunebaum, Weiss, Gallant, and Cohler (1974) administered the Children's Embedded Figures Test and I.Q. tests to groups of 3-, 5- and 6-year-old children of schizophrenics, schizo-affectives, nonschizophrenic psychiatric patients, and normal controls. The 5- and 6-year-olds also were given the Continuous Performance Test. Among 5-year-olds, the schizophrenics' offspring made significantly more CPT omission errors than children in the other three diagnostic groups. Differences in errors of commission and I.Q. were not significant. The 5-year-old children of both schizophrenic and schizo-affective mothers failed more stimuli on the CEFT than did children of nonschizophrenic psychotics and normal mothers. These data appear to support the notion that attentional difficulties are either an early precursor of schizophrenic disorder or a concomitant of the associated genetic predisposition. However, Grunebaum et al. did not find differences between the

6-year-old children in the same groups, and a limited follow-up of the children 3 years later found that the initial between-groups differences for 5-year-olds had diminished.

Another strategy aimed at the identification of schizotypic signs has been explored by Holzman and his colleagues (Holzman, Proctor, Levy, Yasillo, Meltzer, & Hurt, 1974) in studying the importance of schizophrenics' deviant eye-tracking movements, which *may* be related to attentional abilities (Shagass, Roemer, & Amadeo, 1976). Holzman had previously demonstrated that schizophrenics' smooth-pursuit eye movements in tracking a moving stimulus were deviant in comparison to both normals and patient controls. In particular, schizophrenics exhibit more frequent "velocity arrests" than the other groups. Holzman et al. (1974) found that a highly disproportionate number of schizophrenics' clinically unaffected first-degree relatives also manifested such deviant patterns. If these data are reliable, they may indicate that deviant smooth-pursuit eye movements represent a genetic "marker" for schizophrenia. That is, because the first-degree relatives share 50% of their genes with the probands in this study, and because a large percentage of these relatives show pathological tracking movements of a variety that may be specific to schizophrenia, the phenotypic manifestation of abnormal eye-tracking may be related to the presence of genotypic material associated with the predisposition to schizophrenia.

The task then would be to determine the nature of this relationship. Two possibilities exist. One is that the two phenotypic characteristics are genetically related (represented on the same chromosome) but functionally independent in the sense that deviant eye-tracking may not affect other manifestations of the disorder, such as deviant verbal behavior. On the other hand, the genetic material associated with schizophrenia could be translated into biochemical and physiological patterns that directly account for eye-tracking dysfunction and that, in turn, interfere with the person's ability to perceive and organize data from his environment to such an extent that he may become schizophrenic if put under particular stress.

This design has not yet been employed in the study of distraction. Coupled with data from high-risk investigations, however, these data would provide a more coherent picture of the importance and role of distractibility in schizophrenic disorder.

THE EFFECTS OF ANTIPSYCHOTIC MEDICATION

The effects of antipsychotic medication in reducing the behavioral symptoms of schizophrenia have been well documented. Indeed, the advent and success of psychopharmacologic treatment has represented the single most important advance in our understanding of the disorder. However, this development has, until recently, also caused difficult problems for investigators concerned with cognitive processes. In comparisons of schizophrenic and control samples on performance tests, diagnostic differences have invariably been confounded with variations in drug status, thus preventing firm attribution of obtained differences to the disorder itself. However, a few investigators have begun to exploit the use of antipsychotic drugs to their advantage with the hope of clarifying the role of cognitive and perceptual abilities in schizophrenia. Their logic is as follows. If a particular psychological deficit is causally related to clinically disordered behavior, and if antipsychotic drugs have been observed to improve gross aspects of schizophrenic behavior, then these same drugs must have an effect on the more subtle cognitive abilities. Thus, performance on tasks designed to index these abilities should improve when patients are receiving routine doses of antipsychotics and deteriorate when they are withdrawn. Of course, the correlational nature of this design does not allow conclusions concerning causal relationships. Nevertheless, such a pattern of results is consistent with, and represents a minimal necessary condition in support of, the notion that such variables are directly related to, for example, disordered speech.

Goldberg (1972) has outlined a number of problems associated with this sort of investigation. He has specified that the investigator must demonstrate that a deterioration in task performance following the withdrawal of medication is not caused by general changes in the patient's behavior that affect the ability to follow instructions, cooperativeness or interest in the test procedure. In addition, a control group must be employed to account for the effects of repeated testing. Finally, a task must be employed that is sufficiently easy to avoid the loss of a substantial proportion of patients when their behavior deteriorates off medication, an effect which would obviously place severe limitations on the generality of the results.

We have recently completed an investigation of the effects of antipsychotic medication on distractibility that fulfills these requirements and sheds further light on the importance of this phenomenon (Oltmanns et al., in press). Fifteen chronic schizophrenics were withdrawn from standard dosages of antipsychotic medication for a period of 2 weeks. They were administered the two pairs of neutral and distractor tasks that had been previously matched on discriminating power (Oltmanns & Neale, 1975) one week prior to the switch to placebo and again at the end of the withdrawal period. Fifteen chronic schizophrenics who remained on medication were tested at identical intervals to control for repeated testing. Only one patient in each group became untestable at follow-up because of exacerbation of symptoms.

The mean percentage of relevant digits correctly recalled in each condition by these groups are presented in Figures 5.1 and 5.2. The performance of the control patients, who were not distractible on either pair of tests, did not change upon retesting. The experimental schizophrenics who were also not distractible at first testing, did not change on the neutral tests at follow-up, suggesting that

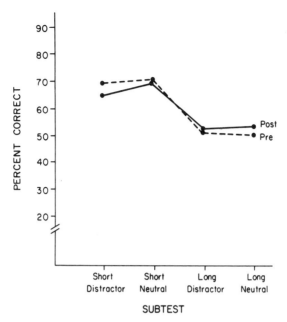

FIG. 5.1 Mean accuracy of performance on four digit-span subtests by 14 chronic schizo-phrenics tested at 2-week intervals (patients on antipsychotic drugs at both times).

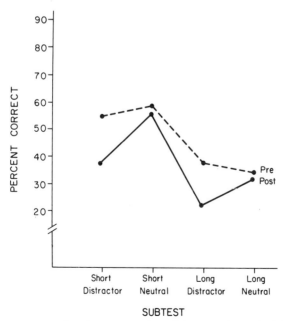

FIG. 5.2 Mean accuracy of performance on four digit-span subtests by 14 chronic schizo-phrenics tested on antipsychotic drugs (Pre) and two weeks later while off drugs (Post).

there was no change in either their willingness to cooperate or their ability to follow instructions. However, their accuracy on the distraction tests deteriorated significantly, suggesting that phenothiazines have the specific effect of reducing distractibility.

There are other data which corroborate this result. Orzack et al. (1967) administered increasing dosages of carphenazine to 18 chronic schizophrenics over a 16-week period. The patients were tested using the Continuous Performance Task (CPT) and the Digit Symbol Substitution Test (DSST) and also rated by ward observers on the Lorr Rating Scale. Orzack et al. observed a steady decrease in errors on the CPT which was correlated with improvement in ratings of pathological behavior. There was no significant change in DSST performance. In a similar, but less well-controlled study, Pigache and Norris (1973) observed the effects of chlorpromazine on the behavior and distractibility of 20 chronic schizophrenics over a 1½-year period, including a 10-week drug-withdrawal period. They noted that, "in a number of patients pronounced clinical deteriorations and improvements occurred and these closely coincided with changes in attention test performance." Although this study did not demonstrate a *differential* performance deterioration upon drug withdrawal, it is consistent with the two other studies that did. Shorter term administration of smaller doses of antipsychotic drugs do not appear to affect distractibility in schizophrenia (Rappaport, 1967, 1968).

Thus, it appears that the long-term administration of large to moderate dosages of antipsychotic medication facilititates the ability of schizophrenics to process auditory information in the presence of distraction, a specific ability in which they have been shown to be deficient, particularly during acute phases of the disorder. This pattern of data provides further support for the suggestion that distractibility is related to schizophrenic thought disorder in the fashion implied by Maher (1972). As Spohn (1972) argued:

> Spheres of psychological functioning in which antipsychotic drugs appear to remedy ... psychological deficit or dysfunction as symptomatic improvement is manifest *are* likely to be critically mediating functions of schizophrenic pathology. (p. 206)

Beyond the implication of relationships between distractibility and language disturbance, the data on drug effects indicate potentially fruitful biochemical and neurophysiological models of schizophrenia. That is, these more objective measures of psychological or behavioral disturbance may be helpful in understanding the specific action of antipsychotic medication and the mechanism by which they produce symptomatic improvement. A few currently appealing models of biochemical dysfunction implicate and draw on the distractibility data.

Snyder (1974) has summarized the persuasive evidence that indicates that antischizophrenic drugs accomplish their effect by blocking the postsynaptic reception of the neuro-transmitter dopamine. More particularly, the dopamine pathway in the brain which seems to be most primarily involved is that which connects the substantia nigra and the corpus striatum. This inference is based on the following logic. One of the best known side effects of the phenothiazines, and one which correlates highly with their clinical efficacy, is their production of extra pyramidal symptoms similar to the tremors seen in patients suffering from Parkinson's disease. Furthermore, this disease seems to be caused by a natural deterioration of the dopamine pathway between the substantia nigra and the corpus striatum. Thus, if phenothiazines act by blocking dopamine reception and in the process produce Parkinsonian symptoms, the major locus of their action may be at postsynaptic sites in the corpus striatum. Snyder goes on to point out that Ungerstedt (1971) has tentatively demonstrated that this same dopamine pathway may be involved in attention-related abilities. Ungerstedt found that rats in which this tract had been unilaterally ablated were inattentive to ipsilateral stimuli, although they were not insensitive to sensory stimulation. Noting that perceptual distractibility is an important element of schizophrenia, Snyder cautiously suggests the following integration of biochemical, pharmacologic, and phenomenological data. "By dampening the influence of perceptions on the patients' psychic life, the phenothiazines might be restoring the 'filter' which seems to have been disarranged in the 'perceiving' machinery of the schizophrenic mind" (p. 252).

INFORMATION PROCESSING: SOME POSSIBLE MECHANISMS

The data reviewed thus far indicate that distractibility may indeed play an important role in schizophrenia. Judging by patients' own subjective accounts, it is a prominent aspect of their perceptual experience during acute phases of the disorder. Using a conservative set of criteria for the disorder, laboratory measures of distractibility are significantly correlated with clinical manifestations of disordered speech. Longitudinal studies point to a covariation between these phenomena, and it seems that the same drugs which reduce the principal behavioral aspects of schizophrenia also moderate the cognitive disturbance caused by distracting stimuli. This overall pattern suggests that distractibility may be an important mediating variable in the production of disordered speech.

At present, however, this inference is a rather large one. Distractibility, as it has been operationalized thus far, is a very broad phenomenon. The argument relating these general phenomena to overt patterns of speech would be much more persuasive if distractibility were more specifically defined in terms of currently accepted aspects of human information processing. Although no single model of information processing has proven entirely adequate in dealing with the vast amount of data that has been generated concerning the performance of normal subjects, several general principles have been established. These broadly applicable aspects of information-processing models may help to locate and define a more specific notion of distractibility. We consider a few of them in the following paragraphs. For our purposes, "information" will be considered in the limited realm of verbal stimuli.

A series of perceptual and cognitive operations intervenes between the sensory reception of verbal stimuli and the generation of a behavioral response. During this process, the information is recoded into a useable form, translated by contact with previously learned material in memory, and stored in a form suitable to the expected delay of response (Broadbent, 1971; Keele, 1973; Norman, 1969). This almost continuous flow of information may be divided into several general stages.

Spoken words are retained for a very brief period (1–10 seconds, depending on the complexity of the stimuli) in a form duplicating that of the original speaker's voice. That is, auditory stimuli are briefly stored in an acoustic form. This stage is known as "sensory storage" or "echoic memory." This level of processing is completed in a parallel fashion, with many stimuli being handled simultaneously.

Beginning immediately, the stimuli in echoic memory are recoded into alternate forms and retained in short-term memory. In the case of auditory stimuli, they are translated from their original acoustic form into an articulatory form. A clear example of this process is the manner in which a telephone number is rehearsed, thereby translating it into an articulatory form and preserving the information at a "higher level" or in a more permanent form. Short-term memory is characterized by its active, "conscious" processes. We are aware of information in short-term memory and are also limited in the amount of information which can be retained in this fashion. Therefore, the operations of this stage are aimed largely at the transformation of information into a more permanent and easily retrievable form, that is, long-term memory.

Information in long-term memory is stored in a highly abstracted form. Verbal stimuli are usually represented semantically. Data concerning the actual form of presentation – language, quality of the speakers voice – are generally not retained. This information is no longer present in "awareness" and must be retrieved by various complex processes.

All models of information processing agree that there are stages in the system which have limited capacities. For example, the serial operations of short-term memory can only handle a relatively small amount of information at a time. Therefore, a *selection* mechanism must be postulated to protect later stages from stimulus overload. The exact location of this selection operation has not been agreed upon. Several theorists (for example, Deutsch & Deutsch, 1963; Morton, 1969; Norman, 1968) suggest that selection occurs after echoic storage and following the recognition of individual stimuli. Other investigators (for example Broadbent, 1971; Treisman, 1969) maintain that selection may also occur at an earlier level of processing and that the salience of some forms of irrelevant stimulation may be attenuated by the individual. Regardless of the location of its operation, the phenomenon of distractibility that we have considered earlier in this chapter clearly refers to the failure or diminished efficiency of this selective process in some schizophrenic patients.

The determination of empirical links between distractibility and other aspects of the disorder would be aided immeasurably by a more specific identification of the locus of this phenomenon in the information-processing chain. Hemsley (1975) has proposed one interesting approach to this problem. Relying on Broadbent's (1971) two-stage model of selective attention, Hemsley suggests that it would be fruitful to determine whether schizophrenics are deficient in the ability to attenuate irrelevant stimuli at an early level of processing (and largely on the basis of their physical properties) or whether the difficulty lies in a later stage of selection. This latter stage relies heavily on the use of semantic cues. As Hemsley suggests, the relationship between the latter alternative and the etiology of disordered speech is intuitively more appealing.

Another alternative to the specification of the peculiar impact of distractibility on schizophrenic cognition is to examine more carefully the manner in which their performance deteriorates. Different tasks rely on particular aspects of information processing. Thus, depending on what sorts of operations are particularly vulnerable to disruption, schizophrenics should appear to be distractible on some tasks and not on others. For example, Korboot and Damiani (1975) found that schizophrenics did not manifest selective problems on a signal-detection task. A related finding was reported by Broen and Nakamura (1972). Tasks that rely heavily on short-term memory, on the other hand, do reveal a differential schizophrenic deficit in selectivity (for example, Hemsley & Zawada, 1976; Oltmanns et al., in press). This discrepancy may indicate that only later stages of processing (the active operations of short-term memory) are abnormally vulnerable to distraction in schizophrenia.

There are, therefore, two general ways of addressing the issue of specificity in selection problems. Hemsley suggests that, given two distinct forms of selection, investigators seek to determine which is particularly deficient. An alternative approach is to ask, given that a problem exists in selection at some point, where its impact is felt most severely. Both approaches should provide a more specific and meaningful insight into the nature of distractibility.

Once this determination is made, it may be easier to ascertain what relationship, if any, exists between distractibility and clinical manifestations of disordered speech. The correlation that we obtained between an index of distraction and ratings of formal thought disorder tentatively supports the notion that these two phenomena are related. More persuasive evidence will depend on finding specific relationships between distractibility, information processing, and the component processes of speech production as well as a longitudinal analysis of covariation in these variables.

CONCLUSIONS

The data which we have reviewed are indicative of an important recent trend in psychological deficit research. An increasing number of investigations have been concerned with establishing the relationship between psychological deficit and various other aspects of schizophrenic disorder. This advance is representative of a growing appreciation among clinical investigators for the work done by colleagues focusing on other specialized topics of inquiry. It has become increasingly apparent that no single key will be found to such a multifaceted disorder as schizophrenia. Single-variable, cross-sectional comparisons of schizophrenic and control populations have provided useful beginnings, but the specification of particular schizophrenic characteristics must be followed up by the establishment of empirical relationships between these phenomena and particular clinical symptoms as well as psychopharmacological effects. Eventually, the role of cognitive deficits in the etiology and long-term course of the disorder must be specified. In short, the simplicity of cross-sectional studies must be abandoned in favor of more complex analyses that will provide a more unified insight into the process of schizophrenia. Isolated theories of cognitive abilities must be elaborated to account for the function of disordered thought in the development and course of schizophrenia.

Studies of distractibility have indicated that this variable may be instrumental in an understanding of schizophrenia, or some large subset of such patients. Laboratory studies have born out the subjective reports of many acutely disturbed patients who describe experiencing problems in perception and thinking associated with the disrupting influence of irrelevant stimuli. A careful analysis of diagnostic criteria indicates that those schizophrenics most susceptible to distraction may be those who also show the strongest genetic predisposition to the disorder. Although acutely disturbed patients are more easily distracted than those who have been hospitalized for some time, even schizophrenics in periods of remission are more distractible than normal people. It remains to be seen whether distractibility is either an early precursor of or a genetic marker for the disorder.

Finally, the same biochemical agents that relieve the clinical signs of schizophrenia also have a facilitating effect on schizophrenic patients' ability to perform cognitive tasks in the presence of distraction. The covariation of incoherent speech and distractibility suggests that the latter phenomenon may be an important mediating variable in the precipitation of the latter. The specification of particular loci of distractibility in information-processing channels may provide a more direct link in this chain of inference. Similarly, the discovery of specific pathways of action for the neuroleptic drugs may ultimately be tied to the biochemical substrate of distractibility. These possibilities and their implications for our understanding of schizophrenia are indeed exciting and may bode well for not too distant advances in both the early identification and treatment of affected and vulnerable individuals.

ACKNOWLEDGMENTS

Preparation of this paper was supported in part by Grant MH 21145 from the National Institute of Mental Health. We would like to thank Sheldon Weintraub and Alec Vachon for their comments on an earlier draft of this paper.

REFERENCES

Andreasen, N. J. C., & Powers, P. S. Overinclusive thinking in mania and schizophrenia. *British Journal of Psychiatry,* 1974, *125,* 452–456.

Andreasen, N. J. C., Tsuang, M. T., & Canter, A. The significance of thought disorder in diagnostic evaluations. *Comprehensive Psychiatry,* 1974, *15,* 27–34.

Bannister, D. The logical requirements of research into schizophrenia. *British Journal of Psychiatry,* 1968, *114,* 181–188.

Bleuler, E. *Dementia praecox or the group of schizophrenias.* New York: International Universities Press, 1950.

Blum, R. A., Livingston, P. B., & Shader, R. I. Changes in cognition, attention and language in acute schizophrenia. *Diseases of the Nervous System,* 1969, *30,* 31–36.

Breakey, W. R., & Goodell, H. Thought disorder in mania and schizophrenia evaluated by Bannister's Grid Test for Schizophrenic Thought Disorder. *British Journal of Psychiatry,* 1972, *120,* 391–395.

Broadbent, D. E. *Perception and communication.* London: Pergamon Press, 1958.

Broadbent, D. E. *Decision and stress.* New York: Academic Press, 1971.

Broen, W. E. *Schizophrenia: Research and theory.* New York: Academic Press, 1968.

Broen, W. E., & Nakamura, C. Y. Reduced range of sensory sensitivity in chronic nonparanoid schizophrenics. *Journal of Abnormal Psychology,* 1972, *79,* 106–111.

Carpenter, W. T., Strauss, J. S., & Bartko, J. J. Use of signs and symptoms for the identification of schizophrenic patients. *Schizophrenia Bulletin,* 1974, *1*(11), 37–49.

Chapman, L. J. Distractibility in the conceptual performance of schizophrenics. *Journal of Abnormal and Social Psychology,* 1956, *53,* 286–291.

Chapman, L. J. Intrusion of associative responses into schizophrenic conceptual performance. *Journal of Abnormal and Social Psychology,* 1958, *56,* 374–379.

Chapman, L. J., & Chapman, J. P. *Disordered thought in schizophrenia.* New York: Appleton–Century–Crofts, 1973.

Cooper, J. E., Kendel, R. E., Gurland, B. J., Sharpe, L., Copeland, J. R. M., & Simon, R. *Psychiatric diagnosis in New York and London: A comparative study of mental hospital admissions.* New York: Oxford University Press, 1972.

Cronbach, L. J., & Meehl, P. E. Construct validity in psychological tests. *Psychological Bulletin,* 1955, *52,* 281–302.

DeSoto, C. B., London, M., & Handel, S. Social reasoning and spatial paralogic. *Journal of Personality and Social Psychology,* 1965, *2,* 513–521.

Deutsch, J. A., & Deutsch, D. Attention: Some theoretical considerations. *Psychological Review,* 1963, *70,* 80–90.

Fischer, M. Genetic and environmental factors in schizophrenia: A study of schizophrenic twins and their families. *Acta Psychiatrica Scandanavica (Supplementum)*, 1973, *238*.

Freedman, B. J. The subjective experience of perceptual and cognitive disturbances in schizophrenia. *Archives of General Psychiatry*, 1974, *30*, 333–340.

Freedman, B. J., & Chapman, L. J. Early subjective experience in schizophrenic episodes. *Journal of Abnormal Psychology*, 1973, *82*, 46–54.

Goldberg, S. C. Advantages and problems in the use of performance tests to study schizophrenic deficit. *Psychopharmacologia*, 1972, *24*, 1–5.

Gottesman, I. I., & Shields, J. *Schizophrenia and genetics: A twin study vantage point.* New York: Academic Press, 1972.

Grunebaum, H., Weiss, J. L., Gallant, D., & Cohler, B. J. Attention in young children of psychotic mothers. *American Journal of Psychiatry*, 1974, *131*, 887–891.

Gurland, B. J., Fleiss, J. L., Cooper, J. E., Kendell, R. E., & Simon, R. J. Cross-national study of diagnosis of the mental disorders: Some comparisons of diagnostic criteria from the first investigation. *American Journal of Psychiatry*, 1969, *125*, 30–39.

Gurland, B. J., Sharpe, L., Simon, R. J., Kuriansky, J., & Stiller, P. On the use of psychiatric diagnosis for comparing psychiatric populations. *Psychiatric Quarterly*, 1972, *46*, 461–473.

Gurland, B. J., Sharpe, L., Stiller, P., & Barrett, J. Trends in patient populations contrasted by two methods of diagnosis. *Psychiatric Quarterly*, 1973, *47*, 184–190.

Harris, J. G. Size estimation of pictures as a function of thematic content for schizophrenic and normal subjects. *Journal of Personality*, 1957, *25*, 651–671.

Hawks, D. V., & Robinson, K. N. Information processing in schizophrenia: The effect of varying the rate of presentation and introducing interference. *British Journal of Social and Clinical Psychology*, 1971, *10*, 30–41.

Hemsley, D. R. A two-stage model of attention in schizophrenia research. *British Journal of Social and Clinical Psychology*, 1975, *14*, 81–89.

Hemsley, D. R., & Zawada, S. L. "Filtering" and the cognitive deficit in schizophrenia. *British Journal of Psychiatry*, 1976, *128*, 456–461.

Heston, L. L. Psychiatric disorders in foster home reared children of schizophrenic mothers. *British Journal of Psychiatry*, 1966, *112*, 819–825.

Holzman, P. S., Proctor, L. R., Levy, D. L., Yasillo, N. J., Meltzer, H. Y., & Hurt, S. W. Eye-tracking dysfunctions in schizophrenic patients and their relatives. *Archives of General Psychiatry*, 1974, *31*, 143–151.

Kallmann, F. J. *The genetics of schizophrenia.* Locust Valley, New York: J. J. Augustin, 1938.

Kallmann, F. J. The genetic theory of schizophrenia. *American Journal of Psychiatry*, 1946, *103*, 309–322.

Keele, S. W. *Attention and human performance.* Pacific Palisades, California: Goodyear Publishing Company, 1973.

Kety, S. S., Rosenthal, D., Wender, P. H., Schulsinger, F., & Jacobsen, B. Mental illness in the biological and adoptive families of adopted individuals who have become schizophrenic: A preliminary report based on psychiatric interviews. In R. R. Fieve, D. Rosenthal, & H. Brill (Eds.), *Genetic research in psychiatry.* Baltimore: Johns Hopkins University Press, 1975.

Kopfstein, J. H., & Neale, J. M. Size estimation in schizophrenic and nonschizophrenic subjects. *Journal of Consulting and Clinical Psychology*, 1971, *36*, 430–435.

Korboot, P. J., & Damiani, N. Auditory processing speed and signal detection in schizophrenia. *Journal of Abnormal Psychology*, 1976, *85*, 287–295.

Lang, P. H., & Buss, A. H. Psychological deficit in schizophrenia: II. Interference and activation. *Journal of Abnormal Psychology*, 1965, *70*, 77–106.

Lawson, J. S., McGhie, A., & Chapman, J. Distractibility in schizophrenia and organic cerebral disease. *British Journal of Psychiatry,* 1967, *113,* 527–535.

Levine, F. M., Pomeranz, D., & Toscano, P. *Non-attending as an adaptive response in chronic schizophrenic patients on a delayed auditory feedback task.* Paper presented at the 45th annual meeting of the Eastern Psychological Association, Philadelphia, April 1974.

Levine, M. Hypothesis behavior by humans during discrimination learning. *Journal of Experimental Psychology,* 1966, *71,* 331–338.

MacDonald, N. Living with schizophrenia. In B. Kaplan (Ed.), *The inner world of mental illness.* New York: Harper & Row, 1964.

Maher, B. A. The language of schizophrenia: A review and interpretation. *British Journal of Psychiatry,* 1972, *120,* 3–17.

McGhie, A. Attention and perception in schizophrenia. In B. A. Maher (Ed.), *Progress in experimental personality research* (Vol. 6). New York: Academic Press, 1970.

McGhie, A., & Chapman, J. Disorders of attention and perception in early schizophrenia. *British Journal of Medical Psychology,* 1961, *34,* 103–116.

McGhie, A., Chapman, J., & Lawson, J. The effect of distraction on schizophrenic performance (1) Perception and immediate memory. *British Journal of Psychiatry,* 1965, *111,* 383–390.

Meehl, P. E. Schizotaxia, schizotypy, schizophrenia. *American Psychologist,* 1962, *17,* 827–838.

Morton, J. Interaction of information in word recognition. *Psychological Review,* 1969, *76,* 165–178.

Neale, J. M. Perceptual span in schizophrenia. *Journal of Abnormal Psychology,* 1971, *77,* 196–204.

Neale, J. M., & Cromwell, R. L. Attention and schizophrenia. In B. A. Maher (Ed.), *Progress in experimental personality research* (Vol. 5). New York: Academic Press, 1970.

Nolan, J. D. Within-subjects analysis of discrimination shift behavior in schizophrenics. *Journal of Abnormal Psychology,* 1974, *83,* 497–511.

Norman, D. A. Toward a theory of memory and attention. *Psychological Review,* 1968, *75,* 522–536.

Norman, D. A. *Memory and attention: An introduction to human information processing.* New York: John Wiley & Sons, 1969.

Oltmanns, T. F., & Neale, J. M. Schizophrenic performance when distractors are present: Attentional deficit or differential task difficulty? *Journal of Abnormal Psychology,* 1975, *84,* 205–209.

Oltmanns, T. F., & Neale, J. M. Abstraction and schizophrenia: Problems in psychological deficit research. In B. A. Maher (Ed.), *Progress in experimental personality research* (Vol. 8). New York: Academic Press, in press.

Oltmanns, T. F., Ohayon, J., & Neale, J. M. Distractibility in schizophrenia: The effect of anti-psychotic medication and diagnostic criteria. *Journal of Psychiatric Research,* in press.

Olver, R. R., & Hornsby, J. R. On equivalence. In J. S. Bruner, R. R. Olver, & P. M. Greenfield (Eds.), *Studies in cognitive growth.* New York: John Wiley & Sons, 1966.

Orzack, M. H., & Kornetsky, C. Environmental and familial predictors of attention behavior in chronic schizophrenics. *Journal of Psychiatric Research,* 1971, *9,* 21–29.

Orzack, M. H., Kornetsky, C., & Freeman, H. The effects of daily administration of carphenazine on attention in the schizophrenic patient. *Psychopharmacologia,* 1967, *11,* 31–38.

Payne, R. W. Hochberg, A. C., & Hawks, D. V. Dichotic stimulation as a method of assessing disorder of attention in over-inclusive schizophrenic patients. *Journal of Abnormal Psychology,* 1970, *76,* 185–193.

Pigache, R. M., & Norris, H. Selective attention as an index of the antipsychotic action of chlorpromazine in schizophrenia. *Bulletin of the British Psychological Society,* 1973, *26,* 160.

Professional Staff of the United States–United Kingdom Cross National Project. The diagnosis and psychopathology of schizophrenia in New York and London. *Schizophrenia Bulletin,* 1974, *1*(11), 80–102.

Rappaport, M. Competing voice messages: Effects of message load and drugs on the ability of acute schizophrenics to attend. *Archives of General Psychiatry,* 1967, *17,* 97–103.

Rappaport, M. Attention to competing voice messages by nonacute schizophrenic patients. *Journal of Nervous and Mental Disease,* 1968, *146,* 404–411.

Rattan, R. B., & Chapman, L. J. Associative intrusions in schizophrenic verbal behavior. *Journal of Abnormal Psychology,* 1973, *82,* 169–173.

Reiss, D. Families and the etiology of schizophrenia: Fishing without a net. *Schizophrenia Bulletin,* 1975, *1*(14), 8–11.

Rosenthal, D. *Genetic theory and abnormal behavior.* New York: McGraw–Hill, 1970.

Rosenthal, D. The concept of sub-schizophrenic disorders. In R. R. Fieve, D. Rosenthal, & H. Brill (Eds.), *Genetic research in psychiatry.* Baltimore: Johns Hopkins University Press, 1975.

Schneider, K. *Clinical psychopathology.* (M. W. Hamilton, trans.). New York: Grune & Stratton, 1959.

Shagass, C., Roemer, R. A., & Amadeo, M. Eye-tracking performance and engagement of attention. *Archives of General Psychiatry,* 1976, *33,* 121–125.

Slater, E. *Psychotic and neurotic illnesses in twins.* London: Her Majesty's Stationary Office, 1953.

Snyder, S. H. *Madness and the brain.* New York: McGraw–Hill, 1974.

Spitzer, R. L., Endicott, J., & Robins, E. *Research diagnostic criteria (RDC) for a selected group of functional disorders* (1st edition). Biometrics Research, New York State Psychiatric Institute, New York, New York, June, 1975.

Spohn, H. E. A strategy for the study of behavioral mechanisms of antipsychotic drug action in schizophrenia. *Psychopharmacologia,* 1972, *14,* 201–208.

Spohn, H. E., Cancro, & Thetford, P. E. Visual scanning and size estimation in acute schizophrenics. In R. Cancro (Ed.), *Annual review of the schizophrenic syndrome* (Vol. 4). New York: Brunner–Mazel, 1976.

Strauss, J. *The Case Record Rating Scale (CRRS).* University of Rochester, Rochester, New York, 1974.

Strauss, J. S., Carpenter, W. T., & Bartko, J. J. Schizophrenic symptoms and signs. *Schizophrenia Bulletin,* 1974, *1*(11), 61–69.

Strauss, M. E. Behavioral differences between acute and chronic schizophrenics: Course of psychosis, effects of institutionalization, or sampling biases? *Psychological Bulletin,* 1973, *79,* 271–279.

Taylor, J. F., & Hirt, M. Irrelevance of retention interval length and distractor-task similarity to schizophrenic cognitive interference. *Journal of Consulting and Clinical Psychology,* 1975, *43,* 281–285.

Treisman, A. M. Strategies and models of selective attention. *Psychological Review,* 1969, *76,* 282–299.

Ungerstedt, U. Stereotaxic mapping of the monoamine pathways in the rat brain. *Acta Physiologica Scandinavica* (Supplement 10), 1971, *367,* 1–48.

Vonnegut, M. *The eden express.* New York: Praeger Publishers, 1975.

Watson, S. J. Effect of delayed auditory feedback on process and reactive schizophrenic subjects. *Journal of Abnormal Psychology,* 1974, *83,* 609–615.

Winokur, G., Morrison, J., Clancy, J., & Crowe, R. The Iowa 500: II. A blind family history comparison of mania, depression, and schizophrenia. *Archives of General Psychiatry,* 1972, *27,* 462–464.

Wishner, J., & Wahl, O. Dichotic listening in schizophrenia. *Journal of Consulting and Clinical Psychology,* 1974, *42,* 538–546.

Wohlberg, G. W., & Kornetsky, C. Sustained attention in remitted schizophrenics. *Archives of General Psychiatry,* 1973, *28,* 533–537.

World Health Organization. *The international pilot study of schizophrenia (Vol. I).* Geneva: World Health Organization Press, 1973.

Zubin, J. Cross-national study of diagnosis of the mental disorders: Methodology and planning. *American Journal of Psychiatry,* 1969, *125,* 12–20.

Zubin, J. Problem of attention in schizophrenia. In M. L. Kietzman, S. Sutton, & J. Zubin (Eds.), *Experimental approaches to psychopathology.* New York: Academic Press, 1975.

6

Personal Constructs Among Schizophrenic Patients

Lawrence G. Space
Rue L. Cromwell

Department of Psychiatry
University of Rochester

The existence of a cognitive disturbance in schizophrenia is not a matter of debate. Since Bleuler's (1911/1950) clinical description of schizophrenia, cognitive disturbance has been part of its definition. Associative deficit, one of the three major symptoms specified by Bleuler, presumes that a person's concepts and thoughts normally exist in an organized pattern.

Ambivalence, another of Bleuler's symptoms, concerns the progression from these thought associations to decisions and then to actions. Even when conflicting forces increase one's vulnerability to "mistakes," a progression in the decision process is normally expected. Unsureness, hesitation, immobilization, and the lower capacity to arrive at opinions or solutions to problems are part of what is observed in schizophrenia. In schizophrenics, the ambivalence, like the associative deficit, may reflect a cognitive disturbance.

The third Bleuler symptom, disturbance in affect, has been traditionally viewed to be separate from cognition. It need not be (Kelly, 1955). The display of emotion and arousal, whether deviant or not, may be understood to be complementary to cognitive activity. When arousing stimuli impinge upon a person, autonomic indicators of affect occur. Orienting and cognitive structures are reflexively activated to acquire, process, understand, and in some cases promote action related to the input. As the input is resolved, the autonomic indicators decrease, and the person returns to a homeostatic but dynamic state. If while the input is being processed, the information is incongruent to the person's conceptual structure, the autonomic responses continue. In other words, if an event, favorable or unfavorable, is not expected or is not so routine as to be uninteresting, emotion is displayed. This emotion is described with such terms as joy, sadness, fear, and anxiety. After the preexisting conceptual structure has accomodated (that is, the implications of the events are processed), the autonomic indicators cease. The conceptual structure remains modified so that similar events in the future may be processed more easily. The change of state is referred to as memory. If similar events in the future become anticipated to be commonplace, the direction of change is called habituation.

If the input fails to be resolved, whether because of an organismic defect or ambiguous, unreconcilable information from the external event, autonomic indicators continue. This continuation is described as an affective or emotional disturbance. Thus, with this view, fostered by Kelly, the autonomic and cognitive manifestations are not independent areas of study but are inherently interrelated. Emotional disorders are cognitive disorders.

Methods to study cognitive disturbance have been limited. Interview, word association, projective techniques, and objective tests have been employed. Concepts such as distance (low commonality) in associative linkage, contamination (assumed interaction or relation) among independent and separate ideas, over and underinclusion, and other concepts have been developed to describe aspects of cognitive disturbance. Yet, much is left to be learned about mapping the content and rules of conceptual structure as well as the disturbances which affect this content and these rules. While schizophrenia, according to the Bleuler criteria, may be assumed to be a cognitive disorder, much is left to be learned about its cognitive aspects. The purpose of this chapter is to present a way of thinking about the disorder as well as a method to facilitate research and widen clinical understanding.

Does cognitive disturbance result from or is it antecedent to the various deficits of schizophrenia? The answer is uncertain, and this chapter does not provide a final answer. Some things, however, are clear. A more complete understanding of the phenomena of conceptual structure and the knowledge of how it relates to the attentional, perceptual, biochemical, social-communication, and other manifestations of schizophrenia is needed.

The idea that conceptual dimensions are organized into a structure is not new. Semon (Stierlin, 1967) recognized that retrievable associations which evolved from experience had to be organized into clusters. Freud popularized the notion of intrapsychic structures. However, except for gross distinctions, he was not concerned with organization among individual conceptual elements. Jung, in developing the word-association test, recognized more fully the relationship among these individual elements. With the clinical work of Rapaport and the developments in Minnesota and elsewhere of norms for word associations, the concept of commonality (associative distance) became a major index to describe thought disturbance in schizophrenia. Osgood's work on semantic differential was directed toward identifying the common denominators of structure within a single language-sharing culture. However, it was not until Kelly (1955) developed the Role Construct Repertory Test (rep grid) that a method was established to map associative structure for separate individuals.

Kelly formulated a theory of personal constructs to account for the development, function, change, and breakdown of an individual's conceptual structure. Personal constructs refer to dimensions of discrimination that individuals devise to anticipate and understand the world about them. Noting how scientists construct theories and make predictions according to formal and explicit rules, he theorized that all people utilize conceptual systems to predict the outcome of events. For practical purposes, Kelly applied the theory to understand how people conceptualize other people.

Unfortunately, Kelly's ideas were largely ignored in his home country. His views were dissonant to and in conflict with reinforcement learning theory, which attempted to explain behavior through the incremental accrual of habit rather than through organization and reorganization of conceptual structure. Theories of information processing, more compatible with his ideas, had not yet become popular. His Role Construct Repertory Test (rep grid), difficult to analyze by hand, came just before the age of computers. His approach to psychological prediction, based on repeated observations of single individuals (idiographic) rather than single variable normative observations across populations (nomothetic), was not fully appreciated by all of his contemporaries. Instead, many psychologists were inclined to treat the psychometric variability resulting from repeated observations of the same individual as a nuisance (error variance).

This chapter acquaints the reader with the rep-grid method and the opportunity it provides to study disturbed cognitive functioning. Data is clinically descriptive and is intended to suggest directions for controlled research.

The authors attempt to demonstrate that content is as reasonable to research as the rules of conceptual structure. After the method is described and illustrated with schizophrenic rep-grid protocols, the implications of the experimental variables and their relation to current understandings of schizophrenia are discussed.

THE KELLY REP-GRID PARADIGM

The rep grid is a paradigm rather than a formal test because the elements and modes of sorting the elements may be changed for various purposes. The method begins by eliciting from or providing to the subject a number of items to be sorted. Although these items may be material objects, depicted situations, photographs, ideas, or other elements, they are most often people. Typically, the names of family members, friends, and acquaintances in the subject's own world, together with the subject himself, are elicited. They are elicited rather than provided because terms produced by an individual have greater associative significance and discriminability for him than other terms from the working vocabulary of the person's culture. Zimring (1969) found that subjects take longer to associate to personal construct terms than to other terms. Cromwell and Caldwell (1962) and Bonarius (1971) demonstrated that subjects rate to greater extremes when their personal constructs rather than other culturally common terms are used in rating scales.

Kelly suggested a set of 22 role titles from which to elicit names of actual people known to the subject. The role titles given below represent a slight modification from Kelly's suggested list:

1. Myself
2. My mother
3. My father
4. My brother
5. My sister
6. My spouse or present boy/girlfriend
7. A boy/girlfriend closest to me prior to my spouse
8. The ideal male (undesignated personal concept)
9. My best same-sexed friend
10. A disappointing same-sexed friend
11. My psychotherapist
12. A person who disliked me
13. A person for whom I feel sorry
14. A person with whom I feel uncomfortable
15. The ideal female (undesignated personal concept)
16. A person whom I would like to know better
17. A teacher whom I admired
18. A teacher with an objectionable point of view
19. An employer I had during a period of stress
20. The most successful person I know
21. The happiest person I know
22. The most ethical person I know

The subject is asked to provide the name of a different person for each of 20 role titles (the two ideal roles are not included). When a role title does not apply, the subject chooses a person in his life who comes closest to fulfilling that role.

The 20 designated names are recorded. Then, three names from the list are presented for a sort. Although the three items selected to initiate each sort may be randomly chosen, they are usually selected to sample particular aspects of the subject's social relationships. For example, one may wish to sample the subject's constructs based upon his childhood family, current close friends, more distant acquaintances, and so on.

To begin the sort, the subject is asked to choose the two persons who are like each other and yet are different from the third person in some important aspect of behavior or personality. The subject then is asked to give a word or short phrase (construct) that characterizes this similarity. The subject then indicates how the third person is different (the contrast). When the contrast is recorded, the subject is then presented another three names. The procedure is repeated until 22 sorts have been completed. The examiner's request for an aspect of behavior or personality is emphasized because psychiatric patients tend to regress toward the use of concrete descriptions (physical characteristics, and so forth) instead of conflict-laden behavioral patterns. In the present procedure, the subject is discouraged from repeating the same construct—contrast pair. After four such reminders, the subject is no longer asked to think of another construct—contrast pair. Although Shubachs (1975) reports that repeated constructs are likely to be more important, the purpose here was to obtain greater breadth of construct sampling.

The subject then returns to the first construct—contrast pair and is simply asked to give the opposite of the construct without respect to the third person in the sort. Very frequently, the characteristic of the third person (contrast) will not be the opposite of the construct. For example, in "people I depend upon vs. unreliable," the term "unreliable" is not necessarily the opposite in the subject's thinking. In response to the request for an opposite, the subject may say "people whom I do not depend upon." For the remainder of the test, only the construct—opposite pair is used.

With the construct—opposite pair, the subject proceeds from one role designation to the next and gives a rating that indicates whether each person more closely fits the construct or the opposite. If the role designee is quite well described by the construct, a rating of 1 is given. If the role designee is quite well

TABLE 6.1
A Partial Rep Grid of a Schizophrenic Subject

		Role designees*									
Construct–opposite pairs		Ted	Helen	Roy	Alvin	Catherine	Alice	Mary	Ideal Male	Carl	Jim	Dr. Rosenbloom
(+) Close to me	Far away	6	3	6	6	1	1	2	1	1	2	1
(+) Love	Hate	6	1	1	1	1	2	2	1	1	1	1
Used to love	(+) Unlove	6	1	1	1	1	2	2	1	1	1	1
(+) Good personality	Bad personality	2	6	1	1	1	1	1	1	1	1	1
(+) Party a lot	Unparty	1	6	1	2	2	2	2	1	1	1	4
(+) Help me	Unhelp me	6	1	1	1	1	2	2	1	1	1	1
(+) Sense of humor	Bad sense of humor	2	6	1	2	1	2	2	2	1	1	1
Kind	(+) Generous	1	1	1	1	1	1	1	1	6	6	6
(+) Help me	Don't help me	1	1	1	1	1	1	1	1	1	1	1
(+) Too good	Better	3	6	6	6	6	6	6	6	6	6	6
(+) Somebody to talk to	Untalk to	6	6	6	3	1	2	2	1	1	1	1

*Names are fictional

described by the opposite, a rating of 6 is given. Ratings of 2, 3, 4, and 5 are given in the cases of a moderate construct fit, slight construct fit, slight opposite fit, and moderate opposite fit, respectively.

For example, the first role designee to be rated is the subject himself. If the construct—opposite pair is honest—dishonest, the subject must indicate on a 6-point scale whether he sees himself to be honest or dishonest. The subject then applies the 6-point scale of honest—dishonest to each of the other 21 role designations. The last role designation, the most ethical person, was replaced at this point with "myself as others see me."

The subject then turns to the second of the 22 constructs (for example, sincere), gives an opposite (for example, insincere), and again applies the 6-point scale to each role designation. This procedure is repeated until all 22 construct—opposite pairs are used to rate each of the 22 role designations.

Finally, the subject indicates which pole, the construct or the opposite, is considered to be more positive. This information may also be obtained by noting how the ideal person is rated, although discrepancies sometimes occur between these two methods.

The final product of the rep grid is a 22 × 22 matrix of numbers ranging from 1 to 6 with each column labeled according to a role designation and each row labeled according to a construct—opposite pair. This grid data may be collected manually or through a computer administration (Space, 1975).

A truncated sample rep grid from a schizophrenic patient is given in Table 6.1.

ANALYSIS OF REP-GRID PROTOCOL

The rep-grid protocol may be analyzed in a number of ways. The following appear useful for schizophrenia research:

1. Descriptive terms used for constructs, contrasts and opposites are examined individually. The number of neologistic, peculiar and concrete terms as well as any themes that may be present or recurring are noted.

2. Idiosyncratic pairings of constructs and contrasts are then noted. For example, "authority figures vs. nice guys," or "true Christians vs. women" can represent idiosyncratic pairings.

3. The construct—opposite pairings are then examined to determine to what extent the pairings were corrected into logical opposites.

4. Next, the rep grid is intercorrelated row by row, and the matrix is submitted to a principal components (communalities equal one) analysis and varimax rotation. With the present procedure, factors are extracted, beginning with the largest first, until the eignevalues reach 1.00; one additional factor is then extracted. For convenience of inspection, the factors are printed out with construct—opposite pairs listed within each factor according to order of magnitude of loadings. If the algebraic direction of the loading is negative, the

construct is reflected. That is, pairing is switched so that the construct is listed in the second column and the opposite is listed in the first column. The minus sign on the factor loading value is thus eliminated. Those construct—opposite pairs with loadings less than .40 in absolute magnitude are eliminated. This value is chosen because factor loadings are akin to correlation coefficients, and with an N of 22, a correlation of .40 is significant to the p = .05 level.

5. The within-factor construct—opposite pairs listed from the previous step are examined within the context of the examiner's cultural and clinical experience to determine if the pairs commonly "go together." Word-association research indicates highly reliable association among various terms used within a given culture. Research in personal construct theory has found that the tightness of relationship between two constructs is indeed reliable for a given individual. For example, for most people in our culture, the use of the terms "honest—dishonest" and "sincere—insincere" is expected to be positively correlated. However, the correlation may vary (for example, .8 for one person and .4 for another).

It is this reliability of associative relationships within single individuals that is the basis on which rep-grid factors rest. Furthermore, good interjudge agreement is possible when estimating whether a construct—opposite pair would ordinarily "go together" in a factor. A lack of "going together" is usually important in understanding the unique way a subject construes people. In addition, unreconciled conflicts may be revealed. That is, two terms in the construct column may be compatibly associated, but the association of their respective opposites would reveal conflict (and vice versa, from the opposite to the construct column).[1]

6. Once the content of each of the factor clusters has been examined, the number of factors is noted. The number of factors is often used to measure cognitive simplicity—complexity. The more factors there are, the more cognitively complex is the individual; the more cognitively complex the individual, the more he is able to differentiate among other people and perceive others as less similar to himself. Relatively complex persons infer the personal constructs of others in social situations more efficiently than cognitively simple persons (for example, Adams-Webber, 1969; Shoemaker, 1955).

7. Next, within-factor inconsistency is examined. This analysis, developed by the authors, examines the integrity of the separate factors. Whether the subject fails consistently to assign himself to one or the other pole of the factor is

---

[1] The reader is reminded that of the ratio of N (number of columns, in this case) to number of variables (number of rows, in this case) is often used as an arbitrary basis for estimating the stability of a factored matrix. However, the ultimate basis is whether the matrix, and the subsequent factor structure, is replicable (in this case, replicable within the same individual). In this respect, the well-documented stability of associative relationships justifies the rep-grid procedure. Nevertheless, stability will vary from one subject to the next. Therefore, confirmation of rep-grid factor structure through controlled replication (using same constructs again) and follow-up inquiry remains important.

referred to as *self-factor* inconsistency. Whether the subject assigns himself to the positively or nonpositively evaluated side of each construct—opposite pair within a factor is referred to as *self-valence* inconsistency. If consistent, the subject will designate himself as either completely positive or completely nonpositive. Whether the subject fails to assign the terms on one side of the factor as all positive or all nonpositive is referred to as *factor-valance* inconsistency.

With only two degrees of freedom, these three aspects of inconsistency are not independent. That is, with one type of inconsistency identified, at least one other must be present. Three, two, or zero, but never one type of inconsistency may occur. However, by examining all these dimensions, important information for understanding the subject's world is revealed. Whether one factor shows consistency or inconsistency is independent of whether or how another factor shows inconsistency. In self-factor inconsistency, the subject is categorizing individuals in his world with dimensions that the subject himself does not fit. Thus, he may see himself as different or estranged.

Self-valence indicates whether the subject sees himself as acceptable within a given factor dimension. A consistently positive self-valence indicates that the subject is comfortable and positive about himself or that he may be exercising denial to avoid dealing with unacceptable aspects of himself. A consistent nonpositive self-valence may also be realistic and even accepted. Or, the nonpositive view may represent a feeling of inadequacy or self-deprecation (that is, incongruent with how the subject ideally wishes to view himself). Pervasive nonpositive self-evaluation across many factors may suggest depression. Inconsistency on a factor indicates a confusion or uncertainty about his own acceptability. In general, self-valence inconsistencies are associated with mood shifts, occasional guilt, occasional depression, and general emotional lability.

Related to self-valence is the more traditional notion of self-concept. Much research has been done on self-concept as measured along a single positive vs. negative dimension of valence. The present paradigm allows the clinician—investigator to identify what areas (factors) are positive, what are nonpositive, and what are inconsistent on a positive—nonpositive dimension.

Factor-valence inconsistency indicates that although certain attributes among people tend to go together, they cannot be consistently evaluated on a good—bad dimension.

The three types of inconsistency just described represent the use of specific probes, self and valence, to be tested for fit against factor structure and each other. Other probes can also be chosen according to particular interest. For example, if the clinician is interested in why the patient has difficulty with a given parent, the parent column (mother or father) can be used as a probe and inconsistency should be revealed on those factors where the patient is having difficulty dealing with that parent. For each type of inconsistency, an index may be generated to reflect the degree of inconsistency within the factor structure (Space, 1976).

To evaluate inconsistency, one must be concerned with its source. Inconsistency within rep-grid protocol has many sources. First, normal protocols are expected to have some inconsistencies because of the complexities of the world we live in. Second, inconsistencies may arise from clerical mistakes of the subject or examiner during testing. Third, it may result as an artifact of the factor-analytic procedure used to understand the rep grid. Fourth, deficits in information processing and retrieval can produce inconsistent factors. Finally, and most germane to this chapter, underlying personal conflicts give rise to inconsistency. Let us examine each separate source of inconsistency.

In a complex world, some inconsistency is expected to occur in a normal protocol. For example, complete factor—valence consistency throughout the protocol may indicate an overemphasis upon "separating the good guys from the bad guys." This may lead to less discriminability among people.

Clerical mistakes of either the subject or examiner are sources of error common to all testing procedures and are part of any test's unreliability.

Inconsistencies arising from the mathematical analysis, although minor, should be understood. To derive the factor structure, a principal components—varimax rotation is employed in the present rep-grid analysis. This mathematical technique is merely a way by which to group construct—opposite pairs that correlate with each other as the subject uses these dimensions to describe people. The technique produces groupings so that maximal interrelationships exist among dimensions within a factor, minimal relationships exist between contructs of different factors, and the mathematically derived factors themselves are orthogonal. The alignment of the self-column data and the positive—nonpositive valence data as applied to each factor represents arbitrary probes to examine congruency within each associative cluster. The self-description column actually contributes to the factor structure and, thus, has a small but mathematically greater probability of being consistent with the factor solution. The valence data is independent. In either case, however, with a complex factor structure it is unlikely that every probe (self, valence or other dimension) will be found consistent on every factor. Some inconsistency is expected and is not to be interpreted as pathology.

Information-processing and retrieval deficits are elusive sources of inconsistency. Recent research has shown schizophrenics to fluctuate in and out of contact (Nideffer, Space, Cromwell, & Dwyer, submitted for publication). Stimulus information may be processed at one time and not at another. The rate of information processing, and lapses therein, may be reflected in rep-grid performance. Shifts in processing rate may be dependent or independent of rep-grid content. Specific content in the rep grid may arouse conflict that in turn temporarily influences processing rate. Long-term effects of conflict on information processing may be present and are noted in the discussion on conflict and inconsistency.

It is important to attempt to identify sources of inconsistency resulting from clerical errors and information-processing deficits. Only a slow unpressured testing process, a slow careful inquiry and repeated testing may identify and resolve these sources. An arbitrary rule that may be used to compensate for potential unreliability and mathematical artifacts is to interpret inconsistency in a factor only when shown by more than one construct. This would not be done if follow-up inquiry or testing revealed the single inconsistency to be stable.

Conflict within a person's conceptual structure leading to inconsistency may be of two general types: transitional or unresolved and self-perpetuating.

Transitional conflict is part of the process of growth and change that individuals experience with psychotherapy and with significant life experiences. When transition in conceptual structure is occurring, it is reflected in certain factor areas. Change over time either toward or away from inconsistency can be traced through repeated testing and provides a fascinating way to study personal growth. These transitional areas are most receptive to being dealt with early in psychotherapy.

In contrast to transitional factors, consistent nonpositive or positive ones are more resistant to change. They should be dealt with later in psychotherapy when such treatment is deemed appropriate. In some cases, consistent nonpositive factors may be realistic self-evaluations (for example, athletics in a poorly coordinated individual) but are not of core significance in the individual's view of himself. A consistent factor that has maladaptive consequences should be changed. When the change occurs and the conceptual structure becomes temporarily inconsistent during the transition, the individual is likely to experience the emotional turmoil so often found when a person in therapy feels for a time that he is getting worse rather than better.

A realistic and consistent factor with positive self-valence represents a stable base for security and a source of support while the person lowers his defenses and explores conflictive and threatening areas in his factor structure. These factors represent islands of security, and the psychotherapist should support their validity and integrity to make the patient's job easier in exploring the transitional, insecure areas.

Instances of conflict-generated inconsistencies other than transitional ones may represent continuing unresolved and self-perpetuating conflict. Although with time transitional factors self-repair toward consistency, disturbed factors do not. They either remain rigidly the same as in paranoid thinking or show an instability which cannot be discriminated from simple unreliability without repeated examination.

If an unresolved conflict is of core significance, that is, if it involves important constructs of self, the conflict may eventually lead to conceptual breakdown. When the latter occurs, thinking becomes loose, spotty, or self-contradictory rather than transparently conflictive and anxious as in the psychoneurotic patient.

Factors with unresolved conflicts initially have constructs with a publicly shared meaning. Later, the meanings may become unique or even bizarre. A completely inconsistent protocol is likely to be *prima facie* evidence for a schizophrenic disturbance. No conflict-free islands are left from which to depart into a conventional "uncovering" psychotherapy. No islands are left to allow the individual to conceptualize coherently and manage his affairs.

Inconsistency does not indicate with certainty the existence of conflict, but conflict, when it occurs, is indeed reflected by inconsistency. Neither inconsistency nor presence of conflict indicate with certainty the more permanent fragmentation in a person's conceptual structure, but where conceptual structure is fragmented, it yields evidence of inconsistency and conflict. In other words, when inconsistency exists, conflict is more probable. When conflict cannot be resolved, conceptual distortion and breakdown is more probable. These assumptions are basic to many of the interpretive comments that occur later in the chapter.

The theoretical positions of both Bannister (1960, 1962) and Radley (1974) suggest these levels of inconsistency may be heirarchical and progressive in the development of schizophrenia. That is, schizophrenics with conflict-laden inconsistency in their conceptual structure may progress from stable self-perpetuation to bizarre meanings to looseness. These progressive levels may be discerned from the condition of transition and conflict just described. First, the cluster may be relatively stable, composed of constructs with meanings that are publicly shared. Any inconsistency that occurs will self-repair with time. Second, the cluster may be stable and conflictual but may also consist of constructs that are bizarre or with idiosyncratic meanings. Finally, the cluster may be weak and unstable, either through looseness of associative membership or shifts in information processing, while containing either publicly shared or bizarre constructs.

We have noted that inconsistency may be either stable or unstable, but a word of caution should be offered at this point. With regard to both instability over time and reliably identified inconsistency, no research has given adequate attention to the separation of performance mistakes (deriving from attention and retrieval impairment) and actual breakdown in memory-stored conceptual structure. For decades clinicians have used terms, such as loosening and fragmentation, that imply that an associational deficit occurs at the level of storage. Indeed, the language of the theoretical comments presented here implies this. Yet, the authors propose that such breakdown in conceptual structure, independent of errors of attention and retrieval, has yet to be demonstrated. This assertion borders closely upon being a parascientific issue because conceptual structure cannot be assessed without examining behavior that involves attention and retrieval. However, the crucial matter is whether the subject, when assessed under conditions which minimize (or average out) performance mistakes, ceases to show unstable or inconsistent responses. Much research has shown schizophrenics to be intact in long-term factual memory. Meanwhile, whether conceptual breakdown in schizophrenia is solely a function of attention and retrieval problems, or is in at least some respects independent of it, is still an open question.

8. The next step in extracting information from the rep grid is through the identification analysis. By comparing (correlating or matching) the self column with other columns, individual role designees can be described in varying degrees of similarity to the subject. Other indices include (a) average correlation of self with all other people, (b) average correlation of self with males vs. females, (c) correlation of self with mother vs. father, (d) correlation of self with the ideal male and ideal female, and (e) correlation of self with "the self as other people see you."

Identification analyses are highly revealing in how the subject sees himself in relation to other people. In the rep-grid procedure, subjects are often unaware of how they have described themselves in relation to others. In schizophrenia, sexual identification and identification with distant vs. close (family, spouse, best friend, and so on) persons are especially important to examine.

Cross-sexual identification is frequent among schizophrenics. This means that the subject sees himself as more similar to the opposite than to his own sex. To a lesser degree, cross-parent identification also occurs.

9. The final step of analysis, the persons factor analysis, involves a factor analysis of columns rather than rows of the rep grid. The rotated factors of this analysis are groups of people (role designees) rather than groups of construct—opposite pairs. The individual's conceptual structure is described in terms of how he groups people rather than of how he associates construct—opposite pairs. Grouping of self, mother, father, spouse, psychotherapist, and distant vs. close individuals is each an important basis of interpretation. The intercorrelation matrix from this analysis is useful for comparing particular individuals of interest. For example, if one were interested in transference within the therapy relationship, whom the patient describes to be most similar to the psychotherapist would be available from the matrix.

PERSONAL CONSTRUCT AND RELATED RESEARCH
WITH SCHIZOPHRENICS

Rep-grid Measures

Early work on the Kelly Role Construct Repertory Test with neuropsychiatric patients focused on two major areas. Jones (1961) demonstrated that these patients had a significant tendency to either overidentify or underidentify with the parents of the opposite sex, as defined by matches between self and parent columns. Underidentification, typical of schizophrenics, generally means cross-

sex identifiction. Using other techniques, cross-sex identification has been demonstrated by Piety (1967) and others. More recently, Winter (1975) also reported a trend toward a lower same-sex parent minus opposite-sex parent score.
This trend, it is pointed out, may disappear when social class is considered.

The second area of research examined the content of constructs chosen by
schizophrenics. When given full freedom in choice of constructs, Rohrer (1952)
demonstrated that schizophrenics tended to choose less abstract (less psychological and emotional) constructs. Physical features, situations, or residence were
more frequently used to describe individuals rather than social, personality and
behavioral features. This work has continued in more recent years. When judging
photographs, schizophrenic subjects with the most severe flattening of affect
made the least use of constructs describing personality or current emotional
state (Dixon, 1968; McPherson, Barden, & Buckley, 1970; McPherson, Bardon,
Hay, Johnsontone, & Kushner, 1970). Williams and Quirke (1972), using both
photographs and people known to the subject, found that nonschizophrenics
used more psychological constructs than schizophrenics. The amount of psychological construing correlated with affect flattening, rating of withdrawal, and
Bannister's measures of intensity and consistency. This relationship was strongest when constructs were generated from people personally known to the
subjects. In a related study, Wright (1973) found that schizophrenics who
showed loosening on the Bannister intensity and consistency scores also tended
to score high in nonabstractness in Rapaport's version of the Object Sorting
Test. McPherson, Barden, Hay, Johnsontone, and Kushner have suggested that
some schizophrenics may lack a coherent system of psychological constructs.
Consequently when they are required to use psychological constructs, they do so
in a vague way that leaves them labeled as affectively flattened.

Bannister (1960, 1962) instituted a program of personal construct research
with schizophrenics. He argued that thought-disordered schizophrenics display a
loosening of association among constructs. This loosening is believed to result
from a failure of the individual's constructs to provide adequate predictions in
social situations. To examine the loosening of construct relationships, Bannister
and Fransella (1966) developed the Grid Test of Thought Disorder. This test is a
modification of the rep grid using photographs and supplied constructs. By
examining the magnitude of intercorrelations among constructs (intensity) and
their repeatability (consistency), Bannister, Fransella, and Agnew (1971) were
able to discriminate thought-disordered schizophrenics from other psychiatric
groups as well as normals. Although their findings have been confirmed by
McPherson, Blackburn, Draffan, and McFadyen (1973), other studies have
suggested that intensity and consistency do not discriminate thought-disordered
schizophrenics when the consistency with which elements are assigned to constructs is considered. Williams (1971) showed that varying the elements in the
Grid Test of Thought Disorder had an effect on the magnitude and discriminability of intensity and consistency. Frith and Lillie (1972) and Haynes and Phillips

(1973) found that intensity and consistency do not discriminate thought-disordered schizophrenics when the consistency with which elements are assigned to the constructs is partialled out. Furthermore, Adams-Webber (1970) indicated that Bannister's measure of intensity is similar to measures of cognitive complexity. Therefore, thought-disordered schizophrenics may appear more cognitively complex than normals, based on the Bannister findings.

Radley (1974) reviewed the evidence regarding a loosening of construct relationships and schizophrenia. He suggested that looseness in schizophrenia may not involve a loosening of associations among constructs. Instead, it may involve a problem in the way the schizophrenic uses constructs in relation to people. Based on Bannister's (1962) finding that high variability in intensity is found in normals, Radley suggests that schizophrenics may be either loose or tight in construct relationships but invariant in their tightness or looseness. This results in less flexibility, which, it is argued, impairs an individual's capacity for integrating conflicting information. When the schizophrenic faces conflicting evidence, he may seek only that evidence which supports his construing.

Radley further suggests that to handle conflicting but unavoidable information, the schizophrenic changes the meaning of his terms. These constructs may acquire a new meaning not commonly shared in the culture. Without a culturally shared meaning, the schizophrenic may lose considerable predictive efficiency in his interactions with the world outside of his family and friends.

The rep grid can provide an approach to understanding how an individual changes his use of terms. As suggested earlier, this change in use may be relevant to schizophrenia. Such an analysis may also reveal why the schizophrenic has a difficulty in interpersonal relationships that frequently leads to withdrawal.

A recent study by Bannister, Adams-Webber, Penn, and Radley (1975) attempted to provide serial validation for thought-disordered schizophrenics over an extended period of time. Their hope was to tighten up the construing of these schizophrenics; however, the experiment did not produce the desired results. One reason given for its outcome was the failure to determine the idiosyncratic meanings of the words they were attempting to validate. They also suggest that bizarreness occurs before construct loosening.

In a landmark work, Bannister and Salmon (1966) compared the intensity and consistency of thought-disordered schizophrenics and normals when construing material objects vs. people. The lower intensity of relationships that discriminated schizophrenics from normals was more apparent when people rather than objects were used as elements in the grid. These findings were also supported by McPherson and Buckley (1970) and Heather (1971). Finally, with greater attention to control of difficulty level and other factors, the finding was confirmed again by McPherson, Armstrong, and Heather (1975).

In another recent work of interest, schizophrenics were reported to have significantly higher self-ideal correlations than either psychiatric controls or parents of both groups (Winter, 1975). The finding of high self-ideal correlation is consistent with the findings of Miskimins, Wilson, Braucht, and Berry (1971), who have found that self-ideal discrepancy does not differentiate some psychotics from normals. They suggest that in some psychotics self-ideal discrepancy is resolved through defenses. However, this results in a widening of the discrepancy in the way the psychotic sees himself as compared to the way others see him.

Double-bind Communication

Among the various psychogenic theories of schizophrenic etiology has been double-bind communication. Double-bind communication refers to messages that occur within the context of an ongoing relationship (Wynne, 1976) and create conflicting ideas, affects, or motivations in the listener: "You are such a despicable boy that only I, your mother, could love you," "Come lie across my lap, dear. I need to spank you." It is not difficult to move from the double-bind hypothesis to Bannister's formulation of schizophrenia. Double-bind messages lead to many invalid predictions of outcome. Also compatible is Radley's belief that invalidation may result in a change in the meaning of terms as used by the schizophrenic. Moreover, it is not difficult to see the relation between the double-bind hypothesis and the Bleulerian symptoms of affective disorder and ambivalence. However, the double-bind hypothesis has been in disrepute for several reasons.

First, no research data exists to demonstrate the development of schizophrenia as a consequence of double-bind communication.

Second, the soundness of research design and operational measures to demonstrate the occurrence of such an effect are, in most cases, unimpressive. Even the most sophisticated research methodologist finds it difficult to formulate a sound experiment to test the double-bind hypothesis.

Third, many advocates of the double-bind hypothesis have needlessly ignored the stress—diathesis model and the evidence of biological-genetic predictors of onset of schizophrenia. The evidence on this side of the picture is formidable.

Fourth and finally, perhaps the greatest reason for the downfall of the double-bind communication hypothesis is the obvious clinical evidence that people who are not schizophrenic had experienced and coped with major double-bind situations often during their lives. Why one individual but not another may be vulnerable to the double-bind stress has not been answered by the theory.

Yet, clinical evidence continues to reveal that certain experiences and types of communication that do not allow the listener reasonable and unequivocal prediction of his own fate is sometimes associated with the impairment of psychological integrity. Goldstein, Rodnick, McPherson, and West (1977) compared parents of adolescents who later became schizophrenic with comparable offspring who did not become schizophrenic. Parents of the schizophrenia-bound group more often offered negative (criticism, complaints, sarcasm, and so forth) and positive comments to their offspring within the same 5-second interval. The tendency for these mixed negative–positive segments exceeded those given by the parents whose offspring did not become schizophrenic. Wynne, Singer, Bartko, and Toohey (1975) have shown parents of schizophrenics to have a greater frequency of communication deviance than parents of neurotics or normals. The frequency of the parents' communication deviance is correlated with severity of illness in the schizophrenic offspring. Moreover, the psychiatric status of the offspring is better predicted by communication deviance in the parents than in their psychiatric status. Wynne, Singer, and Toohey (1975) utilized global communication measures among three classes of parents to make blind predictions about the status of their offspring. These three parent groups consisted of 7 whose biologic offspring had become schizophrenic, 9 whose adoptive offspring had become schizophrenic, and 10 whose adoptive offspring had not become schizophrenic. Perfect prediction of schizophrenic–nonschizophrenic status of offspring was made in all 26 cases by Singer, who conducted the blind analyses of the parent communication records.

In a study of 491 emotionally disturbed children in 17 different treatment centers, Cromwell (cited in Cromwell, Strauss, & Blashfield, 1975) found anticipation of punishment to be an important factor.[2] Children who received parental punishment contingent upon undesirable behavior, and who understood reasons for their punishment were shown two years later to have had neither deliterious nor advantageous effects. On the other hand, comparable children who could not anticipate when they would and would not be punished by their parents showed prodromal signs of schizophrenic deterioration at the 2-year follow-up.

Kringlen (1977), in a study of families in which both parents are schizophrenic, reported a family history which is relevant to the issues of communication and conceptual structure. The two parents, both having been hospitalized with schizophrenia, had three children. Of these, two also became schizophrenic. The third child led a happy and well-adjusted life.

The mother, married at 24 years, worked as a seamstress. Always sensitive, suspicious and extroverted, she developed psychotic symptoms at the age of 27. When first hospitalized at the age of 31 and again at 32, she had hallucinations, bizarre paranoid ideas and confusion. Thereafter, she always had vague paranoid ideas about spiritual connections among people.

The father, a mechanic, had a good work record in his younger years. Married at 25, he was admitted to a mental hospital at the age of 31. At that time he was paranoid and maintained that his wife was the Devil. He was excited and showed other acute psychotic symptoms. He was hospitalized again at the ages of 33 and 42 with hallucinations, paranoid symptoms, and anxiety. In later life, he worked regularly and, upon retirement, received a disability pension.

---

[2] Full research report yet to be published.

The first child, 49 years old at the time of follow-up, was schizophrenic. He recalled his childhood as a very depressive period. Conflicts in the home and quarrels between his parents were frequent. His father often beat him. Not allowed to play with certain other children, he felt lonely. The best time in his childhood was when both parents were hospitalized. After school he worked as a mechanic. Sensitive and suspicious, he tended to withdraw when hardships occurred. Two years after his marriage at 24, he began to display deviant behavior and said that he was not married. He felt that the police were following him. More serious schizophrenic symptoms gradually developed, and he was hospitalized. Although he still has occasional hallucinations and is always paranoid, he has done some casual work in recent years. He receives a disability pension.

The daughter of the family, age 46 at follow-up, also became schizophrenic. As the third child in the family, she remembered her early days as a dismal period of her life. Sensitive and sulky, she often cried when scolded. Like her older brother, she reported that her parents restricted autonomy and interfered with her activities. Describing her father as extremely strict and furious, she often felt his thoughts accompanied her. Nevertheless, she was fond of her father. His quarrelling with the mother was painful to her. Her mother, she felt, really never understood her. The parents' conflicting views on child upbringing were difficult for her to reconcile. For example, frequently her mother would permit her to go to a party and her father would refuse to let her go. As an adult, she worked as a shop assistant and later as a maid. Moving to a new job in Oslo at the age of 23, she gradually developed symptoms of tiredness, somatic complaints, then restlessness and religious excitement. The following year she was hospitalized with paranoid ideas. She felt Jesus had transferred his thoughts to her. Eight hospitalizations followed. Earlier, she was catatonic and paranoid. Later, she became more autistic. In the follow-up interview she was "on guard," sensitive, and troubled with auditory hallucinations. Her condition rendered her unable to work.

The second of the three children, a son, remained normal. He was 48 years old at the time of follow-up. He was married and worked as a foreman. He had never experienced nervous troubles. Like the others, he reported that his parents, and also his uncle who lived in the same house, tried to interfere with his play with other children. He ignored their meddling and admonitions. At an early age, he decided that the home situation was hopeless, so he spent much of his free time in a service garage near his home. This represented quite a different milieu for him. Like his siblings, he felt his father was the dominant figure at home. His mother was more compliant but also manipulating. At an early age, he decided to leave home as early as possible. After elementary school, he started to work. He found a room for himself in the city at the age of 14; he married at 24. Remaining active and competent at work, he has moved up to the rank of foreman in a machine shop. He is relaxed, friendly, independent, and self-assertive. His relations with friends and colleagues are good. Both he and his wife state that their marriage is happy. The follow-up investigators found the visit with him and his wife very comfortable.

Three things are immediately evident from this brief description. The child who did not become schizophrenic did not "buy himself into" the self-perpetuating conflicts within the household. That is, if he had taken a position with respect to the construct dimensions shared within the household, some loss would have been sustained. Having the good fortune of a younger sister requiring care and attention, he was able to escape this environment. In doing so, he was able to formulate a new construct dimension (that the situation at home was hopeless and, at the same time, that it was more attractive or hopeful to be at the service garage or elsewhere). In addition, he apparently had a significant early development toward internal locus of control. That is, he came to view the outcome of events to be dependent upon his own actions. Escaping to the service garage whenever possible (where he undoubtedly acquired other role models for identification), making plans in advance, getting a job early in life, moving to a room in the city at the age of 14, performing vigorously and competently at work to earn advancement, and developing a social role toward others that provided, in return, a warm supportive context for living – all these represented a consistent theme.

Kringlen reported these cases to emphasize the importance of studying individuals who are genetically at risk to become schizophrenic but do not. His succinct description allows an estimation of aspects of the personal-construct structure in the offspring. The construct elements of the two who succumbed to schizophrenia can be estimated as follows:

(+) (S) Obey parents	vs.		Disobey
(S) Share turmoil at home	vs.	(+)	Not share turmoil
(S) Parents make decisions	vs.	(+)	Make own choices
(S) No play with other children	vs.	(+)	Play and fun

The assignment of the self (indicated by S) on the dimensions probably oscillated and reflected a perpetuating conflict. The offspring who remained healthy apparently had a more consistent and stable manner of assigning himself on dimensions:

Home	vs.	(+) (S) Elsewhere, including service garage
Hopeless	vs.	(+) (S) More favorable
Turmoil	vs.	(+) (S) No turmoil
No autonomy	vs.	(+) (S) Autonomy

Returning to the earlier question, why is it that some individuals are vulnerable to double-bind and conflictual communication, although others are not? From the foregoing brief review, the authors suggest that double-bind communication is less important than the conceptual structure of the person who receives it. Some individuals develop a structure which allows them to subsume, revise, or reject conflictual communications; others develop construct clusters that make conflict self-perpetuating (that is, binding). For these latter individuals, double-bind communication *cannot* be coped with because it involves the conflict-laden conceptual structure. In an attempt to reduce conflict, some may produce idiosyncratic constructs that in turn have less predictive and adaptive value. Accordingly, the process of psychosis advances.

How does one identify a self-perpetuating conflict? Unfortunately, for the investigator, a self-perpetuating conflict may occur in almost any sector of an individual's life that he and his culture judge to be important in establishing his identity. Common for conflict are such areas as sexual identity, assertiveness vs. passivity, parental relationships, hostility, and the expressing and receiving of affection. The self-perpetuating nature of the conflict may be further understood by the following examples.

When a young male, in his early experiences with his father or other males, learns to construe the male role to be offensive, constricting, or too demanding, he has a high probability of perceiving the female role to be more satisfying and attractive. At the same time, however, he may construe his own attraction or identification with the female role to be a deviant and objectionable aspect of himself. Thus, regardless of which direction he turns with respect to sex identification, he is unable, regardless of behavior choice, to achieve or anticipate a satisfying (self-acceptable) outcome. In the absence of other coherently positive areas of self-construction, this self-perpetuating conflict may potentially generalize and fragment the young man's thinking on a broader basis.

Another possible self-perpetuating conflict may occur when independence and dependence are construed on opposite sides in the same construct cluster. If the subject views dependent behavior to be strictly for children or to be a sign of weakness, and at the same time independent behavior is viewed to be too threatening and demanding, the subject will then be in conflict regardless of which pole of the construct he chooses to assign himself.

As another example, a subject may learn to construe aggressiveness or hostility to be forbidden or frightening. At the same time, he may view the alternative of passivity, inactivity, or indecision to lead to embarrassment, loss, or deprivation. Under such circumstances, the subject is unable to derive a positive construction of himself with either choice.

An individual may learn to construe affection to be expressed only toward the opposite sex. If positive associations and feelings of attraction have grown with a person of the same sex, these associations may be viewed by him or her to be a sign of pathology. The individual will label himself negatively, and with the conflict left unresolved, a fragmenting of self-constructs may occur. Likewise, if an individual construes a single incident or experience to be reflective of himself as a total person, then, any experience labeled by him to be unacceptable may propel him into irreconcilable and opposing dimensions of self-construction. Depending upon the individual, various aspects of an experience may make the conflict self-perpetuating. For one person, the occurrence of the experience is sufficient to create the conflict. For another, not avoiding the situation may have been crucial in generating the conflict. An individual may label himself to be deviant because, although he resisted or was reluctant, he detected a feeling of satisfaction in the experience. Although no satisfaction was experienced, another person may be aware of his attraction to the people or other aspects of the situation. In short, how the subject construes the meaning of the event and whether a conflict, thus generated, perpetuates itself may be important in understanding the early stages of the conceptual loosening and fragmentation.

An Episode of Hallucinations in a Nonpsychiatric Patient

In a highly detailed and documented self-report by a university professor with no history of a psychiatric disturbance, Goldstein (1976) recounts several visual and auditory hallucinatory experiences. They occurred while he was in the hospital awaiting a slipped-disc operation. In addition to corroborating his own recall of these experiences through the reports of others who observed his behavior, he carefully analyzed hypotheses concerning why the hallucinations occurred. In doing so, he eliminated drugs and sleep deprivation to be possible causes. Also, the author stated quite correctly that his hallucinatory experiences did not have direct reference to him in the usual persecutory or grandiose sense. In addition, when the surgery was over, the hallucinations abruptly ceased. He concluded that the experiences resulted from a state of heightened fear or anxiety.

When he was a child, prior to the age of antibiotics, he had been hospitalized for mastoid surgery and was quite aware of his parents' apprehension regarding his possible death. This earlier experience was associated to the present one. On his way to the hospital for surgery, he had become convinced he would die.

With this information, some of his conceptual structure can be surmised:

(S) Being in hospital	(+) Being elsewhere
(S) Dying	(+) Living
(S) Afraid	(+) Unafraid
(S) Pain	(+) No pain

In terms of the personal constructs reconstructed above, self-perpetuating conflicts are not present; only the anxiety-producing hospitalization is imminent. The cluster is consistent in both self and valence. The self, however, is at the opposite pole from what is positively valued. In general, people do not wish to have a painful illness, to go to the hospital, or to die. Thus, being on the negative pole did not make him unacceptable or different from other people. Completion of successful surgery allowed him to shift to the other pole. By contrast, the inconsistent conceptual structure of the schizophrenic patient leaves a basis for labeling himself to be uniquely unacceptable. He is caught in a conflict where a polar shift brings no resolution toward consistent self-construction. For these reasons, it may be that hallucinatory and delusional experiences of some people are directed toward themselves and persist rather than become obviated by fortunate environmental events. It may also follow that after a person experiences these symptoms and labels them and himself as crazy, the resolution to consistent self-construction becomes even less accessible.

An hallucinatory experience is an innocuous experience of heightened anxiety — both for Goldstein and others — as long as it is conceptualized to have no grave significance. Is it possible that psychosis begins with a conceptual structure that treats such events with having grave personal significance? Is it possible that the biological variables now studied in schizophrenia relate not to its etiology but instead to whether the disorder is expressed by one type of symptom or another?

REP GRIDS OF SCHIZOPHRENICS

To illustrate routine quantifiable data from rep grids, four schizophrenic protocols and analyses are presented. These rep grids were taken from the first four available patients with unequivocal schizophrenia diagnoses when the preparation began for this chapter. In other words, to illustrate the degree of applicability of the technique, no cases were discarded. One author reconfirmed the diagnosis according to DSM II diagnosis and administered the grids. The other author was given only the sex, diagnosis, and computer-analyzed protocols for blind analyses. The reader is given only age, sex, hospitalization history, and rep-grid data. In this way, the reader is not tempted to focus upon how the test data relate to clinical symptoms or history. A comparison set of rep-grid protocols on normal or nonschizophrenic psychiatric patients is not provided because it may leave the improper impression that one can draw valid comparisons from such a small sample. With these restrictions, we expect the rep-grid analyses to illustrate hypotheses one can generate rather than conclusions one can draw about schizophrenia.

For each protocol, a list of constructs, opposites, contrasts, valences and the construct—opposite factor structure is presented. The persons factor structure is presented for the first two protocols only. The raw data and intercorrelation matrices are usually considered intermediate steps toward the more interpretable rotated factor solutions; therefore, they are not given. The intercorrelation matrix for the persons analysis is useful to the psychotherapist who is conversant regarding all the role figures; however, it is not presented here.

Personal constructs with factor loadings equal to or greater than .40 are listed in order of absolute magnitude for each factor. Absolute magnitude is used because constructs with negative factor loadings have been reflected. That is, the construct and opposite listing is reversed. The construct or opposite is labeled with a (+) to indicate the subject's designation of the more positive pole.

Because the other pole is not affirmed to be negative, by implication it is assumed to be "nonpositive."

The listing of the persons factor structure follows the same procedure of order and magnitude. When a negative factor loading is encountered, the role title is listed as the "opposite of" the title.

The identification analysis gives product—moment correlations between the subject and various role figures. Correlations are given in both sign and magnitude.

Case JW

JW is a 23-year-old male who had one 2½-month hospitalization prior to the present one. He was tested on the last day of a 3-week stay. The constructs, opposites, and contrasts that were elicited during examination are given in Table 6.2.

Socially appropriate language is shown in constructs (no excessive concretism or neologisms). However, at least 12 out of the 22 constructs—contrast pairs are judged to be idiosyncratic (for example, very understanding vs. I like him better

TABLE 6.2
Constructs, Opposite and Contrasts for Case JW

Constructs	Opposites	Contrasts
(+) Very understanding	Dumb	I like him better because he's my brother
(+) Nice	Mean	Meaner
Angry	(+) Sad	Nice
Friendly	(+) Unfriendly	Stuck on herself
Confused	(+) Not confused	Dead (Father)
(+) Help me	Unhelp	Just teaches
(+) Friends	Enemies	Enemy
(+) Smarter	Dumb	Dying—he died
Mean	(+) Nice	Good
(+) Good to me	Bad to me	Still bad
Happy	(+) Sad	Not happy
(+) Close to me	Far away	Likes me but too old
(+) Love	Hate	Help
Used to love	(+) Unlove	Now I love
(+) Good personality	Bad personality	Doesn't
(+) Party a lot	Unparty	Don't party with
(+) Help me	Unhelp me	Doesn't help me
(+) Sense of humor	Bad sense of humor	He's dying
Kind	(+) Generous	Tries to be kind but likes me for boyfrie
(+) Help me	Don't help me	Messed up or a queer
(+) Too good	Better	Alright
(+) Somebody to talk to	Untalk to	Down, sick

because he is my brother, confused vs. dead (father), help me vs. just teaches, smarter vs. dying, and so on). When opposites were requested, the subject produced terms which were both concrete and neologistic with 9 of the 22 being idiosyncratic (for example, help me vs. unhelp, used to love vs. unlove, very understanding vs. dumb, sad vs. angry).

Table 6.3 gives the results of the construct factor analysis. On Factor 1, the subject has factor-valence congruency. However, the subject is markedly mixed in assignment of self. Interestingly, on the more strongly loaded constructs (which are not in order of elicitation), the subject ascribes himself with nonpositive valence and on constructs of weaker loadings, with positive valence. Also, some looseness, confusion, or else fine definitional distinctions occur because the subject assigns himself in one direction with "help me vs. unhelp me" and in the other direction with "help me vs. don't help me." This factor seems to be a stereotype by which to view friends. Dimensions of dependency (being taken care of), affection, intelligence, and sociability are included.

Factor 2 is more healthy in terms of self-factor coherency. The factor is consistent in self-valence and factor-valence with one exception (unfriendly being positive and friendly being nonpositive). This exception is very probably an attentional or clerical error. For most people it is more positive to be friendly than to be unfriendly, and sad is an unusual opposite for angry. In spite of the aforementioned healthy aspects, the pattern of constructs, if clerically correct, are probably not highly useful in dealing with a wide variety of situations.

Factor 3 also has only one exception in factor-valence and self-factor consistency. With self-valence, however, the subject is more contradictory. Because of idiosyncratic opposites, this factor is difficult to interpret. An interview would be required to determine more fully what these dimensions mean and whether the meanings are maintained over time.

With Factor 4, the subject returns to a construction of more healthy form. He is consistent with regard to all three aspects of factor structure. The major problem is that the subject assigns himself in the nonpositive direction; thus, a degree of depression is suggested.

Factor 5 is also consistent in all aspects of factor structure. However, because of the idiosyncratic opposite, the factor is difficult to interpret.

In Factor 6, the subject is consistent in factor structure. If the next two constructs, loaded at .39, were included, both self-factor and self-valence inconsistency would be created. With the borderline consistency, it appears that the subject is construing the world about him more coherently than he is construing himself. In short, cognitive disturbance is probably present on this factor.

In the small Factor 7 the subject construes himself as "sad," which is rated by him to be positive. As mentioned previously, this may result from attention lapse or clerical error, but it may also be a stable idiosyncratic construction.

In the persons factor analysis presented in Table 6.4, Factor 1 is characterized by the most strongly loaded people being primarily in a distant or structured

TABLE 6.3
Construct Factor Structure for Case JW

Factor 1

Factor loadings	Construct–opposite pairs	
.92	(+) Friends	S Enemies
.91	(+) Good to me	S Bad to me
.91	(+) Help me	S Unhelp me
.89	(+) Love	S Hate
.74	(+) Smarter	S Dumb
.71	(+) Close to me	S Far away
.69	(+) Somebody to talk to	S Untalk to
.63	(+) S Help me	Don't help me
.57	(+) S Good personality	Bad personality
.46	(+) S Sense of humor	Bad sense of humor

Percentage of variance accounted for: 28%.
Self-factor is inconsistent.
Self-valence is inconsistent.
Factor-valence is consistent.

Factor 2

Factor loadings	Construct–opposite pairs	
.87	Mean	(+) S Nice
.84	Mean	(+) S Nice
.82	Angry	(+) S Sad
.81	(+) Unfriendly	S Friendly
.42	Unparty	(+) S Party a lot

Percentage of variance accounted for: 17%.
Self-factor is consistent.
Self-valence is inconsistent.
Factor-valence is inconsistent.

Factor 3

Factor loadings	Construct–opposite pairs	
.83	(+) Very understanding	S Dumb
.81	Used to love	(+) S Unlove
.80	Better	(+) S Too good
.44	S Kind	(+) Generous

Percentage of variance accounted for: 11%.
Self-factor is inconsistent.
Self-valence is inconsistent.

Factor 4

Factor loadings	Construct–opposite pairs	
.91	(+) Help me	S Unhelp
.45	(+) Generous	S Kind
.44	(+) Close to me	S Far away
.41	(+) Somebody to talk to	S Untalk to

Percentage of variance accounted for: 8%.
Self-factor is consistent.
Self-valence is consistent.

Factor 5

Factor loadings	Construct–opposite pairs	
.86	(+) Not confused	S Confused
.70	(+) Generous	S Kind

Percentage of variance accounted for: 8%.
Self-factor is consistent.
Self-valence is consistent.
Factor-valence is consistent.

Factor 6

Factor loadings	Construct–opposite pairs	
.76	(+) S Good personality	Bad personality
.72	(+) S Party a lot	Unparty
.68	(+) S Sense of humor	Bad sense of humor
.51	(+) S Help me	Don't help me

Percentage of variance accounted for: 12%.
Self-factor is consistent.
Self-valence is consistent.
Factor-valence is consistent.

Factor 7

Factor loadings	Construct–opposite pairs	
.82	Happy	(+) S Sad

Percentage of variance accounted for: 5%.
Self-factor is not applicable.
Self-valence is not applicable.
Factor-valence is not applicable.

TABLE 6.4
Person Factor Structure for Case JW

Factor 1	Factor 4
.90 Admired teacher	.88 Girlfriend
.89 Person like to know better	.87 Ideal male
.88 Happiest person	.79 Sister
.83 Employer during stress	.58 Best same-sexed friend
.82 Most successful	.54 Disappointing same-sexed friend
.66 Person uncomfortable with	.52 Psychotherapist
.62 Ideal female	.48 Girlfriend before present one
.57 Disappointing same-sexed friend	.41 Most successful
.47 Best same-sexed friend	
.44 Psychotherapist	Factor 5
	.60 Psychotherapist
Factor 2	.60 Person for whom I feel sorry
.84 Brother	.57 Opposite of myself (subject)
.64 Girlfriend before spouse	.57 Best same-sexed friend
.59 Ideal female	
.58 Person uncomfortable with	Factor 6
.41 Disappointing same-sexed friend	.84 Teacher with an objectionable point-of-view
.40 Mother	
	Factor 7
Factor 3	.83 Mother
.85 As others see you	
.77 Person who disliked subject	
.66 Myself (subject)	

relationship with the subject. Unfortunately, however, this includes his best male friend. On the whole, the subject appears estranged in social relationships.

Persons Factor 2 groups people from his nuclear family (brother, father, mother) and the prior girlfriend together with ideal female on one hand and various negative role titles on the other; thus, the factor appears contradictory or loose.

Factor 3 appears disturbed because the subject groups himself together with one who dislikes him.

Confusion in sex-role identification is suggested in Factor 4, where the subject's wife and sister are grouped together with the ideal male and the best male friend. Further questions are raised because the ideal male and best male friend are grouped together with a disappointing male friend and the psychotherapist. In general, the factor is loose and difficult to interpret.

In Factor 5, the subject groups the psychotherapist together with a person for whom he feels sorry, the ideal female and the opposite of himself, all fairly rare and surprising.

In Factor 6, the objectionable teacher is grouped alone.

Factor 7 indicates that the subject views the mother in a category by herself. Thus, he has apparently not generated constructs that reconcile his mother with other people in the world.

TABLE 6.5
Identification Analysis for Case JW

Identification	Correlation
Maximum identification	
Person who disliked subject	.52
As others see me	.48
Minimum identification	
Teacher with an objectionable point-of-view	−.30
Psychotherapist	−.30
Parent identification	
Mother	.17
Father	.39
Average female identification (6 females)	.23
Average male identification (12 males)	.06
Ideal-sex identification	
Ideal Male	.15
Ideal Female	.13
Social closeness–estrangement	
Average correlation with 19 people	.12

In the identification analysis shown in Table 6.5, the subject appears more identified with the 6 females than with the 12 males. The match with his father is greater than with his mother. Thus, although some evidence exists for cross-sex identification, it is not complete. Identification with ideal male and female is low but nevertheless is in the expected direction. Average identification with people in general is low. Interestingly, his personal identification is strongest with the person he designates as not liking him. This correlation even exceeds the relationship between self and how others see him. Both the psychotherapist and the teacher with an objectionable viewpoint are significantly in the direction of inverse identification, which probably is revealing about the nature of the therapeutic relationship at this time.

In general, JW's cognitive structure appears to have islands of sanity and coherence amidst islands of madness. The amount of disturbance causes considerable difficulty in understanding and interpreting the protocol. The subject very likely has the same degree of difficulty in understanding and predicting within his interpersonal relationships.

Case DT

DT is a 29-year-old female who was tested on the tenth day of a 14-day first hospitalization.

As shown in Table 6.6, DT had socially appropriate content in the language of the constructs. Only two idiosyncratic construct–contrast pairs appeared (sincerely Christian vs. she is a woman, like outdoors vs. unmarried). These were the

TABLE 6.6
Constructs, Opposites and Contrasts for Case DT

Constructs	Opposites	Contrasts
(+) Sincerely Christian	Athiest	She's a woman
(+) Friendly	Unfriendly	Not so friendly
(+) Like outdoors	Homebody	Unmarried
(+) Good friend to have	Gossipy	Not a good friend of mine
(+) Reserved	Outgoing	Little more outgoing
(+) Like what doing	Miserable	She's a good friend not doing what she likes as a career
Can't keep a secret	(+) Keep a secret	He could
Likes real good houses	(+) Not important what kind of houses	Doesn't matter to her
(+) Have own hobbies	No hobbies at all	Not a lot of hobbies
(+) Likes English lit.	Isn't educated	She wouldn't
(+) Conservative spenders	Spendthrift	The other I don't know about
(+) Likes children	Dislikes children	Probably the other one doesn'
(+) Conserv. governmentwise	Liberal	Probably liberal
Not too much common sense	(+) Common sense	This one would have common sense
Likes to talk–argue	(+) Doesn't like to argue	Quiet, not get into argument
(+) Helpful	Not helpful	Other wouldn't go out of her way
(+) Not so outgoing	Outgoing	Outgoing
(+) Live in country	City life	Live in city
(+) Considerate of feelings	Don't care others feel	This one wouldn't be
(+) Faith to family life	Not faithful to family	Might not be
Not good friend with	(+) Good friends with	Am with this one
(+) Like to visit others	Don't like to visit	This one doesn't care too much about it.

first and third constructs elicited. She corrected these when giving the opposites. She had difficulty in complying with the request for opposites; instead, she continued to give many contrasts (for example, good friend to have vs. gossipy, likes English literature vs. isn't educated).

Table 6.7 gives the construct factor structure for DT. Factor 1, as opposed to the previous case (JW), has complete consistency in factor-valence, self-valence, and self-factor relationship. Moreover, this consistently described self-valence is positive rather than negative. However, in examining the content of the factor, a pastoral quality is suggested. The good, helpful people tend to live in the country and have specific, conservative and intellectual habits. A constriction and rigidity rather than schizophrenic fragmentation is suggested, especially in her dealings with city people. Much of the health of the construct may be judged by whether the positively viewed country people are intimate to her daily life or remote in time, place or fantasy.

Factor 2 suggests that she has trouble with construing socially extroverted vs. introverted people. All three congruency dimensions are inconsistent to some degree. Reserved people tend to be looked upon positively. However, it is also positive to visit with others and to be friendly, which are not characteristic of reserved people. Either a contradiction or a fine distinction is shown in self-assignment; the subject describes herself to be "not so outgoing" when compared to "outgoing" but "outgoing" when compared to "reserved."

Factor 3, like Factor 1, is totally consistent in factor-valence, self-valence, and self-factor relationships; moreover, the self-assignment is positive. The only structural difference from Factor 1 is that the more emergent (construct rather than opposite) pole is nonpositive rather than positive. The high loadings of the factor place more emphasis upon technical intelligence rather than good, helpful, warm friends. Again, city life appears to be stereotyped as downgrading.

Factor 4 is a peculiar and small one that focuses upon arguing. Because it is set apart, arguing may have a special significance in her life.

In Factor 5, the subject returns to an essentially sound and completely consistent factor with completely positive self-assignment. One may expect that it should be useful in anticipating experiences with other people.

Factor 6 is also totally consistent and totally positive in self-valence. The factor appears vulnerable to poor predictions about some people. A tendency may occur to distrust people who do not share her viewpoint.

The persons factor analysis presented in Table 6.8, like the construct factor analysis, begins with a suggestion of rigidity and defensive constriction. The subject groups herself with the ideal male and female, other positive figures, and the opposite of other negative figures. The grouping suggests she may be too rigidly positive to deal with problems about herself.

Factor 2 suggests that DT may have a problem in choosing friends because she sees someone she would like to know better to be similar to someone who disliked and disappointed her.

In Factor 3, it is apparent that successful and objectionable people can have common characteristics.

Factor 4 groups the nuclear family (father, brother, mother, sister) together with the best female friend. Consistent with prior interpretations, this suggests a narrow inner circle of people who are not well-differentiated. She sees herself to be more different from her family than they are from each other.

Factors 5 and 6, however, indicate that the sister is the one family member who is indeed differentiated from the others.

The identification analysis shown in Table 6.9 indicates a high degree of projective assimilation. That is, an unusually large number of role figures (14 of 22) are described to be significantly similar to the subject. This inevitably results from a lack of differentiation among people, together with the tendency to assume that the attitudes, beliefs, and feelings of other people are like one's own. This notion is further borne out because the most highly identified real

TABLE 6.7
Construct Factor Structure for Case DT

	Factor 1			Factor 2	
Factor loadings	Construct–opposite pairs		Factor loadings	Construct–opposite pairs	
.84	(+) S Helpful	Not helpful	.91	(+) Reserved	S Outgoing
.82	(+) S Good friends	Not good friends with	.91	(+) S Not so outgoing	Outgoing
.82	(+) S Likes children	Dislikes children	.40	Don't like to visit	(+) S Like to visit others
.77	(+) S Likes outdoors	Homebody			
.73	(+) S Faithful to family life	Not faithful to family			
.72	(+) S Like what doing	Miserable			
.71	(+) S Have own hobbies	No hobbies at all			
.70	(+) S Sincerely Christian	Athiest			
.64	(+) S Considerate of feelings	Don't care other feel			
.57	(+) S Live in country	City life			
.51	(+) S Friendly	Unfriendly			
.49	(+) S Good friend to have	Gossipy			
.47	(+) S Keep a secret	Can't keep a secret			
.40	(+) S Likes English literature	Isn't educated			

Percentage of variance accounted for: 30%.
Self-factor is consistent.
Self-valence is consistent.
Factor-valence is consistent.

Percentage of variance accounted for: 10%.
Self-factor is inconsistent.
Self-valence is inconsistent.
Factor-valence is inconsistent.

Factor loadings	Construct–opposite pairs	
.87	Spendthrift	(+) S Conservative spender
.82	Not too much common sense	(+) S Common sense
.81	Likes real good houses	(+) S Not important what kind of house
.76	Isn't educated	(+) S Like English literature
.75	Liberal	(+) S Conservative governmentwise
.55	Athiest	(+) S Sincerely Christian
.53	Miserable	(+) S Like what doing
.52	Not faithful to family	(+) S Faithful to family
.44	City life	(+) S Live in country
.44	Can't keep secret	(+) S Keep a secret

Percentage of variance accounted for: 23%.
Self-factor is consistent.
Self-valence is consistent.
Factor-valence is consistent.

Factor loadings	Construct–opposite pairs	
.97	Likes to talk–argue	(+) S Doesn't like to argue

Percentage of variance accounted for: 7%.
Self-factor is not applicable.
Self-valence is not applicable.
Factor-valence is not applicable.

Factor 5

Factor loadings	Construct–opposite pairs	
.71	Can't keep secret	(+) S Keep a secret
.70	Gossipy	(+) S Good friend to have
.40	Don't care others feel	(+) S Considerate of feelings

Percentage of variance accounted for: 9%.
Self-factor is consistent.
Self-valence is consistent.
Factor-valence is consistent.

Factor 6

Factor loadings	Construct–opposite pairs	
.68	(+) S Like to visit others	Don't like to visit
.63	(+) S Friendly	Unfriendly
.51	(+) S Conservative governmentwise	Liberal

Percentage of variance accounted for: 8%.
Self-factor is consistent.
Self-valence is consistent.
Factor-valence is consistent.

TABLE 6.8
Persons Factor Structure for Case DT

Factor 1	Factor 4
.94 As others see you	.90 Father
.94 Ideal male	.77 Brother
.94 Ideal female	.77 Mother
.90 Psychotherapist	.66 Best same-sexed friend
.90 Myself (subject)	.43 Sister
.90 Admired Teacher	.42 Most successful
.90 Spouse	.40 Person like to know better
.83 Happiest person	
.79 Opposite of person uncomfortable with	*Factor 5*
.68 Opposite of boyfriend before spouse	.92 Person for whom feel sorry
.60 Employer during stress	.48 Boyfriend before spouse
.57 Person like to know better	.46 Sister
.55 Most successful	.42 Person uncomfortable with
.42 Sister	
Factor 2	*Factor 6*
.92 Disappointing SS friend	.41 Sister
.85 Person who disliked subject	.41 Most successful
.51 Person like to know better	
Factor 3	
.95 Teacher with an objectionable point-of-view	
.49 Most successful	

people are the admired teacher and the psychotherapist. Each of these roles are socially distant and structured, thus allowing for more projection than with intimate acquaintances.

Despite the high number of positive significant identifications, two are negatively significant. These include the person she feels uncomfortable with and a previous boyfriend.

Identification with father is greater than with mother, and the identification with the 10 males is greater than with the 8 females. Thus, cross-sex identification is clear. Cross-sex identification does not occur in the relationship of self to the ideal male and female. As already indicated, the correlation match with people in general is high.

No evidence of schizophrenic fragmentation of conceptual structure exists in this protocol. In fact, the formal structure of relationships may be described to be orderly and certainly too positive to be considered normal. The normal individual, who continually engages and copes with problems and is usually undergoing refinements in conceptual structure, typically displays as many or more inconsistencies as this patient. Certainly, more negative self-percepts would be shown. The problem in this patient is that the constructs often appear to be constricted to a narrow range of people to insure their validity. They are not

TABLE 6.9
Identification Analysis for Case DT

Identification	Correlation
Maximum identification	
As others see you	.95
Ideal female	.94
Admired teacher	.92
Ideal male	.86
Psychotherapist	.82
Spouse	.77
Most successful	.70
Employer during stress	.67
Person like to know better	.67
Happiest person	.65
Sister	.57
Brother	.46
Best same-sexed friend	.44
Father	.40
Minimum identification	
Person uncomfortable with	−.76
Boyfriend prior to spouse	−.60
Parent identification	
Mother	.24
Father	.40
Average female identification (8 females)	.37
Average male identification (10 males)	.43
Ideal-sex identification	
Ideal male	.86
Ideal female	.94
Social Closeness–estrangement	
Average correlation with 19 people	.41

useful in discriminating herself from others, especially those of more intimate relationship. Consequently, this protocol suggests the patient is vulnerable to either schizophrenic fragmentation or constriction if she is put into highly complex social situations. This type of protocol can also occur with one who has recovered from a schizophrenic fragmentation by imposing highly consistent, highly positive, and defensive constructs onto the self and a constricted portion of the world about her.

Case TS

TS is a 23-year-old male who was hospitalized once prior to the hospitalization at the time of testing. The first stay lasted 1½ months and the second lasted 2½ months. Testing occurred 16 days before discharge.

TABLE 6.10
Constructs, Opposites and Contrasts for Case TS

Constructs	Opposites	Contrasts
(+) Close	Distant	(not elicited)
(+) Sophisticated	Crude	(not elicited)
Lacks confidence	(+) Sure of themselves	(not elicited)
Conformist	(+) Nonconformist	(not elicited)
Don't compromise	(+) Compromise	Compromises a bit
(+) Studious	Wild	Not too studious
(+) Set of rules and values	Undisciplined	Troublemaker
(+) Disciplined	Undisciplined	Not disciplined
Tease	(+) Leave alone–docile	Not like teasing
(+) Scientific	Unscientific	Fun-loving
Insecure	(+) Secure	Secure
(+) Goal directed	Aimless	Lackadaisical
(+) Fun loving	Boring	Straight laced
(+) Outgoing	Introverted	Introvert
(+) Talkative	Quiet	Quiet
(+) Drinkers and hell-raisers	Quiet	Quiet–keep to self
(+) Active	Inactive	Inactive
(+) Headed right	Mixed up	Crazy
(+) Stick to one person	Run around	Runs around with other guys
(+) Ambitious	Lazy	Not ambitious
(+) Settled	Unsettled	Unsettled
(+) Cool	Uncool	Uncool

From Table 6.10, the language of TS's constructs is socially appropriate and without concretism or neologisms. The only idiosyncratic pairing, a mild one, is "scientific vs. fun-loving," and this was corrected in the construct–opposite pairing. A testing error occurred whereby the opposites were elicited for the first four sortings without asking for contrasts. This may have encouraged the subject to continue giving opposites.

From the construct factor analysis of Table 6.11, Factor 1 has factor-valence consistency, self-factor consistency (one exception), and self-valence consistency (one exception). Also, he evaluates himself primarily in the positive direction. The factor essentially describes a self-confident, goal-directed, competent individual. The subject describes himself consistently and positively except for being "unsettled." Other people who fit this positive description tend to be settled. This capability of negative self-description appears healthy. On the other hand, examination of self-descriptions on the construct-opposite list reveals only two nonpositive descriptions, neither of which are strongly negative in our culture. For an individual with two somewhat lengthy hospitalizations, an essentially positive self-image suggests considerable denial or inability to perceive oneself accurately. As noted earlier, some individuals tend to resolve self-ideal discrepancy by seeing themselves in a positive light. The correlation of the subject with the ideal male (.53) does not strongly support this contention, but the unusually positive self-description may reflect denial.

Factor 2 describes the active, drinking, fun-loving, undisciplined person. The subject describes himself to be active and fun-loving but not with the other negatively evaluated dimensions. Inconsistency exists in all aspects of factor structure. The self-valence inconsistency is recorded because of one negative self-assignment (quiet). The factor-valence and self-factor inconsistencies may point to conflict associated with either transition or conceptual breakdown. If one becomes too active or fun-loving, he may take on a number of negative characteristics.

Factor 3 is completely consistent. The factor describes the socially affable, well-adjusted person.

Factor 4 is unusual in content because people described to be "teasing" and "running-around" are also described to be "not compromising." Nevertheless, the construct is subtlely congruent, and the subject describes himself positively to be one who compromises, leaves people alone (docile), and sticks to one person.

Factor 5 has only one loaded construct (conformist vs. nonconformist). The subject describes himself positively to be a nonconformist. One cannot interpret what this means without further data because no other construct is associated with conformism. Obviously, conformism has variance and meaning which is independent of the preceding four factors.

The number of factors in this protocol is small. Interpreted with the traditional dimension of cognitive simplicity—complexity, this subject can be described to be simple in cognitive structure. This means that, with all other things being equal, the subject is less equipped for predicting the behavior of other people than one with a greater number of factors.

The identification analysis of Table 6.12, as in the case of DT, indicates a high degree of projective assimilation (the tendency to see others as having one's own attitudes, characteristics, and feelings). Thirteen of the 22 role figures had a significant identification match. Three figures (disappointing male friend, employer during stress, and person uncomfortable with) are viewed in the negative direction. The strongest positive identifications are with the mother, father and happiest person, suggesting close ties with his parents with a possible failure to fully establish his own separate identity.

Often expected with schizophrenia, identification with mother exceeds that with father. Identification with females exceeds that with males, and the ideal female exceeds the ideal male match. Thus, cross-sex identification is again clear. Overall identification with people is moderate, probably because significant negative identifications helped balance positive identifications.

This protocol, in general, does not reveal schizophrenic fragmentation. Moreover, the structure is less brittle and vulnerable to schizophrenic breakdown than that of DT. Possibly, denial as a defense may represent a means of reconstitution

TABLE 6.11

Construct Factor Structure for Case TS

Factor 1		Factor 2	
Factor loadings	Construct–opposite pairs	Factor loadings	Construct–opposite pairs
.94	(+) S Sure of themselves — Lacks confidence	.93	(+) S Active — Inactive
.93	(+) Settled — S Unsettled	.81	(+) Drinkers and hell-raisers — S Quiet
.90	(+) S Goal directed — Aimless	.72	(+) S Fun loving — Boring
.89	(+) S Ambitious — Lazy	.72	Undisciplined — (+) S Set of rules and values
.89	(+) S Headed right — Mixed up	.70	Undisciplined — (+) S Disciplined
.86	(+) S Secure — Insecure	.64	Tease — (+) S Leave alone–docile
.80	(+) S Cool — Uncool	.62	Unscientific — (+) S Scientific
.77	(+) S Sophisticated — Crude	.61	Run around — (+) S Stick to one person
.74	(+) S Studious — Wild	.57	Wild — (+) S Studious
.64	(+) S Scientific — Unscientific		
.56	(+) S Disciplined — Undisciplined		
.50	(+) S Stick to one person — Run around		
.46	(+) S Set of rules and standards — Undisciplined		
.45	(+) S Close — Distant		

Percentage of variance accounted for: 39%.
Self-factor is inconsistent.
Self-valence is inconsistent.
Factor-valence is consistent.

Percentage of variance accounted for: 22%.
Self-factor is inconsistent.
Self-valence is inconsistent.
Factor-valence is inconsistent.

Factor 3

Factor loadings	Construct–opposite pairs	
.86	(+) S Talkative	Quiet
.81	(+) S Outgoing	Introverted
.67	(+) S Close	Distant

Percentage of variance accounted for: 12%.
Self-factor is consistent.
Self-valence is consistent.
Factor-valence is consistent.

Factor 4

Factor loadings	Construct–opposite pairs	
.88	Don't compromise	(+) S Compromise
.67	Tease	(+) S Leave alone–docile
.49	Run around	(+) S Stick to one person
.31	Undisciplined	(+) S Disciplined

Percentage of variance accounted for: 9%.
Self-factor is consistent.
Self-valence is consistent.
Factor-valence is consistent.

Factor 5

Factor loadings	Construct–opposite pairs	
.92	Conformist	(+) S Nonconformist

Percentage of variance accounted for: 6%.
Self-factor is not applicable.
Self-valence is not applicable.
Factor-valence is not applicable.

TABLE 6.12
Identification Analysis for Case TS

Identification	Correlation
Maximum identification	
Mother	.84
Father	.69
Happiest person	.59
Brother	.58
Ideal female	.57
Girlfriend before present one	.54
Ideal male	.53
Most recent girlfriend	.52
Sister	.51
Most successful	.46
As others see you	.46
Admired teacher	.45
Teacher with an objectionable point of view	.42
Minimum identification	
Employer during stress	−.52
Person uncomfortable with	−.42
Disappointing same-sexed friend	−.42
Parent identification	
Mother	.84
Father	.69
Average female identification (6 females)	.44
Average male identification (12 males)	.23
Ideal-sex identification	
Ideal male	.53
Ideal female	.57
Social closeness—estrangement	
Average correlation with 19 people	.31

following a breakdown. The subject would likely show an inability to handle complex situations and would resort to passive dependency (would lean on someone with a more adequate construct system than his own).

Case NN

NN is a 41-year-old female with two hospitalizations lasting one week and three weeks, respectively. At the time of testing, she had been hospitalized for 10 days and was discharged 10 days later. The constructs, opposites, and contrasts that were elicited during examination are given in Table 6.13.

The terms NN used to describe her personal constructs are socially appropriate (not too concrete or neologistic). However, an unusually high number of idiosyncratic construct—contrast pairs are given (for example, dislikes Italians vs.

TABLE 6.13
Constructs, Opposites and Contrasts for Case NN

Constructs	Opposites	Contrasts
(+) Jolly	Sad	Mediocre jolly
Aggressive	(+) Nice	Nice
(+) Outgoing	Shunning	Quiet
Dislike Italians	(+) Like	Different period
Drank	(+) Sober	Hollering and talking
Not showy	(+) Quiet	Showy
Grudges	(+) Easy going	Doesn't have grudges
(+) Loves children	Hate	Don't bother with them
Fake	(+) Real	Harsh (fake also)
(+) Outside	Inside	By where she was
(+) Make things (cooking)	Pretend	Cook but not like them
(+) With people	Without people	Not with people
(+) Put front easily	Shy away	Regular person
(+) Pass self off easily	Not so easy	Shy
(+) Sex with	No Sex	This was my father
(+) Good hearted	Rotten	Good hearted too, but I don't know him all these years
(+) Close	Far apart	Not as close
Business	(+) Regular job	Children and the house
Talk about people	(+) Not gossip	Don't remember my dad doing that
(+) Close to me	Far away	Closer to Sam than to John
(+) Recent	Past	Long ago
(+) Nothing to do with	Always together	Not same type of relationship

different period; drank vs. hollering and talking; fake vs. harsh (fake also); outside vs. right where she was). Approximately 10 of the 22 construct–contrast pairs would be judged to be idiosyncratic by most observers. However, when NN is asked to give the opposite of the construct, most of these idiosyncracies are corrected. Most judges would view only 2 (for example, not showy vs. quiet) of the 22 construct–opposite pairs to be idiosyncratic.

Table 6.14 gives the results of the construct factor analysis. Factor 1 indicates that "putting up a front easily," "passing oneself off easily," "being with people," "outgoing," and "jolly" have a common association. At the opposite pole of the same construct, "shying away," "having a shunning nature," and "sad" have a common association. The subject assigns herself exclusively to the latter rather than the former pole.

The subject views herself in a negative light on all the constructs, which is likely to reflect some degree of depression. Otherwise, this factor appears intact and free of cognitive disturbance.

On the second factor, the subject is consistent about which pole is positively and nonpositively viewed; however, she is at conflict concerning where to assign

TABLE 6.14

Construct Factor Structure for Case NN

	Factor 1		
Factor loadings	Construct–opposite pairs		
.95	(+)	Puts front easily	S Shy Away
.90	(+)	Pass self off easily	S Not So Easy
.85	(+)	With people	S Without People
.57	(+)	Outgoing	S Shunning
.40	(+)	Jolly	S Sad

Percentage of variance accounted for: 16%.
Self-factor is consistent.
Self-valence is consistent.
Factor-valence is consistent.

	Factor 3		
Factor loadings	Construct–opposite pairs		
.88	(+)	S Closer to me	Far away
.88	(+)	S Close	Far apart
.70	(+)	S Recent	Past
.45	(+)	S Goodhearted	Rotten
.43	(+)	S Sad	Jolly
.42	(+)	S Loves children	Hate

Percentage of variance accounted for: 14%.
Self-factor is consistent.
Self-valence is inconsistent.
Factor-valence is inconsistent.

	Factor 2		
Factor loadings	Construct–opposite pairs		
.83	S Grudges	(+)	Easy going
.77	Dislikes Italians	(+)	S Like
.74	S Fake	(+)	Real
.64	S Aggressive	(+)	Nice
.59	S Sad	(+)	Jolly
.41	Not showy	(+)	S Quiet

Percentage of variance accounted for: 14%.
Self-factor is inconsistent.
Self-valence is inconsistent.
Factor-valence is consistent.

	Factor 4		
Factor loadings	Construct–opposite pairs		
.91	(+) S Regular job	Business
.77	(+) Outside	S Inside

Percentage of variance accounted for: 10%.
Self-factor is inconsistent.
Self-valence is inconsistent.
Factor-valence is consistent.

Factor 5

Factor loadings	Construct–opposite pairs	
.81	(+) S Sex with	No sex
.64	S Shunning	(+) Outgoing
.62	Rotten	(+) S Goodhearted
.61	(+) S Quiet	Not showy
.50	S Aggressive	(+) Nice

Percentage of variance accounted for: 11%.
Self-factor is inconsistent.
Self-valence is inconsistent.
Factor-valence is inconsistent.

Factor 6

Factor loadings	Construct–opposite pairs	
.80	(+) Make things (cooking)	S Talk about people
.77	(+) Not gossip	

Percentage of variance accounted for: 8%.
Self-factor is consistent.
Self-valence is consistent.
Factor-valence is consistent.

Factor 7

Factor loadings	Construct–opposite pairs	
.88	(+) S Nothing to do with	Always together
.48	(+) S Quiet	Not showy

Percentage of variance accounted for: 6%.
Self-factor is consistent.
Self-valence is consistent.
Factor-valence is consistent.

Factor 8

Factor loadings	Construct–opposite pairs	
.90	S Drank	(+) Sober
.60	(+) S Loves children	Hate
.41	(+) S Recent	Past

Percentage of variance accounted for: 8%.
Self-factor is consistent.
Self-valence is inconsistent.
Factor-valence is inconsistent.

herself. People described as "grudges," "disliking Italians," "fakes," "aggressive," "sad," "not showy," and who "hate children" are viewed to be nonpositive. The respective opposites are viewed to be positive. The subject assigns herself on the positive side twice and the nonpositive side four times. Besides being in conflict about where to assign herself on this factor, it is also interesting that she associates sadness with being aggressive.

The third factor describes recent acquaintances and herself as goodhearted but sad. This construct is possibly a source of conflict because it precludes the possibility of being both goodhearted and jolly. If NN were to choose jolly to be a self-description, she may expect herself also to become "rotten" and not be close to those around her. Such a conflict would tend to maintain "sadness" as a self-construction.

Factor 4 presents consistency in factor-valence only. NN assigned herself to be positive on "regular job" and nonpositive on "inside". The following possible interpretations can be made: (1) The subject may have committed a clerical error in assigning "inside" a nonpositive and "outside" a positive valence. Without knowing the personal meaning of "outside–inside," it is difficult to judge the liklihood of a clerical error. (2) The subject may have committed a clerical error in assigning herself to be "inside" instead of "outside." (3) The subject may be in a state of transition or revision of personal constructs, thus having temporary conflict about whether to view herself to be "outside" or "inside." Inquiry is necessary to establish whether idiosyncratic meanings are ascribed to such dimensions.

Factor 5 concerns those with whom she has had sex. It is more disturbed than the preceding factors. Those with whom she has had sex tend to be described as "shunning" and "quiet" but also as "rotten" and "aggressive." She views herself to be like them in behavior except that she is goodhearted rather than rotten. There is self-valence inconsistency, factor-valence inconsistency and self-factor inconsistency. With possible perpetuating cognitive disturbance, the people she has had sex with are viewed to be rotten and aggressive.

Factor 6 is consistent with respect to both valence and assignment of self. The only problem here is that the subject assigns herself completely with negative valence. The factor appears to concern productive non-gossipy people opposed to those who "pretend" and are "gossipy." Most clinicians utilizing personal construct analyses interpret a consistently negative self-concept on a factor to be less vulnerable to fragmentation than the inconsistent (mixed) relationship.

Although Factor 7 has an idiosyncratic pairing (quiet vs. not showy), it indicates that the subject sees herself to be quiet and possibly isolated from people.

Factor 8 is inconsistent with respect to valence (both factor and self). It appears to reveal a value conflict regarding drinking. People who drink are viewed to be nonpositive, but drinking people are viewed to be loving of children, a positive trait, and are among her recent acquaintances.

TABLE 6.15
Identification Analysis for Case NN

Identification	Correlation
Maximum identification	
As others see me	.71
Brother	.65
Person I feel sorry for	.56
Minimum identification	
Teacher with an objectionable point-of-view	−.38
Parent identification	
Mother	.00
Father	.25
Average female identification (8 females)	−.05
Average male identification (10 males)	.10
Ideal-Sex identification	
Ideal male	−.06
Ideal female	−.18
Social Closeness–estrangement	
Average correlation with 19 people	.03

The identification analysis, given in Table 6.15 indicates a closer identification with males than females and with father than mother. As noted earlier, this cross-sex identification has been suggestive of schizophrenia. (To some degree it occurs in all the protocols reported here.) The match with people in general would indicate considerable estrangement. The subject tends to see herself to be opposite of the ideal but not significantly so. Going beyond this, the high identification with her brother indicates her perceived closeness to him in contrast to other members of her family. Usually, role figures identified significantly in the negative direction have had a history of strong conflict and rejection with the subject. In this case, the nun whom she describes to be a teacher with an objectionable viewpoint approaches this category.

A VIEWPOINT ABOUT SCHIZOPHRENIA

Very little can be said with certainty about the etiology of schizophrenia. Most investigators accept a stress diathesis model; yet, no one can assert that both stress and constitutional vulnerability must be present in an uncommon degree in all cases. The evidence for biological transmission contributing to schizophrenia is clear; yet, no research has identified the relevant chromosomes, the mode of inheritance, or what is inherited. Are schizophrenia-specific genes directly inherited? Or, are numerous unrelated physical and neural shortcomings inherited that deprive individuals in different ways of good social functioning and development of conceptual structure? If the latter is so, the stressors rather than schizophrenia may possess the genetic relevance. In other words, schizophrenia can be the common outcome from various sources of stress. Dopamine and other biochemical hypotheses are offered, but no biochemical substance can yet be asserted as a necessary schizophrenia-specific antecedent. Various arousal disorders have been identified in both schizophrenics and high risk individuals for schizophrenia; yet, no research has determined whether these disorders bring on the schizophrenic disorder or whether they are the outcome of stressful experience prior to and during psychosis. Impairment in attention and information processing has also been well demonstrated. No evidence yet exists that these impairments are related to specific underlying genetic or biochemical factors that potentially result in schizophrenia. No research distinguishes whether the development of arousal problems is the immediate antecedent and cause of the attention and information-processing impairment or whether the individual, once becoming impaired, then develops an arousal disorder.

THE ROLE OF CONCEPTUAL BREAKDOWN

The purpose of this chapter is to illustrate aspects of conceptual breakdown in schizophrenics. We have illustrated that it occurs in varying degrees and in relationship to quite different aspects of life experience. In addition, we have illustrated how some areas may be left intact and how the dimensions of breakdown can be quantified and potentially normed for purposes of research and clinical study. We have suggested the breakdown of conceptual structure may be a progressive process, starting with inconsistent and conflictual associative clusters that become self-perpetuating. In an attempt to reduce conflict, constructs assume new and idiosyncratic meanings. Finally, looseness and instability occur as the final effort for conflict resolution.

It may be that the conceptual breakdown described here is a secondary outcome in individuals who are already taxed with genetic, biochemical, arousal, attentional, or other impairment which has already determined the schizophrenia. If so, the material described here may play no important role in the etiology of schizophrenia. Cognitive breakdown may be one of the many outcomes of a foregoing process. Consequently, the most relevant question becomes whether the analysis of cognitive structure is useful in assessing severity of psychosis and in pointing to ways to facilitate the defense and coping against a schizophrenic disorder.

On the other hand, cognitive breakdown, as described here, may have a more central role in the etiology of schizophrenia. It may be that certain ways the individual comes to construe himself and the world relegate him to the *anti-hedonic* position wherein punishment and dissatisfaction is one alternative and satisfaction or gratification associated with guilt and self-condemnation is the other alternative. This irreconcilable bind may occur in one area for one schizophrenic and in a different area for another. Possibly, the process of invalidation of the conceptual system caused by poor predictions may lead to withdrawal and the constriction or obstruction of information processing, (a state of increased stimulus redundancy). This constriction may lead to even less efficient predictions. Thus, the individual has increasing difficulty navigating in a world with social complexities at every level – work, family and social-recreational. If so, the assessment of conceptual structure is important to indicate both vulnerability and areas of preventive intervention.

When an individual has undergone a prolonged period of inconsistency among his various self-concepts – so that in no area of life can he say, "This is me, and I am glad" – his entire conceptual structure begins to loosen independently of whatever validations or invalidations have occurred from the outside world. Once this has happened, the disturbed metabolism, attentional and processing impairments, and arousal disorders may follow in course. The current state of our knowledge cannot rule out this possibility.

REFERENCES

Adams-Webber, J. R. Cognitive complexity and sociality. *British Journal of Social and Clinical Psychology*, 1969, *8*, 211–216.

Adams-Webber, J. R. An analysis of the discriminant validity of several repertory grid indices. *British Journal of Psychology*, 1970, *61*, 83–90.

Bannister, D. Conceptual structure in thought disordered schizophrenics. *Journal of Mental Science*, 1960, *106*, 1230–1249.

Bannister, D. The nature and measurement of schizophrenic thought disorder. *Journal of Mental Science*, 1962, *108*, 825–842.

Bannister, D., Adams-Webber, J. R., Penn, W. I., & Radley, A. R. Reversing the process of thought disorder: A serial validation experiment. *British Journal of Social and Clinical Psychology*, 1975, *14*, 169–180.

Bannister, D., & Fransella, F. A grid test of schizophrenic thought disorder. *British Journal of Social and Clinical Psychology*, 1966, *5*, 95–102.

Bannister, D., Fransella, F., & Agnew, J. Characteristics and validity of the grid test of thought disorder. *British Journal of Social and Clinical Psychology*, 1971, *10*, 144–151.

Bannister, D., & Salmon, P. Schizophrenic thought disorder: Specific or diffuse? *British Journal of Medical Psychology*, 1966, *39*, 215–219.

Bleuler, E. *Dementia praecox or the group of schizophrenias.* New York: International University Press, 1950. (Originally published, 1911.)

Bonarius, J. C. J. *Personal construct psychology and extreme response style: An interaction model of meaningfulness, maladjustment and communication.* Amsterdam: Swets & Zeitlinger, N. V., 1971.

Cromwell, R. L., & Caldwell, D. F. A comparison of ratings based on personal constructs of self and others. *Journal of Clinical Psychology*, 1962, *18*, 43–46.

Cromwell, R. L., Strauss, J. S., & Blashfield, R. K. Theoretical position. In N. Hobbs (Ed.), *Issues in the classification of children: A handbook of categories, labels, and their consequences.* Los Angeles: Josey Bass, 1975.

Dixon, P. M. *Reduced emotional responsiveness in schizophrenia.* Unpublished doctoral dissertation, University of London, 1968.

Frith, C. D., & Lillie, F. J. Why does the repertory grid test indicate thought disorder? *British Journal of Social and Clinical Psychology,* 1972, *11,* 73–78.

Goldstein, A. G. Hallucinatory experience: A personal account. *Journal of Abnormal Psychology,* 1976, *84*(4), 423–429.

Goldstein, M. J., Rodnick, E. H., Jones, J. E., McPherson, S. R., & West, K. L. Intrafamilial patterns observed in groups at risk for schizophrenia spectrum disorders in early childhood. In L. C. Wynne & R. L. Cromwell (Eds.), *The nature of schizophrenia.* New York: John Wiley & Sons, Inc., 1977.

Haynes, E. T., & Phillips, J. P. N. Inconsistency, loose construing and schizophrenic thought disorder. *British Journal of Psychiatry,* 1973, *123,* 209–217.

Heather, B. B. *A test of the serial invalidation hypothesis by varying constructs and elements.* Unpublished masters thesis, University of Leeds, 1971.

Jones, R. E. Identification in terms of personal constructs. *Journal of Consulting Psychology,* 1961, 275–276.

Kelly, G. A. *The psychology of personal constructs* (2 vols.). New York: Norton, 1955.

Kringlen, E. Adult offspring of two psychotic parents. In L. C. Wynne & R. L. Cromwell (Eds.), *The nature of schizophrenia,* New York: John Wiley & Sons, Inc., 1977.

McPherson, F. M., Armstrong, J., & Heather, B. B. Psychological construing, "difficulty" and thought disorder. *British Journal of Medical Psychology,* 1975, *48,* 303–315.

McPherson, F. M., Barden, V., & Buckley, F. The use of "psychological constructs" by affectively flattened schizophrenics. *British Journal of Medical Psychology,* 1970, *43,* 291–293.

McPherson, F. M., Barden, V., Hay, A. J., Johnsontone, D. W., & Kushner, A. W. Flattening of affect and personal constructs. *British Journal of Psychiatry,* 1970, *116,* 39–43.

McPherson, F. M., Blackburn, I. M., Draffan, J. W., & McFadyen, M. A further study of the grid test of thought disorder and personal construct subsystems. *British Journal of Social and Clinical Psychology,* 1973, *12,* 420–427.

McPherson, F. M., & Buckley, F. Thought process disorder and personal construct subsystems. *British Journal of Social and Clinical Psychology,* 1970, *9,* 380–381.

Miskimins, R. W., Wilson, L. T., Braucht, G. N., & Berry, K. L. Self-concept and psychiatric symptomatology. *Journal of Clinical Psychology,* 1971, *27,* 185–187.

Nideffer, R. M., Space, L. G., Cromwell, R. L., & Dwyer, P. *Speed vs. accuracy in the choice reaction time of good and poor premorbid schizophrenic and normal subjects.* Manuscript submitted for publication.

Piety, K. R. Patterns of parent perceptions among neuropsychiatric patients and normal controls. *Journal of Clinical Psychology,* 1967, *23,* 428–433.

Radley, A. R. Schizophrenic thought disorder and the nature of personal constructs *British Journal of Social and Clinical Psychology,* 1974, *13,* 315–327.

Rohrer, J. W. *A study of predictive utility of the role construct repertory test.* Unpublished doctoral dissertation, Ohio State University, 1952.

Shoemaker, D. J. *The relation between personal constructs and interpersonal predictions.* Unpublished doctoral dissertation, Ohio State University, 1955.

Shubachs, A. P. W. To repeat or not to repeat? Are frequently used constructs more important to the subject? A study of the effect of allowing repetition on constructs in a modified Kelly Repertory Test. *British Journal of Medical Psychology,* 1975, *48,* 31–37.

Space, L. G. A console for the interactive on-line administration of psychological tests. *Behavior Research Methods and Instrumentation,* 1975, *7,* 191–193.

Space, L. G. *Cognitive comparison of depressives, neurotics, and normals.* Unpublished doctoral dissertation, Wayne State University, 1976.

Stierlin, H. Bleuler's concept of schizophrenia: A confusing heritage. *American Journal of Psychiatry*, 1967, 123, 996–1001.

Williams, E. The effect of varying the elements in the Bannister–Fransella grid test of tought disorder. *British Journal of Psychiatry*, 1971, *119*, 207–212.

Williams, E., & Quirke, C. Psychological construing in schizophrenics. *British Journal of Medical Psychology*, 1972, *45*, 79–84.

Winter, D. A. Some characteristics of schizophrenics and their parents. *British Journal of Social and Clinical Psychology*, 1975, *14*, 279–290.

Wright, D. M. Impairment in abstract conceptualization and Bannister and Fransella's grid test of schizophrenic thought disorder. *Journal of Consulting and Clinical Psychology*, 1973, *41*, 474.

Wynne, L. C. On the anguish, and creative passions, of not escaping double binds: a reformulation. In C. E. Sluzki & D. C. Ransom (Eds.), *The double bind: The foundation of the commercial approach to family*. New York: Grune & Stratton, 1976.

Wynne, L. C., Singer, M. T., Bartko, J. J., & Toohey, M. L. Schizophrenics and their families: Recent research on parental communication. In J. M. Tanner (Ed.), *Psychiatric research: The widening perspective*. New York: International University Press, 1975.

Wynne, L. C., Singer, M. T., & Toohey, M. L. *Communication of the adoptive parents of schizophrenics*. Paper presented at the Fifth International Symposium on the Psychotherapy of Schizophrenia, Oslo, Norway, 1975.

Zimring, F. M. Structure of constructs systems and word association latencies. *Journal of Experimental Psychology*, 1969, *79*(2), 353–357.

7
Hemispheric Asymmetry and Schizophrenic Thought Disorder

Algimantas Shimkunas

University of Missouri—Columbia

THE PLURALITY OF THOUGHT DISORDER

After more than thirty years of research since Hunt and Cofer's (1944) classic review, investigators have no clear understanding of the nature and significance of schizophrenic thought disorder. Countless investigations have probed facets of the problem, and numerous reviewers (Broen, 1968; Buss & Lang, 1965; Chapman & Chapman, 1973; Lang & Buss, 1965; Maher, 1966; Payne, 1961; Salzinger, 1973) have assessed the many hypothetical constructs purported to describe or explain schizophrenic thinking. Although many promising explanations have been offered, no single one seems to characterize schizophrenic thought. Is it a loss of abstraction (Goldstein, 1944; Wright, 1975), overinclusion of concepts into categories (Cameron, 1947; Chapman & Taylor, 1957), accentuated response bias (Chapman & Chapman, 1973), lawful disorganization by collapse of response hierarchies (Broen, 1966, 1968), immediacy of stimuli (Salzinger, 1973), or autism (Shimkunas, Gynther, & Smith, 1967)? This question is not new and has been posed a number of times, both implicitly and explicitly (Buss & Lang, 1965; Chapman & Chapman, 1973; Salzinger, 1973).

A typical approach toward clarification has assumed that schizophrenic thought processes should break down to one or a few basic mechanisms. For example, empirical tests following this assumption have contrasted Broen and Storms' and Chapman's theories (Boland & Chapman, 1971; Hamsher & Arnold, 1976). Although Boland and Chapman (1971) found support for Chapman's theory over that of Broen and Storms', these results have failed in replication (Hamsher & Arnold, 1976), and there is some question whether Boland and Chapman's (1971) findings were, in fact, contradictory to the Broen and Storms position (Hamsher & Arnold, 1976; Storms & Broen, 1972). Theoretical

193

critiques have not fared better. Thus, Buss and Lang (1965) concluded that loss of abstraction, resulting in concrete associations, is not a valid interpretation of thought disorder. The studies they reviewed showed schizophrenics to be no more concrete than normals. A recent reassessment of that literature (Wright, 1975), however, has shown that Buss and Lang's (1965) negative view of the Goldstein—Vigotsky position on impairment of abstraction was incorrect and that strong evidence supports the abstraction-deficit hypothesis.

Such discrepancies and other difficulties have prevented clarification of interactions among thought-disorder constructs. They suggest that traditional theoretical and empirical evaluations may not suffice and that other means of analysis may be required to help understand the problem. An alternative may include a comprehensive construct validation of schizophrenic thought in which analogy serves as a vehicle.

CONSTRUCT VALIDITY OF SCHIZOPHRENIC THOUGHT

An implicit assumption regarding thought disorder is that it should be reducible to one or a few constructs. There appears to be no suggestion that many or all of the major dimensions describing thought disorder may fill functional roles in the overall articulation of the problem. This may reflect excessive reliance on the "principle of parsimony" that states that only as many constructs as are necessary to explain a scientific problem should be used (Russell, 1959). However, the rule of parsimony fails to provide guidelines for the determination of how much description is necessary for a given problem. The very nature of the problem creates that criterion, which, of course, is unknown. Extremely complex problems may defy parsimonious description. Excessive parsimony may increase the likelihood of a Type II theoretical error if potential constructs are rejected by premature judgments of their validity. Considering the often noted heterogeneity of schizophrenic behaviors and the multiplicity of its cognitive, perceptual and physiological deficits, broader conceptualizations appear necessary.

A comprehensive understanding of thought-disorder constructs accords with established principles of theory construction. Cronbach and Meehl (1955) outlined an approach to construct validation, which permits a broad integration of constructs to take the place of a criterion when meaningful criteria are lacking. Construct-validation procedures provide a means of escaping "the 'infinite frustration' of relating every criterion to some more ultimate standard (Cronbach & Meehl, 1955, p. 282)." Construct validity is based on the development of a nomological network that posits an "interlocking system of laws" (p. 290) constituting a theory. Such laws typically relate (a) observables to each other (b) constructs to observables, or (c) different constructs among themselves Cronbach and Meehl argue that direct observational contrasts between the

operations of two constructs *need not* be made. Theorists may accept intranet-
work proofs that the two operations reflect the same property as defined by the
network. It may appear that such an approach would permit surplus meaning
about the phenomenon in question. However, the network must accept potential
relations among constructs for predictive theorizing, not all of which may enjoy
the level of empirical validity that may be required.

> The hypothesized network goes 'beyond the data' only in the limited sense that it
> purports to *characterize* the behavior facets which belong to an observable but as yet
> only partially sampled cluster; hence it generates predictions about hitherto unsampled
> regions of the phenotypic space (p. 292).

The implications of Cronbach and Meehl's construct-validation procedures for
research on thought disorder are direct. Thought-disorder variables must be
articulated nomologically in order to determine whether a number of them can
be meaningfully unified to define a higher order construct of thought disorder.
If thought disorder includes a plurality of dimensions, this would be reflected in
its construct validity. If, on the other hand, thought disorder is limited to a
singular dimension, the network would permit this to be established. In either
case, such an effort would aid the development of construct validity for the
construct of schizophrenia, which is also in question (Braginsky, Braginsky, &
Ring, 1969; Rosenhan, 1973; Salzinger, 1973).

AN ANALOGY FOR SCHIZOPHRENIC THOUGHT

Initially, theoretical integration of existing thought-disorder constructs appears
to lack feasibility even though it may be appropriate. A preliminary schematic is
necessary. Without it, familiar paradigms, which provide no new information, are
the only alternatives. In his consideration of the nature of science from the
perspective of modern physics, Oppenheimer (1956) suggested the importance
of analogy. By the use of analogy, it may be possible to find parallels between
structures or constellations of particulars, in which one form provides the basis
for theoretical articulation of another form. Analogical theorizing presupposes
some sense of unity in nature that is similarly expressed in a variety of natural
forms. An appropriate analogy may suggest a new way of approaching a
phenomenon in question.

However, the attempt to find an analogue for schizophrenic thought disorder
is immediately faced with the question of where to look. Thought disorder
appears as an unusual and alien phenomenon to investigators with "normal"
thought processes, and a standstill is quickly reached. By contrast, research on
depression (Seligman, 1975) has benefited from experimenters' personal understanding of common depressed-mood states. The uncommon quality of thought
disorder seems to preclude personal understanding by other than the schizo-

phrenics themselves. Given this "limitation," only obvious structures can be pursued.

Perhaps the most obvious is the brain, presumably the very source of thought. Although much research has been done on central nervous system processes in schizophrenia, little attention has been paid to the nature of normal brain function and its possible implications for schizophrenic thought. This is understandable inasmuch as sufficient descriptors of both thought disorder and neuropsychological functioning must be established before the latter can serve as an analogical basis for the former. As both are now becoming reasonably well described, it would appear that such steps may be appropriate.

An analogy between the psychological functions of the nervous system and schizophrenic thought appears potentially fruitful. Thought disorder is presumably derived from some kind of brain functioning. If a global characterization of mental activity as performed by various brain structures can be developed, it may be capable of generating parallels to the process of schizophrenic thought. This structural model of mental activity may help direct empirical efforts in articulating a nomological network that could suggest interrelationships among thought-disorder constructs. The analogy to neuropsychological structures must necessarily include some consideration of both their psychological functions and the interactions among different elements of the structure.

Structural approaches to the brain and nervous system focus on a number of different neuroanatomical divisions. A logical starting point for present concerns is the cerebral cortex inasmuch as it represents the most highly evolved element of the central nervous system and mediates the most sophisticated forms of mental activity (Luria, 1966, 1973; MacLean, 1967). Considerable research in recent years (compare to Dimond & Beaumont, 1974a; Galin, 1974; Kinsbourne & Smith, 1974) has articulated the asymmetrical nature of the cerebral hemispheres with respect to function and their probable modes of interaction. Qualitatively different styles of thinking between hemispheres have been identified, and an understanding of interhemispheric communication, attentional orientation and information processing is beginning to emerge. A consideration of this literature and its implications for cognitive processes forms a preliminary basis for a neuropsychological model of schizophrenic thought.

PATTERNS OF ASYMMETRY IN CORTICAL FUNCTIONS

Asymmetry is a salient feature of locomotor and neural control operations in all vertebrates (Kinsbourne, 1973). Sensory functions, including auditory (Gordon, 1974a; Kimura, 1967), visual (Bogen, 1969; DeRenzi & Spinnler, 1966; Kimura, 1966), tactual (DeRenzi, Faglioni, & Scotti, 1971; DeRenzi & Scotti, 1969; Nebes, 1971), and olfactory modalities (Gordon, 1974b) have asymmetrical representation in the cerebral hemispheres. Neural pathways from sensory receptors project into the cortex in asymmetrical fashion and are mediated by either hemisphere, with their proportion of input depending on the particular sense modality. Vision is equally asymmetrical for each hemiretina so that the left visual field is mediated by the right hemisphere, while right visual-field mediation is carried out by the left hemisphere (Kimura, 1966; Kimura & Durnford, 1974). Auditory pathways, while overlapping, produce stronger responses in the cortex contralateral to the stimulated ear (Kimura, 1967; Rosenzweig, 1951; Tunturi, 1946). Tactile stimulation also projects primarily to the contralateral cortex while olfaction projects ipsilaterally (Gordon, 1974b). As sense modality connections to cortical hemispheres are reasonably differentiated, investigators can reliably present stimulus information to the left or right side of the brain to demonstrate asymmetry of psychological functions between hemispheres.

This task is not as simple as it appears. The hemispheres are connected by a bundle of nerve fibers known as the corpus callosum, which serves as a communication transfer system between them (Joynt, 1974). Hence, information processed by one hemisphere is rapidly transferred to the other. To minimize such effects, investigators have used brief tachistoscopic stimulus presentation to visual hemifields (Dimond, Gibson, & Gazzaniga, 1972; Kimura, 1966) or simultaneous presentation of auditory stimuli in dichotic listening paradigms (Kimura, 1967; Shankweiler & Studdert-Kennedy, 1967). Auditory stimuli have also been presented to one hemisphere, with white noise serving as a masking device to partially inactivate the other hemisphere. This is possible because of stronger contralateral than ipsilateral connections in audition; one hemisphere processes the signal with greater intensity, while the other responds more intensely to masking noise.

Such experimental strategies are important when subjects with intact brains are used. Research with "split-brain," or commissurotomized (surgically sectioned corpus callosum), patients makes experimental procedures simpler because interhemispheric transfer is totally eliminated. Through the study of commissurotomized patients, advances have been made in understanding cortical mediation of perceptual, motor and cognitive functions (Gazzaniga, 1970; Gazzaniga, Bogen, & Sperry, 1962; Gazzaniga, Bogen, & Sperry, 1965). With hemispheres disconnected, one side of the cortex is literally unaware of that the other is processing; hence, a familiar object held in the left hand (right hemisphere mediated) by a commissurotomized subject with left hemisphere dominance for speech (right hand dominant) cannot be identified verbally, even though it is recognized to be familiar (Gazzaniga, 1967). Studies of hemispherectomized (Smith, 1974) and lobectomized (when restricted to one hemisphere) subjects (Jones, 1974) and subjects with unilateral lesions (Efron, 1963b; Perret, 1974) also simplify the determination of hemispheric specialization. Studies using various of these subject selection and stimulus presentation strategies have begun to establish patterns of asymmetry in a number of psychological (cognitive, perceptual, emotional) functions between hemispheres and in their modes of interaction.

LEFT-HEMISPHERE FUNCTIONS

The left cortical hemisphere is dominant for speech in approximately 90% of normal right-handers and 60% of normal left-handers (Branch, Milner, & Rasmussen, 1964). Differences in patterns of hemispheric asymmetry have been found to be consistent with this estimate (Bryden, 1965; Satz, Achenbach, Pattishall, & Fennell, 1965). Numerous studies of left-hemispherectomized subjects (Kohn & Dennis, 1974; Smith, 1974) have shown severe language impairment. Smith (1974) reported severe aphasia following left hemispherectomy. A subject could produce isolated words, but was unable to reply meaningfully to questions, and responded with short emotional phrases and expletives. While speech and speech-related abilities return slowly, some degree of verbal impairment remains. Right-sided hemispherectomies, on the other hand, produce no discernible effect on language functions (Dandy, 1928, 1933). Rowe (1937) reported a case in which a Stanford–Binet IQ of 115 remained unchanged six months following surgery. Such findings have led to the assumption that the left hemisphere is the "verbal hemisphere."

Investigations using the principle of asymmetry in the design of experimental procedures have begun to articulate the details of the verbal nature of the left hemisphere. Kimura (1966) presented normal subjects with groups of letters, a dot pattern and a nonsense figure in a tachistoscopic binocular viewing task. Stimuli were presented to either left or right visual fields, while subjects maintained center fixation. Center fixation is required by this paradigm to insure that only one hemisphere's retinal pathways are stimulated at a time. Results indicated that the left hemisphere was superior in the identification of the letter arrangements and the right hemisphere in identification of the dot pattern. No hemispheric differences were found in identifiction of nonsense figures. Kimura (1961) found that patients with left temporal-lobe lesions performed poorly in reporting digits presented dichotically (different digits to each ear simultaneously), relative to patients with right temporal lesions. Moreover, following surgery, left temporal-lesion patients' performance deteriorated significantly, while patients with right temporal lesions did not change. Left-hemisphere superiority on dichotic digits tasks has been found in both sexes as early as age 5 in upper-middle-class children (Kimura, 1963) and at age 5 in girls and age 6 in boys of low-to-middle socioeconomic class (Kimura, 1967). In another study in which different unisyllabic words were presented to each ear dichotically, with subjects required to report the words for one ear only, the left hemisphere showed a distinct advantage (Kimura, 1967). No differences between hemispheres were found for monaural presentation. Dichotic studies presenting nonsense syllables of low association value also showed distinct left hemisphere superiority in both oral reports and in multiple choice recognition (Kimura, 1967). These studies clearly demonstrate left-hemisphere superiority for a variety of verbal materials ranging from low (letters, nonsense syllables) to higher (numbers, words) levels of conceptual organization and meaningfulness.

A study by Shankweiler and Studdert-Kennedy (1967) provides an indication of the level of language structure at which left-hemisphere superiority occurs. Normal subjects were presented with either consonant—vowel syllables (for example, pa, ka, da) or steady-state vowels in a dichotic listening task. Left-hemisphere advantage was found for recognition of consonant—vowel syllables. No hemispheric differences were found for recognition of vowels. These findings suggest that speech dominance operates at a level of speech sound structure in view of the left hemisphere's advantage for syllables exhibiting phonemic contrasts (stop-consonants).

Experiments using words as stimuli have elaborated on the verbal facility of the left hemisphere. Perret (1974) used a modified Stroop Test with right-handed patients with unilateral cortical lesions. Patients with left-hemisphere lesions showed poor test performance when naming colors of color names that had inconsistent print colors, while no hemispheric differences were found in naming colors of dot patterns nor noncolor words. Patients with left frontal-lobe lesions also showed poorest performance in a test of word fluency in which they were required to call out target words from an array. Caplan, Holmes, and Marshall (1974) presented three classes of words tachistoscopically to either right or left visual fields of normal right-handers. All words across conditions were of the same length and ended in the same suffix. Left-hemisphere superiority was found for recognition of agentive nouns (for example, helper), relative to either simple nouns (river) or ambiguous noun—verbs (father). The right hemisphere recognized more agentive and ambiguous words than simple nouns. Seamon and Gazzaniga (1973) presented two simple English words simultaneously on a back projection screen followed by a recognition memory probe to a single hemisphere via left or right visual field. Memory probes were pictorial representations of either one of the words presented or of an unrelated object. Subjects (normal right-handers) were given either rehearsal or relational imagery instructions. Rehearsal instructions required subjects to rehearse the two words subvocally throughout the presentation. Relational imagery instructions required subjects to form an imaginal representation of each word and place the two images in a single interactive scene. Results indicated shorter reaction times for the left hemisphere when subjects used the rehearsal strategy and shorter reaction times for the right hemisphere when relational imagery mediated recognition.

Although there is considerable support for the left hemisphere's mediation of speech and language, it is not clear whether verbal ability is the basic element of its activity. Abbs and Smith (1970), for example, presented self-generated sound feedback of subjects' own voices by means of a hybrid computer system to one hemisphere while the other was stimulated by a masking noise. Articulation errors of substitution, addition and omission were measured. No differences in speech errors were found between hemispheres at 0.0- and 0.1-second delays. However, the left exceeded the right hemisphere in errors at 0.2- and 0.3-second delays. Berlin, Lowe-Bell, Cullen, Thompson, and Loovis (1973) used dichotic task presentation of stop-consonants paired with the letter "a." Stimuli were paired so that onsets were 15, 30, 60, or 90 milliseconds apart. Results indicated a significant left-hemisphere advantage of 14% at simultaneity. A temporal offset of 15 msec still indicated left hemisphere superiority, but at 30 msec differences between hemispheres were no longer found. A retest with the same subjects one year later showed the same left-hemisphere advantage at 15 msec with a drop off at 30 msec.

These studies strongly confirm the expectation of left-hemisphere mediation of verbal processes at various levels of complexity, from simple speech sounds to categorical conceptualization and subvocal learning strategy. Yet, verbal processes break down, and the left hemisphere loses its processing advantage when feedback or stimuli are separated by *time*. However, other explanations may be possible. The findings of Abbs and Smith (1970) may be interpreted in terms of an interference phenomenon. Thus, longer delays in the feedback of one's own expressive speech would tend to increase interference because earlier speech would conflict with present attempts to formulate concepts. Inasmuch as the left hemisphere processes in a verbal style, such conflict or interference should increase with increased separation between feedback and expression. In the Berlin et al. (1973) study, left-hemisphere advantage dropped off at a 30-msec separation between stimulus onsets. A 30-msec delay may have effectively removed the dichotic effect of competition between hemispheres for processing the relevant information. Still, both studies involved a separation in time between elements. If the general nature of language is considered in this context, it may be viewed to be primarily time-based. Words, concepts and sentences appear to be elements along a linear progression. Concepts are typically expressed one after another just as time proceeds from one moment to the next. The verbal specialization of the left hemisphere may have as its foundation a temporal processing mechanism.

There are a number of studies that suggest a temporal mechanism. Efron (1963a) used both light and shock stimuli presented to the subject's right or left hemisphere. The left-hemisphere stimulus was presented 100 msec prior to the right, after which latency was reduced by 5 msec on each succeeding trial until true simultaneity was reached. Order of stimuli was then reversed. Right-handed normal subjects were compared with normal left-handers, with expectations assuming greater left-hemisphere dominance in the former group. Results indicated that right-handers experienced simultaneity when the left stimulus preceded the right (by 3.81 msec for light, 3.32 msec for shock), but that left-handers perceived simultaneity only when true simultaneity occurred. Hence, increasing left cortical dominance resulted in poorer judgments of non-temporal (that is, simultaneous) experience. In another study, Efron (1963b) compared subjects with left-hemisphere lesions and normal controls on temporal judgments of two light flashes and two tones separated by varying time intervals. Subjects were required to indicate which light or which tone occurred first. Performance of control subjects exceeded that of experimental subjects in both tasks. Carmon and Nachshon (1971) compared subjects with right- or left-hemisphere lesions and normal controls. Sequences of three, four or five light and sound stimuli were presented to subjects who were instructed to choose any stimulus in an ongoing sequence as a starting point and to identify the order of stimuli continuing in sequence. Subjects with left-hemisphere lesions were severely impaired in stimulus sequence identification, although those with right-hemisphere lesions showed no difference from controls. Thus, temporal sequencing that has no verbal content appears to be a critical feature of left-hemisphere activity. The left brain is unable to judge events when they occur simultaneously (Efron, 1963a), and its functioning is essential to the differentiation of physically real events that occur in sequence (Efron, 1963b; Carmon & Nachshon, 1971).

Is the temporal dimension of left-hemisphere activity related to its verbal dimension? A study by Cohen (1973) provides a preliminary answer. Normal right-handers viewed irregular clusters of upper-case letters, either to left or right of center fixation with rapid tachistoscopic presentation. Viewing was monocular with the right eye only. Letters were presented in various sized clusters, and the subjects were required to indicate whether the array contained all letters of the same kind or whether they were different. When judgments of sameness of stimuli were elicited, left-hemisphere reaction times were faster than those of the right hemisphere. Additionally, left-hemisphere reaction times increased significantly with cluster size (two, three or four letters), while the right hemisphere's reaction times were uniform across clusters. No differences were found with regard to judgments of whether the letters in the clusters were different. In a second experiment, normal right-handers followed the same procedure, but the stimuli used were unnameable shapes. Results showed that the left hemisphere processed sameness judgments with faster reaction times than the right, as before. In processing different sized clusters, the right hemisphere showed no differences in latency across shapes, as with letters, thus indicating parallel or simultaneous judgments. Although left-hemisphere reaction times were shorter for two than three shapes, neither differed from the latency for four shapes. Hence, the left hemisphere's serial processing orientation as a general process was still in question. A third experiment repeated the earlier procedure, but with cluster sizes up to five items exposed for a longer time (200 msec vs. 100 msec previously), and one-half the stimuli were letters while the remainder were shapes. Judgments of sameness for letter clusters by the left hemisphere reflected the expected serial effect. Clusters of five and four showed longer latencies than clusters of three and two and clusters of three longer than two. The right hemisphere, on the other hand, showed no differences across cluster sizes. Hemispheres did not differ with cluster size in reaction to shapes. With regard to reaction times to "different" judgments, the right hemisphere was faster for both letters and shapes; for letters, the right hemisphere was faster for cluster sizes of five and four than three and two, while the left hemisphere showed a mixed pattern of latencies across clusters. Overall, this study failed to differentiate the verbal from the temporal dimensions of left-hemisphere processing. The left hemisphere serially processes only letters not shapes that are processed holistically. The right hemisphere processes shapes holistically, but fails to process letters serially.

In sum, verbal and temporal aspects of cortical processing appear to be salient features of left cerebral-hemisphere function, although the right hemisphere does poorly in both. These two aspects may be extremely difficult to separate, if that is at all possible, given that language appears to be structurally temporal. It is clear, however, that the right hemisphere is relatively inferior in these functions, although it should presumably excel in nonverbal situations in which simultaneous and immediate elements must be discriminated. To clarify the functional significance of left-hemisphere verbal–temporal processing in the context of its relation to the right hemisphere, it is important to first consider, in more detail, the nature of right-hemisphere activity. Following this, some inferences may be possible concerning hemispheric interaction.

RIGHT HEMISPHERE FUNCTIONS

The right cerebral hemisphere has historically been consigned to the status of "second-class citizenship" in the central nervous system. Since Broca's (1865) assertion that speech was localized in the left hemisphere, investigators have paid little attention to the right hemisphere. Early neurological studies of localization of functions in the left hemisphere reflected the importance of speech and language to the human being (Smith, 1974). However, Hughlings Jackson anticipated the necessity for concern with functions of the "minor" hemisphere as early as 1864: "If then, it should be proved by wider evidence that the faculty of expression resides in one hemisphere, there is no absurdity in raising the question as to whether perception – its corresponding opposite – may not be seated in the other" (Jackson, 1958, p. 148). In spite of Jackson's observation, little consideration was paid to right-hemisphere functions until the mid-1920's (Bogen, 1969). Recent studies on cortico-hemispheric specialization, which were stimulated by Sperry's work on the split-brain, have begun to strongly establish the functions and nature of right-hemisphere activity.

Hughlings Jackson's initial observations concerning the perceptual quality of right-hemisphere function represent an accurate view of one of its major roles. Contemporary views focus on its "spatial" or "perceptual" nature (Bogen, 1969; Galin, 1974). These views are based on the observation that patients with right-hemisphere lesions show deficits in appreciation of spatial composition and in the recognition of faces (Hécaen & Angelergues, 1963; Milner, 1958). Cortico-hemispheric studies have supported the spatial–perceptual nature of the right brain. It is recalled here that Kimura's (1966) work on visual perception indicated right-hemisphere superiority in recognition of dot patterns. In another of these studies, Kimura (1966) presented normal right-handers with patterns of nonsense figures (forms) or capital letters to the right and left visual fields. Each pattern had six characters of two types. Subjects were requested to report how many similar forms or letters were seen and, in subsequent trials, how many different forms or letters were seen. Results indicated a strong right-hemisphere advantage for simple enumeration of forms. No differences between hemispheres were found in the enumeration of different forms or of same or different letters. Kimura's (1967) dichotic listening studies also support the perceptual hypothesis concerning the right brain. Normal subjects were dichotically presented with two different melodies heard in a post-task recognition procedure. The right hemisphere showed a decided advantage for the identification of both familiar and unfamiliar melodies. The same subjects showed the typical left-hemisphere advantage in a dichotic digits task. The right-hemisphere effect for response to, and recognition of, music has been demonstrated by numerous studies (Gordon, 1974a; Kimura, 1961; McKee, Humphrey, & McAdam, 1973; Milner, 1962).

Using commissurotomized epileptics (split-brain patients), Nebes (1971) investigated right-hemisphere functioning with regard to the perception of part–whole relations. The task required the subject to choose from among three sizes of completed circles the size circle from which a given arc (ranging from 80° to 280°) had been removed. Three conditions were employed: (1) a somesthetic–visual condition, in which subjects could see the three circles and identify the circle containing the arc, which the subject held in the right or left hand behind a screen so that it could not be seen, (2) a visual–somesthetic condition, in which the arc was seen, but the circles could only be touched, and (3) a somesthetic–somesthetic condition in which arc and circles were all out of view and manipulated tactually. Results indicated a strong right-hemisphere superiority in part–whole matching and a basic incompetence in the left hemisphere's performance of these tasks.

This spatial-style processing has been elaborated by studies of maze learning and related tasks. Milner (1965) used subjects with unilateral cortical excisions and normal controls. The task was a visual maze consisting of 10 by 10 array of bolts wired so that a click was heard whenever the stylus touched the wrong bolt. Subjects were required to follow a predetermined path from the lower left to upper right corner. Results indicated that trials to criterion and error rate did not differ between normals and left-hemisphere lesion groups. However, patients with right-hemisphere lesions showed severely impaired performance. Corkin (1965) used tactually guided mazes with patients who had surgery for relief of cerebral seizures. Results showed that patients with right-hemisphere lesions were significantly inferior to patients with left-hemisphere lesions. Kohn and Dennis (1974) studied a small sample of subjects who had undergone hemidecortication 7 to 9 years earlier. Right hemidecortication resulted in severe deficits on Porteus and WISC mazes and on tests of map-reading and directionality. However, no hemispheric differences were found on tests of visual—spatial organization, left—right discrimination and physical shape matching.

The spatial function of right-hemisphere activity is reasonably apparent in studies of visual and tactile perception. Two- and three-dimensional spaces, such as geometric forms and maze patterns, appear to be coded and processed in terms of recognition, compositional qualities and directional orientation. Auditory processing, particularly regarding the musical superiority of the right brain, is more difficult to conceptualize in relation to the spatial nature of this hemisphere. It is recalled that several studies have established the right hemisphere's responsiveness to music, particularly melodies. However, these findings suggest an additional problem: namely, how can melodies represent a spatial dimension? Melodies involve an element of rhythm and timing, characteristics that should be more consistent with the temporal nature of the left brain. Gordon (1974a) provides some clarification of this problem. Several epileptic patients about to undergo major brain surgery were given the Wada Test (Wada & Rasmussen, 1960) to determine speech dominance. this test involves the injection of sodium amobarbitol into the right or left carotid artery, resulting in immediate cessation of virtually all hemispheric functions on the same side of the cortex for a period of 3 to 5 minutes. The contralateral hemisphere, however, retains all of its functions during this time; hence, the test can successfully identify which hemisphere is dominant for speech. Following injection, Gordon (1974a) requested subjects to sing songs familiar to them. Right carotid-artery injection resulted in singing that became severely deficient in six of seven subjects tested. Patients who were able to sing showed striking amelodic patterns, including unnatural pitch changes in contrast to their pre-injection singing performance. Gordon noted, however, that rhythm was not particularly affected by this immobilization of the right hemisphere. Thus, rhythm and timing dimensions of melodic processing appear to be mediated elsewhere, perhaps in the left hemisphere.

In another study, Gordon (1970) attempted to elaborate the nature of musical processing by contrasting melodic presentations with musical chords. Normal subjects who were amateur musicians were dichotically presented with a melodies test and a chords test. Results indicated that only the chords test showed significant right-hemisphere dominance. Melody recognition failed to differentiate hemispheres, which is inconsistent with previous well-established findings of the right brain's superiority for melodies (Kimura, 1967). However, sample characteristics of Gordon's study were probably responsible for these null results. Subjects were reasonably accomplished musicians. A recent study by Bever and Chiarello (1974) has shown that musically naive subjects show the typical right-hemisphere advantage for melodies, although musically sophisticated subjects have a left-hemisphere superiority. Musically sophisticated subjects may have developed the ability to organize melodic sequences by the relationship of their component parts, hence reflecting left-hemisphere activity. Although Gordon's subjects failed to show any hemispheric asymmetry for melodies, the sophisticated vs. naive dimension may have confounded melodic recognition in his subjects.

Gordon's (1974a) findings with the chords test, however, suggest a possible understanding regarding the spatial quality of auditory processing that appears relevant to the right hemisphere. It may be difficult to conceptualize a musical chord as being displaced in space, although a chord played on an organ, as it was in this case, does seem, to the listener, to "spread out." Nevertheless, as Gordon noted, the most obvious quality lacking in the chord presentation is that of time. Although a melody shows a temporal progression of notes and pitch changes, a chord is simply a group of tones occurring at the *same time.* Hence, chords are simultaneous and immediate, rather than temporal and sequential. The stimulus quality of chords appears logically consistent with the simultaneous and immediate nature of right-hemisphere processing that has been noted by a number of investigators and reviewers (Carmon & Nachshon, 1971; Efron, 1963b; Galin, 1974; Ornstein, 1972). Thus, processing of musical stimuli appears to engage both the left hemisphere, for its melodic–temporal aspect, and the right hemisphere, for its spatial–simultaneous aspect.

This nontemporal, simultaneous processing feature of the right hemisphere was confirmed by Halperin, Nachshon, and Carmon (1973), who presented subjects with three-tone sequences in a dichotic listening paradigm. The number of transitions varied with presentation, so that zero-transitions were a succession of three high or three low pitches, whereas a two-transition sequence was one in which pitches varied (for example, low, high, low). Subjects were to report as many of the tones in a sequence as possible. Results indicated that more zero-transitions were recalled by the right hemisphere, while the left hemisphere was superior for two-transition sequences. Thus, the temporal quality of left and the nontemporal, simultaneous quality of right hemisphere were confirmed.

Simultaneous processing of right-hemisphere activity and its spatial–perceptual nature appear quite consistent. Perception clearly seems to involve processing at a *particular moment in time.* This certainly appears to be the case in visual perception insofar as environmental stimuli are simultaneously present. Parallel operations are probably reflected in tactile, olfactory and certain aspects (for example, the spatiality of chords) of the auditory modalities. Language and cognitive operations, as already suggested, appear to be dependent on a temporal–sequential mode of processing.

Another nontemporal function that appears to be right-hemisphere mediated is emotionality. Preliminary studies show a strong emotional component in right-hemisphere processing. Carmon and Nachshon (1973) dichotically presented normal right-handers with all possible pairs of human nonverbal sounds including crying, shrieking and laughing of a child, an adult male and an adult female. Subjects identified the emotional stimulus from a choice of pictorial representations of a child, man or woman crying, shrieking, laughing. Results indicated a very strong right-hemisphere superiority in identification of these nonverbal emotional qualities; 76% of subjects reported more accurately when processing with the right hemisphere, 24% when processing with the left. Other studies (Haggard & Parkinson, 1971; King & Kimura, 1971) support these findings with demonstrations of right-hemisphere superiority in the identification of nonverbal human sounds and emotional intonation.

Blumstein and Cooper (1974) presented sentences, which were low-pass filtered to make them 100% unintelligible, to normal right-handers in a dichotic listening paradigm. Sentences such as, "It has come" were spoken in different intonations to conform with a grammatical representation of the sentence as declarative, interrogative, imperative, or conditional. Subjects were either requested to identify the verbal content of the sentence (even though unintelligible) or to identify the intonation contour that the sentence assumed. Results indicated that identification of verbal content showed no effect for either hemisphere, but there was a distinct right-hemisphere advantage in the identification of nonverbal intonation contours. In a second experiment, filtered vs. nonfiltered speech was presented in the same four intonation-contour patterns. Consonant–vowel syllables in sets of three were spoken, assuming the four intonation patterns to insure that no syntactic or semantic information would be used in processing. Results showed no differences between filtered and nonfiltered speech, but the expected right-hemisphere advantage was again found in the nonfiltered speech condition. Inasmuch as vocal intonations are primary carriers of emotionality in human communication, the right hemisphere appears to play a salient role in the mediation of emotional experiences.

Schwartz, Davidson, and Maer (1975) used a conjugate lateral eye-movement paradigm to assess response to emotional vs. nonemotional reflective questions. This procedure had been used in a number of previous studies that had demonstrated left-hemisphere mediation of response to verbal questions and right-hemisphere mediation of spatial questions (Bakan, 1969; Gur, Gur, & Harris, 1975; Kinsbourne, 1972). The rationale for these studies relies on lateral orientation and movement of the head and eyes, mediated by frontal cortical areas (Crosby, 1953; Robinson, 1968; Sherrington, 1906) in such a manner that balanced attention reflects cortically balanced activation with head and eyes directed straight ahead. Movement of head and eyes to the left or right reflects contralateral cortical activation. Hence, moving the eyes to the right should reflect left-hemisphere activity, while moving the eyes to the left, should reflect right-hemisphere activity. Schwartz et al. (1975) asked normal subjects four kinds of reflective questions: verbal–nonemotional, verbal–emotional, spatial–nonemotional, spatial–emotional. Results replicated earlier studies by indicating more right-eye movements to verbal questions and left movements to spatial questions. Emotional questions also elicited greater left-eye movements, while nonemotional questions stimulated more right movements. Spatial–emotional questions produced most left movements; verbal–nonemotional questions produced most right movements. Thus, emotionally, as well as spatially oriented cognitive activity reliably shows right-hemisphere advantage, while the left hemisphere appears to be engaged by verbal and nonemotional conceptual processes.

Many of the studies reported here further indicate that either hemisphere is particularly unsuited for activity that is not consistent with its natural proclivity. When a hemisphere attempts to process in a manner inconsistent with its capabilities, deviant responses may be expected. Thus, Dimond and Beaumont (1974b) presented subjects with words from the Kent–Rosanoff word-association procedure and asked them to produce associates to these stimuli as rapidly as possible. Results showed that left-hemisphere processed words were significantly more often common associates than right-hemisphere responses, which were more uncommon. This finding is consistent with the contention (Galin, 1974; Ornstein, 1972; Levy, Trevarthen, & Sperry, 1972; Seamon & Gazzaniga, 1973) that the right hemisphere's cognitive activity may be characterized by imaginal, nonlinear modes of association, which fail to conform to the demands of a logical, sequential problem-solving orientation. The latter is more the province of the left hemisphere. Right-hemisphere cognitive activity, influenced by spatial–perceptual and emotional factors, and the tendency toward simultaneous processing, is likely to be characterized by imagery, fantasy and affect and lacking in rational cognitive constraints.

INTERHEMISPHERIC INTERACTION

Given the strong qualitiative disparity between the functions of the two hemispheres, it is important to understand their mode of interaction. This is not specifically known, but theoretical explanations have been advanced. A predominant one is that of competition between hemispheres (Galin, 1974; Kinsbourne, 1973, 1974). Galin (1974) suggests that the hemispheres may operate in alternation, with situational demands determining the excitation of one over the other.

This contention is supported by a number of electrophysiological studies that have shown higher alpha blocking in either hemisphere when the subject performs a task relevant to that hemisphere (Galin & Ornstein, 1972; McKee, et al., 1973). Thus, the left hemisphere engages in alpha blocking (an index of attention) when subjects perform verbal tasks, and the right hemisphere blocks alpha rhythm during spatial and musical tasks. Conjugate lateral eye-movement studies (Bakan, 1969; Gur et al., 1975; Kinsbourne, 1972) also suggest differential hemispheric activation by orientation to left or right depending upon hemisphere-relevant psychological activity. The dominating hemisphere may disconnect or force inhibition of the other, nonrelevant, hemisphere.

Attention becomes a critical mechanism to hemispheric interaction. Hemispheres appear to collaborate by balancing attention between opposing directionalities in space and focus attention by preattentive structuring of the field, followed by selective focusing within the field in temporal sequence appropriate to the problem (Kinsbourne, 1974). Thus, spatial information arrives at an input stage, presumably through initial right-hemisphere action, followed by a process of selecting the appropriate information in the perceptual field, resulting in focal attention and problem solving by the left hemisphere. In addition to this general progression, verbal—temporal vs. spatial—emotional characteristics of the specific situation would be operative in emphasizing which hemisphere is to be dominant.

The hemispheres are linked by callosal commissures, and when decisions are formulated within each half of the brain, information flow along transverse commissures coordinates these decisions so that the output mechanism can receive unequivocal messages (Kinsbourne, 1974). If there is a conflict between the two sides, transcallosal inhibitory action should produce definite priorities for the entire organism by magnifying small initial imbalances until they are decisively resolved.

Environmental circumstances should play an important role in determining the nature of interhemispheric competition. Temporal—verbal and spatial—emotional characteristics of situational demands would be the basic triggering mechanisms that bring either hemisphere into activation. Hence, conflict and problem situations should stimulate initial perceptual activity oriented toward information intake with right-hemisphere excitation. Once the situation is assessed perceptually, excitation should transfer to left-hemisphere processing so that alternate response strategies to the problem may be evaluated. If an appropriate response is readily available, both hemispheres should coordinate to effect a solution. The left hemisphere would provide the problem-solving strategy while the right may serve as a perceptual feedback system to aid in problem solution and as a mediator of intensity (emotional) of response. If an appropriate response cannot be found by left activation, an oscillation between hemispheres should ensue with alternations between additional information intake, emotional response and problem-solving attempts.

It is important to remember, however, that neither hemisphere is probably ever fully inactive at any moment in time in normal circumstances. Galin's (1974) characterization of the inactive hemisphere to be "idling" is cogent to this point. Even when idling, the inactive hemisphere is probably in a state of readiness to perform. Kinsbourne's (1974) distinction between preattentive and focally attentive processes suggests that the right hemisphere may be gathering general gestalts from the perceptual field while it is inactive, whereas the left hemisphere shows its readiness by attentive focusing in preparation for making problem-solving decisions. Thus, they may be conceived of as two autonomous but interacting engines in a vehicle sharing a common drive train. While developing decision strategies, one idles while the other attempts various solutions within its sphere of activity until a unitary decisive approach strategy is reached. At that point, they may jointly engage the drive train into movement toward goal achievement. The corpus callosum and related commissures may serve as a kind of gear assembly that permits engaging hemispheres into synchronous activation as well as an information relay system that informs each side regarding the other side's functional status.

LATERAL ASYMMETRY IN SCHIZOPHRENIA

Flor-Henry (1969) initially suggested a relationship between left-sided lesions in temporal lobe epilepsy and schizophrenia. Gruzelier and Venables (Gruzelier, 1973; Gruzelier & Venables, 1973; Gruzelier & Venables, 1974) reported a series of findings indicative of excessive asymmetry in autonomic arousal in schizophrenics.

Like many sensory functions, electrodermal activity appears to be projected contralaterally to the cortex. Animal studies have demonstrated that electrodermal activity is regulated by both inhibitory and excitatory cortical mechanisms (Wang, 1964; Wang & Brown, 1956) that are distributed contralaterally (Bechterew, 1905; Langworthy & Richter, 1930; Schwartz, 1937; Wang, 1964). Similar findings have been noted in humans. Sourek (1965) found higher skin-potential response amplitudes contralateral to the side of unilateral brain lesions. Holloway and Parsons (1969) showed that unilaterally brain-damaged subjects had markedly higher skin-conductance levels contralateral to the side of the lesion, primarily in response to passive sensory stimulation. Such effects did not occur in controls nor in bilaterally brain-damaged subjects. These results are consistent with the concept of a cortical release mechanism by which brain damage releases reticular and autonomic systems from normal cortical tonic inhibition, resulting in greater autonomic firing (Dell, 1963; Holloway & Parsons, 1969; Parsons & Chandler, 1969). When lesions are unilateral, as they were in the cases of Sourek's (1965) and Holloway and Parson's (1969) samples, the cortical release of autonomic activity predominates on the side contralateral to the side of damage.

The findings of the Gruzelier–Venables studies may be evaluated in terms of these asymmetrical patterns of cortically mediated autonomic responses.[1] If schizophrenic deficit involves asymmetrical cortical functioning, schizophrenics should manifest asymmetrical patterns of electrodermal activity, with greater activity on the side of the body that is contralateral to that of the malfunctioning hemisphere.

In the first of these studies, Gruzelier (1973) compared acute (hospitalized for less than 5 years) and chronic (hospitalized for more than 5 years) schizophrenics who were classified either as responders or nonresponders, depending on whether or not they showed skin-conductance orienting responses, with a group of normal controls. All subjects were left-hemisphere dominant as determined by a handedness questionnaire, and all schizophrenics were on phenothiazine medication with similar dosage levels across groups. Results indicated fewer right-hemisphere-mediated orienting responses in chronic responders at the same time

---

[1] It should be noted that Gruzelier (1973) and Gruzelier and Venables (1973, 1974) mistakenly assumed ipsilateral, not contralateral, hemispheric mediation of electrodermal activity. This interpretation was based on the findings of two reports of asymmetrical skin-conductance activity in unilaterally brain-damaged subjects. In the first, Luria and Homskaya (1963) found a patient with a left frontal lobe tumor to show an absence of electrodermal orienting responses on the left hand. Gruzelier and Venables interpreted this to indicate an ipsilateral connection to the damaged left hemisphere. However, insofar as cortical mediation of skin-conductance activity is contralateral in both excitatory (Bechterew, 1905; Langworthy & Richter, 1930) and inhibitory effects (Bechterew, 1905; Schwartz, 1937), the opposite conclusion is also tenable. Thus, left-handed skin-conductance orienting responses should reflect differentially lowered right-hemisphere responding because the damaged left hemisphere is presumably responding excessively on the basis of the cortical release mechanism and predominating over the right hemisphere. Of course, this does not explain this patient's lack of right-hemisphere orienting responses because it was the left hemisphere that was damaged. Regardless, substantive conclusions can hardly be made solely on the basis of data from an N of one.

The second report was Sourek's (1965) study that was cited earlier. The Gruzelier–Venables articles support their claim of ipsilateral mediation by Sourek's finding of lower skin-potential response amplitudes on the side of the body ipsilateral to the lesions. However, this is the same as saying that these subjects had *higher* response amplitudes on the contralateral side, exactly what would be expected on the basis of the various animal studies (Bechterew, 1905; Langworthy & Richter, 1930; Schwartz, 1937; Wang, 1964) and the findings with humans (Holloway & Parsons, 1969).

All things considered, it appears that Gruzelier and Venables' error in assuming ipsilateral cortical–electrodermal connections stems from a misunderstanding of the nature of asymmetrical CNS–ANS connections. However, this shortcoming did not in any way affect the adequacy of their experimental design nor the applicability of their findings. Insofar as Gruzelier (1973) and Gruzelier and Venables (1973, 1974) clearly indicated the manner in which either the left or right hand responded electrodermally in their various diagnostic groups, their results can be interpreted clearly. Hence, my interpretation of their findings is based on the corrected assumption that such autonomic activity is contralateral.

that these patients were slower to habituate left-hemisphere orienting responses. Furthermore, skin-conductance levels were higher for all responders' left hemispheres, but higher for nonresponders' right hemispheres, suggesting greater verbal—temporal activation in the former and spatial—emotional activation in the latter. Bilateral differences of this kind are highly deviant because they do not occur in normals (Gruzelier, 1973). Response amplitudes and response frequencies were found to be generally higher for the left hemisphere in all schizophrenic groups, relative to normal controls, again indicating excessive verbal—temporal activation.

Gruzelier and Venables (1973) again studied responder and nonresponder acute and chronic schizophrenics, but in comparison to psychiatric patients with depression and personality disorders. Two-tone stimuli of 1000 and 2000 hz were presented in random and 30- and 60-second intervals, with subjects required to make a response to the 1000-hz signal tone. Results for electrodermal response frequency showed no laterality differences in personality disorders nor depressives on either tone. However, nonresponder schizophrenics showed a greater left-hemisphere response to the signal tone as did responders to the neutral tone. Response amplitude was higher for the left hemisphere in the acute schizophrenic group to the neutral tone; no other differences for response amplitude were found. Left-hemisphere response latency was faster for acute responders, although right-hemisphere latency was faster for chronic responders. Skin-conductance levels for the right hemisphere were higher in nonresponder schizophrenics and personality disorders during the tone discrimination task. Depressed patients showed elevated skin-conductance levels mediated by the right hemisphere. In a replication study, Gruzelier and Venables (1974) again found higher left-hemisphere mediated electrodermal response amplitude for responder schizophrenics, although depressives showed the reverse (higher right-hemisphere mediated amplitude). Skin-conductance levels were elevated for the left hemisphere in acute schizophrenics, while depressives showed higher right-hemisphere skin conductance.

The overall findings of the three Gruzelier—Venables studies reveal two significant patterns of hemispherically mediated general and reactive arousal in schizophrenia. Heightened general arousal, as indicated by skin-conductance levels, appears to be primarily mediated by the left hemispheres of acute and responder schizophrenics (Gruzelier, 1973; Gruzelier & Venables, 1973). To the contrary, the right hemisphere appears to mediate heightened general arousal in chronic and nonresponder schizophrenics and depressed patients (Gruzelier, 1973; Gruzelier & Venables, 1973; Gruzelier & Venables, 1974). Although all schizophrenics tend to show greater left-hemisphere-mediated reactive arousal in terms of response amplitude and frequency (Gruzelier, 1973), reactive arousal patterns show greater consistency with the acute—responder vs. chronic—nonresponder distinction as indicated above. Thus, acute and responder schizophrenics showed greater left-hemisphere-mediated response amplitudes, frequencies and faster latencies (Gruzelier, 1973; Gruzelier & Venables, 1973; Gruzelier & Venables, 1974), although chronic responder schizophrenics had faster response latencies (Gruzelier & Venables, 1973), and depressives had greater response amplitudes (Gruzelier & Venables, 1974), all mediated by the right hemisphere.

Gruzelier and Venables' finding of asymmetry in cortically mediated emotional arousal and reactivity has strong implications for understanding the role of arousal and, by implication, the nature of thought disorder in schizophrenia. The drive and arousal theories that have attempted to explain schizophrenic process have all shown various deficiencies as explanatory models (Epstein & Coleman, 1970). Some of these deficiencies may stem from previous ignorance of the asymmetrical nature of autonomic nervous-system functioning in schizophrenia.

The implications for schizophrenic thought disorder may be even more complex. Drive–arousal theories typically assume some kind of response interference or performance decrement with increasing arousal (Hebb, 1955, 1958; Hull, 1943; Lindsley, 1951, 1957; Malmo, 1957, 1958). A number of drive–arousal theories of schizophrenia postulate that disorganized thinking in schizophrenia represents this performance deficit in response to a high arousal state (Broen & Storms, 1966; Mednick, 1958). A general assumption of these and related neuroattentional models (Fischer, 1971; Silverman, 1964, 1972) is that intensity of information processing increases with increasing arousal. At some point, rate of information input exceeds the schizophrenic's ability to process information. Here, cortically mediated information processing is assumed to shut down via cognitive gating mechanisms (Silverman, 1964) that may be based on the schizophrenic's subjective reduction of stimulus intensity until there is little or no attentional response (Silverman, 1972). At this stage, the schizophrenic is left with no input from the external environment and presumably turns to internal programs generated by subcortical activity (Fischer, 1971). These internal programs typically reflect little, if any, structure and are marked by intense imagery, symbolism and hallucination.

Gruzelier and Venables' findings appear to be reasonably consistent with this general model. Their acute and responder schizophrenics showed higher left-hemisphere-mediated arousal and reactivity to stimuli. Intensified left-hemisphere activity would be expected in response to increased demands for information processing because verbal–temporal problem-solving strategies should be best suited for selecting relevant information and rejecting irrelevant cues. Verbally mediated discrimination should permit catetorization of cues, whereas contiguity and sequence define the temporal context of relevant and irrelevant cues. The predominance of left-hemisphere activation in acute and responsive schizophrenics appears to reflect an extremely active problem solving orientation. The intensity of this activity may produce high levels of information overload as suggested by Fischer (1971), but restricted to left-hemisphere processes. If the left hemisphere is overloaded in acute schizophrenia, then any further demands on cognition, concept formation and other verbal abilities should result in failure, perhaps in the form of disorganized thinking. Insofar as the right hemisphere is still functioning at a lower level of arousal, it may partly compensate for the immobilized left brain. However, because of its specialization for spatial, emotional and imaginal processes, the right-hemisphere compensation may only produce additional "noise" into the system. Futile attempts by the left hemisphere to process information may be further contaminated by the intrusion of emotional and imaginal responses.

Some support for this suggestion of a weakened left hemisphere in schizophrenics may be found in a recent signal detection study (Bahzin, Wasserman, & Tonkonogii, 1975). Bahzin et al. (1975) contrasted paranoid schizophrenics with auditory hallucinations of varying severity with nonhallucinating paranoids and normal controls. All subjects were right-handers. The task was a measure of absolute auditory threshold as a function of signal duration. Thresholds for 1000-hz tone of 1000-, 100-, 10-, and 1-msec durations were determined by the method of limits, alternating right and left ears. Tone intensity gradually changed from audible to inaudible, with the threshold being the lowest intensity of signal tone heard by the subject over three repetitions. Results showed no differences in signal detection between hemispheres in normals and nonhallucinating paranoids. However, significant increases in auditory thresholds were found for left-hemisphere processing in hallucinating schizophrenics as the signal shortened in duration from 10 to 1 msec. Such a performance deficit would be expected in a hemisphere that was excessively aroused.

An overactivated right hemisphere in chronic and nonresponder schizophrenics is consistent with Fischer's (1971) suggestion that the ultimate resolution of the schizophrenic process involves cortical processing of internal programs generated by subcortical structures. The acute stage may be characterized by an overuse of the left hemisphere in attempts to problem solve, leading to an ultimate shutdown of central attentional processing of external stimuli (Silverman, 1964, 1972). The chronic stage may then represent a shift from the inadequately functioning left hemisphere to predominant right-hemisphere activity. Because the right hemisphere specializes in perceptual and emotional activity, it would be an appropriate mediator for subcortically generated programs. Instead of mediating perception of the external world, the right brain may now process internal (emotional) images. Inasmuch as internal imagery and fantasy are continuously available, the chronic schizophrenic could presumably maintain a consistent activation of the right brain, as indicated by the Gruzelier–Venables findings.

BILATERAL TRANSFER AND CONCEPTUAL DISORGANIZATION IN SCHIZOPHRENIA

To more fully evaluate the implications of cortical asymmetry in schizophrenic functioning, it is important to consider the possible role of callosal transfer of information between hemispheres. A preliminary indication of callosal defect in schizophrenics was demonstrated in an autopsy study by Rosenthal and Bigelow (1972). These investigators performed brain autopsies on schizophrenics and a control group of character disorders, neurotics and normals, none of whom showed evidence of cortical atrophy nor ventricular dilation. Unfortunately, this study suffers from the shortcoming that only the right hemisphere and the corpus callosum were autopsied; left-hemisphere sections were used for microscopic examination and were not included in the study. Measurements included brain weight, volume of various cortical structures, cortical mantle width, and corpus callosum width. Results indicated no differences in any structure, except that corpus callosum width was significantly greater in schizophrenics than controls. Rosenthal and Bigelow (1972) concluded with the observation that certain diseases of the corpus callosum bear resemblance to psychosis. Neoplasm in the corpus callosum often results in mental and emotional deterioration, and Marchiafava's disease (focal degeneration of the corpus callosum) produces mental and emotional disorders often indistinguishable from schizophrenia in terms of presenting symptoms.

One study of callosal transfer in schizophrenic cognition is presently available. Beaumont and Dimond (1973) compared acute schizophrenics with psychiatric controls and normal controls. Subjects were presented with letter, digit and abstract-shape stimuli to the right or left visual fields concurrent with central fixation. Results indicated that schizophrenics did not differ from controls in simple identification of stimuli for either hemisphere. This is consistent with Bull and Venables (1974) failure to show hemispheric differences in schizophrenics in the perception and identification of English words. However, Beaumont and Dimond (1973) found schizophrenics to be significantly poorer than all controls when matching letters and shapes *across* hemispheres. Consistent with this, a study by Young (1974) showed that schizophrenics failed to benefit from bilateral, as opposed to unilateral, presentation of verbal matching stimuli presented visually. Nonpsychotic controls gave shorter reaction times when stimuli were presented bilaterally, suggesting that they process information more efficiently when both hemispheres are given access to stimuli, whereas bilateral processing in schizophrenics is no faster than unilateral processing. However, caution must be taken in interpreting this finding, which was statistically significant ($p < .05$) but was part of a nonsignificant ($p > .10$) ANOVA interaction. In addition, Beaumont and Dimond's (1973) schizophrenics were poorer than psychiatric controls in matching digits and shapes within the right hemisphere.

These preliminary results concerning interhemispheric processes in schizophrenia show considerable consistency. An overloaded left hemisphere, which may be incapable of effective verbal and conceptual processes, appears to function in parallel with a potentially highly arousable right hemisphere (in chronic patients) that may intensify response to internal emotional processes. At the same time, cross-hemispheric communication appears diminished, so that the asymmetrical processing strategies of the two brains cannot be integrated and resolved. Dimond and Beaumont's (1974b) interpretation of schizophrenic defect as a modified disconnection syndrome is thus plausible. Schizophrenia, classically conceptualized (Bleuler, 1950) as a splitting of thought from affect, appears to be developing an empirical basis in neuropsychology.

HEMISPHERIC ASYMMETRY AND COGNITIVE DEFICIT IN SCHIZOPHRENIA

Given the asymmetrical nature of schizophrenia as just described, how can the role and function of schizophrenic thought disorder be understood? The research on cognitive deficit in schizophrenia appears to divide into three basic areas, namely attentional–perceptual, cognitive and motivational operations. This ordering would appear to characterize their structural positions in the process of experience. Hence, attentional and perceptual processes should precede cognition, which characterizes the reality that is perceived. Both may be influenced by the emotional state of the individual at the time that information processing occurs. It is assumed, of course, that all three functions also influence each other reciprocally in an integrated organism.

The following discussion of cognitive deficit and its relation to schizophrenic cortical asymmetry proceeds through this sequence of functions. Because of limitations on space, only a sampling of prevailing theoretical positions are considered within each area at this time. The greatest emphasis in the discussion is placed on cognitive processes of schizophrenics in relation to cortical asymmetry because cognitive operations are assumed to be most central to cortical functioning. However, the brevity of the evaluations of perceptual and motivational operations in the following sections does not indicate that they are any less important from the standpoint of asymmetry. Similarly, other cognitive processes than those discussed here may also have considerable relevance with regard to asymmetry. Again, present space limitations prohibit any further discussion of the vast variety and complexity of many other psychological processes found in schizophrenics.

ATTENTIONAL–PERCEPTUAL OPERATIONS

Studies by McGhie and Chapman (Chapman & McGhie, 1962; Lawson, McGhie, & Chapman, 1964; McGhie & Chapman, 1961) have suggested that schizophrenics show defects in filtering out irrelevant environmental cues. Both anecdotal accounts by schizophrenic individuals (McGhie & Chapman, 1961) and empirical studies (Chapman & McGhie, 1962; Lawson et al., 1964) have shown that schizophrenics have difficulty filtering out nonessential information in the process of selecting focal information. This deficit may ultimately relate to schizophrenic left-hemisphere immobilization. It is recalled that selective focusing is one possible outcome of hemispheric interaction as indicated by Kinsbourne (1974) and would appear to be primarily engaged by left-hemisphere functioning. As acute schizophrenics show a weakening of left-brain functioning, a breakdown in focusing on relevant cues should result. Irrelevant information would then presumably flood the schizophrenic's consciousness, as was clearly described by McGhie and Chapman's (1961) classic first-person accounts. The extensiveness of this deficit is reflected in the findings of the Lawson et al. (1964) study, in which contextual constraints failed to improve schizophrenics' verbal performance. This is also consistent with their cortical asymmetry in that contextual constraints, as used in this study, were verbal contexts, the very kind of constraint least likely to control the performance of a left-hemisphere immobilized individual.

Another attentional impairment in schizophrenics is their tendency to respond to stimuli that are immediate or have occurred most recently (Salzinger, 1971a, b). Studies by Salzinger have shown that schizophrenics' psychophysical judgments (Salzinger, 1957) and verbal behavior (Salzinger, Portnoy, Pisoni, & Feldman, 1970) are strongly influenced by their most recent experience. Salzinger's findings and immediacy theory are entirely consistent with schizophrenics' cortical asymmetry. The left hemisphere shows a strong temporal processing orientation, as already indicated. Without its adequate functioning in the acute schizophrenic, we would expect some kind of disorganization in the processing of timing, duration and recency. With the right brain compensating for the immobilized left, there should also be an increased tendency to orient toward the immediate present. This would be expected on the basis that the right brain processes information immediately and simultaneously, which are characteristics of its perceptual and emotional nature, as previously indicated. Hence, the temporal ability of the left brain, which may permit use of more remote information, is decreased, while the immediate orientation of the still-functioning right brain moves into greater prominence. The net effect should result in the increased reliance on present events, as Salzinger has shown.

COGNITIVE OPERATIONS

Two historically prominent explanations of schizophrenic thought disorder, which have strongly influenced contemporary research, are loss of abstraction and overinclusion. Although abstraction appeared earlier in the literature chronologically (Bolles & Goldstein, 1938; Goldstein, 1939; Vigotsky, 1934), it ran afoul of severe criticism as a valid construct relevant to schizophrenic thought (Buss & Lang, 1965). However, it has recently shown more promise both in terms of its original tie to concreteness as a characteristic of schizophrenic thought (Wright, 1975) and as the possible cognitive mechanism that malfunctions to result in autistic thinking in schizophrenics (Shimkunas, 1970; Shimkunas, et al., 1967). Overinclusion, on the other hand, has enjoyed reasonably continuous prominence as a viable description of schizophrenic thought since its introduction by Cameron (1947). These two concepts have also been in competition concerning which is the more accurate and valid explanation of thought disorder (Cameron, 1944; Hanfmann & Kasanin, 1942). Hence, some consideration of the nature and possible interaction of abstraction and overinclusion appears important to an evaluation of asymmetrical cortical functioning and schizophrenic thought. However, a proper analysis of the two constructs would move well beyond the scope of this chapter. Research on each is marked by considerable disagreement in operational definition and construct validity (compare to Buss & Lang, 1965; Chapman & Chapman, 1973; Wright, 1975). A forthcoming paper by this author will consider the relationship between abstraction, overinclusion and recent extensions of overinclusion in detail. For the present, only a brief evaluation of these constructs, with particular emphasis on their cortico-hemispheric implications, is offered.

It appears best to start with a consideration of the fundamental nature of categorical inclusion. Cameron (1947) originally observed the unusual way in which schizophrenics constructed their cognitive classes or categories. They appeared to "overinclude" various irrelevant objects and environmental cues. In object-sorting procedures, schizophrenics would frequently group objects, which were perceptually available, beyond the boundaries of a particular category. It appeared that they were relatively unable to limit attention to task-relevant stimuli. Cameron (1947) viewed this tendency to be an excessive broadening of conceptual classes to incorporate stimuli falling beyond the boundaries defined by relevant cues. Since Cameron, overinclusion has been thoroughly researched by means of object-sorting tasks (Payne, Matussek, & George, 1959), concept-sorting procedures (Chapman, 1961; Chapman & Taylor, 1957), synonym tests (Moran, 1953), and other means (Epstein, 1953; Payne & Hewlett, 1960; Payne et al., 1959).

In their evaluation of this literature, the Chapmans' (Chapman & Chapman, 1973) have concluded that *similarity* may be the critical dimension that forms the basis of overinclusion. Thus, in object-sorting tasks (Payne et al., 1959), the subject is asked to hand over all objects that belong with, or can be grouped with, a test object. Similarity is the criterion for grouping, and inclusion of irrelevant objects may be considered to be an inappropriate extension of the category. This overinclusion appears to result from judgments of similarity that are excessive because items that depart from the definition of the category are assumed by the schizophrenic to be similar. Moran's (1953) task, which required subjects to give synonyms to stimulus words, appears to be based on similarity of linguistic meaning. Schizophrenics gave more inadequate synonyms, suggesting their inability to discriminate similarities with precision. Chapman's concept-sorting procedure yielded strong indications of overinclusion when objects in similar categories (for example, fruit, vegetables) were sorted at the same time (Chapman, 1961; Chapman & Taylor, 1957). Much of Chapman's later work also appears to involve the similarity dimension. Thus, schizophrenics' excessive use of the preferred or strongest meanings of words, even when that meaning is inappropriate in context (Chapman & Chapman, 1965; Chapman, Chapman, & Miller, 1964), can be viewed to be an inability to distinguish between two meanings of the *same* word. Schizophrenics' choice of associative intrusions (Chapman, 1958; Rattan & Chapman, 1973) shows their preference for the most dominant meaning of a word, which is carried by a word associate rather than more correct definitional or categorical meanings. Here, the more preferred meaning direction of the *same* word is selected.

In all these studies, the schizophrenic appears unable to discriminate classes of objects, associations and definitional meanings. Categories that are distinct but that are close to each other become blurred so that similarity is attributed to stimuli that are not quite similar. It thus appears that the similarity continuum becomes subjectively distorted by the schizophrenic. These may be the same kinds of distortions that normals make in response bias (Chapman & Chapman, 1973), but the schizophrenic's distortion of similarity is more extreme. It clearly goes beyond the normal limits of conceptual behavior, resulting in a thought process that lacks the precision necessary to make adaptive evaluations and decisions. Concept and word meanings lose their focal distinctiveness and are no longer capable of stabilizing the schizophrenic's conception of reality. Environmental cues, appearing more similar than they are, may merge into confusing patterns that defy separation and analysis because the schizophrenic cannot find the boundaries of individual concepts.

It is difficult to understand from the research and theory on overinclusion and related concepts which mechanism may provide the means by which the conceptual boundaries of the schizophrenic are extended as they are. In the present view, this mechanism may be found in the operations of the process of abstraction. Goldstein (Bolles & Goldstein, 1938; Goldstein, 1939; 1944) proposed the major classic theory of abstraction deficit in schizophrenia. Because his formulations have been frequently subject to misinterpretation (compare to Shimkunas et al., 1967; Wright, 1975), only his major statements as presently relevant are discussed. Goldstein viewed normal thinking to be characterized by an abstract attitude, which utilizes a reflective evaluation of qualities abstracted, or taken from, an object. Abstraction is a voluntary reflection on the nature of the object and its various characteristics, leading to a selection of a quality followed by some elaboration of it. The concrete attitude, on the other hand, is an involuntary, unreflective response to immediate sense experience relative to the object. Because the concrete attitude orients the individual to respond immediately to the whole object, there is an inability to determine commonalities among objects or concepts that are *similar* in some ways but *different* in others. Insofar as Goldstein (1944) attributed the concrete attitude to schizophrenics, he viewed them to be deficient in reflecting on the various features of stimuli that shared similarities with other stimuli, but which were also different from them.

Subsequent research on abstraction led to the conclusion that Goldstein's formulation was incorrect because schizophrenics failed to show excessive concreteness in their conceptual behavior (Buss & Lang, 1965). However, further research (Shimkunas et al., 1967; Shimkunas, 1970) demonstrated that, while concreteness seemed to play a questionable role in schizophrenic thinking, their abstracting ability was impaired by autism. In an evaluation of cognitive-deficit research, Shimkunas (1972) agreed with Goldstein (1944), suggesting that the abstraction process could be better understood as based in the mechanism of *generalization.*[2] Accordingly, concrete responding is characterized by excessive adherence to the stimulus features of the object, with the result that only the immediate characteristics of the object determine the response; this represents a virtual lack of generalization. Increased generalization permits abstraction by means of a departure from the specific or literal aspects of the stimulus. In proverb interpretation, for example, an abstract response reflects the essential meaning of the proverb and postulates a *general* situation or set of events. The proverb itself is concrete, making reference to specific or literal events. Autism or idiosyncratic thinking is seen to be extreme generalization, tantamount to overabstraction. Hence, the generalization process can be viewed to proceed from concreteness to abstraction to autism, with schizophrenics often conceptualizing at the upper limits of generalization (that is, autism).

Direct evidence of a relationship between abstraction and generalization is available in a study by Kirschner (1964). Schizophrenics, organics and neurotics were separated into abstract and concrete groups on the basis of their performance on a color—form sorting test and block-design test. Abstract and concrete subjects were equally distributed among diagnostic groups. The tests were chosen to best approximate Goldstein's concepts of abstract and concrete attitude. Concrete and abstract subjects then participated in a visual stimulus-generalization task. Kirschner (1964) found that abstract subjects displayed a higher, flatter gradient of stimulus generalization than concrete subjects. No significant main effects for diagnosis nor interaction between concreteness and diagnosis were found, and none were expected. Thus, abstract subjects responded more to peripheral stimuli than concrete subjects, who were more bound to the training stimulus. Although abstraction appears related to generalization, categorical inclusion does not. Al-Issa (1972) compared schizophrenics

---

[2] Although Shimkunas (1972) entertained the possibility that overinclusion also was based on a generalization dimension, this position is considered to be incorrect in light of the present argument.

and normals on a stimulus-generalization task and found that, although schizophrenics showed greater stimulus generalization, overinclusion and generalization were unrelated (r = .076).

These data present a fairly clear statement of the relationship between abstraction and generalization. It is expected, on the basis of the present argument, that a test performance-defined autistic group in Kirschner's (1964) study would have shown a flatter generalization gradient than his abstract subjects. Consistent with this are Tutko and Spence's (1962) findings with the passive sorting procedure (Part II) of Rapaport, Gill, and Shafer's (1945) version of the Goldstein—Scheerer Object Sorting Test. Passive sorting on this task is a direct measure of abstraction because the examiner requires subjects to indicate *why* a group of objects belong together. The subject must then find what general or abstract quality characterizes the object. Tutko and Spence (1962) categorized errors into those that were restrictive because of inability to indicate similarities and expansive because of overly broad, vague or idiosyncratic qualities. Their restrictive errors appear to parallel the usual meaning of concrete responses, although their expansive errors parallel McGaughran and Moran's (1956, 1957) "open-private" response and Shimkunas et al's. (1967) autistic response. Tutko and Spence (1962) found that process schizophrenics were predominantly expansive. This is consistent with Watson's (1973) finding that process schizophrenics show more concreteness on proverb interpretations, although reactives show more autism. Taking Tutko and Spence's (1962) findings into consideration with Kirschner's (1964) stimulus generalization effects, it may be possible to consider Tutko and Spence's restrictive and expansive errors to represent extremes on the generalization continuum. The restrictive, concrete response admits to no similarity among objects because each object is unique, hence, *different* from any other. Increased generalization to the point of normal abstraction would permit the finding of certain commonalities among objects. However, this level was not measured by Tutko and Spence. Expansive or autistic errors are carried by excessive generalization to the point where concepts become vague and unconnected. A similar view can be taken of McGaughran and Moran's (1956, 1957) categories, with closed—public reflecting normal concreteness, open—public as normal abstractness, closed—private as autistic concreteness,[3] and open—private as autistic abstractness. In these studies, schizophrenics most frequently gave open—private responses, suggesting that they conceptualize at extremely high levels of abstraction bordering autism. Such levels of abstraction reflect a strong orientation toward generalization from central to peripheral concepts.

---

[3]This appears contradictory in light of the present consideration of the relationship between abstraction, autism and generalization. However, it is theoretically possible to find oppositional processes in nature to occur at the same time (for example, crying while smiling in humans). A more detailed consideration of this paradox will be given in a later evaluation of this theory.

How does such a generalization process relate to the similarity continuum previously discussed? The relationship appears to be a polar one, meaning it represents oppositional properties that reciprocally influence each other. An example of polarity well known to assertive mailmen and long-distance runners is fear and rage and their reconciliation in the dog. As increments of rage reach sufficient proportions, the dog attacks. However, if the dog is made to fear his "prey," with fear increasing to the same level as rage, the dog will cease its attack and retreat. A model that predicts this sudden change from rage to fear (to flight), thus one polarity to another (Zeeman, 1976), is highly complex and is not presented here. It does, however, illustrate a possible parallel to the operations governing the relationship between similarity and generalization, hence, between overinclusion and abstraction deficit in schizophrenia.

Generalization involves a movement from the specific or particular to the general. This has been termed inductive reasoning in the philosophy of logic and scientific method (Cohen & Nagel, 1934). The specific is the concrete object, projected via the generalization process to its broader category. Hence, dogs are mammals. However, in order to establish the category mammal, the similarity continuum is needed. Thus, zoologists and other naturalists have historically observed similarities among different varieties of animals and have determined that dogs have characteristics that are shared by most other animal species that fall into the genus mammal, namely, hair, mammary glands and the os penis. These mammalian characteristics define the parameters of its category by *similarity*. Dogs, cows and apes are similar because they all bear those qualities, and those qualities, in turn, define them as mammals. They also differ from birds, fish and other animals by virtue of those characteristics.

Similarity appears to define the category, although generalization permits the relation of the specific object to a particular category. Judgments of similarity appear to correspond to the process of deductive reasoning or movement from the general to the specific (Cohen & Nagel, 1934). In tests of overinclusion, an object is presented along with other objects, some of which are similar to it. The subject is to select those that belong with it, with belongingness implying similarity. The subject presumably generates a category (or is given the idea to do so), which then serves as a criterion of the selection of the remaining items. Once the category is present, the deductive process ensues, enabling the subject to choose only those objects that fit that category. The criterion of fitness is the similarity of objects that originally defined that category.

Generalization works hand in hand with the similarity continuum. By means of induction, specific object characteristics are generalized, or projected, to the larger categories to which they pertain. Thus, in abstraction, a dog in the context of an ape is considered to be a mammal. If a dog is considered with a bird, the degree of generalization must be greater, hence, the abstraction vertebrate. Considered with a butterfly, the dog is now within the still broader category of animal, and so on. Levels of abstraction are crossed by increasing amounts of generalization. Thus, abstraction defines the *level of the category* (for example, mammal, vertebrate, animal, and so forth), although inclusion defines the *category itself* (for example, three four-legged creatures with hair, mammary glands, and so on). Similarity-based inclusion and generalization-based abstraction are thereby seen as interacting mutually to define the other's point of departure. The resultant process appears to represent a fundamental cognitive program that permits the structuring of external reality processed by the individual's perceptual system. If the perceptual system is flawed, which appears to be the case in the schizophrenic, the cognitive program simply follows the incorrect information it receives *as if it were valid.* This, of course, would result in the establishment of inappropriate categories by the process of overinclusion because schizophrenics' excessive perceptual input would demand a restructuring of categories to accommodate the increased input. The broadening of categories would demand increased flexibility in abstraction via generalization. Hence, if cows and robins are overincluded, the individual is faced with postulating a meaningful category for it. To do so, it would be necessary to check on various levels of generalization away from the specific (robin, cow) to determine whether these two could fit any category at some level of abstraction. Because the precise categories for these specifics are mutually exclusive (birds are not mammals and vice versa), a *new* category is constructed by means of autism, or overabstraction. This may take some bizarre form, such as a "milk giving creature which can jump over the moon," or that may cause the "milkman to lose his job because she can deliver the milk herself, airmail." Autistic and otherwise incomprehensible statements that are so common among schizophrenics thus become understandable as attempts to combine different levels of abstraction to enable the individual to sustain a comprehensive grasp of his or her stimulus inundated external reality.

The polar, interactional nature of categorical thinking is particularly salient in the present view of schizophrenic thought. The nature of polarity, by definition, involves a shifting between oppositional properties. In schizophrenics, the shifting between similarity decisions and categorical generalizations is theoretically consistent with their tendencies toward overinclusion and autism. It would appear that such shifts could have mutually reinforcing effects so that increased overinclusion would facilitate increased overabstraction, and vice versa. A self-perpetuating program of this sort is conceivable as a foundation of the intransigent nature of schizophrenic thought disorder. As a polar model, however, this formulation appears incomplete. Polarity implies opposition, and there does not appear to be direct opposition between similarity and generalization but rather a disjunction. Their general operations appear parallel as well, because each augment the other in the process of categorical broadening. Hence, it is likely that another variable or variables in combination with the above need to be considered before a clear polarity can be postulated.

Nevertheless, the present formulation is sufficient to consider the role of hemispheric asymmetry and interaction in schizophrenic thinking. Given the nature of the functions of the cerebral hemispheres, the schizophrenics' cognitive orientation toward similarity generalization appears best described to be primarily a left-hemisphere operation. The left brain's focal directionality (Kinsbourne, 1974) would be consistent with the active nature of cue selection inherent in categorical inclusion and progression through levels of abstraction. Overinclusion may be particularly salient as a left-hemisphere activity inasmuch as Cohen (1973) found a distinct left-hemisphere advantage for sameness judgments for both verbal and pictorial stimuli. The process of similarity generalization should rapidly seek resolution concerning incoming perceptual data. The processing of these data, however, is a right-brain function as previously indicated. Hence, it appears necessary to consider both hemispheres to be ultimately interacting in the overall process that starts with perception and ends with some cognitive resolution. The verbal nature of the left hemisphere restricts it to conceptualizing largely in terms of words, concepts and names. These are the materials that form the substance of categorical inclusion and abstraction. But left-brain focal conceptual processes should act in response to right-hemisphere imagery, which forms the substance of its mediation of perceptual data. Images of the objects that have been perceived must be successfully communicated across the corpus callosum to the left hemisphere so that it can transform them into words. These words or names then enter into similarity–generalization continua for structuring and categorization. Preattentive structuring by the right hemisphere orients it toward pictorial–schematic representations of the external environment and cannot, in and of itself, do the verbal conceptual work of the left brain.[4] It can only restructure cues that may not have been adequately conceptualized by the left brain. Thus, poorly conceptualized images should be sent back to the right hemisphere for restructuring, followed by a return to the left hemisphere for another attempt at conceptualizing.

With the possible immobilization of the left hemisphere in acute schizophrenics (Gruzelier, 1973; Gruzelier & Venables, 1973, 1974), similarity generalization should be inefficient, resulting in return to the right brain for restructuring. If perceptual processing is still distorted, distorted imagery should be reprocessed to the left brain, which can perform no better inasmuch as it is still immobilized by arousal. Repeated reversals between hemispheres may characterize schizophrenics' continued attempts to understand and communicate their perceptions of reality. The deficit observed in schizophrenic corpus callosum functioning (Beaumont & Dimond, 1973; Rosenthal & Bigelow, 1972) may either reflect an inherent defect in the structure or a result of excessive right–left-brain approximations. If conceptual problems fail to resolve because of left-brain immobilization, increased intercommunication between hemi-

---

[4] Although the right brain is capable of some verbal functions, its effectiveness is limited to passive repetition of words and verbal decoding while the left brain (assuming left dominance for language) uses language expressively (Kinsbourne, 1974).

spheres should result. This may lead to a "jamming" of transcallosal fibers contributing to the interhemispheric transfer problems that have been observed (Beaumont & Dimond, 1973).

With chronicity, schizophrenics show a shift in hemispheric overexcitation to the right brain (Gruzelier, 1973; Gruzelier & Venables, 1973, 1974), although the left brain still shows heightened reactive arousal. This may be associated with structural changes in experience and behavior that accompany later stages of intransigent forms of the disorder. In this case, the perceptual and emotional responsiveness of the right hemisphere may be exaggerated to a degree of interference with left-hemisphere processing. While the left hemisphere appears to be partially recovered from its previous immobilization in the acute stage, the right brain may now be sending it exaggerated and personalized perceptual or emotional imagery. If primary right-brain stimulation is perceptual, the schizophrenic's expressive language may reflect increased reliance on concrete, pictorial images, which are now left-hemisphere-translated into concrete verbal responses. It is recalled that both Tutko and Spence (1962) and Watson (1973) found more restrictive, concrete responses in process schizophrenics, but expansive and autistic responses in reactives on tests of abstracting ability. If there is any resemblance between chronic and process schizophrenia and acute and reactive schizophrenia in terms of neuropsychological functioning as there appears to be with regard to neuroattentional mechanisms (Silverman, 1972), these findings may support the present argument. Thus, verbal expressions of concrete imagery are expected to be salient among chronic schizophrenics. This again reflects potential interference with the left hemisphere's use of generalization. Adherence to unique, concrete images among chronic patients would be expected to be a result of a normally aroused left-hemisphere receiving grossly distorted and intensified concrete images from the overaroused right hemisphere. Whereas the stimulus overload of the left hemisphere in acute schizophrenics is primarily verbal—conceptual in nature, the situation in chronicity may be one of right-hemisphere imagery overload. Because the left hemisphere is still overreactive, intense right-hemisphere imagery is likely to continue to influence left-hemisphere disorganization.

This is consistent with the alternate possibility of right-hemisphere overexcitation of an emotional rather than perceptual type. In this case, the chronic schizophrenic may respond with exaggerated emotionality and lose control entirely or withdraw to experience internal subcortical programs (Fischer, 1971), particularly at extremely high levels of stimulus intensity reduction (Silverman, 1972). Stimulus-intensity reduction characterizes attentional responding by which stimulation is perceived as less intense than it actually is. Nonparanoid, process and probably chronic schizophrenics are typically reducers, whereas paranoids, reactives and acutes augment stimulus intensity (Silverman, 1972). Reduction of stimulus intensity permits withdrawal as perceptual processing is muted. Within this withdrawal state, accompanied by an overactive right hemisphere, the chronic schizophrenic should be intensely involved with personalized, concrete imagery.

The attempt to integrate schizophrenics' asymmetrical cortical functioning with abstraction deficit and overinclusion runs into difficulties when consideration is made of the nature of schizophrenic samples used to measure thought disorder. Abstraction deficit has been found in acute schizophrenics (Shimkunas, 1970; Shimkunas et al., 1967) and in chronics (Flavell, 1956). Both acutes (Harrow, Tucker, Himmelhoch, & Putnam, 1972; Payne et al., 1959) and chronics (Chapman, 1961; Chapman & Taylor, 1957; Harrow et al., 1972) have also shown overinclusion. If these processes are basically left-hemisphere mediated, the evidence is paradoxical with regard to the differential asymmetrical cortical patterns of acute and chronic schizophrenics. However, it can be resolved by considering the interactional nature of the cortical hemispheres, namely, that a unitary bilateral decision is prerequisite to the comprehensive functioning of the organism (Kinsbourne, 1974). Flexible interaction between left-hemisphere verbal–cognitive and right-hemisphere imaginal–perceptual properties would result in normal cortically expressed conceptualizations. Inasmuch as both acute and chronic schizophrenics appear asymmetrical and inflexibly overexcited in opposite hemispheres, unitary thought processes characterized by similarity generalization would be impossible to stabilize. Abstraction would appear to require both left-hemisphere words and right-hemisphere images to permit a generalization from one (unique image) to the other (abstract word). Similarly, categorical inclusion should require left-hemisphere words (category names) and right-hemisphere image decoding processes (separation of objects into categories). Hence, both abstraction and inclusion can be expected to malfunction when hemispheres are asymmetrically inflexible and communicate poorly with each other.

However, the left hemisphere would appear to retain executive function in both cases. Focal attentional and conceptual processes serve to culminate information processing. Hence, another explanation would consider the original left-hemisphere immobilization of the acute schizophrenic as the initiation of the abstraction–inclusion disturbance. As the acute schizophrenic becomes chronic, he or she may simply rely on disorganized patterns of similarity generalization that were learned during the acute stage of the disorder. Furthermore, because the chronic schizophrenic's left hemisphere is still overreactive, some distortion in discriminating similarities and crossing levels of generalization should remain. Overinclusion and abstraction deficit patterns may represent vestigial remains of early schizophrenia in the chronic patient, who is now more preoccupied with internal CNS processes. This appears consistent with the common clinical observation of some extremely regressed chronic patients who continually perseverate the same idiosyncratic conceptualizations for months and years.

MOTIVATIONAL OPERATIONS

A basic assumption underlying the present conceptualization of schizophrenia is that intensified emotional arousal serves as a catalyst for thought disorder. Overexcitation of the left hemisphere appears to initiate disturbed verbal conceptualizations by means of altering the cortical interpretation of perceptual input. Levels of excitation of both the left hemisphere in acute schizophrenics and the right hemisphere in chronics are assumed to reach maximal ergotrophic proportions (Fischer, 1971), hence, exceeding the normal limits of the inverted U performance function.

Schizophrenia research has generated a number of drive–arousal theories. However, many of these formulations have been criticized (Epstein & Coleman, 1970; Lang & Buss, 1965), often because the specific mechanisms they postulate have not been adequately demonstrated or are difficult to cross-conceptualize with contemporaneously occurring perceptual and cognitive mechanisms. Knowledge of the nervous system's internal interactions (among arousal, perception and cognition) is presently insufficient for such precise delineations at an empirical level. Therefore, a more appropriate way of understanding CNS–ANS activation processes may be to consider such functioning from a broader perspective. The present approach takes this direction to permit a better integrated, though perhaps less specifically accurate, conceptualization.

Hullian drive-theory-based models include the theories of Mednick (1958, 1959) and Broen and Storms (Broen, 1968; Broen & Storms, 1966; Storms & Broen, 1969). Mednick's theory assumes that acute schizophrenics are functioning in a heightened drive state. This eventuates in (a) a flattening of the stimulus generalization gradient, resulting in semantic generalization and (b) the raising of competing responses above response threshold, resulting in interference with dominant responses. The acute schizophrenic shows thought disorder by incorporating distantly generalized cues that, when raised above threshold, combine randomly with dominant cues. Mednick's formulation is generally consistent with the present model. Here, schizophrenics are viewed to overgeneralize beyond the limits of abstraction to produce autism, while they utilize excessive similarity, hence attending to competing stimuli to produce overinclusion. This deficit in similarity generalization is conceived to result from an overactivated thus immobilized, left hemisphere. The excessive drive or arousal of the left brain disrupts normal cognitive functions that would lead to appropriate abstrac tions and categorical inclusions.

In Broen and Storms' views (Broen, 1968), an increasing number of appropriate and inappropriate responses reach similar ceilings, hence producing near equal response probabilities for both. As in Mednick's theory, this response-competition model assumes ceiling effects to occur because of heightened drive strength. Broen and Storms' ceiling effect and Mednick's suprathreshold response tendency may permit alternate explanations of the mechanism by which various cognitive processes, including overinclusive autism, function. As cognitive operations increase in speed or intensity with increasing left-hemisphere arousal, potential responses further along generalization gradients should increase in associative strength. The intensity of this CNS–ANS activity may also increase the relative associative strength of cues and meaning responses along various similarity continua. Overabstraction and overinclusion would characterize the thought process potentiated by these competitive response reorganizations.

Venables' (1964) input-dysfunction model describes an attentional mechanism that is also important to the present argument. This model assumes low resting arousal in acute schizophrenics with high reactive arousal that permits their excessively broadened attention to stimuli. Their excessive reactivity reflects the heightened attentional response orientation previously described by McGhie and Chapman (1961). Chronic schizophrenics, on the other hand, show narrowed attention as reflected in reduced reactivity, in response to higher resting arousal. These theoretical expectations are consistent with the asymmetry of schizophrenic thought disorder. With overaroused left hemispheres, acute schizophrenics are free to process perceptual data as mediated by the right hemisphere. With the loss of its executive function by overexcitation, the left hemisphere can no longer effectively orient focally to specific cues that are presented via preattentive structuring by the right hemisphere (Kinsbourne, 1974). Without focal control over perceptual input mediated by the right hemisphere, the random nature of broadened attention, as observed in acute schizophrenics, would be expected. The narrowed attention of chronic schizophrenics can be understood in terms of excessive right-hemisphere mediated arousal. Preattentive structuring of the external environment by right-hemisphere mediation of perceptual input may become intensified beyond the left hemisphere's ability to cope focally with perceptual cues. With high excitation, perceptually mediated internal images could reach levels of potency sufficient to draw the schizophrenic's attentional response entirely to them. The chronic schizophrenic may then respond only to these images, rejecting external perception because it lacks sufficient strength to compete with internal processes. This conceptualization of the shift from the broadened attention of the acute stage to the narrowed focus in chronicity parallel Silverman's (1967, 1972) attention–response model, which has already been related to the present formulation.

CONCLUSION

This presentation has offered a tentative nomological mapping of the structure of schizophrenic thought disorder. Schizophrenia is conceptualized to be an asymmetrical dysfunction in cortico-hemispheric integration. Overexcitation of the left hemisphere during the acute stage disrupts effective verbal–conceptual reasoning and focal attentional information processing. Right-hemisphere over-excitation during chronicity intensifies perceptual—emotional mediation, poten-tiating narrowed attention to subcortically stimulated imagery in the context of behavioral withdrawal. During acute stages of schizophrenic disorganization, left-hemisphere verbal—temporal information-processing strategies break down, seeking compensation in right-hemisphere perceptual—emotional mediation. The right hemisphere's orientation toward simultaneous processing potentiates in-creased attention to temporally immediate environmental cues. Failures in hemispheric integration and left-hemisphere discrimination of conceptual simi-larity and generalization lead to overinclusive autistic verbal behaviors. With chronicity, asymmetrical shifts in cortically mediated arousal may leave the schizophrenic with vestigial remains of disorganized thinking learned during acute stages and maintained by high left-hemisphere reactivity.

Intensified right-hemisphere-mediated internal imagery and hallucination fur-ther distort thinking and potentiate withdrawal behaviors. In both cases, an integrated organismic response to the external environment is further handi-capped by the malfunctioning of interhemispheric nerve fibers. This serves to disconnect conceptual from perceptual and emotional mediation, resulting in the discontinuity between thought and emotion that has been observed in schizo-phrenia.

The asymmetrical model of schizophrenic thought disorder departs from the typical style of current theorizing in this area of psychological research. It does not pretend to make precise statements incorporating the myriad of conflicting, often contradictory findings of empirical investigations. Empirical precision is the cornerstone of theory construction within research areas delineating specific theoretical dimensions. The present approach represents an attempt to find a thread of compatible meaning across a variety of specific problem areas relevant to different psychological functions. Functional interactions within the structure of the schizophrenic's nervous-system activity may thus become potentially understandable. Given the complex psychobiological problem that schizophrenia represents, broad, structurally oriented theorizing appears to be a necessary step in the ultimate construct validation of the phenomenon. The asymmetrical model of schizophrenic thought is a rudimentary step in that direction.

ACKNOWLEDGMENTS

I am grateful to Robert Boice, William Brown, Robert Daniel, and Mark Zipper for their helpful suggestions and critical comments concerning this chapter.

REFERENCES

Abbs, J. H., & Smith, K. U. Laterality differences in the auditory feedback control of speech. *Journal of Speech and Hearing Research*, 1970, *13*, 298—303.
Al-Issa, I. Stimulus generalization and overinclusion in normal and schizophrenic subjects. *Journal of Consulting and Clinical Psychology*, 1972, *39*, 182—186.

Bahzin, E. F., Wasserman, L. I., & Tokonogii, I. M. Auditory hallucinations and left temporal lobe pathology. *Neuropsychologia,* 1975, *13,* 481–487.

Bakan, P. Hypnotizability, laterality of eye movements and functional brain asymmetry. *Perceptual Motor Skills,* 1969, *28,* 927–932.

Beaumont, J. F., & Dimond, S. J. Brain disconnection and schizophrenia. *British Journal of Psychiatry,* 1973, *123,* 661–662.

Bechterew, W. Der einfluss der hirnrinde auf die thranen schweiss und harnabsonderung. *Archiv für Anatomie und Physiologie,* 1905, 297.

Berlin, C. I., Lowe-Bell, S. S., Cullen, J. K., Thompson, C. L., & Loovis, C. F. Dichotic speech perception: An interpretation of right-ear advantage and temporal offset effects. *Journal of the Acoustical Society of America,* 1973, *53,* 699–709.

Bever, T. G., & Chiarello, R. J. Cerebral dominance in musicians and nonmusicians. *Science,* 1974, *185,* 537–539.

Bleuler, E. *Dementia praecox or the group of schizophrenias.* New York: International Universities Press, 1950.

Blumstein, S., & Cooper, W. E. Hemispheric processing of intonation contours. *Cortex,* 1974, *10,* 146–158.

Bogen, J. E. The other side of the brain: II. An appositional mind. *Bulletin of the Los Angeles Neurological Society,* 1969, *34,* 135–162.

Boland, T. B., & Chapman, L. J. Conflicting predictions from Broen's and Chapman's theories of schizophrenic thought disorder. *Journal of Abnormal Psychology,* 1971, *78,* 52–58.

Bolles, M., & Goldstein, K. A study of the impairment of "abstract behavior" in schizophrenic patients. *Psychiatric Quarterly,* 1938, *12,* 42–65.

Braginsky, B. M., Braginsky, D. D., & Ring, K. *Methods of madness: The mental hospital as a last resort.* New York: Holt, Rinehart & Winston, 1969.

Branch, C., Milner, B., & Rasmussen, T. Intracaroitid sodium amytal for the lateralization of cerebral speech dominance. *Journal of Neurosurgery,* 1964, *21,* 399–405.

Broca, P. Sur la faculte du langage articule. *Bulletins de la Sociéte D'Anthropologie de Paris,* 1865, *6,* 493–494.

Broen, W. E., Jr. Response disorganization and breadth of observation in schizophrenia. *Psychological Review,* 1966, *73,* 579–585.

Broen, W. E., Jr. *Schizophrenia: Research and theory.* New York: Academic Press, 1968.

Broen, W. E., Jr., & Storms, L. H. Lawful disorganization: The process underlying a schizophrenic syndrome. *Psychological Review,* 1966, *73,* 265–279.

Bryden, M. P. Tachistoscopic recognition, handedness, and cerebral dominance. *Neuropsychologia,* 1965, *3,* 1–8.

Bull, H. C., & Venables, P. H. Speech perception in schizophrenia. *British Journal of Psychiatry,* 1974, *125,* 350–354.

Buss, A. H., & Lang, P. J. Psychological deficit in schizophrenia: I. Affect, reinforcement, and concept attainment. *Journal of Abnormal Psychology,* 1965, *70,* 2–24.

Cameron, N. Experimental analysis of schizophrenic thinking. In J. S. Kasanin (Ed.), *Language and thought in schizophrenia.* New York: Norton, 1944.

Cameron, N. *The psychology of behavior disorders.* Boston: Houghton–Mifflin, 1947.

Caplan, D., Holmes, J. M., & Marshall, J. C. Word classes and hemispheric specialization. *Neuropsychologia,* 1974, *12,* 331–337.

Carmon, A., & Nachshon, I. Effects of unilateral brain damage on perception of temporal order. *Cortex,* 1971, *7,* 410–418.

Carmon, A., & Nachshon, I. Ear asymmetry in perception of emotional nonverbal stimuli. *Acta Psychologica,* 1973, *37,* 351–357.

Chapman, J., & McGhie, A. A comparative study of disordered attention in schizophrenia. *Journal of Mental Science,* 1962, *108,* 487–500.

230   A. SHIMKUNAS

Chapman, L. J. Intrusion of associative responses into schizophrenic conceptual performance. *Journal of Abnormal and Social Psychology*, 1958, *56*, 374–379.

Chapman, L. J. A reinterpretation of some pathological disturbances in conceptual breadth. *Journal of Abnormal and Social Psychology*, 1961, *62*, 514–519.

Chapman, L. J., & Chapman, J. P. The interpretation of words in schizophrenia. *Journal of Personality and Social Psychology*, 1965, *1*, 135–146.

Chapman, L. J., & Chapman, J. P. *Disordered thought in schizophrenia.* New York: Appleton–Century–Crofts, 1973.

Chapman, L. J., Chapman, J. P., & Miller, G. A. A theory of verbal behavior in schizophrenia. In B. A. Maher (Ed.), *Progress in experimental personality research* (Vol. 1.). New York: Academic Press, 1964.

Chapman, L. J., & Taylor, J. A. Breadth of deviate concepts used by schizophrenics. *Journal of Abnormal and Social Psychology*, 1957, *54*, 118–123.

Cohen, G. Hemispheric differences in serial versus parallel processing. *Journal of Experimental Psychology*, 1973, *97*, 349–356.

Cohen, M. R., & Nagel, E. *An introduction to logic and scientific method.* New York: Harcourt, Brace, 1934.

Corkin, S. Tactually guided maze learning in man: Effects of unilateral cortical excisions and bilateral hippocampal lesions. *Neuropsychologia*, 1965, *3*, 339–351.

Cronbach, L. J., & Meehl, P. E. Construct validity in psychological tests. *Psychological Bulletin*, 1955, *52*, 281–302.

Crosby, E. C. Relations of brain centers to normal and abnormal eye movements in the horizontal plane. *Journal of Comparative Neurology*, 1953, *99*, 437–479.

Dandy, W. E. Removal of right cerebral hemisphere for certain tumors with hemiplegia. Preliminary report. *Journal of the American Medical Association*, 1928, *90*, 823–825.

Dandy, W. E. Physiological studies following extirpation of the right cerebral hemisphere in man. *John Hopkins Hospital Bulletin*, 1933, *53*, 31–51.

Dell, P. Reticular homeostasis and critical reactivity. In G. Moruzzi, A. Fessard, & H. H. Jasper (Eds.), *Progress in brain research* (Vol. I.). Amsterdam: Elsevier, 1963.

DeRenzi, E., Faglioni, P., & Scotti, G. Judgment of spatial orientation in patients with focal brain damage. *Journal of Neurology, Neurosurgery, Psychiatry*, 1971, *34*, 489–495.

DeRenzi, E., & Scotti, G. The influence of spatial disorders in impairing tactual discrimination of shapes. *Cortex*, 1969, *5*, 53–62.

DeRenzi, E., & Spinnler, H. Visual recognition in patients with unilateral disease. *Journal of Nervous and Mental Disease*, 1966, *142*, 515–525.

Dimond, S. J., & Beaumont, J. G. (Eds.). *Hemisphere function in the human brain.* New York: John Wiley & Sons, 1974. (a)

Dimond, S. J., & Beaumont, J. G. Experimental studies of hemisphere function in the human brain. In S. J. Dimond & J. G. Beaumont (Eds.), *Hemisphere function in the human brain.* New York: John Wiley & Sons, 1974. (b)

Dimond, S. J., Gibson, A. R., & Gazzaniga, M. S. Cross field and within field integration of visual information. *Neuropsychologia*, 1972, *10*, 379–381.

Efron, R. The effects of handedness on the perception of simultaneity and temporal order. *Brain*, 1963, *86*, 261–284. (a)

Efron, R. Temporal perception, aphasia, and déjà vu. *Brain*, 1963, *86*, 403–424. (b)

Epstein, S. Overinclusive thinking in a schizphrenic and a control group. *Journal of Consulting Psychology*, 1953, *17*, 384–388.

Epstein, S., & Coleman, M. Drive theories of schizophrenia. *Psychosomatic Medicine*, 1970, *32*, 113–140.

Fischer, R. A cartography of the ecstatic and meditative states,. *Science*, 1971, *174*, 897–904.

Flavell, J. H. Abstract thinking and social behavior in schizophrenia. *Journal of Abnormal and Social Psychology*, 1956, *52*, 208–211.

Flor-Henry, P. Psychosis and temporal lobe epilepsy. *Epilepsia*, 1969, *10*, 363–395.

Galin, D. Implications for psychiatry of left and right cerebral specialization: A neurophysiological context for unconscious process. *Archives of General Psychiatry*, 1974, *31*, 572–583.

Galin, D., & Ornstein, R. Lateral specialization of cognitive mode: An EEG study. *Psychophysiology*, 1972, *9*, 412–418.

Gazzaniga, M. S. The split brain in man. *Scientific American*, 1967, *217*, 24–29.

Gazzaniga, M. S. *The bisected brain*. New York: Appleton–Century–Crofts, 1970.

Gazzaniga, M. S., Bogen, J. E., & Sperry, R. W. Some functional effects of sectioning the cerebral commissures in man. *Proceedings of the National Academy of Science*, 1962, *48*, 1765–1769.

Gazzaniga, M. S., Bogen, J. E., & Sperry, R. W. Observations on visual perception after disconnection of the cerebral hemispheres in man. *Brain*, 1965, *88*, 221.

Goldstein, K. The significance of special mental tests for diagnosis and prognosis in schizophrenia. *American Journal of Psychiatry*, 1939, *96*, 575–587.

Goldstein, K. Methodological approach to the study of schizophrenic thought disorder. In J. S. Kasanin (Ed.), *Language and thought in schizophrenia*. New York: Norton, 1944.

Gordon, H. W. Hemispheric asymmetries in the perception of musical chords. *Cortex*, 1970, *6*, 387–398.

Gordon, H. W. Auditory specialization of the right and left hemispheres. In M. Kinsbourne & W. L. Smith (Eds.), *Hemispheric disconnection and cerebral function*. Springfield, Illinois: Charles C. Thomas, 1974 (a)

Gordon, H. W. Olfaction and cerebral separation. In M. Kinsbourne & W. L. Smith (Eds.), *Hemispheric disconnection and cerebral function*. Springfield, Illinois: Charles C. Thomas, 1974. (b)

Gruzelier, J. H. Bilateral asymmetry of skin conductance orienting activity and levels in schizophrenics. *Biological Psychology*, 1973, *1*, 21–41.

Gruzelier, J. H., & Venables, P. H. Skin conductance responses to tones with and without attentional significance in schizophrenic and nonschizophrenic psychiatric patients. *Neuropsychologia*, 1973, *11*, 221–230.

Gruzelier, J., & Venables, P. Bimodality and lateral asymmetry of skin conductance orienting activity in schizophrenics: Replication and evidence of lateral asymmetry in patients with depression and disorder of personality. *Biological Psychiatry*, 1974, *8*, 55–73.

Gur, R. E., Gur, R. C., & Harris, L. J. Cerebral activation, as measured by subjects' lateral eye movements, as influenced by experimenter location. *Neuropsychologia*, 1975, *13*, 35–44.

Haggard, M. P., & Parkinson, A. M. Stimulus and task factors as determinants of ear advantages. *Quarterly Journal of Experimental Psychology*, 1971, *23*, 168–177.

Halperin, Y., Nachshon, I., & Carmon, A. Shift of ear superiority in dichotic listening to temporally patterned nonverbal stimuli. *Journal of the Acoustic Society of America*, 1973, *53*, 46–50.

Hamsher, D. deS., & Arnold, K. O. A test of Chapman's theory of schizophrenic thought disorder. *Journal of Abnormal Psychology*, 1976, *85*, 296–302.

Hanfmann, E., & Kasanin, J. Conceptual thinking in schizophrenia. *Nervous and Mental Disease Monographs*, 1942, *67*, 1–115.

Harrow, M., Tucker, G., Himmelhoch, J., & Putnam, N. Schizophrenic "thought disorders" after the acute phase. *American Journal of Psychiatry*, 1972, *128*, 824–829.

Hebb, D. O. Drives and the C.N.S. (Conceptual nervous system). *Psychological Review,* 1955, *62,* 243–254.

Hebb, D. O. *A textbook of psychology.* Philadelphia: Saunders, 1958.

Hécaen, H., & Angelergues, R. *La cecite psychique: Etude critique de al notion d'agnosie.* Paris: Masson, 1963.

Holloway, F. A., & Parsons, O. A. Unilateral brain damage and bilateral skin conductance levels in humans. *Psychophysiology,* 1969, *6,* 138–148.

Hull, C. L. *Principles of behavior.* New York: Appleton–Century, 1943.

Hunt, J. McV., & Cofer, C. N. Psychological deficit. In J. McV. Hunt (Ed.), *Personlaity and the behavior disorders* (Vol. II.). New York: Ronald, 1944.

Jackson, J. H. In J. Taylor (Ed.), *Selected writings of John Hughlings Jackson.* New York: Basic Books, 1958.

Jones, M. K. Imagery as a mnemonic aid after left temporal lobectomy: Contrast between material-specific and generalized memory disorders. *Neuropsychologia,* 1974, *12,* 21–30.

Joynt, R. J. The corpus callosum: A history of thought regarding its function. In M. Kinsbourne & W. L. Smith (Eds.), *Hemispheric disconnection and cerebral function.* Springfield, Illinois: Charles C. Thomas, 1974.

Kimura, D. Some effects of temporal-lobe damage on auditory perception. *Canadian Journal of Psychology,* 1961, *15,* 156–165.

Kimura, D. Speech lateralization in young children as determined by an auditory test. *Journal of Comparative and Physiological Psychology,* 1963, *56,* 899–902.

Kimura, D. Dual functional asymmetry of the brain in visual perception. *Neuropsychologia,* 1966, *4,* 275–285.

Kimura, D. Functional asymmetry of the brain in dichotic listening. *Cortex,* 1967, *3,* 163–178.

Kimura, D., & Durnford, M. Normal studies on the function of the right hemisphere in vision. In S. J. Dimond & J. G. Beaumont (Eds.), *Hemisphere function in the human brain.* New York: John Wiley & Sons, 1974.

King, F. L., & Kimura, D. *Left-ear superiority in dichotic perception of vocal nonverbal sounds* (Research Bulletin 188). London, Ontario: University of Western Ontario, Department of Psychology, June, 1971.

Kinsbourne, M. Eye and head turning indicates cerebral lateralization. *Science,* 1972, *176,* 539–541.

Kinsbourne, M. The control of attention by interaction between the cerebral hemispheres. In S. Kornblum (Ed.), *Attention and performance IV.* New York: Academic Press, 1973.

Kinsbourne, M. Mechanisms of hemispheric interaction in man. In M. Kinsbourne & W. L. Smith (Eds.), *Hemispheric disconnection and cerebral function.* Springfield, Illinois: Charles C. Thomas, 1974.

Kinsbourne, M., & W. L. Smith (Eds.), *Hemispheric disconnection and cerebral function.* Springfield, Illinois: Charles C. Thomas, 1974.

Kirschner, D. Differences in gradients of stimulus generalization as a function of "abstract" and "concrete" attitude. *Journal of Consulting Psychology,* 1964, *23,* 160–164.

Kohn, B., & Dennis, M. Patterns of hemispheric specialization after hemidecortication for infantile hemiplegia. In M. Kinsbourne & W. L. Smith (Eds.), *Hemispheric disconnection and cerebral function.* Springfield, Illinois: Charles C. Thomas, 1974.

Lang, P. J., & Buss, A. H. Psychological deficit in schizophrenia: II. Interference and activation. *Journal of Abnormal Psychology,* 1965, *20,* 77–106.

Langworthy, O. R., & Richter, C. P. The influence of efferent cerebral pathways upon the sympathetic nervous system. *Brain,* 1930, *53,* 179–193.

Lawson, J. S., McGhie, A., & Chapman, J. Perception of speech in schizophrenia. *British Journal of Psychiatry,* 1964, *110,* 375–380.

Lindsley, D. B. Emotion. In S. S. Stevens (Ed.), *Handbook of experimental psychology.* New York: John Wiley & Sons, 1951.

Lindsley, D. B. Psychophysiology and motivation. In M. R. Jones (Ed.), *Nebraska Symposium on Motivation* (Vol. 5). Lincoln: University of Nebraska Press, 1957.

Levy, J., Trevarthen, C., & Sperry, R. W. Perception of bilateral chimeric figures following hemispheric disconnection. *Brain,* 1972, *95,* 61–78.

Luria, A. R. *Higher cortical functions in man.* New York: Basic Books, 1966.

Luria, A. R. *The working brain: An introduction to neuropsychology.* New York: Basic Books, 1973.

Luria, A. R., & Homskaya, E. G. Disturbance of the regulating activity with lesion of the frontal lobes of the brain. In *The human brain and psychic processes.* Moscow: Izd. APN RFSR, 1963.

MacLean, P. D. The brain in relation to empathy and medical education. *Journal of Nervous and Mental Disease,* 1967, *144,* 374–382.

Maher, B. A. *Principles of psychopathology.* New York: McGraw–Hill, 1966.

Malmo, R. B. Anxiety and behavioral arousal. *Psychological Review,* 1957, *64,* 276–287.

Malmo, R. B. Measurement of drive: An unsolved problem. In M. R. Jones (Ed.), *Nebraska Symposium on Motivation* (Vol. 6). Lincoln: University of Nebraska, 1958.

McGaughran, L. S., & Moran, L. J. "Conceptual level" vs. "conceptual area" analysis of object-sorting behavior of schizophrenic and nonpsychiatric groups. *Journal of Abnormal and Social Psychology,* 1956, *52,* 43–50.

McGaughran, L. S., & Moran, L. J. Differences between schizophrenic and brain-damaged groups in conceptual aspects of object sorting. *Journal of Abnormal and Social Psychology,* 1957, *54,* 44–49.

McGhie, A., & Chapman, J. Disorders of attention and perception in early schizophrenia. *British Journal of Medical Psychology,* 1961, *34,* 103–116.

McKee, G., Humphrey, B., & McAdam, D. Scaled lateralization of alpha activity during linguistic and musical tasks. *Psychophysiology,* 1973, *10,* 441–443.

Mednick, S. A. A learning theory approach to research in schizophrenia. *Psychological Bulletin,* 1958, *55,* 316–327.

Mednick, S. A. Learning theory and schizophrenia: A reply to a comment. *Psychological Bulletin,* 1959, *56,* 315–316.

Milner, B. Psychological defects produced by temporal lobe excision. *Proceedings of the Association for Research on Nervous and Mental Disease,* 1958, *36,* 244–257.

Milner, B. Laterality effects in audition. In V. B. Mountcastle (Ed.), *Interhemispheric relations and cerebral dominance.* Baltimore: Johns Hopkins University Press, 1962.

Milner, B. Visually-guided maze learning in man: Effects of bilateral, hippocampal, bilateral frontal, and unilateral cerebral lesions. *Neuropsychologia,* 1965, *3,* 317–338.

Moran, L. J. Vocabulary knowledge and usage among normal and schizophrenic subjects. *Psychological Monographs,* 1953, *67* (20, Whole No. 370).

Nebes, R. D. Superiority of the minor hemisphere in commissurotomized man for the perception of part–whole relations. *Cortex,* 1971, *7,* 333–349.

Oppenheimer, R. Analogy in science. *American Psychologist,* 1956, *11,* 127–135.

Ornstein, R. E. *The psychology of consciousness.* San Francisco: Freeman, 1972.

Parsons, O. A., & Chandler, P. Electrodermal indicants of arousal in brain damage: Cross validated findings. *Psychophysiology,* 1969, *5,* 644–659.

Payne, R. W. Cognitive abnormalities. In H. J. Eysenck (Ed.), *Handbook of abnormal psychology.* New York: Basic Books, 1961.

Payne, R. W., & Hewlett, J. H. G. Thought disorder in psychotic patients. In H. J. Eysenck (Ed.), *Experiments in personality* (Vol. 2.). London: Routledge & Kegan Paul, 1960.

Payne, R. W., Matussek, P., & George, E. I. An experimental study of schizophrenic thought disorder. *Journal of Mental Science*, 1959, *105*, 627–652.

Perret, E. The left frontal lobe of man and the suppression of habitual responses in verbal categorical behavior. *Neuropsychologia*, 1974, *12*, 323–330.

Rapaport, D., Gill, M., & Schafer, R. *Diagnostic psychological testing* (Vol. 1.). Chicago: Year Book Publishers, 1945.

Rattan, R. B., & Chapman, L. J. Associative intrusions in schizophrenic verbal behavior. *Journal of Abnormal Psychology*, 1973, *82*, 169–173.

Robinson, D. A. Eye movement control in primates. *Science*, 1968, *161*, 1219–1224.

Rosenhan, D. L. On being sane in insane places. *Science*, 1973, *179*, 250–258.

Rosenthal, R., & Bigelow, L. B. Quantitative brain measurements in chronic schizophrenia. *British Journal of Psychiatry*, 1972, *121*, 259–264.

Rosenzweig, M. R. Representations of the two ears at the auditory cortex. *American Journal of Physiology*, 1951, *161*, 147–158.

Rowe, S. N. Mental changes following the removal of the right cerebral hemisphere for brain tumor. *American Journal of Psychiatry*, 1937, *94*, 604–612.

Russell, B. *Wisdom of the west*. Garden City, New York: Doubleday, 1959.

Salzinger, K. Shift in judgment of weights as a function of anchoring stimuli and instructions in early schizophrenics and normals. *Journal of Abnormal and Social Psychology*, 1957, *55*, 43–49.

Salzinger, K. An hypothesis about schizophrenic behavior. *American Journal of Psychotherapy*, 1971, *25*, 601–614. (a)

Salzinger, K. The immediacy hypothesis of schizophrenia. In H. M. Yaker, H. Osmond, & F. Cheek (Eds.), *The future of time: Man's temporal environment*. Garden City, New York: Doubleday, 1971. (b)

Salzinger, K. *Schizophrenia: Behavioral aspects*. New York: John Wiley & Sons, 1973.

Salzinger, K., Portnoy, S., Pisoni, D. B., & Feldman, R. S. The immediacy hypothesis and response produced stimuli in schizophrenic speech. *Journal of Abnormal Psychology*, 1970, *76*, 258–264.

Satz, P., Achenbach, K., Pattishall, E., & Fennell, E. Order of report, ear asymmetry and handedness in dichotic listening. *Cortex*, 1965, *1*, 377–396.

Schwartz, G. E., Davidson, R. J., & Maer, F. Right hemisphere lateralization for emotion in the human brain: Interactions with cognition. *Science*, 1975, *190*, 286–288.

Schwartz, H. G. Effect of experimental lesions of the cortex on the "psychogalvanic reflex" in the cat. *Archives of Neurology and Psychiatry*, 1937, *38*, 308–320.

Seamon, J. G., & Gazzaniga, M. S. Coding strategies and cerebral laterality effects. *Cognitive Psychology*, 1973, *5*, 249–256.

Seligman, M. E. P. *Helplessness*. San Francisco: Freeman, 1975.

Shankweiler, D., & Studdert-Kennedy, M. Identification of consonants and vowels presented to left and right ears. *Quarterly Journal of Experimental Psychology*, 1967, *19*, 59–63.

Sherrington, C. S. *Integrative action of the nervous system*. New Haven: Yale University Press, 1906.

Shimkunas, A. M. Reciprocal shifts in schizophrenic thought processes. *Journal of Abnormal Psychology*, 1970, *76*, 423–426.

Shimkunas, A. M. Conceptual deficit in schizophrenia: A reappraisal. *British Journal of Medical Psychology*, 1972, *45*, 149–157.

Shimkunas, A. M., Gynther, M. D., & Smith, K. Schizophrenic responses to the Proverbs Test: Abstract, concrete, or autistic? *Journal of Abnormal Psychology*, 1967, *72*, 128–133.

Silverman, J. The problem of attention in research and theory in schizophrenia. *Psychological Review*, 1964, *71*, 352–379.

Silverman, J. Variations in cognitive control and psychophysiological defense in the schizophrenias. *Psychosomatic Medicine,* 1967, *29,* 225–251.

Silverman, J. Stimulus intensity modulation and psychological dis-ease. *Psychopharmacologia,* 1972, *24,* 42–80.

Smith, A. Dominant and nondominant hemispherectomy. In M. Kinsbourne & W. L. Smith (Eds.), *Hemispheric disconnection and cerebral function.* Springfield, Illinois: Charles C. Thomas, 1974.

Sourek, K. *The nervous control of skin potentials in man.* Pravda: Nakladatelstvi Ceskoslovenske Akademie Ved., 1965.

Storms, L. H., & Broen, W. E., Jr. A theory of schizophrenic behavioral disorganization. *Archives of General Psychiatry,* 1969, *20,* 129–144.

Storms, L. H., & Broen, W. E., Jr. Intrusion of schizophrenics' idiosyncratic associations into their conceptual performance. *Journal of Abnormal Psychology,* 1972, *79,* 280–284.

Tunturi, A. R. A study on the pathway from the medial geniculate body to the acoustic cortex in the dog. *American Journal of Physiology,* 1946, *147,* 311–319.

Tutko, T. A., & Spence, J. T. The performance of process and reactive schizophrenics and brain injured subjects on a conceptual task. *Journal of Abnormal and Social Psychology,* 1962, *65,* 387–394.

Venables, P. H. Input dysfunction in schizophrenia. In B. A. Maher (Ed.), *Progress in experimental personality research* (Vol. 1.). New York: Academic Press, 1964.

Vigotsky, L. S. Thought in schizophrenia. *Archives of Neurology and Psychiatry,* 1934, *31,* 1063–1077.

Wada, J., & Rasmussen, T. R. Intracarotid injection of sodium amytal for the lateralization of cerebral speech dominance. *Journal of Neurosurgery,* 1960, *17,* 266–282.

Wang, G. H. *The neural control of sweating.* Madison: University of Wisconsin Press, 1964.

Wang, G. H., & Brown, V. W. Suprasegmental inhibition of an autonomic reflex. *Journal of Neurophysiology,* 1956, *19,* 564–572.

Watson, C. G. Abstract thinking deficit and autism in process and reactive schizophrenics. *Journal of Abnormal Psychology,* 1973, *82,* 399–403.

Wright, D. M. Impairment in abstract conceptualization in schizophrenia. *Psychological Bulletin,* 1975, *82,* 120–127.

Young, M. J. *Hemispheric specialization and bilateral integration of cognitive processes in schizophrenia.* Unpublished doctoral dissertation, University of Missouri, Columbia, 1974.

Zeeman, E. C. Catastrophe theory. *Scientific American,* 1976, *234,* 65–68.

8

Language and Cognition in Schizophrenia: A Review and Synthesis

Steven Schwartz

University of Texas Medical Branch

INTRODUCTION

During the past century, substantial interest has been focused on the odd communications that schizophrenics sometimes produce. The following two examples are representative:

> Then, I always liked geography. My last teacher in the subject was Professor August A. He was a man with black eyes. I also like black eyes. There are also blue and gray eyes and other sorts, too. I have heard it said that snakes have green eyes. All people have eyes. There are some, too, who are blind. These blind people are led about by a boy. It must be terrible not to be able to see. There are people who can't see and, in addition, can't hear. I know some who hear too much. One can hear too much. There are many sick people in Burgholzli; they are called patients. (Bleuler, 1950, p. 17)
>
> Oh, it's that thorazine. I forgot I had it. That's Lulubelle. This one's Jean. J-E-A-N. I'll write that down. Speeds up the metabolism. Makes your life shorter. Makes your heart bong. Tranquilizes you if you've got the metabolism I have. I have a distemper just like cats do. Cause that's what we all are, felines. (Chaika, 1974, p. 261)

After reading these samples, it is easy to see why the consensus of most writers on this subject has been that, despite the frequently lamented unreliability of the diagnosis, schizophrenic or at least disordered communications are relatively easy to recognize (Hunt & Jones, 1958).

Unfortunately, just what it is about schizophrenic verbalizations that make them so clearly deviant is not universally concordant. Ignorance in this regard is not caused by a lack of hypotheses. Many papers appear each year, and the literature has been reviewed several times in the recent past (Maher, 1972; Pavy, 1968; Seeman, 1970). Most accomplishments in this area are presented in the other chapters of this volume.

Despite a great deal of progress, an explanation for the term "schizophrenic language" remains elusive.[1] Experimental results are often inconsistent across studies and rarely, even when they are consistent, yield large differences between schizophrenics and other types of psychiatric patients. The reasons for this uncertain state-of-affairs are many. One important problem is that schizophrenia is a vague diagnostic category (see Zubin, 1961). If the subject population used in an experiment is heterogeneous, meaningful results are difficult to obtain, and conflicting results across studies are inevitable. This problem has been recognized for a long time, and most researchers are careful to specify their subject populations with as much precision as possible.

A different sort of problem, and the subject of this chapter, is inherent in the conceptual and methodological apparatus in which most of the work on schizophrenic language is conducted. It is the present thesis that the slow progress in this field is because a majority of the experiments on schizophrenic language suffer from procedural and theoretical problems so severe that their results and the conclusions drawn from their results are highly questionable. These problems are described in detail as they pertain to research on a variety of currently popular hypotheses.

Implicit in the following discussion is the belief that the function of research in any field is, or should be, the creation of and, if necessary, the elimination of theories. Thus, although the work discussed in this chapter spans the past 60 years, no attempt has been made to review everything published on schizophrenic language during that time. Case histories and anecdotal reports are excluded because of the obvious difficulty in drawing conclusions about theoretical hypotheses from uncontrolled studies, although many important hypotheses originated in such materials. Omitted also are articles which merely demonstrate what has been already shown and experiments which study some specific experimental task rather than schizophrenic language. If one's interest is in schizophrenia and not in the particular methods used to study schizophrenia, these latter experiments have little value. After these various classes of articles have been eliminated from further consideration, remaining are those that represent genuine attempts to test theoretical hypotheses and to advance knowledge of schizophrenic thought and language. The degree of success in this endeavor is the subject of the remainder of this chapter.

ASSOCIATIONISTIC APPROACHES TO THE STUDY OF SCHIZOPHRENIC LANGUAGE

The empiricist—associationistic view of how people obtain and use knowledge about the world has been the dominant theme in psychology since its popu-

---

[1] The present discussion is concerned with peculiarities in the manner that schizophrenics express their bizarre ideas. That is, the focus is not on what schizophrenics say but on how they say it.

larization by Hobbes, Locke, and their disciples. According to this view, all knowledge comes through the senses and is subject to the laws of association. Of course, other viewpoints have been propounded. The Gestalt psychologists, for example, proposed a theory based on the inherent organization of perceptual fields. Other constructive theorists, such as Bartlett, have suggested that people actually synthesize their own knowledge to a large degree. By far, most research in schizophrenic language has been conducted within the associationistic tradition, and this work is discussed first.

Verbal Conditioning of Schizophrenics

Reading the literature on verbal conditioning is a dull experience. To get an idea of this literature's flavor, imagine what would have occurred if verbal conditioners instead of physicists had heard of Sir Issac Newton's famous encounter with a falling apple. Hundreds of researchers would have been kept gainfully employed for centuries attempting to determine whether similar results could be obtained with cocoanuts, pineapples and other fruit. All of this repetition would be defended because postulating unobservable forces, such as gravity, is unscientific, therefore necessitating the demonstration of empirical relationships between stimuli and responses.

The findings of the verbal-conditioning literature can be summarized succinctly. If you have something that others want — whether it be food, money, or merely your good will — you may be able to get them to do what you want because they hope to obtain it (provided, of course, that what you want them to do is within their ability). This undramatic finding underlies a seemingly positive approach to ameliorating some schizophrenic symptoms (see, for example, Meichenbaum, 1973). As an explanation for schizophrenic language, however, it merely yields the now familiar tautology, "Schizophrenics exhibit peculiar language because such behavior is reinforced." To be fair, it should be noted that some researchers have used conditioning paradigms as vehicles to assess hypotheses drawn from other theories. These studies are discussed within the various reviews that follow.

Schizophrenic Word Associations

Although Bleuler (1950) described both syntactic and semantic errors as characteristic of schizophrenia, the research emphasis, with certain notable exceptions, largely has been on semantic irregularities. To put it simply, for over one-half of this century researchers have been trying to show that schizophrenics are confused about the meanings of words. This research has involved several different strategies. Perhaps the oldest is the word-association technique.

Nothing, except the psychiatric couch and the inkblot test, symbolizes psychiatry to the lay public more than the word-association technique. However, in the 100 years since Sir Francis Galton first started asking people to respond to a

stimulus word with the first word or words that came to mind, the word-association technique has also become the preoccupation of many experimentally
oriented psychologists. Taken as a whole, the results of these studies have been
interpreted to demonstrate that schizphrenics give fewer common word associations than nonschizophrenics. When each study is examined individually,
however, the support for this contention is unimpressive.

Perhaps the earliest and most widely cited study was reported by Kent and
Rosanoff (1910). They found that the "insane" gave more idiosyncratic associations to stimulus words than they should have according to word-association
norms. Unfortunately, their experimental group was not an acceptable group of
schizophrenics, despite the large number of its members bearing the label
"dementia praecox." Many types of psychopathology, including a large "unclas-
sified" group, were lumped together making it impossible to determine anything
about schizophrenia per se.

In a very similar study, Johnson, Weiss, and Zelhart (1964) examined the word
associations of a heterogeneous group of psychotic patients. The majority
doubtless were schizophrenic but differed from the control group in age, sex,
educational level, and because they were being hospitalized. Any or all of these
differences between the experimental and control groups may have been responsible for the finding that psychotics give fewer common word associations
than normals.

In a more sophisticated experiment, Sommer, Dewar, and Osmond (1960)
compared chronic and acute schizophrenics with normals and nonschizophrenic
psychiatric patients. Although no attempt was made to equate the groups on
educational level, all of the groups were similar in average age and number of
males and females. The nonschizophrenic patients were included as a control for,
among other things, the effects of hospitalization. (This study was apparently
unknown to Johnson et al., although it was published four years earlier.) The
authors concluded that their results indicate that schizophrenics' word-association responses are less common than those of normals and nonschizophrenic
hospitalized controls. The evidence that they provide for this conclusion is far
from compelling. An overall chi-square test performed on the median of the
scores obtained by assigning each association a value equal to its frequency of
occurrence in the Kent–Rosanoff (1910) norms was statistically significant.
Unfortunately, the authors failed to specify the locus of this significant difference. Taking frequencies of less than 100 in the Kent–Rosanoff tables, as the
authors did to indicate relatively uncommon responses, the percentage of
subjects whose median frequencies fell in this range was 74, 35, 82, and 88 for
the normal, nonschizophrenic patients, acute schizophrenics, and chronic schizophrenics respectively. We can readily see that the normal and schizophrenic
subjects scarcely differed. The nonschizophrenic patients were clearly deviant,
and their performance certainly contributed to the significant chi-square test.
Similarly, the difference among the groups in their respective zero-frequency

responses (word associations that never occurred in the Kent–Rosanoff norms) was also statistically significant. This difference, too, seems attributable to the nonschizophrenic patients who gave considerably fewer zero-frequency responses than either the normals or the schizophrenics. The authors were aware that their nonschizphrenic patients seemed to be performing better than their normals. Noting that the associations of the nonschizphrenic patients were more common than those of normals, the authors stated, "Commonness of association by itself does not indicate good mental health" (p. 667). This disclaimer notwithstanding, however, they went on to explain that the reason their schizophrenic groups gave fewer idiosyncratic responses than the Kent–Rosanoff group of "insane" patients to the same words was "either that Kent–Rosanoff selected sicker patients for their insane group or, due to tranquilizing drugs and better hospital milieu, patients are not as sick now as they used to be" (p. 668). Commonness of associations, it appears, does not indicate mental health when patients are compared with normals but does indicate mental health when patients are compared with one another. As if this was not confusing enough, the situation was further confounded because, although the authors reported in their method section that their study employed 43 normal subjects, they reported median Kent–Rosanoff scores on 46 normals. The hope that this is a typographical error is dashed when later on in the study they reported data on 45 normals (p. 668). The 23 acute schizophrenics described in the method section had dwindled to 19 and the 26 chronic schizophrenics to only 23 by the time all of the results were reported. Even if we ignore the problem of getting the number of subjects to total, the finding of this study that nonschizophrenic psychiatric patients give very common responses, while puzzling, provides no support for the hypothesis that schizophrenics give rarer word-associaton responses than normals.

The evidence in support of the notion that schizophrenics give fewer common word-association responses than others is, at least so far, hardly overwhelming. Several additional studies, however, remain to be reviewed. Several experimenters have used a technique developed by Horton, Marlowe, and Crowne (1963) to measure the commonality of college students' word associations. Horton et al. compiled their word-association norms on the basis of data obtained from a sample of college students' associations to the Kent–Rosanoff words. The appropriateness of these norms for use with schizophrenics who largely came from a noncollege population is highly questionable. Nevertheless, articles reporting studies using these norms have been published by Dokecki, Polidoro, and Cromwell (1965) and Ries and Johnson (1967). It is constructive to compare these studies with the one by Horton et al., which reported a commonality score of 14.58 for college students under relaxed conditions (the conditions used in the other studies). Dokecki, et al. reported commonality scores of 16.08 for their nonschizophrenic patient group, 15.30 for good premorbid schizophrenics, and 9.92 for poor premorbid schizophrenics respectively. Whereas the good and poor premorbid schizophrenics differed significantly, the control group of nonschizophrenic patients did not differ from the good premorbid schizophrenics. Because a higher score indicates more common word associations, it is interesting that both the nonschizophrenic and the good premorbid schizophrenic subjects gave more common responses than Horton et al.'s college students. The commonality score reported by Ries and Johnson for schizophrenics hospitalized five years or less was also higher than the score obtained by Horton, et al.'s college students.

Thus, even if one ignores that the norms used in these studies are based not on a representative sample of the population but on college students, one still finds that nonschizophrenic mental patients, good premorbid schizophrenics, and schizophrenics hospitalized for less than five years all give more common associations than college students. If the commonality of word-association responses is characteristic of a mental disorder, then an unselected group of college students must be said to suffer from this disorder more than hospitalized schizophrenics.

There are many other studies concerned in some way with the word-association responses of schizophrenics. Some of these studies used a verbal-conditioning paradigm. Frankel and Buchwald (1969), for example, were unable to condition schizophrenics to make common word associations. Although this finding was interpreted to support the notion that schizophrenics have difficulty learning to make common associations, it should be noted that Deckner and Blanton (1969) found that schizophrenics take longer to learn to choose a *weak* associate of a word than either patients or normals. When the conditioned response was a strong associate, however, schizophrenics could not be differentiated from normals. If the results of these two experiments seem contradictory, it is because they most assuredly are.

The relationship between the commonness of word associations and schizophrenia was also investigated by Fuller and Kates (1969). Using the Kent–Rosanoff norms, they were unable to find any differences between schizophrenics and normals in either the frequencies of their word associatons or in their respective tendencies to give idiosyncratic responses. Similarly, in the results of a study concerned with schizophrenics' ability to inhibit certain responses (a topic dealt with in a later section), Lisman and Cohen (1972) found that "when lumping together the associative response frequency totals . . . schizophrenics were equal to normals, giving support to the assumption that the patients sample from associative repertoires that are essentially the same as normals" (p. 187).

The discussion of studies of the word associations of schizophrenics could continue, but their results would not become clearer. Many of these other experiments are concerned with word associations under peculiar conditions (Faibash, 1961, for example) that obscure the nature of the underlying word-association hierarchies. In any case, the conclusion drawn from the studies reviewed here is both clear and simple. There is no acceptable evidence indicating that schizophrenics give rarer word-association responses than normals. Indeed, their associations may be more common than those of some college students, but this does not mean that schizophrenics are not confused about the meanings of words. Other hypotheses need to be examined.

Schizophrenia and Response Biases: Chapman's Hypotheses

After some early work on Bateson's theory of schizophrenia (Bateson, Jackson, Haley, & Weakland, 1956), Loren Chapman changed his approach and proposed a new theory to account for schizophrenics' alleged confusion about the meanings of words (Chapman & Chapman, 1965; Chapman, Chapman, & Miller, 1964). According to this theory, "a person has, to any one word, a series of meaning responses" (Chapman & Chapman, 1965, p. 139). These responses form hierarchies from strong to weak, and schizophrenics' hierarchies are assumed to be similar to those of normals. They differ only in response biases. That is, schizophrenics tend to rely on a word's strongest denotative meaning to the relative exclusion of its other, weaker meanings. Thus, in judging the meaning of a word, normals are influenced by the context in which a word appears, whereas schizophrenics are much more influenced by the word's strongest meaning irrespective of the context. Frequently, the task used to investigate this hypothesis has involved a kind of multiple-choice vocabulary quiz. The following is an example of an item from such a quiz taken from Chapman et al. (1964):

When the farmer bought a herd of cattle, he needed a new pen.
This means: A. He needed a new writing implement.
              B. He needed a new fenced enclosure.
              C. He needed a new pick-up truck.

The word "pen" was previously scaled for meaning-response strength, and its strongest meaning was determined to be "writing implement." In this example schizophrenics are expected to choose response "A" more often than normals who would know that a weaker response, "B," is correct.

Doing research with schizophrenics is a difficult undertaking, and the experiments conducted by Chapman and his associates are models of care. In each study, a great deal of care was devoted to controlling extraneous variables. When more than one test was used, both were determined to be equally reliable and to possess similar means and variances of item difficulty (see Chapman & Chapman, 1973, for a discussion of how important this can be).

A major difficulty in using any sort of multiple-choice procedure that has not been given sufficient attention is the omnipresent possibility that a subject may simply respond randomly and by chance alone choose the correct alternative. Because of this possibility, the data obtained from multiple-choice tests generally have been subject to a type of "correction for guessing." In the studies conducted by Chapman and his colleagues, this correction has involved the subtraction of some or all of the irrelevant choices from the number of high and low meaning choices respectively. Implicit in this correction procedure is the notion that schizophrenics either attend to the task or, because they "might be uncooperative or have difficulty taking the test,... [they] might mark randomly" (Chapman & Chapman, 1965, p. 137). Because such a random response should result in the choice of an irrelevant meaning as often as one of the others, subtracting the number of irrelevant choices should, they assert, eliminate the effects of random responding. This correction procedure is neither mathematically nor logically acceptable.

There are two basic problems with the correction procedure. First, it ignores the mathematical probability of making a correct choice (choosing the appropriate meaning) by chance, and second, it does not take into consideration the possibility that a subject may have partial information about the correct response. That is, a subject may not be certain about the correct meaning of a particular word but may be able to exclude the irrelevant meaning.

The probability of making a correct choice in a 3-alternative multiple-choice situation by chance is one-third (.33). An illiterate subject responding in a totally unplanned fashion can be expected to do that well. To demonstrate that a subject is choosing his answers according to a rationale, his score should differ from the one he would obtain by chance. Unfortunately, one cannot easily determine what a "chance" score is in the multiple-choice situation without, at the same time, considering the second problem. That is, a subject may have partial information about the correct response and consequently may eliminate some of the alternatives and select from those remaining. It will be shown that irrelevant choices are rarely chosen by normals or by schizophrenics. If schizophrenics are less familiar with the meanings of words than control subjects, they can be expected to merely guess between the remaining alternatives more often than the controls and, therefore, they are more likely to select the wrong meaning.

Although many of the experiments using multiple-choice tests presented only corrected scores, several studies either did not employ a correction procedure or presented sufficient information to permit the reconstruction of the raw, uncorrected data. The results of one such study by Boland and Chapman (1971) indicate that normals and schizophrenics, as expected, rarely choose the irrelevant response. In this case the task was a 3-alternative multiple-choice vocabulary test in which the choices were either: correct; an associative distractor; or an irrelevant meaning.[2] Normals chose the irrelevant response only 1% of the time

---

[2] This study and several of the ones that follow did not use high and low meanings as the responses but used correct meanings and associative distractors. The prediction in these studies (schizophrenics will be more likely to choose the associative distractor than non-schizophrenics) is derived from Chapman's hypotheses as already described.

and schizophrenics only 6% of the time. On the other hand, normals selected the correct meaning 74% of the time and the incorrect "associative-distractor" for 25% of the items. For schizophrenics the relevant percentages were 42 and 52, respectively. These results do not require the postulation of either response biases or associative distraction for their explanation. They may simply be caused by schizophrenics knowing less about the meanings of words than normals. Thus, they may reject totally irrelevant choices and simply guess between the remaining alternatives.

A similar explanation can be advanced to explain the results reported by Rattan and Chapman (1973). In that study, two multiple-choice vocabulary tests were presented to three experimental groups (schizophrenics, firemen and prison inmates). One of the tests contained distractor items associated with the word to be defined among the alternatives, and the other test did not. Great care was taken to ensure that the two tests were equally reliable and that the mean and variance of item difficulty was equal for the two tests. It was found that schizophrenics performed more poorly on the with-associates tests than on the no-associates test. Firemen and prison inmates – the latter group was included as a check for the possible effects of education, I.Q. and institutionalization – did not show this difference. This finding was interpreted to support the hypothesis that schizophrenics are more susceptible to "associative distraction" than non-schizophrenics. Once again, this finding was thought to be independent of any general intellectual deficit in schizophrenics. This conclusion warrants closer examination.

Table 8.1 contains the data on the number of correct and incorrect answers for each type of subject on the with-associates test. As can be seen, firemen chose the associate on 24% of their incorrect answers, almost precisely what would be expected by chance because this test used four alternatives. Schizophrenics and inmates, however, chose the associate on 58% and 49% of their incorrect answers respectively. Both schizophrenics and inmates, then, chose the associate far in excess of what would be predicted if they were merely guessing from among

TABLE 8.1
Means of Test Accuracy and Choice of Associates on the
With-Associates Vocabulary Test

Mean scores	Experimental Group		
	Firemen	Inmates	Schizophrenics
Number correct	39.92	27.89	22.43
Number wrong	20.08	32.11	37.57
Number of associates	4.75	15.85	21.79
Percentage of associates	24%	49%	58%

Note.–Adapted from Rattan & Chapman (1973).

four choices. The difference between their respective tendencies to choose the associate was very small. Thus, we are forced to conclude that if schizophrenics suffer from "associative distraction," so, too, do inmates. Again, why postulate distraction? Both schizophrenics and inmates were operating at lower intellectual levels than firemen. It is quite possible, therefore, that both groups were less familiar with the meanings of words than firemen. They were able to eliminate some of the least likely alternatives and then guess from those remaining. In still another study of associative distraction, Roberts and Schuham (1974) compared schizophrenics with alcoholics on three multiple-choice vocabulary tests. Each test contained correct and neutral choices and either a high, medium or low strength associative-distractor choice. They found that schizophrenics chose the associative distractor more often than alcoholics at each level of associative-distractor strength. A plot of the relative number of associative-distractor choices at each level of distractor strength approximated, for schizophrenics, a straight line function. This last finding was interpreted to support Chapman's theory because Roberts and Schuham asserted that this straight line function reflects a "hierarchy of errors" that schizophrenics possess. (According to Chapman's hypothesis, schizophrenics should have the same hierarchy of errors as normals.) Curiously, the error function for the alcoholics was *not* a straight line at all. This indicates that if Roberts and Schuham were consistent, alcoholics would not have a hierarchy of response errors. Such an assertion seems dubious. Quite possibly, a ceiling effect was responsible for the alcoholics' flat error curve inasmuch as they averaged about 96% correct and consequently made very few associative-distractor choices at any level of strength. Nevertheless, the failure to find a straight line function for alcoholics, although one was found for schizophrenics, is hardly proof that normals and schizophrenics "have the same hierarchy of errors" (p. 426).

Actually, the entire procedure of plotting the number of errors for each test is questionable as a test of Chapman's hypothesis. To illustrate the essential vacuity of the procedure as a test of anything, consider what happens when the number of choices of neutral "fillers" at each level of associative strength, instead of associates, is plotted. Because the authors reported both corrected and uncorrected scores, the number of neutral choices can be easily obtained. The curve of the number of neutral choices at each level of associative strength appears in Figure 8.1.

As can be seen, a plot of neutral responses also yields a straight line function for schizophrenics, although the neutral words are unrelated to the stimulus words. Surely, this is not evidence for a hierarchy of neutral responses (whatever that may be). Rather, it seems that schizophrenics in this study made more errors than alcoholics, and their pattern of performance seems to suggest that they were more easily confused by the presence of associative distractors as choices. The experiment provides no evidence, however, concerning the similarity of schizophrenic and nonschizophrenic response hierarchies.

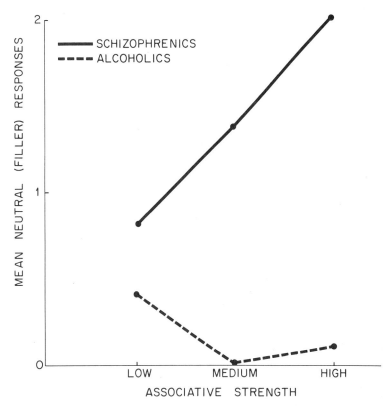

FIG. 8.1   Choices of neutral (filler) alternatives at each level of distractor strength in the Roberts and Schuham experiment.

A substantial number of additional experiments not discussed here have used the multiple-choice procedure. The vast preponderance of this work agrees with the idea that schizophrenics are easily distracted by words that appear to be associatively related to the target word and that they often will respond with a word's strongest meaning irrespective of the context. Unfortunately, the influence of guessing on these tasks is almost impossible to measure because subjects often have partial knowledge about the correct response. Although the weight of evidence seems to favor Chapman's theory, the effects are usually small, and at least two attempts to replicate Chapman et al.'s (1964) results have failed (Neuringer, Fiske, & Goldstein, 1969; Neuringer, Fiske, Schmidt, & Goldstein, 1972). A hypothesis that cannot yet be discounted is that such different findings are simply caused by random fluctuations in the guessing rate of schizophrenics.

A procedure that avoids many of the problems inherent in the multiple-choice test was used by Mourer (1973) to investigate Chapman's theory. One member of a word pair that shared a strong meaning response or of a word pair that shared a weak meaning response (a response low on their respective hierarchies) was presented to normal and schizophrenic subjects in a variant of the method introduced by Shepard and Teghtsoonian (1961). After twice viewing an original list of words, the subjects viewed additional lists in which some of the items were original list words, and some were new words. The subjects were required to respond to each word by pushing a button marked "yes" (the word appeared earlier) or "no" (the word did not appear earlier). Some of the new words were the other members of the "pair." That is, 8 words shared a strong meaning response with the original list words, 8 words shared a weak meaning, and 16 words were unrelated to those on the original list.

In addition to meaning response strength, pairs formed of each original list word and all other words were rated for meaning similarity on a 5-point scale ranging from (1) "They are almost alike in meaning," to (5) "They are not at all alike in meaning." Because meaning response strength was considered independent of meaning similarity, it was possible to divide word pairs into four groups: high meaning response strength, high similarity; high meaning response strength, low similarity; low meaning response strength, high similarity; and low meaning response strength, low similarity.

In accord with his predications, Mourer reported that schizophrenics responded "yes" more frequently than normals to new words sharing a strong meaning response with original list words. Schizophrenics did not differ from normals in the number of falsely recognized weak meaning response words. This finding made inevitable the second predicted result, a greater difference between the number of falsely recognized strong and weak meaning response words among schizophrenics than among normals. Although new words of similar meaning to the old words were falsely recognized more frequenlty than low-similarity words, schizophrenics and normals did not differ in this respect. Thus, only the number of falsely recognized strong meaning response words differentiated schizophrenics from normals. The validity of this finding, however, depends once again on a "correction procedure" of dubious validity. In this case, one-half of the number of falsely recognized control words were subtracted from the number of falsely recognized strong and weak meaning response words. Once again, the stated purpose of this procedure was to "distribute potential acquiescence response bias and random error across the generalization [test] words and the control words" (p. 252). Implicit in this procedure is the notion that, on some word presentation trials, control words could not be clearly recognized as new words. On such trials the subject (operating under the influence of his experience, response sets, and so forth) is thought to guess "yes" at some constant rate, $P(Y|C)$, the probability of responding "yes" to a control word. When the words that are not clearly recognized as new are either strong or weak meaning response "test" words, the subject is thought to guess "yes" at some rate equal to the rate for the control words plus some increment reflecting the contribution of shared meaning response strength, $P(Y|T)$. The correction formula that Mourer used can be easily derived from these assumptions, although his reason for subtracting only one-half of the false recognition rate for control words is somewhat obscure. The correction formula is:

$$P'(Y|T) = P(Y|T) - \tfrac{1}{2}P(Y|C) \tag{1}$$

(where $P'(Y|T)$ represents the "true" guessing rate for test words). It should be clear that this correction procedure is nothing more than a hoary version of the primitive correction-for-guessing procedures once employed in psychophysical research. There is a difference between the typical psychophysical situation and the present one. In the former, the correction is applied to the hit rate, the number of correct responses, whereas Mourer used one guessing rate to correct another. The deficiencies with the procedure and the assumptions upon which it is based, however, are the same in both situations and can be found in any basic experimental text (see Kling & Riggs, 1971, for example). In essence, the problem lies with the assumption that the relationship between $P(Y|T)$ and $P(Y|C)$ is linear. This assumption has frequently been shown to be false (for example, see Swets, 1964) and seems no longer tenable.

Put simply, the notion that a cut-off point exists, above which the subject responds "yes" as a function of meaning response strength and below which he responds by guessing, is unsupported and probably invalid. Rather, it is likely that the subject has no fixed criterion for responding "yes" to test words but employs a variable criterion which changes depending on such factors as stimulus probability and the rewards or costs of "yes" responses.

To get a valid estimate of any bias toward responding "yes" to either strong or weak response words, the hit rate, $P(Y|O)$, the probability of responding "yes" to words that did appear on the original list, needs to be calculated. Then, the criterion for test words (βT) can be estimated by:

$$\beta T = \frac{P(Y|O)}{P(Y|T)} \tag{2}$$

and the criterion for control words may be estimated by:

$$\beta C = \frac{P(Y|O)}{P(Y|C)} \tag{3}$$

Using these formulae[3], the criteria employed by schizophrenics and normals for the various types of words can be calculated and compared to ascertain

---

[3] An alternative set of equations based on a different theory but yielding similar results can be found in R. D. Luce, *Individual choice behavior*. New York: John Wiley & Sons, 1959.

whether any extraordinary bias exists. The procedure is similar to the one employed successfully by investigators of signal detection theory and has also been employed in the false recognition situation considered here (for example, Donaldson & Murdock, 1968).

Mourer's use of an improper correction procedure is further complicated because on more than one occasion the corrected score for weak similarity words was zero or negative. Using the correction formula employed by Mourer, negative corrected scores can be obtained only when the number of "yes" responses to control words exceeds double the number of "yes" responses to low meaning words ($[\frac{1}{2}P(Y|C) - P(Y|T)] < 0$). Negative scores, then, can be conservatively assumed to indicate that some control words and some weak meaning response words do not differ in their meaning response strength. The appropriate index of falsely recognized weak meaning response strength words is some combination of the "yes" responses to control and weak meaning response words, but it is impossible to tell what that combination is. Mourer's use of an improper correction procedure and the arbitrary definition of some words as controls that do not differ from the experimental words in meaning response strength obscured the actual false recognition rate. Thus, the significant difference between the false recognition rates for strong and weak meaning response words found among schizophrenics is therefore called into question. Mourer's procedure, however, unlike the multiple-choice tasks (when informed guessing is likely), does easily lend itself to the use of the statistics derived from decision theory and is thus a potentially powerful paradigm for the assessment of predictions derived from Chapman's theory.

In a somewhat different approach, Deckner and Blanton (1969) reported two experiments designed to test the assumptions of Chapman's theory. One of the experiments, described earlier, indicates that schizophrenics had a difficult time learning to choose weak rather than strong associates. Others, as we have seen, reported the opposite finding. The other experiment used a cloze procedure in which every fifth, eighth or tenth word in a third-grade primer was omitted. Schizophrenics and nonschizophrenic patient controls were asked to determine an appropriate word to replace the one omitted. If schizophrenics had a high meaning response bias, the authors argued that it would be revealed in a group-by-number-of-words-between-deletions interaction. That is, with greater context (more words between deletions) the nonschizophrenics should be better able to guess the appropriate word, whereas schizophrenics should be unaffected by changes in context. Despite the finding that schizophrenics performed poorly at every level of context, there was no interaction obtained between groups and context. Thus, this experiment does not provide support for the notion that schizophrenics are less influenced by context than nonschizophrenics.

To recapitulate, the research performed by Chapman, his students, and his colleagues has consistently supported the hypothesis that schizophrenics tend to be dominated by high meaning responses and subject to associative distraction. On the other hand, several studies performed by others do not support this theory. Moreover, the statistically significant differences found between schizophrenics and others are rarely large. The correction for guessing (random responding) used in most experiments is not a valid procedure for eliminating alternative explanations based on "informed" guessing and partial knowledge. Some experimental paradigms, such as Mourer's for instance, have the potential for correcting the deficiencies of earlier work. With present knowledge, it can only be said that schizophrenics may have a bias toward strong meaning responses. It is certainly not a very strong bias, and it has not been unequivocally demonstrated.

Schizophrenic Confusion About the Meaning of Words: Conclusions

The articles reviewed in the preceding sections share in common a focus on the single word. After reviewing the literature on verbal conditioning, word associations, and response biases, little convincing evidence has been seen that schizophrenics are fond of rare word associations or that they are insensitive to the context in which words occur. They do seem to be less knowledgeable about word meanings, but this is also characteristic of nonschizophrenic hospitalized patients and prison inmates. Although schizophrenics may have a small tendency to respond with a word's strongest meaning, this tendency has not been unequivocally demonstrated.

Even if the correction procedures used by Mourer and the other investigators were without any difficulties, a question about the value of a hypothesis based on meaning responses to words for an understanding of language would still exist. This problem stems from the focus on a single word. In linguistics the pronunciation of a word, its meaning, and its syntactic role only can be determined by a prior general analysis of the sentence in which it appears. Thus, normatively scaling individual words is like studying special (one-word) sentences. Substantial evidence supports the fact that single words or randomized sequences of words are treated very differently from words organized into sentences. The apparent duration of sentences follows a power function lower than randomized sequences, and sentences are also much easier to remember. Evidence also shows that groups of randomly ordered words are treated differently from sentences by the nervous system and may not be processed by the same cerebral hemisphere (see Bever, 1968). In addition, the comprehension process implicit in Chapman's theory, that each word presented to a subject elicits a strong meaning response unless the context demands some weaker meaning, is highly unlikely because of the rapidity with which language is comprehended. The production and comprehension of language is much faster than the time necessary to transmit the number of signals from ear to brain that would be required by a theory such as Chapman's (see Lashley, 1951; Lenneberg, 1967).

Perhaps the biggest drawback in studying individual words is that connected discourse is more complex than the sum of the meanings of its constituent words. The order of words is as important in determining their meaning (a "baby buggy" is not the same as a "buggy baby") as are the rules of syntax. Even when all of the words in a phrase are clear and possess strong meaning responses, the meaning of the utterance still depends on how the various words fit together. Thus, the sentence, "The two men promised me to kill each other" is a meaningful one in English, whereas the sentence, "The two men persuaded me to kill each other" is ambiguous.[4] Clearly, the order of words and the grammar of English sentences need to be considered in understanding language. Any theory based solely on the meanings of words will be unable to account for the inability to interpret the second sentence and is consequently doomed to be inadequate as an account of either normal or disordered language.

Communicability Deficit in Schizophrenia

A somewhat different approach to the study of schizophrenic language but, as we will see, one still heavily influenced by associationistic ideas has as its basis the hypothesis that schizophrenics do not communicate effectively because of a deficit in the organization of what they say. The early work on this hypothesis consisted of word-frequency counts, type-token rations and the like. Although schizophrenics were found to differ from others on a number of dimensions (see Maher, 1966, for a thorough review), this early work did not give rise to much theory, and modern workers have, with few exceptions, turned to other methods.

The work of the most prolific researchers in the area of communication deficit, Cohen and Salzinger, is described in their respective contributions to this volume. Like Chapman, both are scrupulously careful scientists whose techniques can serve as models of experimental work.

Cohen's model of what he calls the "communication process" is derived from a specific experimental task, although several different experimental procedures have been used to assess hypotheses derived from the model. In the prototypical task, schizophrenics and nonschizophrenics are required to serve either as *speakers* or *listeners*. The speaker's task is to give a clue or clues to the listener that allow the listener to choose the one of a pair of stimuli that has been designated by the experimenter as the "referent." According to Cohen, communication in this situation is a two-stage process. The first stage is a sampling stage in which a clue or series of clues is drawn from the speaker's repertoire of clues associated with the referent. This stage is basically associationistic. The probability of any

---

[4] These sentences are taken from Chomsky, N., Psychology and ideology. In N. Chomsky, *For reasons of state.* New York: Vantage Books, 1973.

given clue being sampled is, according to Cohen, proportionate to its associative strength to the referent. The first, sampling, stage is followed by a self-editing or "comparison" stage during which the speaker decides on the adequacy of the sampled clue by comparing its likelihood of eliciting the nonreferent to the likelihood of its eliciting the desired referent from the listener. The outcome of this second stage is either a decision to emit the sampled clue (if the referent is the more likely response) or to resample and repeat the sampling–comparison cycle. The listener who receives the speaker's clue is thought to behave similarly to the speaker in the comparison stage. That is, the listener does not sample clues, but he does compare the clue given to him by the speaker with the two stimuli and attempts to choose the one more highly associated with the clue as his response. Although this model has been operationally defined in terms of a specific task, it is meant to be more widely applicable to communication in general.

An ingenious study by Cohen and Camhi (1967) found schizophrenics to perform poorly in the referential communication task when they played the speaker's role (that is, when they were giving clues) but to do as well as normals when they were in the listener's role (receiving clues). Because the speaker's task required a two-stage process, and the listener's task required only one (the comparison stage), these findings can be interpreted to implicate the sampling stage as being responsible for the schizophrenics' poor performance in the speaker's role. Cohen and Camhi were reluctant to make this interpretation. They pointed out that schizophrenics have similar association hierarchies to normals (an assertion that is clearly in agreement with the preceding discussion of word associations) and that instead of ineffective sampling:

> Faulty comparison in the speaker role, . . . may reflect deficiencies in the ability of schizophrenics to *integrate* the comparison stage with the sampling stage of the two-stage speaker process. Thus, comparison combined with sampling [speaker comparison] may be defective, even though comparison alone [listener comparison] remains relatively unimpaired. (p. 225, emphasis added)

Precisely what is involved in integrating the comparison stage with the sampling stage is not specified.

In a later study, Nachmani and Cohen (1969) sought to assess some hypotheses drawn from the communication model using a different set of experimental tasks. In this study, schizophrenics were compared with nonschizophrenics in memory for words using both a recognition and a recall test. Schizophrenics did approximately as well as nonschizophrenics when memory was tested by recognition but performed poorly when memory was tested by recall. Once again, because recall requires two stages, a sampling (retrieval) stage and an editing stage, whereas recognition requires only the editing stage, these results can be interpreted to implicate the sampling stage as the locus of the schizophrenics' deficit. Nachmani and Cohen, however, were just as reluctant as Cohen and

Camhi to use this explanation. Once again, the integration of the comparison and sampling stages was postulated to be the source of the schizophrenics' problem.

In addition to the number of words correctly recalled or recognized, Nachmani and Cohen also reported "overexclusion" and "overinclusion" scores which, they asserted, largely support their interpretation of the memory test results. Schizophrenics recalled fewer words than nonschizophrenics (overexclusion) and produced many new words semantically related to the originally presented words but not actually presented during learning (overinclusion) than nonschizophrenics. Although these results can just as easily be assigned to faulty sampling as well as to faulty integration between sampling and editing, it is interesting to note that schizophrenics were also overinclusive on the recognition test. That is, they indicated that words semantically related to the original words were actually among the original words. Because presumably only an editing but not a sampling process is involved in recognition, this finding is inexplicable within Cohen's communication model. Nevertheless, this important finding will be referred to later in this chapter.

Noting correctly that the typical procedures described thus far do not allow a clear separation of the sampling and editing stages of the communication process, Smith (1970) sought to rectify this situation by repeating Cohen and Camhi's experiment with an additional experimental condition. In this condition speakers, rather than generate their own clues, were required to choose the better of two clues provided by the experimenter. Smith's results are confusing. The part of his experiment that repeated Cohen and Camhi's experiment failed to find a significant difference between schizophrenics and normals in the speaker's role. Thus, Smith failed to replicate Cohen and Camhi's most important finding, although he used a more powerful statistical test (one-tailed test, $p > .08$).[5] Moreover, schizophrenics did not differ from normals in the commonality of their clues, in their average number of different word types, or in their number of unique speaker-generated clues. All of these differences are significant in the Cohen and Camhi study.

When subjects were required to choose the better of two experimenter-provided clues, the predicted results were obtained. Schizophrenics did not choose the better clue as often as normals. What does this finding mean for Cohen's model of the communication process? When schizophrenics were required to generate their own clues (sampling stage) and choose one (editing stage), they performed as well as normals. On the other hand, when they were given clues by the experimenter, and they could merely compare them (editing stage), they did poorly when compared to normals. Smith concludes that these

---

[5] Smith proceeds, for unknown reasons, to discuss his results as though they had met the usual criteria for statistical significance.

results are caused by a schizophrenic speaker deficit in the comparison stage. This conclusion is not only inconsistent with the one reached by Cohen and his colleagues, who feel it is the integration of the two stages that is important, but it is also illogical. Because the two stages of the communication process are sequential, it is impossible to see how a task that requires only stage 2 leads to poor performance when one that requires both stages does not show any deficit. If the deficit does lie solely in stage 2, how can a task that requires both stages be superior to a task that requires only one? Smith, in further analyses of his results, shows that when the experimenter provided the clues, schizophrenics had a particularly difficult time choosing the better clue when such a choice required multiple comparisons of the clue with the referent and nonreferent stimulus words. The possibility that schizophrenics lack the sustained attentional ability required for these comparisons is a viable explanation for their poor performance.

In the Lisman and Cohen (1972) study mentioned in an earlier discussion, schizophrenics and normals were asked, in addition to giving free word associations, to give associations that they felt few others would give to the stimulus words. Under normal conditions, schizophrenics gave less common word associations than normals. The "idiosyncratic" instructions, however, elicited more common associations from the schizophrenics than from the normals. Lisman and Cohen asserted that these findings indicate that the schizophrenics are deficient in their ability to inhibit associations inappropriate to the task, whether common or unusual. The evidence from the idiosyncratic condition certainly seems to implicate some decision-making process, but a "common" condition in which subjects were asked to respond with what they thought to be the most common associate would have been a helpful addition. Thus, it is not clear why these results by themselves cannot be attributed as easily to faulty response hierarchies as to a deficit in editing.

In summarizing the discussion to this point, it is safe to say that, although Cohen and his colleagues have demonstrated quite clearly that schizophrenics do poorly in the referent communication situation, their early model does not seem adequate to deal with the various experimental results. Realizing that the model needed elaboration, Cohen, Nachmani, and Rosenberg (1974), on the basis of additional evidence, proposed a "perseverative-chaining" model of referent communication, which has as its basis the idea that schizophrenics sample each clue they generate from a "repertoire of associations to the immediately preceding response [clue] rather than the referent" (p. 11). According to this view, the schizophrenic is thought to say each clue aloud although he has rejected it. The schizophrenic then continues this process until a response "passes the probabilistic self-editing" stage, and he stops talking. This new approach does not entirely clarify the discrepancies in findings that have been indicated. However, because this new approach is virtually identical in its implications and predictions to the theory proposed by Salzinger, it is appropriate to turn to his work.

Salzinger, like Cohen, has tried to go beyond the empirical fact that schizophrenics produce verbalizations often hard to understand, to determine the underlying schizophrenic deficit. Using the cloze procedure, Salzinger, Portnoy, and Feldman (1963) found that normal judges were less able to guess the words omitted from the first 100 words of a schizophrenic's transcript than those omitted from the transcripts of nonschizophrenic patients. The judges' performances were even worse for the second 100 words of the schizophrenic transcript, although for nonschizophrenic transcripts the judges actually improved during the second hundred words. Further experimentation (see the chapter by Salzinger, Portnoy, and Feldman in this volume) indicated that judges were able to guess words omitted from schizophrenic transcripts as well as those omitted from the transcripts of nonschizophrenics when they were provided with only a few words of context (for example, the four words surrounding the omitted word). When lengthy context was provided (14 surrounding words), it was easier to guess the words omitted from the nonschizophrenic than those omitted from the schizophrenic transcripts. These findings were interpreted to support an "immediacy hypothesis" that is very similar to Cohen's perseverative-chaining model. From Salzinger's viewpoint, schizophrenic behavior, verbal or otherwise, is primarily controlled by stimuli immediate in the environment. Thus, for schizophrenics small amounts of context afford high guessability because they represent the immediate stimuli which control responding. Large amounts of context do not measurably improve the ability to guess words omitted from schizophrenics' transcripts because schizophrenics are not responding to stimuli remote in time.

Surely, some of these findings can be attributed to a "floor" effect. At low levels of context it is indeed difficult to guess any of the omitted words correctly irrespective of whose protocol they come from. Perhaps most striking is the data for what Salzinger calls "function" words (conjunctions mostly, but some prepositions) in which schizophrenic speech was actually more predictable than nonschizophrenic at low levels of context but less predictable when considerable context was provided. Because conjunctions occur at those points in a sentence that are most vulnerable to distraction or shifts in attention, there is a strong possibility that Salzinger's findings are to a large extent a reflection of the inability to sustain attention.

It is difficult to quarrel with any of Salzinger's findings or to find fault with his methods. However, conceptual difficulties exist in both his position and the one taken by Cohen and his colleagues. Because their work is intended to apply to schizophrenic communications in general (beyond the confines of a particular experimental task), it is appropriate to examine Cohen's and Salzinger's theories with this larger goal in mind. Cohen's work presents an obvious problem in this regard because referential communication as he defines it is not communication in general. Thus, even if their model was clear about what it means to integrate sampling with editing, the many significant utterances which have no definite referent would be ignored. At a much deeper and a considerably more important level, both Cohen's and Salzinger's views encounter problems because of their basically associationistic nature.

According to Salzinger, the "speaker in emitting his words must react not only to the word that he has just uttered but to the last two words, the last three words, usually to many words uttered previously" (Salzinger, Portnoy, & Feldman, 1966, p. 172). It is interesting that Salzinger chooses words to be the building blocks of language but quite understandable because smaller linguistic elements (morphemes, for example) have very few associative relationships, and the specific neuromuscular responses necessary to produce speech (movements of the tongue and jaw, for instance) possess no associative relationship at all. In fact, for muscular movements at least, proceeding sounds in a sequence are more important determinants of how the muscular apparatus will be arranged than preceding sounds (Hörmann, 1971).

Unfortunately, as already discussed, the meaning of a sentence does not derive from summing the meanings of its constituent words and, therefore, any model based on the single word as the fundamental unit of language is inadequate. It can also be demonstrated that the order of words in a sentence cannot be derived from a knowledge of the various strengths of associations existing among its constituent words (Miller & Chomsky, 1963). Even when the inadequacies of the purely associationistic model of natural language are compensated for by the introduction of a Markov model, remaining is the difficulty that such models require astronomical learning capacities of anyone learning to speak English. The problem has been illustrated quite well by Miller & Chomsky who presented the following sentence as an example of the amount of learning a finite-state model of language involves:

> The people who called and wanted to rent your house when you go away next year are from California.

In this sentence, the second and seventeenth words are related, and an appreciation of their relationship is crucial to an understanding of the sentence. The finite-state model (implicit in both Salzinger's and Cohen's theories but never explicated) would have to conclude that the speaker of this sentence learned a unique set of transitions, over 15 words and 15 grammatical category changes. Miller and Chomsky have conservatively estimated that learning to speak English by learning such sequences of transitions between words would require that we learn "the value of 10^9 parameters [transitions] in a childhood lasting only 10^8 seconds" (p. 430).

Even if neurologically possible (which is doubtful according to Lashley, 1951), a finite-based model of language based on the associations between words would require an astronomical amount of learning and then could still never account for the infinite number of possible sentences or the number of words that could be included in a sentence. Indeed, the nonfinite nature of language is one of its most important attributes. Thus, although both Cohen and Salzinger pay greater attention to the structure of language than those experimenters who focus solely on the single word, their associationistic approach is still inadequate to deal with the complexities of natural language.

Associationistic Approaches to Schizophrenic Language: Summary and Conclusions

Associationistic approaches to the study of schizophrenic language for many years have claimed the allegiance of a large number of talented investigators. Unfortunately, as a whole, these studies have not given a clear picture of what is wrong with schizophrenics. Beginning with verbal-conditioning experiments, which were not reviewed because they rarely are designed to improve our theoretical understanding of schizophrenia, the focus shifted to studies of word associations. Contrary to widely held beliefs, schizophrenics do not give rarer word associations than normals. If their associations differ at all, the differnece appears to be in the direction of being more common rather than less common. While this conclusion seems consistent with Chapman's hypothesis, his work goes beyond this point in asserting that schizophrenics tend to give the strongest meaning response irrespective of the context. (They have response biases in favor of the strong meaning.) To the extent that these response biases affect self-editing, and they should, Chapman's hypothesis is congenial with Cohen's who, in addition, locates the problem in the integration of the sampling and comparison stages of a two-stage referential communication process. However, Cohen's results appear murky on this point. Chapman's correction procedures make many of the findings reported in favor of his hypothesis problematic, and almost all of the work done on hypotheses derived from Cohen's theory is open, as we have seen, to alternative explanations. Perhaps most important is the single-word approach of many of the researchers which is only tangentially related to natural language. Although Cohen and Salzinger seem aware of this, their associationistic approach is also inadequate to account for the complexities of language as ordinarily spoken.

It is difficult to feel that the associationistic approach has much value as a theory of language. Although there is no doubt that work in this tradition will continue and that many of the methodological and conceptual difficulties described here will be overcome, the future looks doubtful insofar as further theoretical advances are concerned. This is not to say that the phenomena studied by these researchers are unimportant. Certainly, the findings of Chapman, Cohen, and Salzinger require explanation. An idea of where such explanations can be expected to come from in the future is the subject of the remainder of this chapter.

NONASSOCIATIVE APPROACHES TO SCHIZOPHRENIC LANGUAGE

It is a difficult task to categorize the various nonassociative approaches to the study of schizophrenic language. Many of the articles grouped together in this section bear little resemblance to one another and share in common only their nonassociative stance. Much of this work has been performed not by psychologists but by psychiatrists, other students of mental illness, and linguists. To some experimental psychologists, nonassociationistic approaches have been an anathema and have been viewed as loose minded and "clinical." Recent advances in cognitive psychology have provided new methodologies and a powerful framework for research in language and verbal behavior, which is beginning to change the attitudes of most experimentalists. Indeed, a number of experimental psychologists have begun to apply these methods to the study of schizophrenia. Before I discuss this work, it is important that it is put in a clear historical and conceptual perspective.

The Decline and Rise of Cognitive Psychology

Despite the fact that the study of cognitive processes was the dominant focus of the early experimental psychologists (James, 1890) for most of this century, experimental psychologists turned away from cognitive phenomena. Many succumbed to the influence of Watson's brand of behaviorism and his strongly held conviction that mental phenomena were not a proper area for experimentalists to study. Many of the criticisms that Watson and his followers offered to the cognitive psychologists of their day were well taken. Much of the work on cognition was vague, unreliable and inconsistent. Moreover, much of what was called cognitive psychology consisted of mere armchair speculations about the contents of the mind rather than the controlled experimentation favored by the behaviorists. The speculative, cognitive approach, when applied to schizophrenic language, rarely resulted in empirically verifiable theories. Although no one can doubt that armchair speculations often are a rich source of ideas, it is easy to see why experimentalists might be unenthusiastic about such an approach to psychology.

It should be noted that even during Watson's time cognitive psychologists of an experimental bent, such as Bartlett, Piaget, and the various members of the Gestalt school, were busily working to reveal the limitations of Watson's views. There were also numerous attempts in America to extend the theoretical work on animal learning to thinking and problem solving in man. The influence of cognitively oriented psychologists such as Tolman challenged the prevalent view that learning is a passive process in which events occur in the presence of a learner and simply leave a record of their occurrence. Instead, all of the various cognitive theorists converged in the belief that learning is an active process and that the learner constantly devises strategies and develops cognitive structures during the process of learning.

Although cognitive research and theorizing existed throughout the Watsonian era, it was not until the introduction of cybernetic theory, information theory and the general availability of large digital computers that the field of cognitive psychology substantially began to grow. Books by Broadbent (1958); Miller, Galanter, and Pribram (1960); and Neisser (1967) marked important steps in the legitimizing of modern cognitive psychology. Although each book was heavily influenced by the then available technology, each contributed to the modern view of man as an information processor. At present, the study of cognition is more intense than at any previous time in the history of experimental psychology. With the recognition that complex internal processing is involved in most learning, an expansion of cognitive psychology's subject matter has occurred. Not only are the major academic skills included under cognition but also much that was classically considered a part of perception.

Modern studies of cognition based on an information-processing viewpoint have attempted to develop working models of the thinking processes. Employing the jargon of computers, this approach has tried to extend the data-processing analogy to a variety of mental abilities and, by implication, human intellect as well. This interest in cognition has brought forth new ways of looking at intellectual functioning and many insights into the ways in which information is processed. These information-processing models of cognition have the advantage over their forerunners because they are clearly stated and open to empirical disconfirmation.

There are, of course, many different information-processing models of memory and cognition. Each model has its unique features, but all share many characteristics as well. Such models are generally stated in terms of a series of stores (for example, Broadbent, 1971). Incoming information is first held in a sensory specific store (buffer). These buffer stores have large capacities, but information held within them decays rapidly and is lost unless some attention is paid to the stored information. The result of "paying attention" is that information is passed to a limited-capacity short-term memory store where it is either "rehearsed" or displaced by new information. Rehearsal results in the transferring of information to an almost permanent long-term memory store where capacity is apparently limitless, and forgetting is a result of an inability to retrieve stored information. The physical reality of the various stores is highly doubtful, and one can easily conceive of the various stores as stages or "levels of analysis" (Craik, 1973) without doing much damage to the model or to the present description.

Information-processing models usually posit two broad dimensions along which intellectual functioning can be described. The first dimension, memory structure, refers to processes that are sometimes referred to as "wired-in." These remain mostly constant across situations. The second dimension, control processes, refers to cognitive processes that vary from person to person and across situations. These dimensions are usually elaborated as follows.

Three structural components are usually identified: a sensory register or buffer store; a short-term memory store; and a long-term memory store. Information is thought to flow from the environment through the sensory system where it is held only briefly (perhaps several hundred milliseconds) in the sensory register. Information is then transferred to the short-term store that has a limited capacity and depends heavily on auditory codes.

Selected information is transferred from the short-term store to the long-term store, which has a virtually unlimited capacity and serves as a permanent information repository. The influence of attention and "set" is felt here. Little is known about the actual information structure of the long-term memory store, but certain retrieval effects have been described. Many studies have demonstrated that retrieval from the long-term store is subject to a variety of interference effects, and it seems clear that the organization of the various long-term store data bases will determine whether a particular piece of information is easy or difficult to retrieve.

The various strategies and techniques used in solving problems and in processing information are collectively known as control processes. Among the most important control processes are the coding strategies used in short-term memory. Such terms as "chunking," "organization," "rehearsal" and the like refer to short-term memory coding processes. Search and decision rules are also important control processes, particularly with regard to the retrievel of information from the long-term store. In general, control processes can be thought of as roughly equivalent to a computer program. The "software" tells the computer what to do with the information it has or is about to receive. The memory structure is roughly equivalent to the computer itself, the "hardware" that actually performs the data processing.

Information-processing models of cognition not only view the organism as a sort of computing system in which information from the environment is assumed to pass through a series of stores (or encoding stages) but also view each stage as involving an active recoding of input. These recodings take place in the light of past experience and depend on knowledge already resident in long-term memory. For example, perception is influenced by what is expected (based on past experience) to occur in a given situation. One's knowledge thus affects the ways in which the world is perceived, encoded, and stored, and it is also used to solve problems.

Memory Structure and Schizophrenic Language

Very few investigators have been concerned with schizophrenic memory structure; they prefer instead to concentrate on control processes. A possible exception to this general trend is the long-standing interest in schizophrenics' "span of apprehension." Most recently, this work has involved time-dependent, information-processing tasks designed to determine how much information is apprehended in a given unit of time (see Neale, 1971, for example). As this work is inextricably intertwined with the study of selective attention, it is discussed with the research on control processes.

At least one study had as its concern the storage structure of schizophrenics' long-term memory (Koh, Kayton, & Schwarz, 1974). Schizophrenic and non-schizophrenic patients as well as normals were required to sort a deck of cards, each card bearing a common word, into piles on the basis of perceived similarity. Although overinclusion has long been thought to characterize schizophrenics, cluster analyses revealed that the structure of each group's sorts were similar. This was true even under time pressure. Although these findings are in accord with the evidence reviewed to this point that schizophrenics do not have strange word-association repertoires, it should be mentioned that Koh, et al.'s schizophrenic subjects tend to be younger and more highly educated than those generally serving in such experiments. These differences, particularly the educational difference, may be important when the structure of long-term memory is studied. Moreover, the categorizing of words, although clearly tapping long-term memory, does not do justice to its complexity as a vast repository of information and to rules for acting on the stored information. The intricately related structure of long-term memory is not completely reflected even in complex models such as the one suggested by Collins and Quillian (1972) and is less likely to be reflected in the number and types of piles formed by subjects sorting words.

Control Processes

As opposed to the investigation of memory structure, the study of control processes has been preceding quite rapidly. A large part of this rapidly growing literature has been devoted to explicating the problem of selective attention. Because the ability to attend selectively to aspects of the environment is essential for language learning, this literature is relevant to the present discussion. Fortunately, this work has been ably reviewed by McGhie (1970) and Neale and Cromwell (1970). The advantages and disadvantages of the various experiments are also discussed in the present volume, particularly in the chapter by Oltmanns and Neale. These discussions are not repeated here. Instead, the present focus is on some of the procedures used in these studies and the implications of these procedures for the study of schizophrenic language.

Much of the most interesting work in this area has been performed by Neale and his colleagues using tachistoscopically presented visual displays. Although this research is probably less relevant to a temporal phenomenon such as language than studies using auditory stimuli, it is interesting to note that the results of these studies do not clearly delineate a schizophrenic information processing deficit. Rather, they have been interpreted (see Davidson & Neale, 1974, for example) as an indication that the information-processing operations of both schizophrenics and nonschizophrenics are similar but that schizophrenics perform them at a slower rate.

Attention to auditory stimuli has been studied extensively with dichotic listening tasks in which words or other stimuli are alternated between (or sometimes presented simultaneously to) the two ears, and subjects are asked to shadow some of the stimuli while ignoring the rest (Friedrich, Emery, & Fuller, 1974; Payne, Hochberg, & Hawks, 1970; Wishner & Wahl, 1974). The results of these studies are generally predictable. Schizophrenics omit more shadowed words than nonschizophrenics or normals and recall fewer of the shadowed words on subsequent recall tests. Schizophrenics are also much more likely to make intrusion errors (saying or recalling a word that they were instructed to ignore). In a study using fast and moderate presentation speeds, Wishner and Wahl (1974) obtained the typical findings and concluded that slow information-processing speed and defective filtering are the two most important determinants of the schizophrenics' performance. They continued to argue that schizophrenics and nonschizophrenics must differ at a central stage of information processing rather than at sensory input because the nonschizophrenics did not achieve their superior performance by ignoring unshadowed materials. They actually remembered more of the unshadowed words than the schizophrenics but did not confuse these with the words they were supposed to shadow. In addition, both groups were able to recognize the shadowed words equally well on a subsequent recognition test. The conclusions of Friedrich, et al. are similar. This interpretation of the findings, although logically clear, is semantically confusing because it obscures the meaning of the term "filtering" and as a consequence falsely characterizes the actual schizophrenic deficit.

The term filtering as used by Broadbent (1958) is applied to a stimulus "set" in which the materials to be attended to can be differentiated from the unimportant materials on the basis of a common physical feature (for example, acoustic similarity or spatial location). In his more recent view, Broadbent (1971) has introduced an additional attentional mechanism, "pigeonholing." Pigeonholing occurs when a person adopts a "response set," selecting from a large number of items (for example, a list of words), those constituting a subvocabulary (for example, the names of colors). Thus, filtering leads to stimulus selectivity, whereas pigeonholing results in response selection. As Hemsley (1975) has pointed out, much of the work on attention in schizophrenia has confused filtering with pigeonholing. For example, although Wishner and Wahl interpret their results to support the hypothesis that schizophrenics are deficient in filtering, it appears that in their study, at least, schizophrenics were deficient in pigeonholing. That is, both schizophrenics and nonschizophrenics attended to both the shadowed and nonshadowed words (as evidenced by the results of their subsequent recall and recognition tests). The nonschizophrenics, however, rarely gave these nonshadowed words as responses, and the schizophrenics often did. As indicated by Hemsley, results such as these and the results reported by Lawson, McGhie, and Chapman (1964) that schizophrenics are less able to make use of the structure of language as an aid to memory than nonschizophrenics are not consistent with a filtering defect but with a defect in pigeonholing. The Nachmani and Cohen finding, reported earlier, that schizophrenics allowed semantically related words to intrude into their recognition more often than nonschizophrenics (a finding at odds with their model) is also quite consistent with the hypothesized defect in pigeonholing. In accordance with this, the evidence from studies of selective attention, although somewhat confusing, seems to support the hypothesis that schizophrenics do have a defect in attention, but it is not at the level of the intake of sensory information. The defect, it seems, lies after the intake of information in the response stage and can be understood in Broadbent's terms as a defect in pigeonholing. The possibility that schizophrenics are slower information processors than nonschizophrenics is also quite likely but needs to be investigated using experimental paradigms which allow information-processing speed to be measured directly (for example, Posner, Boies, Eichelman, & Taylor, 1969). The influence of the psychotropic drugs taken by virtually all schizophrenics has to be considered when their relative information-processing speed is investigated.

Once information does reach a processing stage, it needs to be retained and used effectively. Most of the work on the encoding of information by schizophrenics has been performed by Koh and his associates and is described in detail in the chapter by Koh in this volume. Using a free-recall paradigm, Koh, Kayton, and Berry (1973) found that schizophrenics tend to recall fewer words than nonschizophrenics and tend not to cluster their recall together on the basis of semantic categories to the extent that nonschizophrenics do. Schizophrenics also do not tend to organize their recall subjectively (build higher order organizational units over successive trials). It is well known that the fewer words a person remembers, the fewer he can recognize and, in most cases, the clustering score is lower. Because there is doubt that the clustering score used by Koh, et al. (1973) is independent of the number of words recalled (Roenker, Thompson, & Brown, 1971), their findings simply may be the result of the schizophrenics' often noted poor performance on memory tasks. Koh, et al. (1973) also reported the results of recognition tasks which indicated that schizophrenics do not differ from nonschizophrenics in their ability to recognize previously presented words. This fairly ubiquitous finding points to a problem in recall or retrieval strategy that is possibly caused by poor encoding organization which is responsible for the schizophrenic memory deficit. An intriguing aspect of their recognition study is the analysis of the results using signal-detection parameters (Swets, 1964). This analysis indicates that schizophrenics and nonschizophrenics do not differ in their respective sensitivities (d') to the originally presented words. This finding is directly relevant to the problems of selective attention already discussed because signal detection parameters may be directly related to Broadbent's two-stage model of attention. When an operating characteristic is derived, relating the probability of a correct recognition response to the probability of an incorrect response (actually a false alarm), pigeonholing produces an increase in the number of correct responses with a constant false-alarm rate. In decision-theory terms, filtering (whether in perception or memory) affects d', whereas pigeonholing affects β. This latter statistic is the critical value of the likelihood ratio above which a subject's response is favorable. Thus, the finding that schizophrenics do not differ from nonschizophrenics in sensitivity (d') indicates once again that their problem is not in filtering but in some more central pigeonholing activity.

Schizophrenics' Knowledge of Linguistic Rules

A favorite approach to the study of schizophrenic language has been applying the rules of logical or linguistic analysis to transcripts of schizophrenic speech. This approach is exemplified by many of the papers in Kasanin's (1944) famous collection and shows all the signs of continued life (for example, Chaika, 1974). The problem with this approach is essentially the same as that of the case history method. It is difficult to make decisions about the merits of various theoretical hypotheses based on uncontrolled studies. Particular criticisms have been levelled at one linguistic approach by Fromkin (1975) and are generally applicable to the whole field. Thus, although important hypotheses have been derived from such work, purely formal studies of individual cases are not reviewed. It is sufficient to say that the consensus of psycholinguistic investigators is that schizophrenic language is nonexistent, although schizophrenic thought abounds (for example, Brown, 1973).

Effects of Schizophrenics' General State of Arousal

No review of the literature concerned with any aspect of schizophrenia can be considered complete without mention of the general psychophysiological state of schizophrenics. The hypothesis that schizophrenics have a defect in a hypothetical arousal-control mechanism is old (see Mednick, 1958). Although it seems probable that subgroups of schizophrenics differ in their arousal function (Venables, 1964) and that arousal control is a complex and heterogeneous construct (Claridge, 1972), the hypothesis remains important, particularly in the study of the beneficial effects of tranquilizing medication. Thus, it is useful to review briefly knowledge of the effects of arousal on memory and language.

Before proceeding, it is wise to note that the concept of a "general arousal level" is the focus of much controversy. Disagreement about the nature and measurement of arousal has resulted in some writers identifying three different kinds of arousal (Lacey, 1967) while others refer to two (Bradley, 1958) and still others refer to one (Berlyne, 1967). In addition, although most investigators conceptualize arousal as primarily a physiological construct (for example, Sokolov, 1964), others define changes in arousal on the basis of behavior (Broadbent, 1971, p. 413). When the often noted failure of various autonomic arousal indices is added to these disparate views, it becomes clear why some investigators reject completely the usefulness of a concept such as general level of arousal.

As Berlyne (1967) has pointed out, however, arousal level may still serve as a useful theoretical construct when it is viewed as an intervening variable tied to a variety of psychological and environmental antecedents and is likely to affect many physiological and behavioral variables. From this viewpoint, an arousal index, whether physiological or behavioral, will mirror not only the effects of the intervening variable but also the effects of various factors specific to the measure employed. Blood pressure, for example, may be a measure of arousal, but it is also a function of the organism's state of health. Blood pressure, therefore, should correlate imperfectly with other arousal indices that are less dependent on physical health. For present purposes, arousal is considered a general dimension of covert excitement measured by imperfectly correlated indices. It is assumed that arousal is greater than usual when an individual is exposed to threat, stress, strong stimulation, or prolonged periods of deprivation and is less than usual when the individual is fatigued or sleeping. Arousal narrows the range of cues utilized by the organism. Easterbrook (1959) accounted for the frequently reported finding that arousal's effect, as measured by various behavioral indices, is often nonlinear by postulating that for some tasks a focus in the range of cue utilization causes irrelevant cues to be excluded (thereby enhancing performance), whereas for tasks requiring attention to wide range of cues, such a decrease in cue utilization, disrupts performance. For any particular task, then, there is an optimal range of cue utilization (and arousal). This postulate was employed to explain the results of dozens of experiments ranging from Bursill's (1958) finding that arousal results in a "funnelling" in the field of awareness to changes in the recognition-duration thresholds for taboo words (Postman & Bruner, 1948). Although Easterbrook did not propose a specific mechanism by which arousal exerts its effect, it seems clear that any mechanism would involve a loss of information with increasing emotionality.

A similar explanation for the effects of arousal has been suggested by Hockey (1970). From his viewpoint, the effect of arousal is to narrow the focus of attention to the sources which are most dominant (most likely to produce important signals) and to exclude less important sources. The implications of this viewpoint for memory are simple to deduce. If increasing arousal decreases the amount of information apprehended, then less of what occurred during arousing conditions should be remembered under nonarousing conditions. Experimental evidence from a variety of sources indicates that although arousal may have apparent attentional effects, its effect on subsequent memory is quite complex and is not at all consistent with such a simple hypothesis.

Arousal and Memory Consolidation

Some investigators (Kleinsmith & Kaplan, 1963, 1964; Walker & Tarte, 1963) have reported that arousing paired-associate items are harder to remember when recall is tested immediately after acquisition but easier to recall when retention is tested after delays lasting as long as one week. This finding is thought to support the hypothesis that arousal protects a neural trace from interference by rendering it inaccessible until it is consolidated (Walker, 1958).

Although similar results have been reported by others (Berlyne, Borsa, Craw, Gelman, & Mandell, 1965; Berlyne, Borsa, Hamacher, & Koenig, 1966; Levonian, 1967; McLean, 1969), conflicting evidence suggests that the consolidation hypothesis is incorrect. Archer and Margolin (1970); Corteen (1969); Hörmann and Todt (1960); Maltzman, Kantor, and Langdon (1966); and Schönpflug (1966) have reported that under some conditions an increase in arousal during acquisition facilitates immediate as well as delayed recall. Thus, although it appears that arousal during acquisition influences subsequent memory, the precise arousal–recall relationship is unclear. One point, however, seems certain. Since memory, in some experiments, improved from immediate to delayed recall, arousal during acquisition could not have resulted in a permanent information loss. Clearly, explanations based solely on narrowing the focus of attention (that is, purely filtering explanations) need to be made more complex.

Recently, in an attempt to reconcile some of the discrepant results discussed to this point, Levonian (1972) advanced a hypothesis centering on a proposed distinction between arousal's postulated effect on retentivity (linear and positive) and its effect on accessibility (initially negative). He accounted for the discrepant findings in terms of different experimental procedures which possibly resulted in varying rates of habituation (and arousal) for different list items. It seems quite plausible that, because memory sometimes improved from immediate to delayed recall, arousal affected the accessibility of stored information. Unfortunately, Levonian's explanation, although more complex than Easterbrook's, is still not sufficiently complex to explain other, as yet undiscussed findings.

Arousal and Recall Order

An unusual finding was reported by Hörmann and Osterkamp (1966). In their experiment white noise-induced arousal led to a decrease in semantic category clustering in free recall. Mueller and Goulet (1973) and Zubrzycki and Borkowski (1973) reported similar results for anxious when compared to nonanxious individuals. A related and equally interesting finding is associated with the work of Hockey and Hamilton (Hamilton, Hockey, & Quinn, 1972; Hockey & Hamilton, 1970). In their experiments arousal was found to improve immediate recall when order cues were useful for retrieval (for example, a list presented in the same order on successive learning trials) and not when such cues were irrelevant to recall. In these experiments as well as in the "clustering" experiments, the effect of arousal was to increase the tendency for subjects to respond in a verbatim, rote fashion. Clearly, such findings require an explanation somewhat different from any advanced this far.

Arousal and Memory

The effects of arousal on memory can be summarized briefly. Arousal may influence subsequent memory in either a negative or positive direction. Its effect is likely to be positive when order cues are relevant to recall. Arousal may also lead to a decrease in semantic clustering. Finally, the negative effects of arousal may dissipate or even reverse and become facilitative with time. A complete explanation of arousal's effect on recall should be capable of handling all of these findings. Although a complete explanation is yet unavailable, much progress has recently been made. Schwartz (1974, 1975) found that arousal affects pigeonholing by changing the criterion that subjects employ in making a response. (It increases the number of false alarms and the number of intrusion errors.) M. W. Eysenck (1974, 1975) has shown that arousal affects memory in recall but not in recognition tasks (as in schizophrenia). This differential effect of arousal on recall and recognition was interpreted to indicate that arousal affected the retrieval component of recall. Because under high arousal subjects performed better at retrieving common semantic category members but poorly at recalling less frequent category members, these results were thought similar to those reported earlier by Hockey (1970). These experiments are intriguing because they suggest that normal subjects who are aroused behave curiously like schizophrenics. They make more intrusion errors, tend to give dominant category members (which are similar to Chapman's high meaning responses), and have difficulty in recall but not in recognition. Clearly, these similarities are quite suggestive and doubtless should be pursued further.

Nonassociative Approaches to the Study of Schizophrenic Language: A Summary

The amount of research surveyed here is considerably less than the amount included in the discussion of associative approaches. There are several reasons for this. Perhaps the most important is that the information-processing approach focused on here is fairly new and has not yet caught on to the extent that it has in general experimental psychology. Despite the relative youthfulness of this approach, much progress has been made. It now seems fairly clear that schizophrenics and normals do not differ in their respective abilities to take in sensory information. Although schizophrenics do have some difficulties in performing the typically used selective-attention tasks (for example, dichotic listening), this difficulty does not seem to stem from a defect in filtering but rather from a combination of slow information-processing speeds combined with a difficulty in what investigators, following Broadbent, have called pigeonholing. The influence of the psychotropic drugs taken by all hospitalized schizophrenics on both of these parameters (but, most particularly, information-processing speed) remains to be investigated.

Schizophrenics (at least the relatively well-educated ones used by Koh) do not encode verbal materials for recall in the same way as nonschizophrenics; yet, their long-term memory structures appear to be the same as those of normals. The difficulty here is, as has already been mentioned, the possibility that isolated words are treated differently from meaningful word strings and that poor encoding performance on the memory-for-words task does not necessarily imply a strange long-term memory structure.

Schizophrenics, it seems clear, have difficulty when their memory is tested by recall but not when recognition tests are used. This finding is ubiquitous in the literature and strongly suggests that schizophrenics have poor or inefficient memory retrieval strategies.

Finally, it is most intriguing to note the similarities between schizophrenics and nonschizophrenics who are placed in states of high arousal. Both show poor performance on recall but not on recognition tests, both show a great deal of intrusion errors, and both show a tendency to make "dominant" (strong meaning or category member) responses.

Taking these findings as a whole and combining them with what has already gathered from my review of the associationistic literature, it seems obvious that certain convergences emerge. Schizophrenics are easily distracted, biased toward strong meanings of words, and sensitive to only a limited amount of verbal context. It is plausible that lying at the basis of these problems is a central defect in pigeonholing (adopting a response set) which in turn is the result of over-arousal. Thus, when a task can be performed merely on the basis of filtering, schizophrenics perform approximately as well as normals, but when a task requires that schizophrenics use their knowledge of the likelihood of words and probabilities being correct, in other words to selectively alter their response biases, performance falls. This decrease in performance is also noted in nonschizophrenics who are highly aroused and may be the reason that much of the schizophrenic thought disorder is reduced by tranquilizing medications. Of course, this is highly speculative, and much work remains to be done.

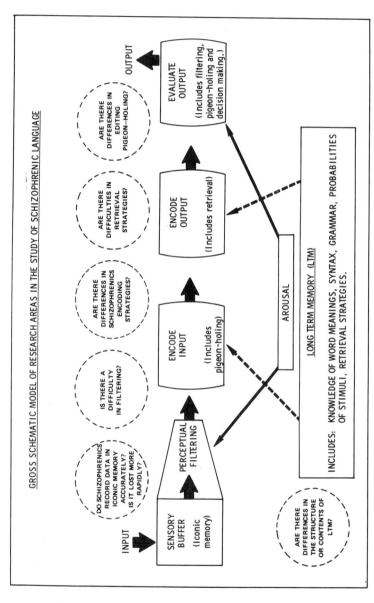

FIG. 8.2 Schematic representation of a research strategy for the investigation of schizophrenic language.

Within the figure, the following text appears:

GROSS SCHEMATIC MODEL OF RESEARCH AREAS IN THE STUDY OF SCHIZOPHRENIC LANGUAGE

INPUT

SENSORY BUFFER (Iconic memory)

PERCEPTUAL FILTERING

ENCODE INPUT (Includes pigeon-holing)

ENCODE OUTPUT (Includes retrieval)

EVALUATE OUTPUT (Includes filtering, pigeon-holing and decision making.)

OUTPUT

DO SCHIZOPHRENICS RECORD DATA IN ICONIC MEMORY ACCURATELY? IS IT LOST MORE RAPIDLY?

IS THERE A DIFFICULTY IN FILTERING?

ARE THERE DIFFERENCES IN SCHIZOPHRENICS ENCODING STRATEGIES?

ARE THERE DIFFICULTIES IN RETRIEVAL STRATEGIES?

ARE THERE DIFFERENCES IN EDITING PIGEON-HOLING?

ARE THERE DIFFERENCES IN THE STRUCTURE OR CONTENTS OF LTM?

AROUSAL

LONG TERM MEMORY (LTM)

INCLUDES: KNOWLEDGE OF WORD MEANINGS, SYNTAX, GRAMMAR, PROBABILITIES OF STIMULI, RETRIEVAL STRATEGIES.

270

A SCHEMA FOR THE STUDY OF SCHIZOPHRENIC LANGUAGE

Based on the preceding review and on the materials presented, Figure 8.2 presents in schematic form the schizophrenic communication process. Enclosed in circles are those questions that may differentiate schizophrenics from nonschizophrenics and help to pinpoint the locus of the schizophrenic deficit. Some of these questions have already been tentatively answered. For others, extensive work remains to be done.

Schematically, input, in this case usually verbal, is seen to reside first in a sensory buffer store from which it either is lost (by decay or by the onset of new stimuli) or is attended to. Studies of iconic memory in schizophrenia have not been performed, and, although there is no reason to suspect a deficit, there is yet no evidence to rule one out. Perceptual filtering comes next, and, as has been discussed, a large number of researchers see this stage as the locus of the schizophrenic problem. Although a later pigeonholing stage seems a more likely place to look for the schizophrenic attentional defect based on the present review, much more research is required in this area, research that clearly separates filtering from pigeonholing. The encoding stage that follows involves considerably complicated processing. Knowledge stored in long-term memory needs to be used to enable the individual to recognize that what he is hearing or seeing are words and what the words mean. In semantic category clustering, for example, the individual must use information already resident in long-term memory to accomplish his task. Output encoding involves much of the same processing as does output evaluation. Here, response biases, task demands, and pigeonholing come into use. Each of these encoding and evaluation stages requires a certain amount of processing "capacity," which may be reduced with increases in arousal. The encoding and evaluation stages, the control of arousal, and arousal's affect on capacity are all possible locuses of the schizophrenic deficit. The answers to these questions posed throughout this chapter and illustrated schematically in Figure 8.2 will constitute a theory of schizophrenic language and cognition.

ACKNOWLEDGMENTS

The preparation of this chapter was greatly aided by U.S. Public Health Service Grant MH28369 from the National Institute of Mental Health. I have received many helpful criticisms of the various ideas in this chapter from students and colleagues. I would particularly like to acknowledge my intellectual debt to H. J. Eysenck, M. W. Eysenck and D. E. Broadbent, whose ideas and suggestions are reflected explicitly and implicitly throughout, and to Carolyn Schwartz, whose mark has been left on every aspect of the chapter.

REFERENCES

Archer, B. U., & Margolin, R. R. Arousal effects in intentional recall and forgetting. *Journal of Experimental Psychology,* 1970, *86,* 8–12.

Bateson, G., Jackson, D. D., Haley, J., & Weakland, J. H. Toward a theory of schizophrenia. *Behavioral Science,* 1956, *1,* 251–264.

Berlyne, D. E. Arousal and reinforcement. In D. Levine (Ed.), *Nebraska Symposium on Motivation, 1967.* Lincoln, Nebraska: University of Nebraska Press, 1967.

Berlyne, D. E., Borsa, D. M., Craw, M. A., Gelman, R. S., & Mandell, E. E. Effects of stimulus complexity and induced arousal on paired-associate learning. *Journal of Verbal Learning and Verbal Behavior,* 1965, *4,* 291–299.

Berlyne, D. E., Borsa, D. M., Hamacher, J. H., & Koenig, I. D. V. Paired-associate learning and the timing of arousal. *Journal of Experimental Psychology,* 1966, *72,* 1–6.

Bever, T. J. Associations to stimulus–response theories of language. In T. R. Dixon & Horton, D. C. (Eds.), *Verbal behavior and general behavior theory.* Englewood Cliffs, New Jersey: Prentice–Hall, 1968.

Boland, T. B., & Chapman, L. J. Conflicting predictions from Broen's and Chapman's theories of schizophrenic thought disorder. *Journal of Abnormal Psychology,* 1971, *78,* 52–58.

Bleuler, E. *Dementia praecox or the group of schizophrenics.* New York: International Universities Press, 1950 (original, 1911).

Bradley, D. B. The central action of certain drugs in relation to the reticular formation of the brain. In H. H. Jasper, et al. (Eds.), *Reticular formation of the brain.* Boston: Little Brown, 1958.

Broadbent, D. E. *Decision and Stress.* New York: Academic Press, 1971.

Broadbent, D. E. *Perception and communication.* Oxford: Pergamon Press, 1958.

Brown, R. Schizophrenia, language and reality. *American Psychologist,* 1973, *28,* 395–403.

Bursill, A. E. The restriction of peripheral vision during exposure to hot and humid conditions. *Quarterly Journal of Experimental Psychology,* 1958, *10,* 113–129.

Chaika, E. A linguist looks at "schizophrenic" language. *Brain and Language,* 1974, *1,* 257–276.

Chapman, L. J., & Chapman, J. P. Interpretation of words in schizophrenia. *Journal of Personality and Social Psychology,* 1965, *1,* 135–146.

Chapman, L. J., & Chapman, J. P. *Disordered thought in schizophrenia.* Englewood Cliffs, N. J.: Prentice–Hall, 1973.

Chapman, L. J., Chapman, J. P., & Miller, G. A. A theory of verbal behavior in schizophrenia. In B. A. Maher (Ed.), *Progress in experimental personality research.* New York: Academic Press, 1964.

Claridge, G. S. The schizophrenias as nervous types. *British Journal of Psychiatry,* 1972, *121,* 1–17.

Cohen, B. D., & Camhi, J. Schizophrenic performance in a word-communication task. *Journal of Abnormal Psychology,* 1967, *72,* 240–246.

Cohen, B. D., Nachmani, G., & Rosenberg, S. Referent communication disturbances in acute schizophrenia. *Journal of Abnormal Psychology,* 1974, *83,* 1–13.

Collins, A. M., & Quillian, M. R. How to make a language user. In E. Tulving & W. Donaldson (Eds.), *Organization of memory.* New York: Academic Press, 1972.

Corteen, R. S. Skin conductance changes and word recall. *British Journal of Psychology,* 1969, *60,* 81–84.

Craik, F. I. M. A "levels of analysis" view of memory. In P. Pliner, L. Krames, & T. Alloway

(Eds.), *Communication and affect: Language and thought.* New York: Academic Press, 1973.

Davidson, G. S., & Neale, J. M. The effects of signal-noise similarity on visual information processing of schizophrenics. *Journal of Abnormal Psychology,* 1974, *83,* 683–686.

Deckner, C. W., & Blanton, R. L. Effect of context and strength of association on schizophrenic verbal behavior. *Journal of Abnormal Psychology,* 1969, *74,* 348–351.

Dokecki, P. R., Polidoro, L. G., & Cromwell, R. L. Commonality and stability of word association responses on good and poor premorbid schizophrenics. *Journal of Abnormal Psychology,* 1965, *70,* 312–316.

Donaldson, W., & Murdock, B. B., Jr. Criterion change in continuous recognition memory. *Journal of Experimental Psychology,* 1968, *76,* 325–330.

Easterbrook, J. A. The effect of emotion on cue utilization and the organization of behavior. *Psychological Review,* 1959, *66,* 183–201.

Eysenck, M. W. Extraversion, arousal, and retrieval from semantic memory. *Journal of Personality,* 1974, *42,* 319–331.

Eysenck, M. W. Effects of noise, activation level, and response dominance on retrieval from semantic memory. *Journal of Experimental Psychology: Human Learning and Memory,* 1975, *1,* 143–148.

Faibash, G. M. Schizophrenic response to words of multiple meaning. *Journal of Personality,* 1961, *29,* 414–427.

Frankel, A. S., & Buchwald, A. M. Verbal conditioning of common association in long-term schizophrenics: A failure. *Journal of Abnormal Psychology,* 1969, *74*(3), 372–374.

Friedrich, D., Emery, K., & Fuller, G. Performance of paranoid schizophrenics on a dichotic listening task. *Journal of Consulting and Clinical Psychology,* 1974, *42,* 583–587.

Fromkin, V. A. A linguist looks at "A linguist looks at 'Schizophrenic Language.' " *Brain and Language,* 1975, *2,* 495–500.

Fuller, G. D., & Kates, S. L. Word association repertoires of schizophrenics and normals. *Journal of Consulting and Clinical Psychology,* 1969, *33,* 497–500.

Hamilton, P., Hockey, G. R. J., & Quinn, J. G. Information selection, arousal and memory. *British Journal of Psychology,* 1972, *63,* 181–189.

Hemsley, D. R. A two-stage model of attention in schizophrenia research. *British Journal of Social and Clinical Psychology,* 1975, *14,* 81–89.

Hockey, G. R. J. Effects of loud noise on attentional selectivity. *Quarterly Journal of Experimental Psychology,* 1970, *22,* 28–36.

Hockey, G. R. J., & Hamilton, P. Arousal and information selection in short-term memory. *Nature,* 1970, *226,* 866–867.

Hörmann, H. *Psycholinguistics.* Heidelberg: Springer–Verlag, 1971.

Hörmann, H., & Osterkamp, U. Uber den Einfluss von kontinuierlichem Lärm auf die Organisation von Gedachnisinhalten. *Zeitschrift für Experimentelle und Angewandte Psychologie,* 1966, *13,* 31–38.

Hörmann, H., & Todt, E. Lärm und lernen. *Zeitschrift für Experimentelle und Angewandte Psychologie,* 1960, *7,* 422–426.

Horton, D. L., Marlowe, D., & Crowne, D. P. The effect of instructional set and need for social approval on commonality of word-association responses. *Journal of Abnormal and Social Psychology,* 1963, *66,* 67–72.

Hunt, W. A., & Jones, N. F. Clinical judgment of some aspects of schizophrenic thinking. *Journal of Clinical and Consulting Psychology,* 1958, *14,* 235–239.

James, W. *The principles of psychology.* New York: Dover, 1890 (reprinted 1950).

Johnson, R. C., Weiss, R. L., & Zelhart, P. F. Similarities and differences between normal and psychotic subjects in response to verbal stimuli. *Journal of Abnormal and Social Psychology,* 1964, *58,* 221–226.

274   S. SCHWARTZ

Kasasin, J. S. *Language and thought in schizophrenia*. Berkeley: University of California Press, 1944.

Kent, G. H., & Rosanoff, A. J. A study of association in insanity. *American Journal of Insanity*, 1910, *67*, July and October, 37–96.

Kleinsmith, L. J., & Kaplan, S. Paired-associate learning as a function of arousal and interpolated interval. *Journal of Experimental Psychology*, 1963, *65*, 190–193.

Kleinsmith, L. J., & Kaplan, S. Interaction of arousal and recall interval in nonsense syllable paired-associate learning. *Journal of Experimental Psychology*, 1964, *67*, 124–126.

Kling, J. W., & Riggs, L. A. *Woodworth and Schlossberg's experimental psychology* (Third edition). New York: Holt, Rinehart & Winston, 1971.

Koh, S. D., Kayton, L., & Berry, R. Mnemonic organization in young nonpsychotic schizophrenics. *Journal of Abnormal Psychology*, 1973, *81*, 299–310.

Koh, S. D., Kayton, L., & Schwarz, C. The structure of word storage in the permanent memory of nonpsychotic schizophrenics. *Journal of Consulting and Clinical Psychology*, 1974, *42*, 879–887.

Lacey, J. I. Somatic response patterning and stress: Some revisions of activation theory. In M. H. Appley & R. Turnbull (Eds.), *Psychological stress: Some issues in research*. New York: Appleton–Century–Crofts, 1967.

Lashley, K. S. The problem of serial order in behavior. In L. A. Jeffress (Ed.), *Cerebral mechanisms in behavior*. New York: John Wiley & Sons, 1951.

Lawson, J. S., McGhie, A., & Chapman, J. Perception of speech in schizophrenia. *British Journal of Psychology*, 1964, *110*, 375–380.

Lenneberg, E. H. *Biological foundations of language*. New York: John Wiley & Sons, 1967.

Levonian, E. Retention of information in relation to arousal during continuously presented material. *American Educational Research Journal*, 1967, *4*, 103–116.

Levonian, E. Retention over time in relation to arousal during learning: An explanation of discrepant results. *Acta Psychologica*, 1972, *36*, 290–321.

Lisman, S. A., & Cohen, B. D. Self-editing deficits in schizophrenia: A word-association analogue. *Journal of Abnormal Psychology*, 1972, *79*, 181–188.

Maher, B. *Principles of psychopathology*. New York: McGraw–Hill, 1966.

Maher, B. The language of schizophrenia: A review and interpretation. *British Journal of Psychiatry*, 1972, *120*, 3–17.

Maltzman, I., Kantor, W., & Langdon, B. Immediate and delayed retention, arousal and the orienting and defense reflexes. *Psychonomic Science*, 1966, *6*, 445–446.

McGhie, A. Attention and perception in schizophrenia. In B. A. Maher (Ed.), *Progress in experimental personality research* (Vol. 5), New York: Academic Press, 1970.

McLean, P. D. Induced arousal and time of recall as determinants of paired-associate recall. *British Journal of Psychology*, 1969, *60*, 57–62.

Mednick, S. A. A learning theory approach to research in schizophrenia. *Psychological Bulletin*, 1958, *55*, 316–327.

Meichenbaum. D. Cognitive factors in behavior modification: Modifying what clients say to themselves. In C. Franks & T. Wilson (Eds.), *Annual review of behavior therapy: Theory and practice*. New York: Bruner–Mazel, 1973.

Miller, G. A., & Chomsky, N. Finite models of language users. In R. D. Luce, R. R. Bush, & E. Galanter (Eds.), *Handbook of mathematical psychology* (Vol. 2). New York: John Wiley & Sons, 1963.

Miller, G., Galanter, E., & Pribram, K. H. *Plans and the structure of behavior*. New York: Holt, Rinehart & Winston, 1960.

Mourer, S. A. prediction of patterns of schizophrenic error resulting from semantic generalization. *Journal of Abnormal Psychology*, 1973, *81*, 250–254.

Mueller, J. H., & Goulet, L. R. The effects of anxiety on human learning and memory. Paper delivered at the annual meeting of the American Psychological Association, Montreal, August, 1973.

Nachmani, G., & Cohen, B. D. Recall and recognition free learning in schizophrenics. *Journal of Abnormal Psychology*, 1969, *74*, 511–516.

Neale, J. M. Perceptual span in schizophrenia. *Journal of Abnormal Psychology*, 1971, *77*, 196–204.

Neale, J. M., & Cromwell, R. L. Attention and schizophrenia. In B. A. Maher (Ed.), *Research in experimental personality research* (Vol. 5). New York: Academic Press, 1970.

Neisser, U. *Cognitive psychology.* New York: Appleton–Century–Crofts, 1967.

Neuringer, C., Fiske, P. J., & Goldstein, G. Schizophrenic adherence to strong meaning associations. *Perceptual and Motor Skills*, 1969, *29*, 394.

Neuringer, C., Fiske, P. J., Schmidt, M. W. & Goldstein, G. Adherence to strong verbal meaning definitions in schizophrenics. *Journal of Genetic Psychology*, 1972, *121*, 315–323.

Pavy, D. Verbal behavior in schizophrenia: A review of recent studies. *Psychological Bulletin*, 1968, *70*, 164–178.

Payne, R. W., Hochberg, A. C., & Hawks, D. V. Dichotic stimulation as a method of assessing disorder of attention in overinclusive schizophrenic patients. *Journal of Abnormal Psychology*, 1970, *76*, 185–193.

Posner, M. I., Boies, S. J., Eichelman, W. H., & Taylor, R. L. Retention of visual and name codes of single letters. *Journal of Experimental Psychology Monograph*, 1969, *79*(1, Pt. 2).

Postman, L., & Bruner, J. S. Perception under stress. *Psychological Review*, 1948, *53*, 314–324.

Rattan, R. B., & Chapman, L. J. Associative intrusions in schizophrenic verbal behavior. *Journal of Abnormal Psychology*, 1973, *82*, 169–173.

Ries, H. A., & Johnson, M. H. Commonality of word associations in good and poor premorbid schizophrenics. *Journal of Abnormal Psychology*, 1967, *72*, 487–488.

Roberts, M. A., & Schuham, A. I. Word associations of schizophrenics and alcoholics as a function of strength of associative distractor. *Journal of Abnormal Psychology*, 1974, *83*, 426–431.

Roenker, D. L., Thompson, C. P., & Brown, S. C. Comparison of measures for the estimation of clustering in free-recall. *Psychological Bulletin*, 1971, *76*, 45–48.

Salzinger, K., Portnoy, S., & Feldman, R. S. Verbal behavior of schizophrenic and normal subjects. *Annals of the New York Academy of Sciences*, 1963, *105*, 845–860.

Salzinger, K., Portnoy, S., & Feldman, R. S. Verbal behavior in schizphrenics and some comments toward a theory of schizophrenia. In P. H. Hoch & J. Zubin (Eds.), *Psychopathology of schizophrenia.* New York: Grune & Stratton, 1966.

Schönpflug, W. Paarlernen, Behaltensdauer und Aktivierung. *Psychologishe Forschung*, 1966, *29*, 132–148.

Schwartz, S. Arousal and recall: Effects of noise on two retrieval strategies. *Journal of Experimental Psychology*, 1974, *102*, 896–898.

Schwartz, S. Individual differences in cognition: Some relationships between personality and memory. *Journal of Research in Personality*, 1975, *9*, 217–225.

Seeman, M. V. Analyses of psychotic language: A review. *Diseases of the Nervous System*, 1970, *31*, 92–99.

Shepard, R. N., & Teghtsoonian, M. Retention of information under conditions approaching a steady state. *Journal of Experimental Psychology*, 1961, *62*, 302–305.

Smith, E. E. Associative and editing processes in schizophrenic communication. *Journal of Abnormal Psychology*, 1970, *2*, 182–186.

Sokolov, E. N. *Perception and the conditioned reflex.* New York: Pergamon Press, 1964.

Sommer, R., Dewar, R., & Osmond, H. Is there a schizophrenic language? *Archives of General Psychiatry,* 1960, *3,* 665–673.

Swets, J. A. *Signal detection and recognition by human observers.* New York: John Wiley & Sons, 1964.

Venables, P. H. Input dysfunction in schizophrenia. In B. A. Maher (Ed.), *Progress in experimental personality research* (Vol. 1). New York: Academic Press, 1964.

Walker, E. L. Action decrement and its relation to learning. *Psychological Review,* 1958, *65,* 129–142.

Walker, E. L., & Tarte, R. D. Memory storage as a function of arousal and time with homogeneous and heterogeneous lists. *Journal of Verbal Learning and Verbal Behavior,* 1963, *2,* 113–119.

Wishner, J., & Wahl, O. Dichotic listening in schizophrenia. *Journal of Consulting and Clinical Psychology,* 1974, *42,* 538–546.

Zubin, J. *Field studies in the mental disorders.* New York: Grune & Stratton, 1961.

Zubrzycki, C. R., & Borkowski, J. G. Effects of anxiety on storage and retrieval processes in short-term memory. *Psychological Reports,* 1973, *33,* 315–320.

Author Index

A

Abbs, J. H., 200, *228*
Achenbach, K., 198, *234*
Adams-Webber, J. R., 151, 158, *189*
Agnew, J., 157, *189*
Al-Issa, I., 219, *228*
Amadeo, M., 131, *142*
Anderson, J. R., 71, *95*
Andreasen, N. J. C., 124, *139*
Angelergues, R., 203, *232*
Archer, B. U., 267, *272*
Armstrong, J., 158, *190*
Arnold, K. O., 193, *231*
Atkinson, R. C., 56, 76, *95*
Auster, P., 19, *33*

B

Back, K. W., 25, *33*
Bahzin, E. F., 213, *228*
Bakan, P., 206, 208, *229*
Banks, W. P., 78, *95*
Bannister, D., 124, *139*, 155, 157–158, *189*
Barclay, J. R., 55, *95*
Barden, B., 157, *190*
Bartko, J. J., 123–124, *139, 142*, 160, *191*

Bateson, G., 243, *272*
Bauman, E., 90, *95*
Beaumont, J. F., 196, 207, 214–215, 223–224, *229, 230*
Bechterew, W., 209–210, *229*
Bent, D. H., 62, *98*
Berlin, C. I., 200, *229*
Berlyne, D. E., 226, *272*
Berry, K. L., 159, *190*
Berry, R., 64, 71, *97*, 264, *274*
Bever, T. G., 205, *229, 251, 272*
Bigelow, L. B., 214, 223, *234*
Bjork, R. A., 57, 77, *95, 96*
Blackburn, I. M., 157, *190*
Blaney, P. H., 114, *116*
Blanton, R. L., 242, 250, *273*
Blashfield, R. K., 160, *189*
Bleuler, E., 1, 23, *33*, 117, *139*, 145, *189*, 215, *229* 237, *239, 272*
Blum, R. A., 128, *139*
Blumstein, S., 206, *229*
Bogen, J. E., 196–197, 202–203, *229, 231*
Boies, S. J., 264, *275*
Boland, T. B., 193, *229*, 244, *272*
Bolles, M., 216, 218, *229*
Bonarius, J. C. J., 148, *189*
Borkowski, J. G., 267, *276*
Borsa, D. M., 267, *272*
Boucher, J., 68, *95*

Bousfield, A. K., 65–67, *95*
Bousfield, W. A., 65–67, 73, *95*
Bower, G. H., 71, *95*
Bradley, D. B., 266, *272*
Braginsky, B. M., 195, *229*
Braginsky, D. D., 195, *229*
Braida, L. D., 83, *96*
Branch, C., 198, *229*
Bransford, J. D., 55, 66, *95*
Braucht, G. N., 159, *190*
Breakey, W. R., 124, *139*
Briggs, G. E., 86, *95*, 113, *115*
Broadbent, D. E., 55–56, 64, *95*, 125,
    136–137, *139*, 260, 263, 265–266, *272*
Broca, P., 202, *229*
Broen, W. E., Jr., 2, 11, 21, *33*, 111,
    113–114, *115, 116*, 118, 120, 137, *139*,
    193, 212, 226, *229, 235*
Brown, A. L., 74, 76, *95*
Brown, R., 265, *272*
Brown, S. C., 70, *98*, 264, *275*
Brown, V. W., 209, *235*
Bruner, J. S., 266, *275*
Bryden, M. P., 198, *229*
Buchwald, A. M., 242, *273*
Buckley, F., 157–158, *190*
Bull, H. C., 214, *229*
Bursill, A. E., 266, *272*
Buss, A. H., 2, 8, *33*, 120, *140*, 193–194,
    216–219, 226, *229, 232*

C

Caldwell, D. F., 148, *189*
Camhi, J., 8, 9, 11, *33*, 111, 113, *116*,
    253–254, *272*
Cameron, N., 193, 217, *229*
Cancro, R., 118, *142*
Canter, A., 124, *139*
Caplan, D., 199, *229*
Carmon, A., 201, 205–206, *229, 231*
Carpenter, W. T., 123–124, *139, 142*
Chaika, E. A., 237, 265, *272*
Chandler, P., 209, *233*
Chapman, J., 50, *51*, 89, *97*, 118, 126,
    128, *141*, 215–216, 227, *229, 232, 233*,
    264, *274*
Chapman, J. P., 3, 10–11, 19, *33*, 41, *51*,
    64, 89, *96*, 101–103, 105, 109, 111–115,
    116, 119, 122, *139*, 193, 217–218, *230*,
    243–244, *272*

Chapman, L. J., 3, 10–11, 19, *33*, 38, 41,
    51, 64, 89, *96*, 101–103, 105, 109,
    111–115, *116*, 119–120, 122, 126, *139*,
    142, 193, 217–218, 225, *229, 230*,
    243–247, 250–252, 258, 268, *272, 275*
Chiarello, R. J., 205, *229*
Chomsky, N., 55–56, *96*, 257, *274*
Clancy, J., 130, *143*
Claridge, G., 91, *96*, 265, *272*
Cofer, C. N., 193, *232*
Cohen, B. D., 4–12, 16, 20, 22–23, 26, *33*,
    90, *98*, 107, 111–113, 115, *116*, 242,
    252–258, 264, *272, 274, 275*
Cohen, G., 201, 223, *230*
Cohen, M. R., 221, *230*
Cohler, B. J., 130, *140*
Coleman, M., 212, 226, *230*
Collins, A. M., 262, *272*
Colotla, V. A., 88, *99*
Cooper, J. E., 121, 124, *139, 140*
Cooper, W. E., 206, *229*
Copeland, J. R. M., 121, *139*
Corkin, S., 204, *230*
Corteen, R. S., 267, *272*
Craik, F. I. M., 57–58, 72, 77, *96, 97*,
    260, *272*
Craw, M. A., 267, *272*
Cromwell, R. L., 15, 19, 24, *34*, 38, *51*,
    101, 111–114, *116*, 118, *141*, 148, 153,
    160, *189, 190*, 241, 262, *273, 275*
Cronbach, L. J., 119, *139*, 194–195, *230*
Crosby, E. C., 206, *230*
Crowe, R., 130, *143*
Crowne, D. P., 241, *273*
Cullen, J. K., 200, *229*

D

Damiani, N., 137, *140*
Dandy, W. E., 198, *230*
Daut, R. L., 114, *116*
Davidson, R. J., 206, *234*, 263, *273*
Davis, K. M., 114, *116*
Dean, P. J., 65–66, 70, 88, *98*
Deckner, C. W., 242, 250, *273*
Dell, P., 209, *230*
Dennis, M., 198, 204, *232*
De Renzi, E., 196, *230*
De Soto, C. B., 125, *139*
Deutsch, D., 136, *139*
Deutsch, J. A., 136, *139*

Dewar, R., 240, *276*
Dimond, S. J., 196–197, 207, 214–215, 223–224, *229, 230*
Dixon, P. M., 159, *190*
Dokecki, P. R., 15, 19, *34,* 38, *51,* 111–114, *116,* 241, *273*
Donaldson, W., 74, *99, 250, 273*
Draffan, J. W., 157, *190*
Duker, J., 60–61, *96*
Durlach, N. I., 83, *96*
Durnford, M., 197, *232*
Dwyer, P., 153, *190*

E

Easterbrook, J. A., 266, *273*
Eckerman, C., 41, *52*
Efron, R., 197, 200–201, 205, *230*
Eichelman, W. H., 264, *275*
Emery, K., 263, *273*
Endicott, J., 122, 125, *142*
Epstein, S., 212, 217, 226, *230*
Ericksen, C. W., 58, *96*
Estes, W. K., 55, *96*
Eysenck, M. W., 268, *273*

F

Faglioni, P., 196, *230*
Faibash, G. M., 242, *273*
Farnsworth, D., 6, 26, *34*
Feldman, R. S., 41–42, 44–45, 48, 50, *52,* 216, *234,* 256–257, *275*
Fennell, E., 198, *234*
Fischer, R., 212–213, 224, 226, *230*
Fisher, M., 129, *140*
Fiske, P. J., 247, *275*
Flavell, J. H., 74, *96,* 225, *231*
Fleiss, J. L., 124, *140*
Flor-Henry, P., 209, *231*
Frankel, A. S., 242, *273*
Franks, J. J., 55, *95*
Fransella, F., 157, *189*
Freedman, B. J., 125–126, *140*
Freeman, H., 118, *141*
Friedrich, D., 263, *273*
Frith, C. D., 157, *190*
Fromholt, P., 64, 94, *97*
Fromkin, V. A., 265, *273*
Fuller, G. D., 242, 263, *273*

G

Galanter, E., 260, *274*
Galin, D., 196, 203, 205, 207–209, *230*
Gallant, D., 130, *140*
Garmezy, N., 21, *34*
Garner, W. R., 58, *96*
Gazzaniga, M. S., 197, 199, 207, 230, *231, 234*
Gelman, R. S., 267, *272*
George, E. I., 217, *234*
Gibson, A. R., 197, *230*
Gilberstadt, H., 60–61, *96*
Gill, M., 220, *234*
Goldberg, S. C., 132, *140*
Goldstein, A. G., 164, *190*
Goldstein, G., 247, *275*
Goldstein, K., 3, *34,* 193, 216, 218–219, *229, 231*
Goldstein, M. G., 159, *190*
Goodell, H., 124, *139*
Gordon, A., 6, *34*
Gordon, H. W., 196–197, 204–205, *231*
Gottesman, I. I., 121, 129, *140*
Gottschalk, L. A., 42, *51*
Goulet, L. R., 267, *274*
Green, D. M., 78, *96*
Greeno, J. G., 57, *96*
Grinker, R. R., 60, 94, *96*
Grunebaum, H., 130, *140*
Gruzelier, J., 209–213, 223–224, *231*
Guilford, J. P., 77, 81, 83, *96*
Gur, R. C., 206, *231*
Gur, R. E., 206, 208, *231*
Gurland, B. J., 121, 124, *139, 140*
Gynther, M. D., 193, *234*

H

Haber, R. N., 55, *96*
Haggard, M. P., 206, *231*
Hake, H. W., 58, *96*
Haley, J., 243, *272*
Halperin, Y., 205, *231*
Hamacher, J. H., 267, *272*
Hamilton, P., 268, *273*
Hammer, M., 41, 43–44, *51, 52*
Hamsher, K. deS., 193, *231*
Hanfmann, E., 217, *231*
Handel, S., 125, *139*
Harris, J. G., 120, *140*

Harris, L. J., 206, *231*
Harrow, M., 225, *231*
Hawks, D. V., 118, *140, 141,* 263, *275*
Hay, A. J., 157, *190*
Haynes, E. T., 157, *190*
Heather, B. B., 158, *190*
Hebb, D. O., 212, *232*
Hécaen, H., 203, *232*
Helson, H., 83, *96*
Hemsley, D. R., 137, *140,* 263, *273*
Herrmann, D. J., 57, *95*
Heston, L. L., 130, *140*
Hewlett, J. H. G., 217, *233*
Himmelhoch, J., 225, *231*
Hirt, M., 118, 122, 123, *142*
Hochberg, A. C., 118, *141,* 263, *275*
Hochhaus, L., 78, *96*
Hockey, G. R. J., 266, 268, *273*
Hollingshead, A. B., 59–60, *96*
Holloway, F. A., 209–210, *232*
Holmes, J. M., 199, *229*
Holzman, P. S., 60, *96,* 131, *140*
Hörmann, H., 257, 267, *273*
Hornsby, J. R., 128, *141*
Horton, D. L., 241–242, *273*
Hull, C. H., 62, *98*
Hull, C. L., 212, *232*
Humphrey, B., 203, *233*
Hunt, E. B., 55, *96*
Hunt, J. McV., 193, *232*
Hunt, W. A., 237, *273*
Hurt, S. W., 131, *140*
Hyde, T. S., 72, *96*

J

Jackson, D. D., 243, *272*
Jackson, J. H., 202–203, *232*
Jacobsen, B., 129, *140*
Jacoby, L. L., 58, 77, *96, 97*
James, W., 259, *273*
Jenkins, J. G., 62, *98*
Jenkins, J. J., 72, *96, 97*
Johnson, A. M., 86, *95*
Johnson, M. H., 241–242, *275*
Johnson, R. C., 240, *273*
Johnson, S. C., 74, *97*
Johnson, W., 41, *51*
Johnsontone, D. W., 157, *190*
Jones, J. E., 159, *190*
Jones, M. K., 197, *232*
Jones, N. F., 237, *273*

Jones, R. E., 156, *190*
Joynt, R. J., 197, *232*

K

Kallmann, F. J., 129, *140*
Kantor, W., 267, *274*
Kantorowitz, D., 6, 20, 23, *34*
Kaplan, S., 267, *274*
Kasanin, J. S., 41, *51,* 217, *231,* 265, *274*
Kates, S. L., 242, *273*
Kayton, L., 63–64, 66, 68–69, 71–75,
    77–79, 87, 89–91, *97,* 262, 264, *274*
Keele, S. W., 136, *140*
Kelly, G. A., 145–148, *190*
Kendell, R. E., 121, 124, *139, 140*
Kent, G. H., 240–242, *274*
Kety, S. S., 129, *140*
Kimura, D., 196–199, 203, 205–206, *232*
Kinchla, R. A., 77, *97*
King, F. L., 206, *232*
Kinsbourne, M., 196, 206–209, 216, 223,
    225, 227, *232*
Kintsch, W., 71, 74, 87, *97*
Kirschner, D., 219–220, *232*
Kleinsmith, L. J., 267, *274*
Kling, J. W., 249, *274*
Koenig, I. D., 267, *272*
Koh, S. D., 64–69, 71–80, 83, 87, 89–93,
    97, 262, 264, 269, *274*
Kohn, B., 198, 204, *232*
Kopfstein, J. H., 118, *140*
Korboot, P. J., 137, *140*
Kornetsky, C., 118, 128–130, *141, 143*
Kringlen, E., 160, 162, *190*
Kurianski, J., 121, *140*
Krauss, R. M., 14, *34*
Kushner, A. W., 157, *190*

L

Lacey, J. I., 266, *274*
Lang, P. H., 120, *140,* 193–194, 216–217,
    219, 226, *229, 232*
Langdon, B., 267, *274*
Langworthy, O. R., 209–210, *232*
Larsen, S. F., 64, 94, *97*
Lashley, K. S., 251, 257, *274*
Lawson, J. S., 89, *97,* 118, 128, *141,*
    215–216, *232,* 264, *274*
Lenneberg, E. H., 251, *274*
Levine, F. M., 118, 125, *141*

Levonian, E., 267, *274*
Levy, D. L., 131, *140*
Levy, J., 207, *233*
Levy, R., 89, *97*
Lieberman, A. M., 94, *97*
Lillie, F. J., 157, *190*
Lindsley, D. B., 212, *233*
Lisman, S. A., 9–10, 12, *34*, 113, *116*, 242, 255, *274*
Livingston, P. B., 128, *139*
Lockhart, R. S., 57–58, 72, *96, 97*
London, M., 125, *139*
Loovis, C. F., 200, *229*
Lowe-Bell, S. S., 200, *229*
Luria, A. R., 196, *233*
Lykken, D. T., 58, *97*

M

MacDonald, N., 125, *141*
MacLean, P. D., 196, *233*
Maer, F., 206, *234*
Maher, B. A., 117, 119, 129, 134, *141*, 193, *233, 237, 274*
Malmo, R. B., 212, *233*
Maltzman, I., 267, *274*
Mandell, E. E., 267, *272*
Mandler, G., 65–66, 70, 88, 90, *97, 98*
Margolin, R. R., 267, *272*
Markham, B., 6, *34*
Marks, L. E., 66, *98*
Marlowe, D., 241, *273*
Marshall, J. C., 199, *229*
Martin, E., 72, 74, *98*
Mattingly, I. G., 94, *97*
Matussek, P., 217, *234*
Maxwell, A. E., 89, *97*
McAdam, D., 203, *233*
McFadyen, M., 157, *190*
McGaughran, L. S., 220, *233*
McGhie, A., 50–51, 64, 89, 91, *97, 98,* 118, 122–123, 126, 128, *141,* 215–216, 227, *229, 232, 233,* 262, 264, *274*
McKee, G., 203, 208, *233*
McLean, P. D., 267, *274*
McNeill, D., 55–56, *98*
McPherson, F. M., 157–159, *190*
Mead, G. H., 7, *34*
Mednick, S. A., 19, 21, *34,* 111, *116,* 212, 226, *233,* 265, *274*
Meehl, P. E., 68, *98,* 109, *116,* 119, 127, 129, 130, *139, 141,* 194–195, *230*

Meichenbaum, D., 239, *274*
Melton, A. W., 72, 74, *98*
Meltzer, H. Y., 131, *140*
Miller, G. A., 55–57, 64, 66, *98,* 114, *116,* 218, *230,* 243, 257, 260, *272, 274*
Milner, B., 198, 203, *229, 233*
Miskimins, R. W., 159, *190*
Moran, L. J., 217, 220, *233*
Morrison, J., 130, *143*
Morton, J., 136, *141*
Mourer, S. A., 247–251, *274*
Mueller, J. H., 267, *274*
Murdock, B. B., 56, *98,* 250, *273*
Murray, D. J., 90, *95*

N

Nachmani, G., 6, 9, 26, *34,* 90, *98,* 111, 113, *116,* 253–254, 264, *272, 275*
Nachson, I., 201, 205–206, *229, 231*
Nagel, E., 221, *230*
Nakamura, C. Y., 118, 137, *139*
Neale, J. M., 118, 122, 132, *140, 141,* 262–263, *273, 275*
Nebes, R. D., 196, 203, *233*
Neisser, U., 55, 84, *98,* 260, *275*
Neuringer, C., 247, *275*
Newell, A., 55, *98*
Nideffer, R. M., 153, *190*
Nie, H. N., 62, *98*
Nolan, J. D., 118, *141*
Norman, D. A., 57, *98,* 136, *141*
Norris, H., 134, *142*

O

Oahayon, J., 122, *141*
Oltmanns, T. F., 119, 122, 126, 128–129, 132, 137, *141*
Olver, R. R., 128, *141*
Oppenheimer, R., 195, *233*
Ornstein, R. E., 205, 207–208, *230, 233*
Orzack, M. H., 118, 129–130, 134, *141*
Osgood, C. E., 68, *95, 98*
Osmond, H., 240, *276*
Osterkamp, U., 267, *273*

P

Parkinson, A. M., 206, *231*
Parsons, O. A., 209–210, *232, 233*
Pattishall, E., 198, *234*

Pavy, D., 237, *275*
Payne, R. W., 118, 141, 193, 217, 225, *233, 234,* 263, *275*
Penn, W. I., 158, *189*
Perret, E., 197, 199, *234*
Peterson, R. A., 69, 72, 80, 83, 90–93, *97*
Phillips, J. P. N., 157, *190*
Piaget, J., 7, *34*
Piety, K. R., 157, *190*
Pigache, R. M., 134, *142*
Pisoni, S., 38, 41, 43, 48, *52,* 216, *234*
Polgar, S. K., 43, *51, 52*
Polidoro, L. G., 241, *273*
Pomeranz, D., 118, *141*
Portnoy, S., 41–45, 48, 50, *52,* 216, 234, 256–257, *275*
Posner, M. I., 264, *275*
Postman, L., 266, *275*
Powers, P. S., 124, *139*
Pribram, K. H., 260, *274*
Proctor, L. R., 131, *140*
Professional Staff of the Cross National Project, 121, *142*
Putnam, N., 225, *231*

Q

Quillian, M. R., 262, *272*
Quinn, J. G., 268, *273*
Quirk, C., 157, *191*

R

Radley, A. R., 155, 158, *189, 190*
Rado, S., 68, *98*
Rapaport, D., 94, *98,* 220, *234*
Rappaport, M., 127, 134, *142*
Rasmussen, T. R., 198, 204, *229, 235*
Rattan, R. B., 120, *142,* 218, *234,* 245, *275*
Richter, C. P., 209–210, *232*
Redlich, F. C., 59–60, *96*
Reiss, D., 119, *142*
Ries, H. A., 241–242, *275*
Riggs, L. A., 249, *274*
Ring, K., 195, *229*
Ritzler, B., 91, *98*
Roberts, M. A., 246–247, *275*
Robins, E., 122, 125, *142*
Robinson, D. A., 206, *234*
Robinson, K. N., 118, *140*
Rodnick, E. H., 21, *34,* 159, *190*

Roemer, R. A., 131, *142*
Roenker, D. L., 70, *98,* 264, *275*
Rohrer, J. W., 157, *190*
Rosanoff, A. J., 240–242, *274*
Rosenbaum, G., 91, *98*
Rosenberg, S., 4–7, 9, 26, *34,* 72, *98,* 111, 113, *116,* 254, *272*
Rosenhan, D. L., 195, *234*
Rosenthal, D., 129, *140, 142*
Rosenthal, R., 214, 223, *234*
Rosenzweig, M. R., 197, *234*
Rothberg, M., 10, *34*
Rowe, S. N., 198, *234*
Russell, B., 194, *234*

S

Salmon, P., 158, *189*
Salzinger, K., 1, 19, *34,* 36–38, 40–45, 48, 50, *51, 52,* 101, 111, 114, *116,* 193, 195, 216, *234,* 252, 256–258, *275*
Salzinger, S., 40, *52*
Satz, P., 198, *234*
Schafer, R., 220, *234*
Schiller, W. J., 72, *98*
Schmidt, M. W., 247, *275*
Schneider, K., 117, *142*
Schönpflug, W., 267, *275*
Schuham, A. I., 246–247, *275*
Schulsinger, F., 129, *140*
Schwartz, G. E., 206–207, *234*
Schwartz, H. G., 209–210, *234*
Schwartz, S., 268, *275*
Schwarz, C., 66, 74–75, *97,* 262, *274*
Scotti, G., 196, *230*
Seamon, J. G., 199, 207, *234*
Seeman, M. V., 237, *275*
Seligman, M. E. P., 195, *234*
Shader, R. I., 128, *139*
Shagass, C., 131, *142*
Shankweiler, D., 197, 199, *234*
Shannon, C. E., 86, *98*
Sharpe, L., 121, *139, 140*
Shephard, R. N., 72, *98,* 248, *275*
Sherrington, C. S., 206, *234*
Shields, J., 121, 129, *140*
Shiffrin, R. M., 56, 76, *95*
Shimkunas, A. M., 193, 217–220, 225, *234*
Shoemaker, D. J., 151, *190*
Shubachs, A. P. W., 149, *190*
Sidman, M., 39, *52*

Silverman, J., 212–213, 224, 227, *234, 235*
Simon, H. A., 55, *98*
Simon, R., 121, 124, *139, 140*
Singer, M. T., 160, *191*
Slater, E., 129, *142*
Smith, A., 197–198, 202, *235*
Smith, E. E., 84, *98,* 254, *275*
Smith, K., 193, *228, 234*
Smith, K. U., 200, *228*
Smith, W. L., 196, *232*
Snyder, S. H., 38, *52,* 134–135, *142*
Sokolov, E. N., 266, *275*
Solso, R. L., 55, *98, 99*
Sommer, R., 240, *276*
Sourek, K., 209–210, *235*
Space, L. G., 152–153, *190*
Spence, J. T., 21, *34,* 220, 224, *235*
Spence, K. W., 21, *34*
Sperry, R. W., 197, 202, 207, *231, 233*
Spinnler, H., 196, *230*
Spitzer, R. L., 122, 125, *142*
Spohn, H. E., 118, 134, *142*
Starkweather, J. A., 42, *52*
Steinbrenner, K., 62, *98*
Sternberg, S., 77, 83, 92, *99*
Stevens, S. S., 78, *99*
Stierlin, H., 146, *191*
Stiller, P., 121, *140*
Storms, L. H., 2, 21, *33,* 111, 113–114, *116,* 193, 212, 226, *229, 235*
Strauss, M. E., 23, *34*
Strauss, J. S., 123–124, 128, *139, 142,* 160, *189*
Streiker, S., 77, 79–80, 90, 93, *97*
Studdert-Kennedy, M., 197, *199*
Sullivan, H. S., 3, 7, *34*
Sutton, S., 37, *53*
Swanson, J. M., 113, *115*
Swets, J. A., 78, *96,* 249, 264, *276*
Szoc, R., 83, 90–92, *97*

T

Tarte, R. D., 267, *276*
Taylor, J. A., 193, 217–218, 225, *230*
Taylor, J. F., 118, 122–123, *142*
Taylor, R. L., 264, *275*
Taylor, W. L., 43, *53*
Teghtsoonian, M., 248, *275*
Thetford, P. E., 118, *142*
Thompson, C. L., 200, *229*

Thompson, C. P., 70, *98,* 264, *275*
Thompson, D. M., 72, 90, *99*
Todt, E., 267, *273*
Tokonogii, I. M., 213, *229*
Toohey, M. L., 160, *191*
Toscano, P., 118, *141*
Traupmann, K. L., 64, 90, *99*
Treisman, A. M., 136, *142*
Trevarthen, C., 207, *233*
Truscott, I. P., 89, *99*
Tsuang, M. T., 124, *139*
Tucker, G., 225, *231*
Tulving, E., 57–58, 72, 74, 77, 88, 90, *96, 99*
Tunturi, A. R., 197, *235*
Turvey, M. T., 94, *97*
Tutko, T. A., 220, 224, *235*

U

Ungerstedt, U., 135, *142*

V

Venables, P., 19, *34,* 91, *99,* 209–214, 223–224, 227, *229, 231, 235,* 265, *276*
Vetter, H., 41, *53*
Vonnegut, M., 126, *142*
Vygotsky, L. S., 7, *34,* 216, *235*

W

Wada, J., 204, *235*
Wahl, O., 118, *143*
Walker, E. L., 267, *276*
Wang, G. H., 209–210, *235*
Waskow, I. E., 42, *53*
Wasserman, L. I., 213, *228*
Watson, C. G., 220, 224, *235*
Watson, S. J., 118, *143*
Weakland, J. H., 243, *272*
Weckowicz, T. E., 38, *53*
Weinheimer, S., 14, *34*
Weiss, J. L., 130, *140*
Weiss, R. L., 240, *273*
Wender, P. H., 129, *140*
Wescourt, K. T., 57, *95*
West, K. L., 159, *190*
Whitehorn, J. C., 41, *53*
Wickens, D. D., 77, 87, *99*
Williams, E., 157, *191*

Wilson, 159, *190*
Winokur, G., 130, *143*
Winter, D. A., 157, 158, *191*
Wishner, J., 118, *143, 276*
Wohlberg, G. W., 128, *143*
Woods, W. L., 22, *34*
World Health Organization, 121, *143*
Wright, D. M., 157, *191,* 193–194,
    217–218, *235*
Wurster, S. A., 37, *53*
Wynne, L. C., 159–160, *191*

Y

Yassillo, N. J., 131, *140*

Yates, A. J., 91, *99*
Young, M. J., 214, *235*

Z

Zawada, S. L., 137, *140*
Zeeman, E. C., 221, *235*
Zelhart, P. F., 240, *273*
Zimring, F. M., 147, *191*
Zipf, G. K., 41, *53*
Zubin, J., 39, *53,* 118, 120–121, *143,*
    238, *276*
Zubrzycki, C. R., 267, *276*

Subject Index

A

Adjusted ratio of clustering, 70, *see also*
    Memory deficits in schizophrenia
Arousal, 211–212, 265–268
    cue utilization and, 266
    definition of, 265–267
    memory consolidation, and, 266
    recall order, effects on, 267–268
Attention, 117–118, 125–126, 208,
    215–216, 261–263, *see also* Brain,
    normal functioning of; Brain,
    abnormalities of function in
    schizophrenia; Distractability;
    Information processing models of
    cognition
dichotic listening measures of, 263
span of apprehension, 262

B

Brain, abnormalities of function in
    schizophrenia, 209–216; 226–227
    attention-perceptual processes, 215–216
    bilateral transfer and conceptual
        disorganization, 213–215
    hemispheric asymmetry, 215
    lateral asymmetry, 209–213
    motivational processes, 226–227
Brain, normal functioning of, 196–209
    asymmetry in, 196–197
    interhemispheric interaction in, 207–209
    left hemisphere functions in, 198–202

Brain (*contd.*)
    right hemisphere functions in, 202–207
    split brain (commissurotomy) studies of,
        197, 203

C

Case record rating scale, *see* Diagnosis of
    schizophrenia
Categorical clustering, *see* Memory deficits
    in schizophrenia
Chapman's dominant response hypothesis,
    3, 10, 19, 111–115, 193, 217, 243–251
    cloze procedure and, 256
    correction for guessing in, 244–245,
        248–250
    hierarchy of errors in, 246–247
Children's Embedded Figure Test, 130
Cloze procedure, 42–44, 46–50, 256,
        see also Chapman's dominant response
    hypothesis; Immediacy hypothesis
Continuous Performance Test, 130
Cognitive deficit, theories of, 110–115,
        see also Chapman's dominant response
    hypothesis; Immediacy hypothesis;
    Memory deficit in schizophrenia;
    Referent Communication
    assumptions about normality, 111–112
    constraint utilization, 113–115
    locus of deficit, 112–113
Commissurotomy, *see* Brain, normal
    functioning of

Concrete thought, 3, 193–194, 216–225,
    see also Brain, abnormalities of function
    in schizophrenia
    asymmetry of brain function and,
        222–225
Control processes, see Information
    processing models of cognition
Constancy, perceptual, 38
Construct validity, 107, 119, 194–195
    nomological net in, 119
Cross National Study, see Diagnosis of
    schizophrenia
Cue utilization, see Arousal

D

Depth of processing, see Information
    processing models of cognition
Diagnosis of schizophrenia, 36–37, 58–63,
    120–125, 238
    Case Record Rating Scale in, 124
    Cross National Study of, 121
    iterative method in, 37
    MMPI in, 60–63
    pathognomic symptoms, 123–125
    Research Diagnostic Criteria in, 122
    Schizophrenia State Inventory in, 60
Diathesis-stress model of schizophrenia,
    129, 159, 187
Dichotic listening, see Attention
Digit Symbol Substitution Test, 134
Disattention deficit, 15, 19, 38, 111
Discrimination power, 102–106
    reliability, influence of, 102–103
    difficulty level, influence of, 103–104
    validity, influence of, 104–106
Distractability, 119–122, 129–135
    course of schizophrenia, and, 127–129
    definition of, 119–120
    drug effects on, 131–135
    genetic factors in, 129–131
    information processing aspects of, 135
Double-bind communication, 159, see also,
    Role Construct Repertory Test

E

Echoic memory, see Information processing
    models of cognition; Memory deficits
    in schizophrenia

Episodic memory, see, Information
    processing models of cognition; Memory
    deficits in schizophrenia
Eye tracking, 131

F

Fantastic auditor, see Referent
    communication
Filtering, 64, 216, 263–264, see also
    Attention; Memory deficits in
    schizophrenia

G

Generalized other, see Referent
    communication
Generalization, 216–225
Grid Test of Thought Disorder, 157–58
    loosening of construct relationships in,
        158

H

Hallucinations, see Diagnosis of
    schizophrenia; Role Construct
    Repertory Test
Hemispheric asymmetry, see Brain,
    abnormalities of function in
    schizophrenia

I

Immediacy hypothesis, 19, 37–40, 44–51,
    111–114, 216, 256
    behavior theory and, 39–40
    bilateral context and, 49–50
    cloze procedure and, 44–47, 50
    drug effects and, 38–39
    lapse-of-attention hypothesis versus,
        50–51
    unilateral context and, 47, 49
Impulsive Speaker Model, see Referent
    communication
Information processing models of
    cognition, 56–58, 135–137, 260–261,
    see also Attention; Filtering;
    Distractability
    control processes in, 57, 261
    depth of processing and, 58, 260

Information (*contd.*)
  echoic memory, 136, 260
  episodic memory, 57
  long term memory, 57, 261
  short term memory, 57, 261
  short term sensory memory, 57, 136
Interference theories, 2, 11
Intertrial Repetition Measure, 65–67, 90,
  see also Memory deficits in
  schizophrenia

K

Korsakoff's syndrome, 124

L

Lapse-of-attention hypothesis, *see*
  Immediacy hypothesis
Lateral asymmetry, *see* Brain, abnormalities
  of function in schizophrenia
Long-term memory, 75–76, *see also*
  Information processing models of
  cognition; Memory deficits in
  schizophrenia
Lorr Rating Scale, 134

M

Memory consolidation, *see* Arousal
Memory deficits in schizophrenia, 61–94,
  264–265
  free recall and mnemonic organization,
    64–76
  affective words, role of, 68–71, 72–74
  categorical clustering in, 65–66, 70,
    74–75, 90, 264
  subjective organization in, 65–66,
    74–76
  nonorganizational and nonlinguistic
    strategies, 86–88
  pleasantness, role of, 80–83
  recognition, 71–72, 76–86, 90–94
  perception, as measured by, 77–80
  signal detection analyses of, 72, 78,
    264–265
  short term memory as measured by,
    91–92
Short term memory scanning, 83–86
Motivation, 226–227

Multiple processing, 84
Munsell color disks, 12, *see also*
  referent communication

N

Nomological net, *see* Construct
  validity

O

Object Sorting Test, 157
Overinclusion, 124, 193, 217–225, *see also*
  Referent communication

P

Perception, subjective accounts of, in
  schizophrenia, 125–126, *see also* Brain,
  abnormalities of function in
  schizophrenia; Information processing
  models of cognition; Memory deficits in
  schizophrenia
Perseverative Chaining Model, *see* Referent
  communication
Perseverative Speaker Model, *see* Referent
  communication
Pigeon-holing, 263, 264
Personal constructs, *see* Role Construct
  Repertory Test

R

Recognition, *see* Memory deficits in
  schizophrenia
Referent communication, 1–26, 108,
  252–255
  associations, role of, 1–5, *see also* Word
    associations
  clinical implications of research in, 21–26
  nonresponse, 23
  referent shifts, 22
  social withdrawal, 24
  treatment, 24–26
  Cohen's research paradigm of, 4–6, 26–33
  Cohen's theory of, 6–7
  comparison in, 6–14
  fantastic auditor in, 3, 7, 15
  generalized other in, 7

Referent communication (*contd.*)
  Impulsive Speaker Model of, 13–17,
    20–23, 26
  listener's role in, 7
  overinclusion in, 13, *see also*
    Overinclusion
  Perseverative Chaining Model of, 19, 26,
    111, 255
  Perseverative Speaker Model, 15–17, 19
  sampling in, 6–15, 21–23
  Tower of Babel Model of, 13
Research Diagnostic Criteria, *see* Diagnosis
  of Schizophrenia
Response set, 253
Role Construct Repertory Test, 146–189
  administration of, 148–150
  analysis of, 150–156
  double-bind communications and,
    159–164
  evaluation of inconsistency in, 153, 156
  factor-valence inconsistency in, 153
  hallucinations and, 164
  schizophrenic performance on, 156–189
  self-factor inconsistency, 152
  self-valence inconsistency, 152

S

Schizophrenic State Inventory, *see*
  Diagnosis of schizophrenia
Semantic encoding, 72–76, 92–93
  incidental versus intentional learning and,
    73–74
Short-term memory, *see* Information
  processing models of cognition; Memory
  deficits in schizophrenia
Signal Detection Theory, 72, 78, 249–250,
  264–265, *see also* Memory deficits
  in schizophrenia
Span of apprehension, *see* Attention
Split-brain, *see* Brain, normal
  functioning of

Stimulus Category Repetition Measure, 65,
  see also Memory deficits in schizphrenia
Stroop Test, 199
Subjective organization, *see* Memory
  deficits in schizophrenia
Stimulus set, 253

T

Tower of Babel Model, *see* Referent
  communication
Tranquilizing Medications, *see*
  Distractability
Type-token ration, 42, 252

V

Verbal behavior, study of, 40–43, 56–57,
  251–252, 257–258, 265
  associative approaches, 257–258
  competence, language, 41, 56–57
  performance, language, 41, 56–57
  rule-governed models, 41, 265
Verbal conditioning, 239

W

Wechsler Adult Intelligence Scale, 60, 63,
  128, *see also* Diagnosis of
  schizophrenia
Word associations, 2–5, 239–243, 251–252,
  see also Referent communication
  autistic, 2
  commonality of, 10, 146, 240–243
  control model of, 2–3
  hierarchic model of, 2
  logical, 2
  loosening of, 2, 117, 123, 145
  repertoire of, 2–5, 255
  selection of, 2–3